# EQUITY AND SUSTAINABLE DEVELOPMENT

U.S.-Mexico Contemporary Perspectives Series, 24
CENTER FOR U.S.-MEXICAN STUDIES
UNIVERSITY OF CALIFORNIA, SAN DIEGO

## Contributors

Tito Alegría
Robert L. Bach
Nora L. Bringas Rábago
Jane Clough-Riquelme
Michael Connolly Miskwish
Angela J. Donelson
John Friedmann
Ruth Gaxiola Aldama
Lawrence A. Herzog
Kathryn Kopinak
Alven H. Lam
Enrique Leff
Silvia López Estrada
Alejandro Monsiváis
Stephen P. Mumme
Laura M. Norman
Keith Pezzoli
Roberto Sánchez R.
Laura Silván
Basilio Verduzco Chávez

# EQUITY AND SUSTAINABLE DEVELOPMENT

## REFLECTIONS FROM THE U.S.-MEXICO BORDER

edited by
Jane Clough-Riquelme and Nora Bringas Rábago

**LA JOLLA, CALIFORNIA**
Center for U.S.-Mexican Studies, UCSD

© 2006 by the Regents of the University of California. Published by the Center for U.S.-Mexican Studies at the University of California, San Diego. All rights reserved under International and Pan-American Conventions. No part of this publication may be reproduced or transmitted in any form or by any means, electronic or mechanical, including photocopy, recording, or any information storage or retrieval system, without prior permission in writing from the publisher.

ISBN: 1-878367-54-4 hardcover
      1-878367-55-2 paperback
Printed in the United States of America

Cover photographs courtesy of El Colegio de la Frontera Norte and the Houston Institute for Culture.

Library of Congress Cataloging-in-Publication Data

Equity and sustainable development : reflections from the U.S.-Mexico
  border / edited by Jane Clough-Riquelme and Nora Bringas Rábago.
    p. cm. -- (U.S.-Mexico contemporary perspectives series ; 24)
  Includes bibliographical references.
  ISBN 1-878367-54-4 (hard cover) -- ISBN 1-878367-55-2 (pbk.)
  1. Sustainable development--Mexican-American Border Region.
2. Poverty--Mexican-American Border Region. 3. Environmental protection--Mexican-American Border Region. 4. Mexican-American Border Region--Economic conditions.    I. Clough-Riquelme, Jane.
II. Bringas, Nora L. III. Series.
HC95.Z9E54 2006
338.972'107--dc22                                    2006001155

# CONTENTS

## Part I. Introduction

1   Testing the Limits of Equity and Sustainable Development
    in the U.S.-Mexico Borderlands                                      3
    JANE CLOUGH-RIQUELME AND NORA L. BRINGAS RÁBAGO

2   The Johannesburg Summit: Implications for the Americas             17
    ENRIQUE LEFF

## Part II. Equity and Urbanization on the Border: Prospects for Sustainable City-Regions

3   Toward a Sustainable Development in the
    U.S.-Mexico Border Region                                          31
    JOHN FRIEDMANN

4   Rethinking Urban Ecologies: Cultural Barriers to
    Sustainable Development?                                           43
    LAWRENCE A. HERZOG

5   Cross-Border Regionalism and Sustainability:
    Contributions of Critical Regional Ecology                         63
    KEITH PEZZOLI

## Part III. Poverty, Vulnerability, and Environmental Management

6   Urban Structure and Social Segregation in Tijuana                  97
    TITO ALEGRÍA

7   Counting the Environment In: Considerations of the
    Risk of Hazardous *Maquiladora* Waste                             125
    KATHRYN KOPINAK

8   Social Vulnerability and Disaster Risk in Tijuana:
    Preliminary Findings                                              149
    NORA L. BRINGAS RÁBAGO AND ROBERTO SÁNCHEZ R.

9   Environment, Poverty, and Gender: Using and Managing
    Environmental Resources in a Tijuana Colonia                 175
    RUTH GAXIOLA ALDAMA

**Part IV. Civil Society in Action in the Border Region**

10  Acquiring Knowledge and Improving Environmental Policy:
    A Binational Agenda for Civic Organizations                  201
    BASILIO VERDUZCO CHÁVEZ

11  Environmental Justice and Border Tribes:
    The Case of San Diego County                                 215
    MICHAEL CONNOLLY MISKWISH

12  Youth and Education for Sustainability on the Border:
    Imagining the Future Citizens of Baja California             243
    ALEJANDRO MONSIVÁIS AND LAURA SILVÁN

13  NGOs, Environment, and Gender in Tijuana                     271
    SILVIA LÓPEZ ESTRADA

14  Accessible Information Technology for Equitable
    Community Planning                                           27
    ALVEN H. LAM, LAURA M. NORMAN, AND ANGELA J. DONELSON

**Part V. Conclusions and Policy Implications**

15  Cross-Border Regional Policy Collaboration:
    Lessons from San Diego–Tijuana                               305
    JANE CLOUGH-RIQUELME

16  Equity and Justice in Binational Environmental Policy        325
    STEPHEN P. MUMME

17  Looking Ahead: Equity in the U.S.-Mexico Border              337
    ROBERT L. BACH

Acronyms                                                         354

Contributors                                                     358

PART I

Introduction

# 1

# Testing the Limits of Equity and Sustainable Development in the U.S.-Mexico Borderlands

JANE CLOUGH-RIQUELME AND NORA BRINGAS RÁBAGO

**THE ELUSIVE SUSTAINABLE DEVELOPMENT PARADIGM**

Nearly thirty-five years ago, at the United Nations Conference on the Human Environment in Stockholm in 1972, the world's leaders for the first time seriously discussed the relationship between prevailing economic models of industrial expansion, depletion of the world's natural resources, and the health and well-being of humanity. Ten years passed before the United Nations finally convened an international commission to determine what could be done to make economic development compatible with environmental protection and improved quality of life worldwide. It was a woman, Norwegian Prime Minister Gro Harlem Brundtland, who led this provocative effort to create a set of global policy strategies that might lead to a new type of development, one that would produce prosperity without jeopardizing the natural resource base for the future and that would distribute prosperity's benefits equitably to the world's people.

It has been almost twenty years since the publication of the seminal United Nations report that called for a new way to think about "our common future" (World Commission on Environment and Development 1987). This report provided an initial framework for a new kind of development—sustainable development—based on the notion of intergenerational stewardship, conservation of natural resources, and the right of every person to human dignity and the satisfaction of basic needs.

Unfortunately, despite decades of international policy development and two global environmental summits (in Rio de Janeiro in 1992 and in Johannesburg in 2002) at which hundreds of nations and thousands of nongovernmental organizations participated, we are still far from a fundamental shift in the economic paradigm that fuels the global economy. The goal of intertwining the three pillars of the sustainable development paradigm at a policy level remains elusive; indeed, the intended aims of these three policy objectives—economic prosperity, environmental protection, and social equity—are often at odds.

Globalization, it was posited, would expand the economic pie for the world's population and distribute prosperity equitably at the same time that the world's natural resource base would be protected or banked for future generations. Yet, with a few notable exceptions, the richest industrial nations, particularly the United States, continue to plunder nonrenewable resources at an alarming rate, while international financial institutions provide assistance to developing nations to compete in the new global economy, but only if they agree to tighten their fiscal belt and limit social programs. The developing economies have, in many cases, improved; however, the poor in these nations have paid the price for their countries' overall increase in prosperity, as evidenced by income distribution coefficients worldwide: "The richest 50 million people in Europe and North America have the same income as 2.7 billion poor people. The slice of the cake taken by 1% is the same size as that handed to the poorest 57%" (Elliot 2002). At the same time, globalization has been fueled not by renewable energy and renewable resources, but rather by fossil fuels and extraction—much as always.

Despite major efforts to develop international agreements on global environmental threats such as global warming and deforestation, these phenomena continue to advance. As evidenced by tsunamis in Southeast Asia, hurricanes in the Gulf of Mexico, earthquakes in South Asia, and shifts in the global environment, the pace of Mother Nature's wrath far out-distances world policymakers' ability to cope. And as various authors in this volume argue, much of the catastrophic loss of life and property is borne by the poorest of the poor because of policy decisions made long before such "natural disasters" strike.

The goal of social equity has proven to be even more elusive than that of protecting the world's natural resources. A consultation draft prepared for the 2002 World Summit on Sustainable Development in Johannesburg stated,

> While it is generally agreed that the various dimensions of poverty and environment are closely linked, there is less agreement on the nature of these linkages and their policy implications. Too often in the past, policies and programmes to reduce poverty and promote growth have been at the expense of ecosystem health and natural resource productivity, while efforts to protect the environment have not always taken into account the interests of the poor (Consultation Draft for World Summit 2002).

Indeed, one of the major rhetorical outcomes of the Johannesburg Summit was the development of a set of specific goals to reduce world poverty by half in the next decade. Whether this goal is attainable in practice and in the agreed-upon time frame remains to be seen.

## SUSTAINABILITY: THE CHALLENGE OF THE U.S.-MEXICO BORDER

The contradictions inherent in the search for sustainable alternatives to modern development can be seen in all of their complexity on the U.S.-Mexico border. There, the industrial and developing worlds are juxtaposed in stark relief over a 2,000-mile-long borderland punctuated by the local realities of city-regions from the Pacific Ocean to the Gulf of Mexico. Despite significant advances in public awareness about the environmental and social costs of industrial development in the region, the creation of cross-border institutions to deal with them, and explicit commitments by the Bush and Fox administrations to facilitate further improvements, most indicators show deteriorating conditions of life and livelihood for the majority of border region inhabitants.[1]

The Center for U.S.-Mexican Studies at the University of California, San Diego has done much to shed light on borderlands issues through its support of research, training, and public education. The Center's Environment and Sustainable Development Program, initiated in 1998, has given international scholars from the natural and social sciences, environmental professionals, and community advocates the opportunity to create a cadre of experts who can inform the planning process in the border region through original policy-driven or community-based research.

---

[1] For a general overview of the issues facing the border, see Ganster 2000.

In December 2002, the Environment and Sustainable Development Program convened a binational conference in Tijuana to reflect on the implications of the Johannesburg Summit for the border region, with a particular focus on social equity and environmental justice. The Center drew on its extensive cadre of former research fellows—including Enrique Leff, regional coordinator for the United Nations Environmental Program for Latin America—to discuss the ways in which the U.S.-Mexico border region concentrates the challenges and contradictions of sustainable development.

The conference, a collaborative effort of the Center for U.S.-Mexican Studies and the Colegio de la Frontera Norte (COLEF) in Tijuana that received funding from the William and Flora Hewlett Foundation, brought together a unique group of theorists, planners, researchers, and advocates who share concern for the future of the border region. In the spirit of equity, the conference drew on the wisdom of eminent scholars such as John Friedmann while also providing a space for young researchers and advocates to share their insights. Participants came from Canada, Mexico, and the United States; from federal, state, and local levels of government; and from nongovernmental organizations. The majority of chapters in this volume are revised versions of presentations made at the conference. Several chapters were added as a result of suggestions made during that event.

One objective of the conference, and of this volume, was to create a framework and collaborative research agenda for equity and sustainable development in the context of borderlands. Enrique Leff's chapter sets the stage by reflecting on the implications of the Johannesburg Summit for Latin America. He charges that the 2002 World Summit was not of the same caliber as the World Summit in Rio in 1992, where a global action plan known as Agenda 21 was laid out. Johannesburg was much more functional in nature. Although major strides have been made, Leff argues that new health crises, military interventions, and abject poverty have often negated those gains. He notes with concern that the dominant economic rationality continues to undermine the goals of Agenda 21. For Latin America, there is no new framework or strategy, but perhaps, Leff suggests, the border region can serve as a place to experiment.

## THEORIZING SUSTAINABLE CITY-REGIONS

In laying out a framework within which to analyze current conditions in the border region, we drew on the theoretical observations of John Friedmann, an eminent theorist of city-regional development and planning. In his chapter, Friedmann criticizes the global discussion of sustainable development as having been ritualized into meaningless rhetoric. The debate has failed to challenge in any substantive way the dominant paradigm of neoliberal economic policies worldwide. Friedmann offers his framework for alternative development, which he elaborated in his seminal *Empowerment: The Politics of Alternative Development* (1992). In it he posits that an alternative form of development based on the household economy, rather than on the "economic man," would empower the poor while creating wealth through democratic systems. He then critiques the current competitive frenzy generated by the new spatial configuration of economic development around transnational city-regions such as San Diego–Tijuana. Rather than kowtowing to the demands of international capital, Friedmann suggests that city-regions invest in and strengthen their endogenous productive assets to create a development that empowers the citizens of the region.

Lawrence Herzog, who coined "transfrontier metropolis" to describe the city-regions that have developed in the "no-man's land" at the boundaries of nation-states, takes a more postmodern view in his chapter. He describes the barriers to achieving a sustainable development in the border region, asking how we deliver the message of sustainability outside of the limited group of scientists and advocates who believe it is possible to have prosperity without selling of the future of upcoming generations. Herzog describes the seven ecologies of the binational region and explains how they limit our vision of the future. He argues that the emerging transfrontier metropolis is creating conditions for a new cross-border ecology that may jolt us into discovering new and innovative ways to transcend these limiting ecologies.

In the following chapter, Keith Pezzoli offers a specific proposal for a progressive approach to cross-border regionalism, which he calls "critical regional ecology." His approach draws on four fields of integrative discourse: new regionalism/institutionalism, sustainability science, informational science, and ethics and culture. Pezzoli discusses this approach through the context of cross-border regional planning, governance, and watershed management in the San Diego–Tijuana urban landscape.

Leff, Friedmann, Herzog, and Pezzoli help to frame the debate on sustainable development in the context of the U.S.-Mexico border, drawing attention to the challenges of moving from theory to practice. They make a case for the utility of focusing on a specific spatial boundary such as the San Diego–Tijuana city-region and examining it empirically as a test for some of these arguments.

## POVERTY, VULNERABILITY, AND ENVIRONMENTAL MANAGEMENT

Over recent decades, humanity has intervened in nature to a high degree, unleashing a series of negative processes such as climate change, deforestation, soil erosion, pollution, drought, and the loss of biodiversity. And these processes, in turn, have affected the frequency and magnitude of natural disasters such as earthquakes and floods. Such processes are intensified by the conditions of poverty in which the majority of the world lives, giving rise to conflicts driven by differential access to resources. Indeed, David Satterthwaite and his colleagues at the International Institute for Environment and Development have long argued that the causal connections between poverty and environmental degradation are spurious:

> There is little evidence of urban poverty being a significant contributor to environmental degradation but strong evidence that urban environmental hazards are a major cause or contributor to urban poverty. Indeed, for much of the poor urban population, environmental hazards are among the main causes of ill-health, injury and premature death (Satterthwaite 1999).

Satterthwaite and his colleagues posit that the health burden borne by poor populations would be greatly reduced by better environmental management if that were understood to include access to potable water, sewage disposal, and other urban services (Hardoy, Mirlin, and Satterthwaite 2002).

The interdependency of the social, environmental, and economic problems that prevail particularly in developing countries constitutes one of the principal challenges to sustainability. Poverty, vulnerability, and environmental degradation present complex issues that development has not resolved. Traditionally, these problems have been viewed as isolated phenomena, but we cannot understand development unless we treat them as they relate to one another.

These phenomena manifest themselves most clearly in urban areas. In border cities like Tijuana and San Diego, we can observe differences in environmental degradation on opposite sides of the border. These differences are attributable to differing types of urban planning, forms of access and land use, opportunities for employment, and income levels. In Tijuana, urban inequalities are directly related to the marginal condition of the population; differential access to resources like credit, social networks, urban land, services, housing, and basic infrastructure serves to aggravate environmental problems in the city.

Many of the empirical studies on poverty and the environment sidestep the interrelationship between urban areas and the processes of the biosphere. For that reason the chapters devoted to the topics of poverty, vulnerability, and environmental management deal directly with urban areas and their inhabitants. Research on these topics requires a multidimensional framework to better comprehend the interrelationships between social, economic, political, and biophysical dimensions as well as the ways in which these interrelationships shape the process of urbanization and how urbanization shapes global environmental change.

Tito Alegría reveals how poverty is concentrated in the outskirts of Tijuana, where residents have reduced access to public services, commercial centers, and sources of employment, further increasing their condition of poverty. Alegría demonstrates a "segregation by location," by which the market pushes the poor out of areas where there are services, leaving only higher-income residents able to afford urban living. Alegría argues that the structure of land use and zoning is generally detrimental to the environment, not only because of the negative redistribution of income but also because the poor are forced to use more energy and put more pressure on urban infrastructure as they travel longer distances from their homes to jobs and services.

Kathryn Kopinak emphasizes the need for a research agenda on social equity and the environment that evaluates the social and environmental costs of industrial development in the *maquiladora* sector. Kopinak has constructed an index of risk for hazardous industrial materials that yields rich information about the kinds of hazards present in border communities and sets a basis for developing an educational program to inform people of these dangers. Oftentimes these dangers are not immediately apparent to families in the border zone who are consumed with the challenges of providing for their families. Kopinak documents the importance of including social costs in any study of *maquiladoras*, with particular emphasis on equity and a concern for environmental impacts.

Nora Bringas Rábago and Roberto Sánchez indicate that what we commonly call natural disasters are often brought on by political and socioeconomic circumstances—inappropriate government policies, distorted economic structures, and poor management of resources. The complexity of urban systems demands an interdisciplinary perspective if we are to understand the range of interactions between environmental change and urban areas in their social, economic, political, and biophysical dimensions. For example, Tijuana's population is extremely vulnerable to cyclical flooding, which is a direct result of a rapid and incomplete urbanization process driven by transnational, national, and local interests. The geographic and social marginalization of Tijuana's poor, which was one outcome of the urbanization process, has put this sector of the city's population at special risk for the consequences of flooding because poor settlements are concentrated on steep slopes and in floodplains. Bringas and Sánchez link vulnerability and disaster risk as unresolved problems of development. Poverty increases vulnerability to disasters, and disasters prolong poverty.

Ruth Gaxiola Aldama examines the distribution of resources and environmental management in a low-income community characterized by a vulnerable location, lack of public services, and health problems related to air, water, and soil contamination. For Gaxiola, the two principal factors that determine resource management practices in the community are gender and access to public services. Factors related to gender equity also influence the manner in which residents of this community manage their resources.

Together, Alegría, Kopinak, Bringas, Sánchez, and Gaxiola demonstrate the complexity of the issues facing the poor and the vulnerable in this city-region that is otherwise blessed with substantial resources. In so doing, they highlight the need for solid and systematic collaborative binational research. Such research could provide an empirical basis that civil society could then use to advocate and to raise awareness among policymakers.

## CIVIL SOCIETY IN ACTION IN THE BORDER REGION

There has been a marked stagnation in citizen participation on environmental issues in Mexico's northern border region in recent years. This may be attributable to the people's general distrust of government and public policy or their failure to understand how public input in policy debates can shape their world. In Mexico, citizen awareness of environmental issues, including the deleterious impacts of human activities, remains muted—despite the fact that citizen participation opens up the possibility of becoming partners in environmental management. This relative apathy has made it difficult for nongovernmental organizations in Mexico to play a meaningful role and has led them to focus more on short-term funding for survival than on long-term programmatic objectives.

In the United States, there is talk of "the death of environmentalism," as the large environmental groups, now squarely in the mainstream, refrain from being critical for fear of alienating their funding sources. Michael Shellenberger and Ted Nordhaus (2005) report that the environmental leaders they interviewed for their now famous article on the politics of global warming were reluctant to characterize the recent worldwide string of hurricanes, earthquakes, and tornadoes as a direct result of global warming. In the foreword to that article, Peter Teague, of the Nathan Cummings Foundation, stated that the authors' reluctance is due, in part,

> to the fact that the conventional wisdom among environmentalists is that we mustn't frighten the public but rather must focus its gaze on technical solutions, like hybrid cars and fluorescent light bulbs.

The limited citizen involvement in environmental programs suggests the need to reassert social capital, raise awareness regarding the distinct role that social actors can play, and develop a true culture of participation, something now more evident in the United States than in Mexico. Nevertheless, environmental agencies in both countries lack the authority and resources—and often the political will—to make substantive, positive changes in the environment.

Basilio Verduzco Chávez emphasizes how high-level institutions control access to information and knowledge. Thus, while civil society has the opportunity to participate "on the ground," it has been unable to influence the production of knowledge. In order to improve environmental knowledge, there must be a co-production of information by both institutions and civil society.

In his chapter, Michael Connolly Miskwish emphasizes the social, economic, and environmental limitations placed on tribal nations in the border areas of San Diego County and the resulting impacts on their ability to prosper as nations within a nation. Despite having overcome some of those limitations through legislation and lawsuits, the tribes continue to be held to an unjust standard, one that frequently forces them to make concessions to local and state governments. And even though the tribes pay various taxes, they never see any of these funds returning to benefit their tribal lands.

Alejandro Monsiváis and Laura Silván look at citizen participation among youth in the border region. Basing their work on a national survey, these authors argue that border youth have relatively low levels of political and civic participation combined with a rather simplistic vision of citizen rights and responsibilities. They suggest encouraging young people to participate in public campaigns for environmental education as a means of engaging them in their world.

Silvia López Estrada examines the connections between gender and the environment in her overview of nongovernmental organizations that work, respectively, on gender issues and on environmental issues. She found a lack of environmental sensitivity among the gender-focused groups and a corresponding lack of gender sensitivity among the environmental groups. López argues that more must be done in both camps to raise public awareness of the connections between gender and the environment in the Tijuana region.

Alven Lam, Laura Norman, and Angela Donelson point to the importance of using GIS and other new technologies to empower border communities. By mapping their own communities, residents in border colonias can assess their strengths and limitations and plan accordingly for the future. These authors discuss a project developed to help colonias in the border sister cities of Douglas, Arizona, and Agua Prieta, Sonora, map their communities, develop their own community plans, and generate resources to support community improvements. Because these closely linked communities sit on opposite sides of the border, the challenge will be to develop decision-making processes that support comprehensive, cross-border policies.

The various authors who discuss civil society in the border region—Verduzco Chávez, Connolly Miskwish, Monsiváis, Silván, López Estrada, Lam, Norman, and Donelson—demonstrate the variety of strategies and issues facing civil society groups in the border region. These authors highlight just a few of the many cases in which border citizens have employed "citizen diplomacy" (Thorup 1993) to make their region a better place to live.

## CONCLUSIONS AND POLICY RECOMMENDATIONS

The North American Free Trade Agreement (NAFTA), signed in 1993, sparked a surge of cross-border collaboration along the U.S.-Mexico border, including a growing trend toward collaboration among local governments to facilitate cross-border planning. Jane Clough-Riquelme looks at the case of the San Diego Association of Governments (SANDAG) and its binational stakeholders working group, which has been facilitating cross-border policy dialogue in the region for more than ten years. This innovative mechanism for interregional planning may serve as a best practice for the rest of the border region.

Although local governments can do much to facilitate dialogue, policy actions must often come at the federal level. Stephen Mumme examines advances in the construction of border environmental policy and the lessons learned. He argues that differences in national approaches to achieving substantive environmental equity affect binational environmental policy. Mumme demonstrates how procedural differences affect the attainment of environmental protection and the protection of vulnerable populations in the border region.

This regional reflection on equity and sustainable development in the U.S.-Mexico border region points up some of the contradictions inherent in the paradigm. As Friedmann notes, a paradigm shift is essential to reducing poverty and protecting resources for future generations. But as Robert Bach noted at the conference that gave rise to this volume, we need to act now. One outcome of the Johannesburg Summit was a push for governments and nongovernmental organizations to take action and be accountable. How this translates into change on the ground remains to be seen.

Much activity has been focused at the national level, but it is in subnational regions that we see the contradictions of sustainable development; this is particularly true on the U.S.-Mexico border, a region that straddles the developed and developing worlds. Clearly there are obstacles to achieving sustainable development in the border region, including institutional ones,[2] but these can be overcome if there is sufficient political will. In many respects the building of personal, professional, and institutional relationships and networks has transformed this transfrontier region into a new landscape.

The contributors to this volume bring to the table a series of doubts, queries, and recommendations that will certainly remain part of the discussions on the border environment in upcoming years. That is, as long as world summits do not go beyond "philosophical" discussions to tackle real mechanisms for achieving international cooperation on local-level proposals to address inequity, protect the environment, and achieve real economic development, these gatherings will bear little fruit.

Environmental problems will persist on the U.S.-Mexico border, and they will become increasingly severe as long as the Mexican portion of the border region continues to absorb the lion's share of the costs generated by the United States' economic and industrial model. We have a huge responsibility in the Tijuana–San Diego region; the dual challenges of building a culture of respect for the environment and formulating policies that work in a binational context are not easily met. But it will be even more difficult to achieve the radical change of direction on which all else depends, and this is the greatest obstacle to be overcome.

A key problem with the prevailing development model is its economic, political, social, and cultural exclusion of the affected population, especially women, youths, the elderly, and indigenous groups. The region

---

[2] See Blatter 2000 for an analysis that suggests cross-border relationships are obstacles to sustainable development.

needs a sea change, a new orientation toward building local competencies through the collective empowerment of civil society. This border region, and Tijuana in particular, needs to search within itself for the assets that will enable it to pursue an endogenous development, one generated by and for the regional society even when the new social and economic relationships are achieved through local and transnational processes.

To this end, an organized civil society must promote and participate in the design of environmental policies. Transparent government is a prerequisite for such social representation and for local and binational alliances to guarantee popular mobilization and participation. Perhaps it will be today's youth who in future years exercise their right to demand a healthy world, and women and indigenous peoples who will promote the best sustainable environmental practices.

**References**

Blatter, Joachim. 2000. "Emerging Cross-Border Regions as a Step towards Sustainable Development? Experiences and Considerations from Examples in Europe and North America," *International Journal of Economic Development* 2, no. 3: 402–39.
Consultation Draft for World Summit. 2002. "Linking Poverty Reduction and Environmental Management." January.
Elliott, Larry. 2002. "A Cure Worse than the Disease," *Guardian*, January 21.
Friedmann, John. 1992. *Empowerment: The Politics of Alternative Development*. Oxford: Blackwell.
Ganster, Paul, ed., 2000. *The U.S.-Mexican Border Environment: A Road Map to a Sustainable 2020*. San Diego, Calif.: San Diego State University Press.
Hardoy, Jorge, Diana Mirlin, and David Satterthwaite. 2002. *Environmental Problems in an Urbanizing World*. London: Earthscan.
Satterthwaite, David. 1999. "The Links between Poverty and the Environment in the Urban Areas of Africa, Asia and Latin America." Paper prepared for the United Nations Development Programme and the European Commission.
Shellenberger, Michael, and Ted Nordhaus. 2005. "The Death of Environmentalism: Global Warming Politics in a Post-Environmental World," *Grist Magazine*, January 13. At www.grist.org/news/maindish/2005/01/13/doe-reprint.
Thorup, Cathryn L. 1993. "Redefining Governance in North America: The Impact of Cross-Border Networks and Coalitions on Mexican Immigration

into the United States." DRU-219-FF. Santa Monica, Calif.: Rand Corporation.

World Commission on Environment and Development. 1987. *Our Common Future: The World Commission on Environment and Development.* Oxford: Oxford University Press.

# 2

# The Johannesburg Summit: Implications for the Americas

ENRIQUE LEFF

Environmental degradation is the expression of a crisis in our present civilization. It is sparking a worldwide debate, from both global and regional perspectives, on strategies and methods for achieving a sustainable world. The views and interests voiced in this debate are extremely complex and diverse, and there is a need to critically analyze how the agenda of sustainable development is being conceived, shaped, and implemented in light of the power strategies in play in the new geopolitics of economic and ecological globalization.

The World Summit on Sustainable Development (WSSD) in Johannesburg in August 2002 is the most recent high-level gathering of heads of state to address these issues. However, Johannesburg was not Rio. The Rio Summit in 1992, held twenty years after the first United Nations Conference on the Human Environment, outlined basic principles, international agreements, and institutional arrangements to bring together ecology and economy, environment and development. In its Agenda 21, Rio delivered a global plan of action. It also established a Commission on Sustainable Development under the United Nations Economic and Social Division, and spurred the creation of a Global Environment Fund as the preeminent funding body for these issues at the global level. The Conventions on Biodiversity and Climate Change were established later to deliver the Cartagena Protocol on Biosafety and the Kyoto Protocol on Climate Change, together with other multilateral environmental agreements.

A set of principles was established at Rio to orient sustainable development, including the principle of common but differentiated responsibilities, the polluter payer principle, and the precaution principle. International conventions and multilateral environmental agreements promoted the goal of dematerializing production, together with pollution control regulations and incentives to gear industrial activity to clean production, setting in motion a new geopolitics of sustainable development. The Clean Development Mechanism set new standards for integrating developing countries into the goals of global sustainability. New functions (opportunities?) were set for tropical and underdeveloped countries as providers of environmental goods and services, under the new comparative advantages incorporated in economic-ecological globalization (see Leff et al. 2002).

We have seen three social actors—the market, the state, and the citizenry—negotiating their roles on the post-Rio path toward sustainability. But there were no clear strategies defined in Johannesburg regarding these actors' roles in achieving the goals set at the WSSD. The market's increased intervention in the valuation of "natural capital"—including environmental goods and services—and in gearing sustainability decisions in an increasingly complex environment has blurred the connections between market performance, poverty alleviation, and ecological balance, especially with regard to collective goods and public services such as education, health care, clean water, and housing.

From Rio to Johannesburg we have witnessed an over-economization of the sustainable development agenda. The slogan "trade, not aid" was coined to justify the lack of willingness among governments in the North to apply 0.7 percent of their gross national product (GNP) to development aid, as had been agreed in Rio 92 (the level achieved was just over 0.2 percent). Yet, based on global and regional social and environmental indicators, it appears unlikely that the free trade agenda—advanced through the North American Free Trade Agreement (NAFTA) and the later trade agreement with Chile, and via negotiations for a Central American agreement and a Free Trade Area of the Americas (FTAA) in 2005—is leading to sustainable development through equitable and just trade. The opportunity to develop innovative financing strategies and mechanisms for sustainable development was lost in Johannesburg, where participants failed to build on the UN Conference on Financing for Development, held in Monterrey, Mexico, a few months earlier.

In the ten years following the Rio Summit, Agenda 21 had developed into a new geopolitics of sustainable development. Research programs and policy mechanisms had been deployed to energize the scientific, technological, and political imagination to dematerialize production, to recycle materials, and to ban toxic and hazardous wastes—all oriented toward making the economy more sustainable. The Clean Development Mechanism was promoted, along with innovative economic theories and instruments for environmental management (including ideas such as optimum pollution and the merchandizing of pollution permits), to redistribute the costs and benefits of sustainable development in a new sharing of comparative advantages between nations wealthy in capital and technology and those rich in biodiversity, natural resources, and environmental services. But this geopolitics of sustainable development also came to house emergent socio-environmental movements that disputed the meanings, means, and ends of sustainable development through new rights and claims for the social appropriation of nature.

The Johannesburg Summit included no evaluation of the strategies and mechanisms of the Rio+10 process nor their social and environmental impacts. Nor was there any debate about the failure to meet the commitments made in Rio, or about new environmental emergencies and new strategies needed to build a sustainable future. Rather, the WSSD took a more functional focus, arriving at a Plan of Implementation for Agenda 21. And that was its major accomplishment.

On the road to Johannesburg, the Worldwatch Institute acknowledged that "steps in the 1990s toward a more just and ecologically resilient world were too small, too slow, or too poorly rooted." The institute's president, Christopher Flavin, went further, affirming,

> Ten years after the Rio Earth Summit, we are still far from ending the economic and environmental marginalization that afflicts billions of people. Despite the prosperity of the 1990s, the divide between rich and poor is widening in many countries, undermining social and economic stability. And pressures on the world's natural systems, from global warming to the depletion and degradation of resources such as fisheries and fresh water, have further destabilized societies.

While it is true that a number of social and environmental improvements had been achieved since Rio—including a decline in deaths from pneumonia, diarrhea, and tuberculosis, and the phasing out of production of ozone-depleting chlorofluorocarbons in industrial countries—a number of health and environmental problems had accumulated. Deaths from AIDS increased more than sixfold over the 1990s, and global emissions of greenhouse gases climbed more than 9 percent. Clearly, the environment continued to be degraded, yet it lost its priority status relative to other issue areas: at the same time that the United Nations Environment Programme (UNEP) struggled to maintain an annual budget of roughly US$100 million, military expenditures by the world's governments exceeded $2 billion per day.

Prior to the Johannesburg Summit, United Nations Secretary General Kofi Annan criticized the obsession with economic growth and noted its potentially disastrous global consequences in terms of environmental degradation and associated social, economic, and cultural costs.[1] An MIT study has shown that economic growth is not compatible with ecological sustainability. With its dynamic of unlimited growth and productive consumption of natural resources, the economic process accelerates environmental/entropic degradation by transforming mass and energy into their more degraded form: heat. Global warming has thus become the indicator of this entropic process driven by an economic rationale. This substantive truth about market rules and the laws of thermodynamics, though rejected by mainstream economics and official discourse on sustainable development, gives scientific support to Annan's comments.

What was new then in Johannesburg? The predetermined objective of the WSSD was to develop an implementation plan to reinforce the efficacy of policies already established in Agenda 21 for solving pressing social and

---

[1] The latest UNEP information shows that natural disasters—primarily weather-related catastrophes that result from economy-driven climate changes—cost the world over US$60 billion in 2003, up from about $55 billion the year before. Other sources have estimated that the economic costs of such "natural" disasters reached $608 billion during the 1990s, more than in all preceding decades. With rising sea levels and increasing climatic extremes, our vulnerability to natural disasters will surely increase (*Vital Signs* 2001).

environmental problems and achieving the goals of sustainable development. However, some "new" issues were highlighted as well and embedded in the international agenda. "WEHAB" was coined to refer to a set of priorities: water, environment, health, agriculture, and biodiversity, with water foremost among these. Nature had appeared superabundant before the UN Conference on the Human Environment in Stockholm in 1972, and the issue of global water scarcity had generally been neglected until the 1990s. This changed in the run-up to Johannesburg. Several sections of the implementation plan address key issues of global water management—from the need to take an ecosystem approach to economic valuation of water resources and services—and concern is growing over privatization actions currently under way as part of the larger process of economic appropriation and merchandizing of nature. Commitments were made in Johannesburg to develop integrated water resources management and water efficiency plans by 2005; to encourage the application by 2010 of the ecosystem approach for the sustainable development of the oceans; and, where possible, to maintain or restore depleted fish stocks by 2015 to levels that can produce the maximum sustainable yield.

Other issues gaining prominence included questions of biodiversity conservation and equitable access to and benefits from genetic resources (the new "green gold"), the problem of escalating soil degradation, and the capitalization of global agriculture. All of these cases are marked by a deepening tension between the economic-scientific-technological alliance (intellectual property rights, market mechanisms, and technology) versus the social reappropriation of nature based on cultural values and collective rights. Continuing to be particularly contentious here are subsidies to highly capitalized agricultural sectors in some of the more "developed" countries in the North and the accelerating spread of transgenic crops in the South. Johannesburg did little to address these issues, and northern countries seem likely to continue their deeply inequitable subsidy practices despite southern objections. On biodiversity, the WSSD agreed to achieve a significant reduction in the current rate of loss of biological diversity by 2010, but not to halt rates of extinction. The participants also agreed to establish an international system for the sharing of benefits from genetic resources with the original owners of these resources and the associated traditional knowledge.

Similarly, discussion of renewable energy sources—a topic pressed by a number of European, Latin American, and Caribbean countries—was generally frustrated by the intransigence of the United States (along with China, India, Japan, Australia, and Arab nations). Commitments on this issue were shallow—namely, to diversify energy supply and substantially increase the global share of renewable energy sources in the total energy supply, and to improve access to reliable, affordable, economically viable, socially acceptable, and environmentally sound energy services and resources. However, no percentages or time spans were set toward achieving this goal. Most disappointing for the Latin American and Caribbean countries was the reluctance to put into action a plan for transitioning to clean and renewable energy sources. A proposal, put forward by Latin American countries under the leadership of Brazil, was to reach an agreement specifying that by 2010, at least 10 percent of the energy consumed on the planet would come from clean energy sources (solar, biomass, wind) to replace the combustion of fuels such as oil and coal, which are the main sources of greenhouse gases.

Financing-for-development questions, including debt cancellation and the northern countries' general failure to live up to their Rio commitments to support global sustainable development efforts, similarly went unresolved. Financing for sustainable development declined after the Rio Summit, as developed nations failed to contribute the agreed-upon 0.7 percent of GDP in foreign aid for sustainable development. Foreign aid spending is now stagnant: despite a 30+ percent expansion in global economic output in the years since Rio, aid spending declined from US$69 billion in 1992 to $53 billion in 2000. Third World indebtedness is worsening; despite pledges at Rio to reduce indebtedness, the total debt burden of developing countries and those in transition climbed 34 percent to reach $2.5 trillion in 2000.

On toxic wastes, the WSSD agreed to strive to produce and use chemicals in ways that do not lead to significant adverse effects on human health and the environment, setting a year goal of 2020, and further, to promote the ratification and implementation of relevant international instruments on chemicals and hazardous waste. These included the Rotterdam Convention, projected to enter into force by 2003, and the Stockholm Convention, projected to be in force by 2004. The question of global warming and atmospheric gases was not effectively addressed. On the positive side was the news that Russia (followed by Canada and China) had agreed to ratify the Kyoto Protocol;[2] Russia later withdrew its commitment, however.

Nevertheless, meetings of Latin American and Caribbean environment ministers in the run-up to Johannesburg produced a regional commitment to sustainable development. The Latin American and Caribbean Initiative for Sustainable Development (ILAC) was approved, and important commitments were made to Africa and to small island nations also struggling with the effects of AIDS, desertification, poverty, and famine. In line with the United Nations Millennium Development Goals (MDGs), participants at Johannesburg committed to halve, by 2015, the proportion of people with incomes below $1 a day, people suffering from hunger, and people lacking access to safe drinking water and basic sanitation. They also agreed to achieve a significant improvement in the lives of at least one hundred million slum dwellers by 2020, as proposed in the "Cities Without Slums" initiative. Further, a world solidarity fund was proposed to eradicate poverty and to promote social and human development in the developing countries.

There was limited debate on education, an issue that was also ignored in the preparatory conferences that preceded the Johannesburg Summit. However, consensus was ultimately reached about the importance of education, with stipulations that, by 2015, all children will be able to complete a full course of primary schooling and that girls and boys will have equal access to all levels of education relevant to national needs; gender disparity in primary and secondary education is to be eliminated by 2005. The WSSD also recommended to the UN General Assembly that it consider adopting a "decade of education for sustainable development," starting in 2005.

Although governments reaffirmed a range of commitments and action targets to achieve more effective implementation of sustainable development objectives (to actively promote corporate responsibility and accountability, including more effective implementation of intergovernmental agreements and measures, international initiatives and public-private partnerships, and appropriate national regulations), no clear strategy or

---

[2] The Kyoto Protocol, established in 1997, proposes a 5.2 percent reduction (from a 1990 base level) in greenhouse gases. It entered into force in February 2005.

"road map" was discussed to link the objectives with concrete policy actions.

Financing of target programs is essential. The pledges that governments made to the WSSD goals are important, but they will not be sufficient.[3] There is nothing to ensure that these goals can be met through economic growth. In fact, there are strong doubts about free trade as the basic mechanism for achieving ecological sustainability and social justice, and substantial social resistance to allowing the market to assume responsibility for value judgments and decision making. This is clearly demonstrated by the proliferation of social movements and grassroots organizations around environmental issues.

However, there was not even a hint in Johannesburg about the possibility of deactivating the machine of unending economic growth and halting the perverse effects of climate change—only some half-hearted attempts to deal with some of the more disastrous impacts that this process has produced. None of the commitments at Johannesburg was allowed to undermine the priority of economic growth over environmental protection. Civil society's views were given due consideration at the summit in recognition of its key role in building partnerships with governments and business for

---

[3] The following are some of the financial commitments. There was agreement to replenish the Global Environment Facility with a total of US$3 billion. Norway pledged an additional $50 million following on the Johannesburg commitments. The United Kingdom announced it was doubling assistance to Africa to £1 billion a year and raising overall assistance for all countries by 50 percent. The European Union announced it would increase its development assistance with more than 22 billion euros in the years to 2006 and by more than 9 billion euros annually from 2006 onward. Germany announced a contribution of 500 million euros over five years to promote cooperation on renewable energy. Canada announced that, as of January 1, 2003, it would eliminate tariffs and quotas on most products from the least developed countries, and that by 2010 it would double development assistance. Japan announced that it would provide at least 250 billion yen in education assistance over a five-year period and would extend emergency food aid amounting to US$30 million to save children in southern Africa from famine; Japan also announced it would provide cooperation in environment-related capacity building by training five thousand people from overseas over a five-year period. Ireland announced that it has allocated almost 8 million euros in emergency funding in response to the humanitarian needs of African countries.

the implementation of the summit's goals. It is yet to be seen, however, how the actions of civil society will blend with those of the state and market to create synergies for sustainable development—particularly because of these actors' opposing views regarding how to attain sustainability. It will require more than goodwill, flexibility, tolerance, and innovating capacities in policy making and social participation to build a new environmental rationale.

Most of the goals set at the WSSD have been undermined by the dominant economic rationale, which privatizes public goods and affects public and social systems on all levels by internalizing short-term profits and externalizing social and environmental costs. Moreover, there has been a prevailing reluctance to heed scientific perspectives on global environmental change and ecological risk management. Yet no one can deny that the costs, even the strictly economic costs, of recent "natural" disasters are enormous. This is not a matter of opinion; the best scientific knowledge from the International Panel on Climate Change confirms the accelerating entropic degradation of our planet.[4] This is a true crisis, demanding a fun-

---

[4] In recent reports, the scientific committee of the International Panel on Climate Change announced the increasing risks of climate change: (1) It is very likely that the 1990s was the hottest decade and 1998 the hottest year at a global scale since 1861. Also, the rise in temperature in the twentieth century was probably higher than in any other century in the past thousand years. (2) In the high and middle latitudes of the Northern Hemisphere, it is quite possible that the snow cover has diminished by about 10 percent since the end of the 1960s, and the annual duration of the ice cover of lakes and rivers shortened by about two weeks during the twentieth century. It is possible that most of the ice cover from the end of summer and beginning of fall in the Arctic has been reduced by 40 percent in recent decades. (3) Since 1750, the concentration of $CO_2$ in the atmosphere has increased 31 percent, from 280 ppm (parts per million) to about 367 ppm today. The present concentration of $CO_2$ had not been reached in the past 420,000 years, and possibly not even during the past 20 million years. (4) Present trends indicate that average global temperature on the earth's surface will increase 1.4° to 5.8°C between 1990 and 2100, on top of the increase of 0.6°C since 1861. These projections are 1° to 3.5°C higher than those reported in the Second Evaluation Report of 1995, mainly due to the fact that it is now expected that future emissions of $SO_2$ (that help to cool the earth) will be lower. (5) The rise in the sea level between 1990 and 2100 has been estimated to measure between 0.09 to 0.88 meters.

damental paradigm shift that must be built through a more open and critical dialogue with all social groups.

Another issue not sufficiently addressed at Johannesburg is environmental security and biosafety. Although questions of ecological risk and food security were touched on in discussions of the costs of natural disasters and poverty alleviation, more complex issues were avoided, such as the paradox that, contrary to the highest scientific ideals, ecological risk arises in part from the over-application of science to nature. And in discussions of the equitable benefits of biotechnology, no consideration was given to biosafety, particularly the social, economic, and environmental risks of transgenic crops.

Happily, there was little focus on population growth as the major cause of environmental degradation, a flawed discourse that blames poor nations for ecological destruction. Presenting the global environmental crisis as the result of the world's population exceeding its carrying capacity had predominated in environment discourse since the 1960s. However, our current problem of an unsustainable world is not strictly a function of a humans-to-ecologies equation. Rather, it is a problem of production and consumption patterns. Exosomatic consumption poses a much greater problem than endosomatic consumption as unsustainable consumption patterns continue to expand in the wealthier countries. Predictions suggest that the world's population will stabilize at between 12 and 14 billion around the middle of the twenty-first century. The planet can handle this population—assuming sustainable production and consumption patterns. But it cannot support such a population under conditions of open-ended economic growth.

As for the implications of the Johannesburg Summit for the Americas, and especially for the Latin American and Caribbean region, the WSSD offered no new visions, frameworks, or strategies. The region's sustainability is now framed under the geopolitics of sustainable development deployed in the Rio+10 process. The only thing agreed upon in Johannesburg that will directly affect Latin America and the Caribbean is the Latin America and Caribbean Initiative for Sustainable Development. However, the fact that the ILAC was included in the Plan of Implementation—and that agreements were reached along the way for regionalization of the Plan of Implementation—gives room for endogenous actions to define and implement an agenda for sustainable development that is better suited to the specific environmental problems and sustainable development priorities of the countries of the region.

Thus the declaration stemming from the Fourteenth Meeting of the Forum of Ministers of the Environment of Latin America and the Caribbean (held in Panama in late 2003) called for the application of decisions taken at the UNEP's Governing Council and at Johannesburg regarding strengthening the regionalization of the Plan of Implementation and the UNEP's work plan. As a step toward such regionalization, the Forum identified eight ILAC points for implementation in 2004–2005: access to genetic resources and equitable sharing of benefits, water resources, human settlements, trade and environment, economic instruments and fiscal policy, renewable energy, climate change, and environmental indicators.[5]

Notwithstanding the importance of actions implemented under these intergovernmental and inter-agency agreements, sustainability in the Latin American and Caribbean region must be pursued within a context shaped by tensions between the following conflicting rationales and interests:

- The region will organize its most concerted efforts for sustainability under the ILAC. However, most decisions and actions will be taken under national policies and in subregional and binational negotiations. The countries of the region will play their cards under the rules of the Clean Development Mechanism, valuing and negotiating their comparative advantages as suppliers of environmental goods and services and anticipating more revenue from the trading of natural capital than from development aid or technology transfers under conditions that are advantageous for the recipient countries.

- Free trade and neoliberal economic policies will continue to shape the world order, setting market and trade conditions for sustainable development through the World Trade Organization (WTO) regimes and the application of economic instruments for environmental management. The plan to establish the FTAA in 2005 and ongoing negotiations for and implementation of other subregional and binational agreements (NAFTA, MERCOSUR, agreements with Chile and Central

---

[5] For the final report of the Forum of Ministers, which establishes the directions, priorities, and mandate for application of the Plan of Implementation in the Latin American and Caribbean region, see www.pnuma.org.

America) have set the scene and written the libretto and score for the various actors who are playing roles in the drama of sustainability.

- The call for a closer partnership among state, market, and citizenry will continue to engender tensions as the process toward sustainability comes to be expressed as a struggle for the social appropriation of nature, where the different visions of the actors involved are apparent in their reluctance to subdue their own interests to the laws of economic and political power governing sustainable development policies. Movements among peasants and indigenous peoples will continue to resist neoliberal policies and will become increasingly "environmentalized," internalizing ecological considerations in their demands for land, cultural rights, and autonomy. These social/environmental movements will receive support from political/academic groups such as LatAutonomy and from grassroots nongovernmental organizations. Regional programs for sustainable development—such as the Mesoamerican Biological Corridor or Plan Puebla-Panamá—will face resistance from local populations and grassroots movements. The debate around transgenic crops will continue, given the failure to establish effective mechanisms for equitable distribution of the benefits of biotechnology, which yields huge profits for the giant agricultural biotechnology companies while displacing an increasing number of peasants and small producers from their land to make way for the new genetic latifundios.

The Johannesburg Summit produced a top-level international agreement to unite efforts toward a sustainable future. The pragmatics of identifying and implementing responses to issues raised in Johannesburg will now unfold in the political arena, where social interests contend for the social reappropriation of nature.

**Reference**

Leff, E., A. Argueta, E. Boege, and C. W. Porto Gonçalves. 2002. "Más allá del desarrollo sostenible. La construcción de una racionalidad ambiental para la sustentabilidad. Una visión desde América Latina." In *La transición hacia el desarrollo sustentable: Perspectivas de América Latina y el Caribe*, ed. E. Leff et al. Mexico: PNUMA/INE-SEMARNAT/UAM.

# Part II

## Equity and Urbanization on the Border: Prospects for Sustainable City-Regions

# 3

# Toward a Sustainable Development in the U.S.-Mexico Border Region

JOHN FRIEDMANN

International development discourse is full of specialized jargon, words that suddenly catch hold of the imagination and for a while become fashionable. Sustainable development is a recent addition. But for someone like me, who has been around the development game for fifty years, the now-popular "sustainable" triggers a memory of W. W. Rostow's metaphor of the "takeoff" into self-sustaining economic growth (1960). In the early 1960s, at the height of Fordism and the Keynesian welfare state, during the dark years of the Cold War, Rostow's anticommunist manifesto did its part in the national propaganda department. It held out the prospect of universal happiness in a world of high mass consumption. At that time we were still living in an era of *national* capitalisms; and according to Professor Rostow's thesis, national economies had to pass through a fixed sequence of "stages" in a successful transition to the final stage of high mass consumption. It was all a matter of having the right combination of policies that would continually raise the value of production above the rate of population growth, chiefly through a shift in the deployment of so-called surplus labor out of agriculture and into secondary industries. The rate of capital accumulation was to play a key role in this structural transformation.

I do not want to single out Professor Rostow for making what was essentially an ideological argument touting the virtues of the capitalist mode of production. He was merely one voice, albeit an influential one, articulating the prevailing wisdom among development economists, even in Latin America. Some readers may remember Raúl Prebisch of the Economic

Commission for Latin America, who succeeded in reducing all the complexities and ambiguities of economic development to the ratio of output to capital.

How far we have traveled in the intervening decades! Our thinking has completely turned around. We old-timers were all Keynesians; now, like it or not, we have had to come to terms with globalism in the new dispensation of a neoliberal world dominated by the United States. In this context, "sustainable" no longer means a flight path into self-sustaining economic growth, but maintaining social relations and the natural environment in a state of dynamic equilibrium. Both are understood as constraints on unregulated markets. It is, therefore, to sustainability in this new dimension, especially as it pertains to localities and regions, that I turn.

After a decade or so, the global discourse on sustainability has become ritualized. Who is seriously going to declare himself in favor of an *unsustainable* development? So the rhetoric, particularly in the public media but in academic utterances as well, must be carefully examined to see what people really have in mind when they say that development must become more "sustainable." Are they challenging neoliberal doctrine as inherently unsustainable, or are they working within the dominant paradigm while treating sustainability as an add-on, a minor modification of standard neoliberal policies, to put a human face on them, to alleviate (but not eradicate) poverty and conjure up Technicolor images of "blue skies and clear water"? If it is the latter, the small print usually says that sustainability is fine so long as it does not cost too much or overly restrict the presumptive right of corporate capital to do pretty much as it pleases.

## IMAGINING AN ALTERNATIVE DEVELOPMENT

I would not be writing these lines if I held with this second meaning. When I wrote *Empowerment: The Politics of Alternative Development* (1992), what I rejected was clear. I wanted to change the way we think about economic development and the mass poverty associated with it. To do so, I began my analysis with a study of the household economy as the fundamental social unit for the production of life and livelihood. At the time, this represented a radical turn away from neoclassical economics, where households play no visible role in the creation of value and the focus is an individual abstracted from all social relations who, in the guise of the notorious fiction of "economic man," is treated, on the one hand, as a "factor of production" and, on the other, as a "consumer" with potentially unlimited desires. (In neoclassical theory, the role of households in social reproduction is only implicit, and their economic function as a subsidy to capital is not explored—a matter of accounting practice.)

Positing the household as the basic unit for the production of life and livelihood accomplishes a number of things for a model of an alternative development. First, insofar as the production of anything is always a social process, the household economy is treated analytically as a network of social relations of extended family, friends, neighbors, work mates, and social organizations. An alternative development, therefore, shifts from the fiction of the autonomous individual to a web of social relations.

Second, households participate simultaneously in two economies: the market where supply and demand interact, and a moral economy of reciprocal obligations. Accordingly, work is not merely that which is accomplished for a monetary return; it also includes unpaid work needed for social reproduction and for maintaining the web of a household's social relations. Much of this unpaid work, which is essential for life and livelihood, is done by women.

Third, in an alternative development, the focus is on the household's self-production of life and livelihood, rather than on the satisfaction of unbounded economic wants. In this context, "life" implies two things that need to be considered separately. It implies, first, that the maintenance of human life at a level of basic subsistence is a primary need of all human beings and, second, that in the context of the moral economy, households must, in addition to merely sustaining life, fulfill certain culturally specific obligations, such as religious and other social observances, that tie households and their individual members into larger networks of social relations. But reference to "life and livelihood" is also meant to suggest that the broader aim of households is to achieve a culturally specified "decent" standard of living above mere survival. Admittedly, "decent" standards are subjective criteria that would normally be defined as a bundle of specific goods and services. Translated into a normative statement, a decent livelihood implies that society's obligations toward households that range below this standard, however these may be defined, cease once the agreed-upon standard has been reached.

Fourth, the household unit is posited as a relatively autonomous political economy with a capacity for deciding on the allocation of the resources available to it and negotiating the different and often conflicting claims of its members. Social relations within households, particularly as drawn along lines of gender and age, are therefore understood to be always in tension and subject to continuous renegotiation.

Finally, the household model of an alternative development places emphasis on access to the means for the self-production of life and livelihood. I refer to these means as a household's bases of social power. At least eight such bases can be identified: a safe life space (including housing and associated community services), surplus time over and above the time necessary for social reproduction, participation in social networks and in organizations, useful knowledge and skills, relevant information, tools of production (including physical and mental health), and financial resources. This multi-stranded concept of social power is intended to substitute for mainstream notions of income poverty. Because many households are relatively disempowered—that is, they are living below a threshold of a culturally and socially defined minimum decent standard of living—a degree of state intervention is necessary to improve their access to at least some of these bases of social power.

But state intervention does not, as a rule, come of its own accord; it requires sustained pressure from below to redeem the claims of specific human and citizen rights. From a household perspective then, this claiming of rights, which is a collective process achieved through social mobilization, can be seen as a social and, ultimately, a political process of empowerment. Though centered in households, political empowerment extends outward toward more inclusive alignments with community and labor struggles, with churches, political parties, voluntary organizations—in short, with the whole of organized civil society. Once it achieves this level of mobilization, radical changes in society, including the redirection of development policies from unlimited accumulation to a genuinely sustainable development, loom as a real possibility.

## TOWARD REGIONAL AUTONOMY: INVESTING IN REGIONAL ASSETS

We need to be clear, however, about what we mean by a genuinely sustainable development in the contemporary sense. Here I will focus on the city-region, because contemporary economic and social developments are no longer effectively bounded by nation-states but are increasingly articulated nationally, transnationally, and indeed globally through intercity networks.[1] This new way of looking at the spatial configuration of economic development has led to a competitive frenzy among city-regions. Here are a few choice sentences from development guru Kenichi Ohmae:

> As a corporate adviser, my role is to advise companies where to invest. The CEOs of major companies are so busy that unless you are on the short list of investment opportunities, you will not even be considered as a possibility. There are dozens of regions and cities that would like to attract the capital and corporate presence of some of my clients, but unless you have made it to the short list, you will be bypassed. To make the short list, you must offer real value and, ultimately, capture the investor's imagination.... It becomes essential, therefore, to segment and objectively assess the potential competition. To make sure that, for a particular purpose, *your* city, *your* region, *your* country is the best—it all comes back to marketing (Ohmae 2000: 34).

City marketing has become a universal obsession. In this perspective, cities are expected to sell themselves to global capital or, as Ohmae puts it, to "offer real value ... to capture the investor's imagination." The "real value" in this case means tax breaks, dedicated infrastructure, and the construction of urban enclaves that cater to the tastes of global investors, from luxury housing to upscale shopping districts. In a broader sense, it also means creating a "friendly business environment" that will open the doors of City Hall to the representatives of international capital and help ensure a docile labor force willing to work for globally competitive wages. Listening to consultants such as Ohmae, a city will be tempted to mortgage its future by promoting itself as a venue for major sporting events, world exhibitions, millennium domes, and similar extravaganzas. Stephen Graham and Simon Marvin have amassed evidence from around the world

---

[1] This section is based on Friedmann 2002: chap. 2, "City Marketing and Quasi City-States: Two Models of Urban Development."

regarding the results of such lopsided kowtowing to international capital. Here is an example from Mumbai (Bombay):

> Mumbai, long a symbol of India's hoped-for progress towards emancipation, has, in effect, become deeply dualised. All aspects of consensus between rich and poor, and their political groups, have broken down. Carefully networked high-rise structures provide a three-dimensional landscape of exclusion and polarisation. They create "localities of the ultra-wealthy and the upper middle class," groups who have benefited enormously from the liberalisation of India's economy and Mumbai's key role in articulating that economy with the rest of the world.
>
> Building works and public subsidy have gone overwhelmingly to serve the living, working, and leisure and transport needs and desires of these groups.... Shanty residents, meanwhile, have to make do with highly inadequate stand pipes or worse still, private water vendors who charge exorbitant rates (Graham and Marvin 2001: 284).

Similar stories could be told about other cities. The point is that policies that are focused on the needs and desires of global capital rather than on a region's inhabitants will leave even household- and community-centered efforts at self-empowerment as meaningless gestures that provide little more than temporary relief from poverty. In effect, they are more welfare programs than an alternative development. The continued disempowerment of large portions of the urban population will ultimately lead to a dualized city, leaving the yawning gap between rich and poor to grow larger and larger. The implication of this scenario is that an alternative development cannot stop at the household level but must seek to create appropriate policies at the meso-level of city and region that will be consonant with people's efforts at self-empowerment. I shall refer to such policies as an endogenous development.

Endogenous development used to mean erecting temporary tariff barriers to protect a country's infant industries and other economic sectors from foreign competition. This was the original thought of Friedrich List, who advocated this policy for an ostensible German Customs Union in

1840. But this is not what I mean. Rather, I have in mind policies at the meso-level of city-region that will direct local investments toward the development of the multiple resource assets that the region possesses. Just as an alternative development seeks to strengthen a household's autonomy by improving its access to the several bases of social power, so an endogenous development seeks to strengthen a city-region's relative autonomy through investment in what I will describe as seven interrelated resource complexes essential for sustaining a city-region's long-term ability to compete globally. These complexes include:

- *Human capital*, or all the things that nurture our ability to grow into healthy and productive human beings: good nutrition, housing and viable neighborhoods, health care, and education.
- *Social capital*, which is a robust, self-organizing civil society deeply engaged with the everyday life of its communities.
- *Cultural capital*, or the region's physical heritage and the distinctiveness and vibrancy of its cultural life.
- *Intellectual capital*, or the quality of the region's universities and research institutions and what Japan calls its "living human treasures"— its leading artists, intellectuals, and scientists who embody the city's creative powers.
- *Environmental capital*, which includes those qualities of the physical environment that are essential for sustaining life itself, such as the air we breathe, the water we drink, and the capacity of the land to sustain permanent human settlement.
- *Natural capital*, or the region's natural resource endowment, such as land, landscapes, beaches, forests, fisheries, and mineral deposits whose use is for production and enjoyment.
- *Urban capital*, commonly referred to as urban infrastructure, which includes facilities and equipment for transportation, energy, water supply, sewage treatment, and solid waste disposal—or, in a more general sense, the built environment.

These seven tightly interwoven resource complexes constitute a city-region's productive assets. The benefits of investing in them must be calculated in social rather than purely economic terms extending over a long period; that is, they must be measured against broad societal goals and values. Nurturing them is not only congruent with an alternative development; it is the sine qua non for a development that puts human life and livelihood ahead of market calculations.[2]

## ON THE BORDER: WHICH REGIONS?

This essay is specifically addressed to interested parties in a city-region divided between two countries. Together, Tijuana and San Diego form a sizable metropolis of between four and five million people, with strong economic and social interdependencies. Some might argue that, given these interdependencies, treating the two as a single city-region—a megacity—would make a lot of sense.[3] But if such a proposal were ever put to a popular vote, I wonder what the outcome would be. Both cities are far from their respective national capitals, and this might be an argument favoring greater autonomy for the border region inasmuch as both Mexico and the United States are federal systems. But each city has its own political culture and, besides, is a constituent part of a larger political entity: Baja California and California, respectively. Moreover, the border divides two very unequal cities: not only does San Diego have more than double Tijuana's population, it has more than fourteen times Tijuana's economic power as measured by the size of the municipal budget alone. Tijuana's economy is in many ways dependent, perhaps excessively so, on San Diego. Much of its population consists of recent arrivals—between 1990 and 2000, Tijuana's annual growth rate was on the order of 5 percent—most of whom are attracted by the prospect of finding a job on the border and/or doing a stint of work in the United States. Although both cities have considerable income poverty, Tijuana's poverty is more desperate and deeper. According to an article in the *New York Times* (February 11, 2001), more than half its population is reported to be living below the official line of poverty.

And so I am inclined to argue that while there can be joint planning and negotiation on many common issues across the border—indeed, a great

---

[2] For more detail, see Friedmann 2002: chap. 2.

[3] For the opposing point of view, see Alegría 2000.

deal is already going on—the conditions for an alternative development in the search for greater regional autonomy must be established through separate political processes in each city-region. I have no illusion that it will be easy for either Tijuana or San Diego to even imagine, let alone embark upon, a more autonomous, endogenous development; yet absent such a development, sustainability cannot be achieved.

September 11, 2001, has had the effect of slowing transborder flows to a crawl, particularly from south to north, and the border has become something like the Great Wall of China to keep out the barbarians. The strong economic and social links between the two cities are still there, and the communication highway is still open. But the wall along the border may also be viewed, at least by the people of Tijuana and Baja California more broadly, as an opportunity for a more endogenous development, for building up Tijuana's regional assets—human, social, cultural, environmental—and for pursuing public policies that will guarantee each local citizen the right to a decent—dare we even to think of a socially guaranteed?—livelihood. The competition among cities for international capital is a race to nowhere. But an autonomous, people-centered, and environmentally responsible development always remains at least a theoretical possibility.

I would like to close with a quotation from a couple of senior economists who have recently published what is probably, for the time being, the most definitive study of growing inequality and poverty during the reform period in China. I do so because the authors use the hard-edged language of economics to say what I have said in more colloquial language. Their advice is aimed at the Chinese central government, and I think similar advice might be given to the central government of Mexico. For in the end, it is the central government that will have to act in both countries to create an equitable and sustainable development. Here is what Azizur Khan and Carl Riskin have to say:

> The key, in our view, is to promote a comprehensive strategy for reduced inequality and poverty that includes consistent actions involving both macroeconomic and institutional policies that influence the overall pattern of development, as well as microeconomic interventions to improve household capabilities.... [F]ostering growth through policies that channel resources away from poor areas and people and then trying

to compensate via a poverty alleviation program turns out to have been an ineffective overall strategy for coping with poverty [in China]; it implies that the government's social welfare function assigns too low a de facto weight to poverty reduction. China, whose anti-poverty approach has been entirely focused on a limited number of designated poor counties, needs to formulate a comprehensive strategy that embraces rural poverty outside the designated counties as well as growing poverty in urban areas (Khan and Riskin 2001: 154).

In the end, poverty reduction in China's galloping economy, no less than in Mexico or the United States, will depend on national commitments along precisely these lines. This is unlikely to happen soon, however. The Rostovian model of aggressive capital accumulation prevails nearly everywhere today, China included. It is based on an ideology that largely succeeds in blaming the victims. The poor are responsible for their own poverty, they say. They are losers. Rather than resetting the policy parameters at the national level in ways that would allow for a development based on principles of social justice, the bottom one-fifth to one-third of society are thrown the bones of charitable neglect. A socially sustainable development is therefore not visible on the horizon, neither on the border nor indeed anywhere. This, alas, is an unhappy conclusion but—without a change in the regime of political economy—a conclusion that leaves us with little hope for a sustainable development.[4]

---

[4] In comments on the first draft of this essay, Lawrence Herzog showed the broader picture of what the single-minded pursuit of the Rostovian model has meant for the culture of cities. He refers to them as the seven ecologies of neoliberalism: an ecology of fear, of which the U.S.-Mexico border wall is the ultimate symbol of U.S. efforts to protect itself against the greater poverty of its neighbor; an ecology of consumerism, symbolized by supermarkets and global franchises; an ecology of global production, symbolized by the twinning of the global factory with its skewed distribution of power: R&D, finance, and marketing strategies to the north of the wall and low-cost assembly work to the south; an ecology of global tourism, which sacrifices real places for ones that erase local cultures and make way for the erotic fantasies of the global imaginary; an ecology of social polarization, in which the rich retreat into their fortified compounds, leaving the city of the poor to the care

## References

Alegría, Tito. 2000, "Juntos pero no revueltos: ciudades en la frontera México–Estados Unidos," *Revista Mexicana de Sociología* 62, no. 2: 89–107.

Friedmann, John. 1992. *Empowerment: The Politics of Alternative Development.* Oxford: Blackwell.

———. 2002. *The Prospect of Cities.* Minneapolis: University of Minnesota Press.

Graham, Stephen, and Simon Marvin. 2001. *Splintering Urbanism: Networked Infrastructures, Technological Mobilities, and the Urban Condition.* London: Routledge.

Khan, Azizur Rahman, and Carl Riskin. 2001. *Inequality and Poverty in China in the Age of Globalization.* Oxford and New York: Oxford University Press.

Ohmae, Kenichi. 2000. "How to Invite Prosperity from the Global Economy into a Region." In *Global City Regions: Trends, Theory, Policy*, ed. Allen J. Scott. Oxford and New York: Oxford University Press.

Rostow, W. W. 1960. *The Stages of Economic Growth: A Non-Communist Manifesto.* Cambridge: Cambridge University Press.

---

of drug lords and police; an ecology of placelessness, in which land has been commodified to the point that it is simply an aggregate of parcels of real estate whose value is set by the market; and an ecology of the global citadel, symbolized by mega-airports and the ubiquitous high-rise office towers supplied courtesy of Global Architecture together with the playgrounds of the rich: brand-name museums, philharmonics, and secluded luxury resorts.

# 4

# Rethinking Urban Ecologies: Cultural Barriers to Sustainable Development?

LAWRENCE A. HERZOG

We face a colossal challenge in addressing the problem of sustainability and urban development. There is a tendency—in the fields of urban planning, sociology of development, or environmental studies—for proponents of sustainability to "preach to the choir." We can write elegant books and articles, construct community outreach strategies, or design Web sites. We have insightful new conceptual tools that point toward the household economy (and not the "rational consumer" of neoclassical economics) as the fulcrum of sustainable life (see John Friedmann's chapter in this volume). We know that sustainability must occur at the intersection of technology, science, art, and social networking.[1]

But how do we deliver the message of sustainability to those outside the boundaries of our circle of intellectuals and believers in sustainability? How do we get the urban masses to rethink their values? How do we deliver a sustainable society to an urban culture that worships SUVs and sprawling suburbs?

What is clear is that "sustainability" is an imprecise notion. It is not merely about the physical environment, nor is it only about politics. Sustainability is, in the end, about culture, values, and a way of life. In this essay, I offer a set of ecologies of urban life in Western society that synthesizes the kinds of cultural barriers we will need to overcome before we can tread down the path of alternative development.

---

Some of this discussion appears in Herzog 2003.

[1] These ideas are articulated in Keith Pezzoli's excellent essay in this volume.

## THE ECOLOGY OF FEAR

> *Si él de Berlin cayó, él de Tijuana, ¿porqué no? [If the Berlin wall fell, why not the one in Tijuana?].* (graffiti on the international boundary fence at Tijuana–San Diego)

For more than a century, Mexican border cities like Tijuana defined their existence by links to the physical boundary. Tijuana, like so many Mexican border cities, occupied a schizophrenic world, dancing between the reality of its economic ties to the United States and its nationalist link to Mexico. The physical boundary—the wall, the fence—stood as a constant reminder of this dual identity.

Today, globalization along the border evokes a critical debate. Does the region's future lie with perpetuation of the wall and all that it symbolizes—national security, sovereignty, defense, and militarization—or does it reside in the propagation of a world of transparent boundaries and transfrontier cities? This theme shapes an underlying tension embedded in the built environment of border cities, a tension that is manifest in the conflicted landscapes of the immediate boundary zone where the two nations meet.

The popular global icon of militarized boundaries is the Berlin Wall—a landscape of bleak, gray images of barbed wire, concrete barriers, soldiers in watchtowers peering through binoculars, and bodies of failed border crossers draped across the no-man's-land between East and West. Before its destruction, the Berlin Wall ran 66 miles in 12-foot-high concrete block and 35 miles in wire and mesh fencing. It had over two hundred watchtowers and blinding yellow night-lights mounted on tall poles.

The Tijuana–San Diego "wall" is 47 miles long and constructed of corrugated metal landing mats recycled from the Persian Gulf War. Migrants have punched it full of holes, so a second parallel wall is under construction a few hundred feet north. The new wall includes 18-foot-high concrete "bollard" pilings topped with tilted metal mesh screens and an experimental cantilevered wire mesh–style fence being developed by Sandia Labs. The fence/wall runs toward the Pacific Ocean, where it becomes a ziggurat of 8-, 6- and 4-foot-high metal tube fence knifing into the sea. It is buttressed by 6 miles of stadium night-lights, 1,200 seismic sensors, and numerous infrared sensors to detect the movement of people after dark.

Like the Berlin Wall, Tijuana's boundary landscapes explode with images of danger and conflict. These images tend to reduce the border to a cliché, a war zone, a place controlled by national governments and their police. Signage on and near the line reinforces an underlying theme: that only governments can decide who crosses. The U.S. government's "Operation Gatekeeper," a strategic 1994 plan launched by the U.S. Immigration and Naturalization Service, is perhaps the most blatant example of a national policy to "Berlinize" the California-Mexico border. Indeed, one official claimed that the operation's goals were to "restore the rule of law to the California–Baja California border."[2] This theme of "militarization" along the border has remained part of the landscape, always threatening to move to the forefront each time a crisis looms. The September 11, 2001, terrorist events in the United States had the immediate effect of resurrecting the policing, enforcement-oriented functions of the international border. This then spiraled into the creation of the Department of Homeland Security.

In San Diego–Tijuana, five million inhabitants share an economy with US$6 billion in annual exports and US$8 billion in cross-border trade. Tourism is booming. Billions will be invested in mega-resorts, luxury marinas, and vacation homes along the coast of nearby Baja California. Some one thousand international assembly plants (*maquiladoras*) employing a quarter-million workers will be here by 2010. This region could be the next Hong Kong. Yet, to poor immigrants huddling at the taco stands along the boundary fence, these dreams reside thousands of miles away in the national capitals. Here on the edge of Mexico, every night as the sun sets, Border Patrol helicopters emerge, like mosquitoes, buzzing the skies and beaming laser spotlights down into the canyons and migrant footpaths. The wall lives.

While images of international walls and the post–9/11 obsession with homeland security dominate the public conscience, the fact is that walls and physical barriers are just as easily imbedded in the internal social ecology of Western cities. Scholars have written about the "mean streets" of urban North America, the fear of urban crime and its impact on the production of horizontal, fragmented suburbs (see, for example, Davis 1990). Urban dwellers have moved away from the city, away from its spontane-

---

[2] Alan D. Bersin, U.S. Attorney, San Diego, cited in Nevins 2000.

ous public spaces, and toward a world of gated communities. The twenty-first-century urban landscape of North America, like the immediate border, is defined by walls and fences. They come in the form of gated communities, or privatized, distant suburbs, or zoning ordinances that protect large lots and effectively keep the working and lower classes from moving to the suburban periphery.

Sustainable development relies on the notion of social conscience and community. Privatized suburbs generally do not enhance a community conscience. Low-density sprawl and the dependence on automobiles tend to isolate suburban dwellers. Until we can reshape the tastes of urban housing consumers, suburban sprawl becomes a reaction to the ecology of fear, and it poses a barrier to a more community-driven, collective consciousness and a sustainable urban future.

## THE ECOLOGY OF CONSUMPTION

One of the guiding principles of global capitalism has been the "culture-ideology of consumerism." Global corporations use advertising and transnational media not merely to sell their products across the globe but to promote a style of consumption that becomes part of a standardized global culture (Sklair 1991). Examples of "globalized consumption" include soft drinks and fast food. Part of the success in marketing these commodities globally can be traced to corporate strategies to homogenize consumer tastes. By constructing globally uniform consumer behavior (through advertising and the construction of recognizable images), multinational corporations can better control the marketing of their products.

This global homogenization of consumer taste arguably exists not only in food products, clothing, and automobiles, but also in the built environment. The design of shopping malls, fast-food restaurants, hotels, resorts, and other urban spaces has become globalized. There are no longer vast differences between shopping mall designs in China, Ireland, Peru, or Mexico. Malls have a standardized site plan and design concept that includes anchor stores, public areas for walking and sitting, food courts, movie theaters, and restaurants. Further, there is a growing trend for global chain stores selling clothing, electronics, and other consumer goods to rent spaces in shopping malls around the world. Hotels and resorts often use standardized designs as well. Indeed, many corporate hotel chains believe that travelers like the predictable, familiar designs of hotel chains in the United States and Western Europe, and developers thus seek to replicate those designs in other cultural settings. Their marketing departments claim that consumers prefer their hotels' familiar images over the less familiar components of local cultures.

These designs are not merely limited to buildings. The new public spaces of the twenty-first century will be privatized streets, festival marketplaces, or giant mall complexes. Increasingly, these consumer spaces seek to replace the traditional downtown as the primary pedestrian-scale gathering place for postmodern city dwellers. The quintessential privatized street is "City Walk," on the west side of Los Angeles, whose architects successfully re-created the scale and feel of a pedestrian street. For example, each store is visually presented as a separate façade, giving the impression of a street lined with individual buildings. City Walk promotes itself as a series of city streets where people can walk and interact. In fact, it is a large private shopping center disguised as a small village of pedestrian spaces, lined with restaurants, clothing boutiques, specialty stores, and movie theaters.

Mexico has embraced the commodified landscape. Four decades ago, a nationalist and proud Mexico rejected most U.S. commercial enterprises within its borders; there were virtually no McDonalds or Burger Kings and no U.S. clothing enterprises anywhere in Mexico as late as the 1980s. But since the signing of the North American Free Trade Agreement (NAFTA), Mexico has opened its doors to U.S. and foreign business. Today, hundreds of U.S. chain stores and hotels have spread across the Mexican landscape—from Blockbuster Video, Office Depot, and Sears to Direct TV, Costco, and Walmart. Most global hotel chains—including Hilton, Hyatt, and Sheraton—have also exploded onto the Mexican scene.

The dominance of the U.S. culture-ideology of consumerism has been particularly intense along the U.S.-Mexico border. In the early 1990s, fast-food outlets invaded border cities like Tijuana virtually overnight. In the span of a couple of years, every major food outlet—McDonald's, Carl's Jr., Burger King, Domino's Pizza, and so on—had embedded themselves in the urban landscape. Around the same time, small, midsize, and large shopping centers began to appear along commercial boulevards and highways. In Tijuana, these mini-malls, with their set-back buildings and parking lots in the front, interrupted the pedestrian scale of the downtown. U.S.-style mega-malls also sprouted along the border; Tijuana now has two regional-sized shopping malls. U.S. and foreign corporate interests have little trouble selling consumption to residents of Tijuana and other border cities. Most can access programming from Southern California via satellite television, allowing advertisers to reach an enormous, captive Mexican audience and teach them "how to consume." As a result, Mexicans living along the border have proven to be highly motivated customers on the U.S. side. Studies have shown, for example, that Mexican consumers have similar (if not better) information and a slightly better understanding than do California residents of the locations and qualities of stores and products in the San Diego region (see Herzog 1999).

A mass consumerist built environment promotes an urban culture that does not think in terms of sustainability. Artificially lit and climate-controlled shopping malls create a wall between city dwellers and their environment. Designed public spaces that foster uncontrolled consumption interfere with other pursuits, such as walking in the natural environment or meeting and conversing with friends and neighbors. A mass consumerist landscape is itself unsustainable, and it becomes a cultural barrier to building a mass consciousness about sustainability.

## THE ECOLOGY OF GLOBAL MANUFACTURING

The "global factory" is one of the great inventions of late-twentieth-century world capitalism. As labor costs impinged on multinational firms' profits in the 1950s and 1960s, the idea arose for global enclaves of cheap labor. Firms discovered they could simply move the factory floor to a less developed nation. Third World countries loomed as the new industrial labor pools for global industrial giants. Thus was born the global factory.

Mexico quickly became a key player through the "twin plant" or maquiladora project. In the 1960s, Mexico's government established a new federal office—the National Border Program, or PRONAF—to promote border economic expansion. The biggest plank in the PRONAF development strategy was reducing unemployment through industrial growth. In 1965, the government introduced the Border Industrialization Program (BIP) to build on the offshore production concepts that U.S. manufacturers had already started in places like Hong Kong and Taiwan. The BIP project envisioned foreign-owned (mainly American) factories relocating their labor-intensive assembly operations to the Mexican border.

And relocate they did. The BIP forever changed the Mexican borderlands. In 1970 there were 160 maquiladoras in Mexico, employing around 20,000 workers. Some twenty-five years later, there were an estimated 2,400 such plants, employing nearly 750,000 workers and with a value-added estimated at roughly US$3 billion. All of these plants are foreign owned; the majority come from the United States, Japan, South Korea, Canada, and Germany.

Maquiladoras brought a dramatic global shift to the Mexican border. They single-handedly legitimated the border region as a place for foreign investment. Asian, European, and U.S. investors facilitated the border's emergence on the radar screen of the global economic community. The construction of assembly plant complexes served to anchor the real estate and development boom of the late twentieth century, bringing roads, sewerage, and other infrastructure to outlying areas of the cities. Maquilas created an alternative job source for millions of Mexican immigrants heading north, and the factories' multiplier effects (they generated linked employment clusters in services) further expanded urban growth. The sheer numbers of new workers amplified pressures on cities like Tijuana to find ways to absorb the incoming migrants.

Within the Mexican border landscape, these factories consolidate around an ecology of the modern industrial park, not unlike the counterpart U.S. suburban industrial parks to the north. As in the United States, the dominant feature is the use of uniform lot sizes and street setbacks, as well as controlled landscaping. There are also sophisticated systems of screening and security as well as large-scale parking facilities.

Maquilas are poorly suited to a sustainable city. For one, they resemble a kind of suburban hacienda compound, an insular space where workers provide labor to the *"patrón"* (the industrial giant) in return for a modest salary. Maquila parks are surrounded by poor colonias, low-income settlements that typically house many of the plants' workers.

A second environmental feature is that maquilas have been notoriously insensitive to the physical environment. Reports abound of air pollution and the dumping of toxic wastes and untreated sewage. Further, the plants' interior environments are poorly designed, such that workers have been exposed to toxins and other unsafe labor conditions (Herzog 1990; Sklair 1995; Pena 1997).

By its very nature, a maquila is a leased space that performs a function for a company located thousands of miles away. This inherently opens the possibility for environmental insensitivity. The maquila as a feature of the built environment is an external imposition. It fosters global manipulation of the local environment. It is the enemy of the concept of "bioregion."

## THE ECOLOGY OF LEISURE

Industrial and postindustrial societies produce a luxury that did not exist in preindustrial societies: leisure time. Leisure time, in turn, created a new tertiary economy—vacation planning and tourism development—which has become one of the fastest-growing economic sectors of the new age of globalization. This multi-billion-dollar industry is largely defined by the distortion of places, regions, and ecology.

Tourism development adheres strongly to the principles of the culture-ideology of consumerism. A central premise of tourism design is the manipulation of a visitor's experience of place so as to maximize profit. Global tourism investors and corporate decision makers tend to view regions as stage sets for generating profit, rather than as genuine places whose identity should be protected. Because global developers generally view investments from distant world headquarter cities like New York, Chicago, or San Francisco, they often lose touch with the places their investments are transforming. The main strategy of tourism development is to enhance marketability and client interest through the production of landscapes that satisfy the needs of projected users (Pena 1997). Tourists prefer comfort, reliability, and pleasure, especially in foreign settings. The architecture designed to accommodate visitors, what one writer calls the "tourism gaze," is a landscape socially constructed for a targeted population (Urry 1990). It has been compared to Foucault's "medical gaze," a strategy of controlled design aimed at a different economic interest group (consumers of medical services and facilities).

Tourism developers seek to create homogenous, readily distinguished, easily consumed built-environment experiences for their client populations. Controlled resort structures with recognizable designs (oceanfront boardwalks, hotels, fast-food outlets, global boutiques, and small, clustered shopping and restaurant complexes) have become the central pillars of tourism landscape design. The value of tourist space is measured by its marketability for short-term tourism visits, rather than by its cultural uniqueness or environmental purity.

Global tourism reveals the dangers of commodification—the transformation of tourism spaces into generic commodities for sale in the world market. As with product marketing, global companies want to standardize the tourism experience. Large-scale tourism resort developments, based on uniform design criteria, are not crafted with the local environment in mind, which is why they are often not sustainable.[3] The tourism industry, controlled from international command centers in wealthy nations, tends to promote distorted images of Third World nations like Mexico, the main destinations of their clients. Global tourism firms have little interest in portraying nations as they really are. For example, it is almost always the case that poverty is minimized or ignored, as are many local customs and practices.

The distinct marketing strategies of the international tourism industry lead to the production of placeless landscapes, devoid or destructive of culture and nature. If tourism is more profitable in built landscapes that are homogenous, then what incentive can there be for tourism developers to preserve the original landscapes of the places in which they invest? Even in ecologically sensitive zones (jungles, mountains) or culturally preserved spaces (colonial downtowns), tourists' demands for cosmopolitan infrastructure—luxury hotels, swimming pools, and lavish shopping spaces—have the effect of diminishing the original cultural landscapes, which become overwhelmed by structures designed for consumption.

In Tijuana, the main commercial street in the old downtown tourism district—Revolution Avenue—is a striking example of a manipulated, commodified space. Revolution Avenue is to Tijuana what Main Street, U.S.A. is to Disneyland—an artificial promenade that sets the mood for a carefully choreographed experience. In Disneyland, the visitor parks the car and walks across the parking lot, through entrance gates, and onto Main Street, a theatrical stage set built at 4/5 scale and lined with cos-

---

[3] Proponents of sustainable development point out that "bioregionalism"—the relationship between settlement formation and nature—must be one of the anchors of economic growth. See, for example, Pena 1997.

tumed characters, from Mickey Mouse to a Barbershop Quartet. In Tijuana, tourists park their cars in vast lots just north of the border, cross the pedestrian entrance into Mexico, and move along a path that leads them to Revolution Avenue.

Tourism tends to reduce places to theme parks like Disneyland, the quintessential "other-directed" landscape, "a world without violence, confrontation, ideological or racial clashes, without politics ... a world that is white, Anglo Saxon, and Puritan-Protestant, often redneck, void of ethnic cast" (Relph 1976: 95). One could argue that Revolution Avenue was designed to be an idealized "Mexico-land," a fantasy exotica of what Americans imagine Mexico to be.

Tourism also breeds "enclavism," the creation of isolated zones for visitors, buffered from the everyday city, that allow an outsider's fantasy of the place to remain distinct from its (usually less exotic) reality. Enclavism leads to the creation of artificial tourism districts that become segregated from the city itself.

Along the beachfront, just south of Tijuana proper, lies an excellent example of an enclave—the village of Puerto Popotla near the town of Rosarito. Popotla was once a small fishing village of fewer than one hundred residents. In the mid-1990s, the Twentieth Century Fox film company leased land adjacent to the village to build a major studio—Fox Baja Studios. The enormous global success of the first film produced there—*Titanic*—has had ripple effects across this part of Baja California. The *Titanic* facilities consisted of massive gray metal warehouses and a giant concrete wall surrounding the site, which townspeople have dubbed "the Berlin Wall." The film production facilities dwarf this village of lobster fishermen, modest wooden shacks, and restaurants for workers. And the compound's high walls and guardhouse evoke the sense of a prison; indeed, security around the site is extremely tight. Here "enclavism" takes an interesting form—an assembly plant for filmmaking or a "movie maquiladora."[4]

This enclave has already brought environmental degradation to the Tijuana/Baja coastline. During construction, underwater explosives may

---

[4] This idea is explored in the 1999 documentary *Factory of Dreams*, produced by Paul Espinosa, KPBS-TV, San Diego.

have been used to grade the beach area and prepare for the construction of several giant pools for filming, causing destruction of marine life for kilometers around the site. Further, according to some observers, the company dumped chlorine into the pools during filming and later emptied them in the ocean, allowing the chlorine to seep into the kelp beds and nearby ecology. Such privately owned, protected, commodified spaces tend to remain closed off from government code enforcers and housing inspectors.

The irony, as one explores the landscape of Popotla, is that Twentieth Century Fox, a company that specializes in creating spectacular, finely crafted images, houses its activities on the edge of the Pacific Ocean in ugly gray warehouses surrounded by concrete walls and barbwire fences.

## THE ECOLOGY OF SOCIAL POLARIZATION

One can envision the Mexican borderlands as overlapping layers of different ecologies. Taken together, the ecologies of fear, consumerism, global production, and leisure create a frenzy of demand for land and urban space. This, in turn, energizes the land market, inflating land values to the point where a smaller and smaller proportion of the population can afford housing. The result is an ecology that is increasingly polarized.

The traditional social geography of Mexican border towns reveals a model that is the inverse of the U.S. pattern. In Mexico, wealthy residents cluster in older established neighborhoods adjacent to downtown, or along a commercial corridor leading out of the central business district. Middle-class, working-class, and poor neighborhoods are arrayed concentrically around the core, with the poorest residents living farthest from the center.

Globalization exacerbates this social geography at the same time that it adds new twists. The biggest changes are the addition of new residential enclaves for transnational investors and visitors. In a city like Tijuana, for example, the valuable coastline just beyond the city offers comparatively inexpensive real estate for U.S. residents, as either second homes or permanent dwellings for retirees. Some 20,000 Americans reside in the coastal corridor between Tijuana and Ensenada, and that number will grow.[5]

---

[5] Mexican property law does not allow foreigners to own land; however, post-NAFTA legislation makes it possible for foreigners to lease land through a trust arrangement (*fideicomiso*) for up to sixty years.

Global real estate projects are aiming to create golf resorts, beachfront condo complexes, and luxury marina housing enclaves for foreign residents. These high-paying land users routinely outbid Mexicans for coastal properties; the result is that the social ecology of the coastal strip is global, dominated by foreign residents.

Meanwhile, the construction of U.S.-style condominiums and suburban housing developments for Mexicans has accelerated across Tijuana. Mexican consumers have become familiar with U.S. housing, both as border crossers and through the media, and global advertising has altered their housing tastes. Wealthy Mexicans want condominiums with Jacuzzis, sunken tubs, and satellite television. Even poor migrants aspire to U.S. house types. A former border architect spoke of his frustration with people who, despite incredibly limited incomes, refuse to live in houses designed to fit their budgets:

> My clients don't want to live in a house designed with recycled metal or junk parts, even if it is excellently constructed. They want a California tract house, with a picture window and a garage. A lot of people can't afford to buy a house in the United States, but they buy the magazines, and then they find a photograph of a house they like. They bring it to the architect in Tijuana, and they say "I want a house like this." But they forget that in Mexico our lot sizes are smaller and narrower. We don't have the space to design with ideal lighting and ventilation. To meet their needs, we end up designing caricatures of American-style houses in miniature (Jorge Ozorno, in Herzog 1999: 206).

As mentioned above, worker housing is dispersed around maquila zones. Migrants to Tijuana live on the edges of the city, near or beyond the zone of maquila workers, in squatter communities of substandard housing known locally as *colonias populares*. This class of marginal, disenfranchised urban poor ultimately may not benefit greatly from globalization, but they respond to its seductive pull. The struggle of the urban poor to survive in booming, globalizing cities constitutes a key debate underlying the globalization protest movements around the globe.

Colonias are pockets of haphazardly constructed houses, self-built by the poor themselves, usually on the worst possible sites in the city: flood-prone canyons, steep hillsides, land adjacent to airports or major highways, or land far removed from the city. Because the poor lack liquid capital with which to buy or even rent a home, many of these settlements were created by illegal land invasions. This means that colonia residents live in a precarious state, burdened by the dual limitations of inadequate construction materials (cardboard, tar paper, scrap wood, scrap metal) and questionable legal ownership. Further, colonias often lack basic services like running water, sewage disposal, paved roads, or street lighting. Most of the households use pirated electricity, stolen from illegal lines connected to nearby electricity grids.

As NAFTA's grip strengthens along the border, more global economic activities—factories, commercial developments, tourism enterprises—create a higher demand for workers in low-paying jobs. This, in turn, attracts ever more migrants from the interior of Mexico. Globalization has exacerbated an already burgeoning northward migration stream, adding to the spread of squalid shanties across the landscape of hills and canyons on the outskirts of Tijuana. Concurrent with the increasing wealth in certain privileged areas (the coast, downtown, the "Zona Río"), there is increasing deprivation in the region's scattered squatter communities.

## THE ECOLOGY OF PLACELESSNESS

We have entered an era in which the city as a physical place is being deconstructed into an array of forms that conform to the postmodern, anti-geographical needs of a global society. Urban dwellers still travel through space, but they are increasingly less aware of or less dependent on its content (Hiss 1991). Today, often only the spectacular spaces, the places with images that mirror those in the electronic space of TV, remain in the mental maps of urban dwellers (Harvey 1989). Technology buffers urbanites from real space, for reasons of both global marketing and security. The result is that people are mainly engaged by public spaces that simulate something, rather than those that are organically embedded in the urban fabric. Turn-of-the-century urbanism—a world of shopping malls, skyways, freeways, TV monitors, historic districts created by local chambers of commerce, and high-tech satellite districts like Silicon Valley—has become ephemeral. This ecology of placelessness[6] is highlighted by sprawling landscapes of fragmented, privatized, and individualized experiences—high-tech offices, condominium complexes, cyber cafes, virtual communities, techno-residential suburbs, and specialized economic districts.

One category of work in planning and urban design in the second half of the twentieth century involved the search for ways to rescue the "sense of place" in cities, since technological change was eclipsing this treasured quality. Some urban design scholars sought to analyze the physical and symbolic landscape cues that make cities more understandable to residents. One classical approach identified five defining structural elements: three define urban places (the district, the landmark, the node); one frames their boundaries (the edge); and one defines the experience of moving through them (the path) (Lynch 1960). Indeed, the field of environmental psychology tries to capture the experience of place and find uniform ways of measuring it (cognitive mapping, for example). More recently, the field of environmental simulation has utilized technology to simulate unique places for the purposes of preserving them in the midst of urban development.

"Sense of place" is a vague notion at best, difficult to measure and highly subjective. Yet seemingly everyone would agree that cities with meaningful spaces are more stimulating than those that are homogenous. One can point to the importance of individual sensibility as a factor in creating a sense of place. Two states of mind have been suggested for city dwellers. "Ordinary perception" is the stream of consciousness that shuts out place and surroundings; it is the conscious state of typical city residents during their daily routines of moving around the city. On the other hand, "simultaneous perception" is a way of taking in one's surroundings and experiencing a place more completely (Hiss 1991). The latter type of perception tends to occur mainly in places with the richest built environment, as, for example, a glittery theater district or a beautiful landscape. The goal of urban designers will be to create urban spaces where users are jolted out of their ordinary perceptive state into a state of simultaneous experience of the urban landscape.

---

[6] See Relph 1976 for an excellent treatment of placelessness.

A pivotal shift in the field of urban design occurred in the early 1970s with the advent of postmodern design theory and its celebration of a different sense of place. In the past, critics had argued that skyscrapers and freeways were destroying sense of place in the city (see, for example, Jacobs 1961). But from a postmodern perspective, the urban highway strip was embellished with signs and symbols that creatively sculpted a new urban tableau tuned to the scale and needs of the automobile. Urban space and time boundaries were being redefined, moving the urban experience out of the ordered, hierarchical grid of modernism to a more anarchic, chaotic, inventive postmodern urban structure (Soja 1989; Dear 2000).

## THE ECOLOGY OF THE GLOBAL/TRANSNATIONAL CITY

While nations continue to militarize borders in some regions of the world, a parallel universe of relatively stable border regions has evolved. On these borders, new kinds of transnational community spaces are forming. The creation of community spaces and places near international borders runs counter to nearly two centuries of history, during which cities were organized as physical entities held territorially within the boundaries of one sovereign nation. This is no longer the case. In a number of global boundary zones—most notably, Western Europe and North America—we find community spaces that sprawl across international boundaries.[7]

The development of a transnational urban ecology is an overlooked dimension of globalization. A century ago, territorial politics dictated that nations rigorously guard their international boundaries. This "shelter func-

---

[7] Important European transfrontier urban agglomerations, with populations ranging between 300,000 and a million inhabitants, include Basel-Mulhouse-Freiburg (Swiss-French-German border); Maastricht-Aachen-Liege (Dutch-German-Belgian border); the Geneva metropolitan area (Swiss-French border); and the Strasbourg metropolitan area (French-German border). In North America, one finds transfrontier urban regions housing between 250,000 and 4 million people along the Canadian-U.S. border (at Vancouver-Victoria-Seattle, Detroit-Windsor, and Toronto-Hamilton-Buffalo), and on the Mexico-U.S. border (at Tijuana–San Diego, Ciudad Juárez–El Paso, Mexicali-Calexico/El Centro, Nuevo Laredo–Laredo, Reynosa-McAllen, and Matamoros-Brownsville).

tion" mentality[8] fostered a common pattern of national settlement: the largest urban population concentrations tended to locate away from the physical edge of the nation-state. In fact, before 1950, boundary regions were mainly viewed as buffer zones that served to defend the larger nation from land-based invasions. Under these conditions, few significant community spaces evolved on or near national boundaries. Indeed, important urban settlements did not appear near borders. A quick glance at a map of Western Europe corroborates this point: the great cities of Paris, Madrid, Rome, Vienna, and Frankfurt all lie in the borderless interior of their respective national settings. Across the Atlantic Ocean, a similar pattern emerges in the Americas: Mexico City, Lima, São Paulo, and Santiago are all positioned at a considerable distance from the nearest international boundary.

Yet today, globalization is opening up border territories to new community formations. Citizens on either side of the Mexico-U.S. boundary are increasingly drawn together; old differences are set aside as urban neighbors become part of a common transnational living and working space. The building blocks of these new transnational communities lie in the social and physical linkages that connect settlements across the boundary. Such linkages in Tijuana–San Diego include the presence of international commuters, transnational consumers, global factories, cross-border land and housing markets, and transnational architecture.

Nearly 300,000 commuters from Mexico legally cross the border on a daily or weekly basis to work on the U.S. side of the transfrontier metropolis. Thousands more cross illegally using a border resident card (which permits Mexican border residents to cross into the United States for nonwork purposes, but which is frequently used illegally to get to work). Billions of dollars in cross-border commercial transactions take place annually. And there are several hundred million border crossings each year, primarily by members of the partnered cities that form the transnational metropolis. Consumers constitute the most active group of legal border crossers, and they are perhaps the primary population that ties together the two sides of this transfrontier metropolis. Collectively, they form a complex regional network of flows north and south across the border. The

---

[8] The notion of "shelter function" is defined in Gottman 1973.

existence of this massive flow is leading to the emergence of what we might term "transnational citizens," people who exist on both sides of the border.

The evolution of a community of transnational citizens who have a presence both north and south of the border is expressed in the region's social ecology. Urban dwellers do not merely consume goods, they consume the built environment itself by purchasing land and housing on both sides of the line. NAFTA has opened the door for the purchase or lease of land by global investors along the border, particularly in Baja California, where there is an array of plans for international resorts, hotel complexes, commercial development, and luxury housing. Baja California already has the second-largest enclave of expatriate American homeowners (the largest is in the Guadalajara region), with between some 15,000 and 20,000 Americans residing in homes along the Baja coast. Meanwhile, increasing numbers of Mexican immigrants, as they regularize their work and immigration status, are purchasing homes on the U.S. side of the border. It is not uncommon to find families in which some members live on the U.S. side of the border, while others remain on the Mexican side. The hard edge of political demarcation—the physical boundary line—begins to blur. The larger transfrontier region becomes the true urban life space of the border dweller, a more precise spatial construct for defining the experience of binational urban families.

The border never really separated the cultural construction of the built environment, but today we are seeing an acceleration in the diffusion of global influences on the built environment of Mexico's border and in Mexican influences north of the border. U.S. influence south of the border even appears in the colonias, in the form of recycled materials purchased in the United States. The rubber tires, used lumber, or scrapped highways signs constitute an important element in the vernacular architecture of Mexican border cities. In sum, we are seeing sets of everyday landscapes—shopping centers, freeways, outdoor markets, commuter lanes—that begin to behave as if the international boundary were invisible.

One of the more vivid examples of transborder community place-making is visible in the strategies border residents employ to "take back" the boundary zone. The wall, legally managed by the U.S. government, is being physically incorporated into the adjacent communities by users, be they local residents, border crossers, artists, or community political groups. Rather than let the boundary zone continue to be a no-man's-land, a zone of insecurity, potential crime, and international bureaucracy, local citizens are choosing to humanize the border. They have erected monuments on the border fence to honor people who died crossing the boundary. They have transformed the fence into a public space that local residents can visit, a sacred place that commemorates the regional struggle at certain moments in history.

This grassroots place-making seeks to redefine the boundary space, turning negative connotations (smuggling, illegal immigration, border police) into positive ones (artworks, monuments, and commemoratives that are part of the community). People who live near the fence use it to define their living space—planting gardens, connecting clotheslines to it, installing telephones for use by clandestine border crossers. The boundary zone becomes more than a part of the everyday neighborhood landscape; it is textured into the built landscape of migration, redesigned as a conduit to help Mexicans who are desperate to cross the frontier and work in the United States. Why not let them make the phone calls to their families north of the border?

## CONCLUSION

It is perhaps fitting to end this essay on a positive note. The gradual spread of cultural landscapes north and south of the border may be the best news possible. The logic of this border bioregion is that it is transnational. Within the emerging "transfrontier metropolis," a new global landscape is taking shape.

Global actors—investors, developers, real estate corporations, business interests, local governments—all seek to remake the borderlands, to prepare it for the global economy of the future. Hundreds of millions of dollars are being spent to build cross-border infrastructure—ports, highways, mass transit, border crossings—to better connect Mexico to the economy north of the border. Global employment centers—factories, shopping malls, tourism projects, housing developments, and commercial enterprises—are further reconfiguring the border.

The result of all this restructuring is the production of a new global cultural landscape. The new social ecology includes innovative building strategies and architectures, along with new kinds of gathering zones, public spaces, community niches, and business districts. Perhaps most notable, there is evidence of enormous contradiction in this landscape: a conflicted transition zone at the boundary line, as opposed to the optimism of the transfrontier NAFTA community; chaos at the border gate, juxtaposed with the promise of new economies; a pedestrian scale in old downtowns versus suburban, car-oriented shopping centers; American-style condo complexes and wealthy suburban enclaves, against the tar-paper shacks and dusty streetscapes of poor colonias. In the end, the global landscape is one of contrast and contradiction—between rich and poor, investment and disinvestment, labor and capital, modernity and postmodernity, planning and spontaneity.

It is our cross-border common ecology that could jolt us into discovering new and innovative ways to transcend the currently limiting urban ecologies of our time. But global equity must be addressed as a long-term problem for this region. NAFTA participants must learn how to resolve the contradictions manifest in the unequal social landscape of border cities. The equity component of NAFTA must be brought into the open and addressed. If this can be done, the cultural landscape of border towns might be reinvented.

## References

Davis, Mike. 1990. *City of Quartz*. New York: Verso.
Dear, Michael. 2000. *The Post-Modern Urban Condition*. Oxford: Blackwell.
Gottman, Jean. 1973. *The Significance of Territory*. Charlottesville: University of Virginia Press.
Harvey, David. 1989. *The Condition of Post-Modernity*. Oxford: Blackwell.
Herzog, Lawrence. 1990. *Where North Meets South*. Austin: Center for Mexican American Studies, University of Texas at Austin.
———. 1999. *From Aztec to High Tech*. Baltimore, Md.: Johns Hopkins University Press.
———. 2003. "Global Tijuana: The Seven Ecologies of the Border." In *Postborder City*, ed. Michael Dear and Gustavo LeClerc. New York: Routledge.
Hiss, Tony. 1991. *The Experience of Place: A New Way of Looking at and Dealing with Our Radically Changing Cities and Countryside*. New York: Vintage.
Jacobs, Jane. 1961. *The Death and Life of Great American Cities*. New York: Random House.

Lynch, Kevin. 1960. *The Image of the City*. Cambridge, Mass.: MIT Press.

Nevins, Joseph. 2000. "The Law of the Land: Local-National Dialectic and the Making of the United States–Mexico Boundary in Southern California," *Historical Geography* 28: 41–60.

Pena, Devon. 1997. *The Terror of the Machine*. Austin: Center for Mexican American Studies, University of Texas at Austin.

Relph, Edward. 1976. *Place and Placelessness*. London: Pion.

Sklair, Leslie. 1991. *Sociology of the Global System*. Baltimore, Md.: Johns Hopkins University Press.

———. 1995. *Assembling for Development*. La Jolla: Center for U.S.-Mexican Studies, University of California, San Diego.

Soja, Ed. 1989. *Post-Modern Geographies*. New York: Verso.

Urry, John. 1990. *The Tourist Gaze*. London: Sage.

# 5

## Cross-Border Regionalism and Sustainability: Contributions of Critical Regional Ecology

KEITH PEZZOLI

Over the past two decades, academics, researchers, and activists around the world have churned out a vast literature analyzing prospects for "sustainable development." The grist for this analytic mill continues to accrue. A range of actors—governmental, corporate, nonprofit, grassroots, religious, tribal, and myriad combinations of these—is engaged in project/policy developments ostensibly aimed at promoting sustainability. Much of the discourse calls for integrating the so-called three Es of sustainability: equity, economic efficiency, and environmental stewardship. The theatre for these efforts spans geographic scales (local, regional, national, city-region, transborder, global), and the formal and informal institutional drivers are also varied: governmental agencies, social movements, public/private-sector collaboratives, corporate associations, international and regional institutions, networks, and research-based consortia, among others. This presents synergistic opportunities. But the border region's jurisdictional fragmentation and uneven development also present serious obstacles.

Transborder city-regions along the U.S.-Mexico border provide dramatic examples of the juxtaposition of wealth and poverty. In the San Diego–Tijuana city-region, San Diego has a population approximately the same size as Tijuana's. Yet Tijuana has a municipal budget one-fourteenth the size of San Diego's—about US$100 million versus approximately $1.4 billion (SDD 2000: 15), making it difficult to develop region-serving infrastructure in this transborder area. The situation is complicated further by lack of understanding or consensus on how to integrate the three Es of sustainability in cross-border settings. This partly explains why advocacy for sustainable development through Agenda 21, the Rio Declaration, the United Nations Millennium Development Goals (MDGs), and countless other declarations and policy prescriptions specific to the U.S.-Mexico border has had little impact. There are contradictory attitudes, beliefs, and expectations on fundamental issues, including trade policy, capital mobility, and the role of the state. The meeting of world leaders at the Johannesburg Summit in 2002 was overshadowed by a disappointing lack of progress and faltering commitment on the part of nations and global institutions.

The quest to balance equity, economy, and environment in sustainable development needs a progressive approach to cross-border regionalism. This volume is evidence of the progressive imagination at work. John Friedmann's essay, for instance, speaks of "imagining an alternative development." Friedmann articulates the progressive challenge as one of enabling an alternative "endogenous" development based on empowerment and local investment in a city-region's productive assets (Friedmann 1992). Stephen Mumme's institutional analysis underscores the need for both substantive and procedural forms of equity in binational policy and decision making. Mumme, along with Jane Clough-Riquelme, Robert Bach, and Basilio Chávez, emphasizes the need to build capacity for civic engagement through strong nongovernmental advocacy/resource organizations. Tito Alegría, Kathryn Kopinak, Nora Bringas, and Roberto Sánchez offer insight into how poverty and environmental systems are interdependent in the U.S.-Mexico border region and beyond. Lawrence Herzog documents cultural barriers to sustainable development and argues the case for "rethinking urban ecologies" (Herzog 1990, 2000). The editors, Jane Clough-Riquelme and Nora Bringas, set the overarching progressive tone of this volume by challenging scholars and activists to join forces in ways that can hold governments and corporations accountable to the sustainability ethic as embodied, for instance, in the United Nations Millennium Development Goals.

My understanding of the term "progressive" is generally in sync with those who define new progressivism as a left-of-center approach to revitalizing social democracy (Etzioni 2000; Giddens 2003; Schrèoder et al. 2002). Yet globalization continues to complicate political categories of left verses right, liberal verses conservative. Interlocking problems stemming from poverty, social injustice, growth-machine politics, mass consumerism, and environmental degradation defy easy solutions. In the quest for sustainable development, we are compelled to search for new understandings that are more nuanced, networked, systems-oriented, globally minded, holistic, ecological, interactive, and relational. There is no singular progressive champion (human agency) to save the day. "Workers of the world, unite" is a nice slogan and bears some merit, but it is an insufficient measure on its own. The same can be said of hopes pinned solely on free market dynamics, the mobilization of civil society, regulatory innovation, technological magic, the entrepreneurial experimentation of globe-girdling corporations, or the ingenuity of the so-called creative class. These caveats complicate efforts to create a working definition of progressive, but it should not stop us from trying.

I define "progressive" as a critical, open-minded, and creatively constructive characteristic of human agency (be it a person, group, network, or some other form of organization) that is trying to improve quality of life and habitat for the common good. "Progressive" is a critical standpoint—at once ecological, globally minded, historically informed, and forward-looking—shared by people and organizations dedicated to eradicating root causes of poverty, social injustice, and/or environmental degradation. Progressive can also be defined in more poetic terms as a characteristic of those who create/share stories and actionable vision in collective struggles to realize the illusive good society. In this conception of progressive, the term ecological is not limited to its scientific meaning as the study of ecosystems, populations, ecotopes, landscapes, and biomes. Rather, ecological also conveys: (1) an important epistemological dimension (the barriers and bridges to producing, integrating, and sharing multidisciplinary *ecologies of knowledge*), and (2) a philosophical dimension (the strengths and weaknesses of using ecological concepts—such as community, stability, diversity, organism, and niche—to understand/improve other systems characterized variously as social, cultural, political, urban, and/or regional). Taking this full range of meanings into account, I suggest that we need a federated ecological approach to inspire and enable progressive cross-border regionalism. I call this approach "critical regional ecology."

## CRITICAL REGIONAL ECOLOGY

Critical regional ecology is an approach to integrating theory and practice for progressive regionalism. More specifically, it provides a conceptual framework for sustainable city-region planning and development. Critical regional ecology cross-fertilizes four fields of integrative discourse: new regionalism/institutionalism, sustainability science, informational science, and ethics and culture. Clearly, this chapter can only scratch the surface of these dimensions and their interrelations.[1] My intent is not to provide some grand meta-narrative or blueprint but rather to sketch the contours (frontiers) of critical regional ecology where promising developments are taking place in our collective capacity to create, integrate, share, translate, and apply knowledge across boundaries. Research universities and activist scholars have an increasingly important role to play in advancing critical regional ecology. The following discussion illustrates dimensions of critical regional ecology through the prism of cross-border regional planning, governance, and watershed management.

## CROSS-BORDER CITY-REGIONS AND PLANNING

> *Planning programs at universities can—and must—raise questions and generate answers about the structure of our society and about how the great transformations underway are to be influenced; otherwise, how do we know towards what are we planning? What are the appropriate questions in these realms for our day and for the future, and how are they best raised and answered?* (Perloff 1981: i)

The invocation quoted above was directed to urban and regional planning theorists, educators, students, and practitioners. Harvey Perloff posed the challenge in the inaugural issue of the *Journal of Planning Education and Research*. I include the quote here to emphasize that planning (as both an academic and a professional field) has a crucial role to play in promoting sustainable development. City-regions are diverse, often conflicting aggre-

---

[1] These themes are developed more fully in Pezzoli n.d.

gations of cities, suburbs, and their environs that need to be organized as integrated systems of networks and infrastructures. Yet globalization, uneven development, and low-density urban sprawl have combined in ways that make traditional planning and policy approaches problematic. The U.S.-Mexico border region is especially challenging in this regard. It covers approximately 2,000 miles, from the Gulf of Mexico to the Pacific Ocean; it is formally defined as the area extending 100 kilometers (62.5 miles) north and south from the international border, making it a 200-kilometer-deep swath of land bisected by the international border. The border region's population has grown rapidly over the past twenty years. Demographers estimate that the current population of 11.8 million will swell to 19.4 million by 2020 (EPA 2005a).

The U.S.-Mexico border has fourteen pairs of "sister cities." Each of these sister-city pairs, as Herzog (1998: 2) points out, "forms a *transfrontier metropolis*, a single cross-border functional living space with U.S. and Mexican dwellers." San Diego–Tijuana is the largest and wealthiest city-region on the U.S.-Mexico border. It has a total population of 4.1 million (2.8 million in the San Diego metropolitan area and 1.3 million in Tijuana). Tijuana's annual growth rate is 4.9 percent, nearly double that of San Diego, and the city-region's population is expected to swell to 8 million by 2030 (Kiy and Kada 2004). Together, the two cities have a total gross regional product of US$125 billion ($120 billion in San Diego; $5 billion in Tijuana).

A report by the International Community Foundation (ICF), titled "Blurred Borders: Transboundary Issues and Solutions in the San Diego/Tijuana Border Region," documents how the San Diego–Tijuana region's rapid growth is causing serious negative impacts: "housing costs are skyrocketing; urban sprawl and a proposed triple border fence threaten rural communities and sensitive habitats of binational ecological importance; transportation infrastructure is insufficient to service the growing traffic; and water and energy supply is becoming an increasingly urgent and hotly contested issue" (Kiy and Kada 2004: 20). What are the prospects for sustainable development under such circumstances? New regionalism/institutionalism—the first of critical regional ecology's integrative discourses—provides some insight along these lines.

## NEW REGIONALISM/INSTITUTIONALISM AND GOVERNANCE

Over the past decade, interest in metropolitan/regional planning and the so-called new regionalism/institutionalism has been rising steadily. Some go so far as to characterize the emphasis on new regionalism as an emerging movement (Wheeler 2002). Stefan Kipher and Karen Wirsig examine the new regionalism from a critical perspective; they recently organized and published a review symposium titled *Progressive Regionalisms in North America*. All five review essays in the symposium concurred that "the latest version of the new regionalism is a useful entry point to discuss the political prospects for a progressive regionalism" (Kipher and Wirsig 2004: 731). But what does progressive mean in this context? How does progressive regionalism—with its emphasis on politics, new institutionalism, and governance—factor into the sustainable development challenge facing city-regions in the context of globalization?

The discourse on new regionalism/institutionalism sheds light on two aspects crucial to sustainable city-region development. First, there is the recognition of the metropolitan scale as a vital geographic unit of analysis for purposes of integrated regional planning. Emphasis is placed on engendering a more whole-systems view of classic planning problems (such as job creation, housing, transportation, urban sprawl, economic development, and so on). This discourse has shed light on how the fate of inner-city development is interdependent with the dynamics of suburban growth—or decline, as the case may be—in outlying suburbs (Calthorpe and Fulton 2001; Wheeler 2002).

Second, the new regionalism/institutionalism discourse sheds light on the need for new approaches to governance. Municipal, district, and other organizational entities have difficulty dealing with various challenges that manifest at the regional scale (for example, the need for jobs-housing balance throughout the metropolis, creation of district-spanning wildlife corridors in the context of species and habitat conservation, and transit-oriented development). In his writing on "regional solutions for 21st-century challenges," Nick Bollman puts it this way: "Only a fundamentally different mode of governance, what we call regional stewardship, will be adequate to the challenge. Stewardship, that is, collaboration among local and state government and the private and civic sectors, is the fundamental building block of 21st-century regionalism" (Bollman 2002: 6).

In his study of the institutional dimensions of environmental change, Oran Young (2002: 5) finds that most contributors to the new institutionalist discourse view "institutions as sets of rules, decision-making procedures, and programs that define social practices, assign roles to the participants in these practices, and guide interactions among the occupants of individual roles." The emphasis is placed on understanding institutions as embedded in organizational cultures including social conventions and systems of rules in use (not just on official documents). A key tenet of the "new institutionalism" is that the economy is shaped by enduring collective forces in the form of both formal and informal social institutions (Amin 1999; Amin et al. 1994). Joachim Blatter (2002: 420) argues that an institutional criterion for sustainable development can be seen in new approaches to urban and regional planning: "It is not comprehensive plans with detailed indicators but the planning processes embedded in institutional settings that are the most important element of successful planning. Intersectoral communication and cooperation, round tables and forums are seen as crucial elements towards innovative and sustainable development."

Along these lines, a recent Social Equity Forum hosted by the Inter-American Development Bank (IDB) concluded with a declaration outlining "institutional challenges for sustainable and equitable social policy in Latin America and the Caribbean." The members of the Social Equity Forum urged "governments, civil society and citizens in the region to increase their efforts to build solid institutions that guarantee sustainable and equitable social policy" (IDB 2004).[2]

---

[2] The Social Equity Forum, an initiative led by the Inter-American Development Bank, was established to enable government leaders, policymakers, academics, and social, labor, and business leaders to increase social equity through economic and social reforms. Members of the forum outlined six priority areas of institutional development: handling social rights with fiscal responsibility; creating institutional spaces for coordinating comprehensive policies for reducing poverty among the various sectoral agents responsible for implementing social policy; guaranteeing institutional continuity of resources, actors, and programs; fomenting access to reliable statistical information, including objective systems for evaluating and monitoring social action and its impact; encouraging leadership aimed at strengthening institutions; and promoting participation by social actors to favor the sustainability of effective social policies.

The merging of new regionalist and new institutionalist perspectives can be seen in the emergent discourse on "governance." UN-Habitat outlines four dynamic trends in city-region governance over the past decade: (1) devolution of power and resources away from centralized governments toward local and regional governments; (2) rising level of citizen participation in policy making; (3) emergence of new forms of multilevel governance (collaborative arrangements joining public, private, and civil society institutions in urban problem solving); and (4) policy- and decision-making structures that are more process driven and territorially based (attuned to regional blocs and area-based interests) (UN-Habitat 2001: 59–62). Evidence of these trends and the quest for effective regional stewardship can be seen in the San Diego–Tijuana cross-border region.

## SANDAG AND THE BORDERS COMMITTEE

In January 2003, the San Diego Association of Governments' (SANDAG) Regional Planning Committee held a joint meeting with SANDAG's Borders Committee, which provides oversight for planning and implementing SANDAG's cross-border initiatives and programs. This includes a binational perspective (dealing with San Diego's relationship to the international border with Mexico); an interregional perspective (dealing with issues involving neighboring Orange, Riverside, and Imperial counties); and collaboration with tribal governments within San Diego County. The Borders Committee works closely with two other SANDAG entities: the I-15 Interregional Partnership and the Committee on Binational Regional Opportunities (COBRO). Intended as input for SANDAG's Regional Comprehensive Plan (RCP), the Borders Committee identified a set of key cross-border priorities, including jobs/housing balance, transportation and trade infrastructure, ports of entry, water supply, energy, and environmental protection and coordination. The Borders Committee now has a set of guiding principles intended to serve as a framework for policy objectives and actions with regard to cross-border regionalism:

- Our region will pursue fair and equitable planning with consideration of interregional impacts and will maintain active and honest communication with our neighboring counties, tribal governments and the Republic of Mexico.

- Our region will promote shared infrastructure, efficient transportation systems, integrated environmental planning and economic development with our neighboring counties, tribal governments and the Republic of Mexico.
- Our region recognizes that it is a unique and dynamic place to live—one that embraces cultural diversity, promotes interregional understanding, and benefits from our varied history and experience (SANDAG 2005).

The final draft of the RCP embraces the guiding principles of the Borders Committee, and it includes a chapter dedicated to borders. A vision statement at the outset of the RCP's border chapter—projecting to the year 2030—offers this forward-looking scenario:

> The greater Southern California–Baja California region boasts a seamless network that connects our economies, infrastructure, transportation, environment and tourism industries.... We work closely with Mexico and our surrounding neighbors to maintain a healthy environment, and both sides of the international border are recognized throughout the world for clean air and water and thriving ecosystems. We have established linkages and common land management practices along our borders (SANDAG 2004: 209).

This is a lofty and optimistic vision, one that is matched by IMPlan across the border in Tijuana.

**IMPLAN: THE MUNICIPAL PLANNING INSTITUTE IN TIJUANA**

The public agency responsible for binational planning on the Mexican side of the San Diego–Tijuana city-region is the Instituto Municipal de Planeación (Municipal Planning Institute). Popularly referred to as IMPlan, this agency recently had its staff slashed from seventy to fewer than twenty full-time employees. It is the only agency in the Tijuana metropolitan area responsible for urban and regional planning. Most of the agency's budget goes to salaries, leaving little available for actual projects. IMPlan has made transborder planning a high priority. In a document that spells out IM-

Plan's transborder planning mission (IMPlan June 2001), the agency lists these goals:

- Promote comprehensive transborder planning with organizations from the public and private sectors on both sides of the border.
- Promote the institutionalization of transborder planning by creating organizations, procedures, laws, and other tools (including financing mechanisms), and by fostering a "transborder planning" culture in society.
- Support organizations with studies, plans, and projects related to transborder planning. Develop joint projects.
- Generate funding for studies, plans, and projects.

Of course, IMPlan's efforts to build capacity for transborder planning will not necessarily result in a progressive regionalist approach to problems of poverty, social injustice, and environmental degradation. The same can be said of SANDAG's efforts. The prospects for progressive regionalism hinge on more than political will and good governance. Inputs from sustainability science, information science, ethics, and culture are also important. In following sections, I review these domains using watershed management as my frame of reference. This usage reflects the increasing importance of watersheds as an organizing concept in transborder affairs.

## SUSTAINABILITY SCIENCE AND WATERSHEDS

> *In a world put at risk by the unintended consequences of scientific progress, social trust in scientific knowledge claims and institutions cannot be taken for granted. Participatory procedures involving scientists, stakeholders, advocates, active citizens and users of knowledge are needed to transform knowledge claims into trustworthy, socially-robust, usable knowledge about the realities which matter in social and environmental change and in the transition to sustainability. In addition, scientists will need to be increasingly sensitive to shifts in patterns of governance that could assist their endeavors.* (Kates et al. 2001: 2)

The preceding quote is from a benchmark declaration of sustainability science that outlines core questions, research priorities, and networking and institutional strategies for linking science to society. Sustainability science aims to understand society-nature interactions and interdependencies from an integrated whole-systems perspective. Kates and colleagues (2001: 4) argue that "Such an understanding must encompass the interaction of global processes with the ecological and social characteristics of particular places and sectors." The severity of environmental problems in the U.S.-Mexico borderlands makes it painfully clear that much more needs to be done to get a handle on the forces driving environmental degradation.

Current environmental laws in the United States and Mexico focus almost entirely on manufacturing facilities, especially the larger industries that have historically been the most heavily polluting (refineries, chemical and power plants, the automobile industry). But new types of environmental problems have emerged. In Southern California and Baja California, non–point source pollution (including, among other things, nutrients, bacteria, sediment, pesticides, and chemicals) runs off millions of backyards, farms, and streets into storm drains. This constitutes one of the biggest environmental threats to the region's coastline. Diffuse sources of pollution also include such things as emissions from gas stations and millions of motor vehicles. Emergent problems that have eluded traditional environmental policy approaches include the atmospheric buildup of carbon dioxide and other greenhouse gases, the potential environmental impacts of genetically modified organisms, urban sprawl resulting in loss of habitat and biodiversity, pesticides that might disrupt human endocrine cycles, and the erosion of the earth's protective ozone layer in the upper atmosphere.

The National Research Council's (NRC) Board on Sustainable Development has identified three high-priority tasks for advancing the research agenda of sustainability science: (1) develop a research framework for the science of sustainable development that integrates global and local perspectives to shape a place-based understanding of the interactions between environment and society; (2) initiate focused research programs on a small set of understudied questions that are central to a deeper understanding of those interactions; and (3) promote better utilization of existing tools and processes for linking knowledge to action in pursuit of a sustainability transition (NRC 1999: 279).

The NRC's priorities underscore the importance of two very important challenges for cross-border regionalism. First, we need to identify appropriate biogeophysical terms of reference (such as watersheds or "waterscapes") useful for place-based views of environment-society interdependencies. Significant progress is being made on this front. Second, while encouraging a diversity of stand-alone research programs, we also need to do much more in the way of building incentives and capacity for knowledge networking and resource sharing across such programs. Progress on this front is much more difficult.

When it comes to defining a particular "region" (as, say, an organizing framework for comprehensive regional planning), it soon becomes apparent that there is no "one-size-fits-all" definition. Depending on the problem or challenge in view, a region may be defined as the contiguously urbanized metropolitan area and its immediate hinterlands, or it might be thought of on a much larger multi-county, multi-state, or even multinational scale. In her classic work, *The Death and Life of Great American Cities*, Jane Jacobs shared this perspective: "A Region, someone has wryly observed, is an area safely larger than the last one to whose problems we found no solution" (cited in Katz 2000).

If conventional definitions of metropolitan areas were applied across the international boundary, San Diego and Tijuana would constitute a "consolidated metropolitan area" comprising two primary metropolitan areas. The San Diego Primary Metropolitan Area would be San Diego County, and the Tijuana Primary Metropolitan Area would be the Tijuana, Playas de Rosarito, and Tecate municipios (Cox 1999). The combined population of this area is 4.5 million people, roughly 1 million of whom live in Tijuana. It is the largest twin-city pair of the fourteen that span the U.S.-Mexico border, and it has the busiest border crossing point (San Ysidro) in the world. This conception of the San Diego–Tijuana city-region is politically configured—that is, it is based on the legal-institutional parameters of a political—not a bioregional or ecological—geography. The newly placed emphasis on watersheds helps bring a more ecological perspective into view.

The EPA defines a watershed as land areas that catch rain or snow and drain to specific marshes, streams, rivers, lakes, or to groundwater (EPA 2005b).[3] Watersheds constitute a bowl or basin-shaped area in which all water within the area (rain, snow) flows to the same outlet point. In the case of the 1,750-square-mile Tijuana River Watershed (two-thirds of which lie in Mexico, and one-third in the United States), the common outlet point is on the U.S. side of the border at the Tijuana River Estuary.

Watersheds provide a useful organizing framework to advance the regional approach to sustainability science as outlined by the NRC: "The major threats and opportunities of the sustainability transition are not only multiple, cumulative, and interactive, but also place-based. In other words, it is in specific regions with distinctive social and ecological attributes that the critical threats to sustainability emerge, and where a successful transition will need to be based" (NRC 1999: 285). The increasingly complex nature of cross-border environmental problems provides a strong catalyst for new integrated approaches centered on cross-border watersheds. Thayer puts it in these terms: "As globalizing economic, technological, and political relationships render arbitrary national boundaries less relevant, we will increasingly deal with the physical realities of environmental, resource, and biodiversity issues by focusing upon natural divisions within physiographic regions" (2003: 19).

A significant and rising amount of work along the U.S.-Mexico border highlights watersheds as an essential organizing framework for tasks involving cross-border environmental research, education, policy, and planning. A good example is the work being done by San Diego State University (SDSU) in partnership with El Colegio de la Frontera Norte (COLEF). This team recently published the *Tijuana River Watershed Atlas* as part of an ambitious transborder watershed research program aimed at harmonizing data across the international boundary. The atlas—including eighty photographs and maps, and with text in both English and Spanish—was published by San Diego State University Press and the Institute for Regional Studies of the Californias, with assistance from SDSU's Department of Geography and the Southwest Consortium for Environmental Research

---

[3] The U.S. Geological Survey provides a standardized definition of regions that subdivides the nation into hydrologic units (watersheds) averaging about 700 square miles.

and Policy (SCERP). Richard Wright, one of the coeditors, points out why this work is significant: "developing information for the entire binational watershed is absolutely essential to plan for the future, to avoid environmental problems that will negatively affect the quality of life of the watershed's 1.4 million residents, and to take advantage of binational synergies for sustainable regional development" (Wright 2005).

Another binational watershed project spanning the U.S.-Mexico border focuses on the Upper San Pedro Basin. The San Pedro River (the basin's major surface-water drainage) enters the basin at the U.S.-Mexico border near Palominas, Arizona. Browning-Aiken and colleagues did an analysis of this case focused on collaborative binational watershed management. They came to this conclusion: "Within the international San Pedro River Basin, disparities between Mexico and the United States regarding economic development and political orientation, combined with a highly variable and complex physical setting, suggest that the successful engagement of scientists with communities and stakeholders will be essential for addressing water management challenges" (Browning-Aiken et al. 2004).

Stephen Mumme (2002) argues that, "Whether speaking of the Colorado River or the Rio Grande, much of the debate on use of the border's scarce water resources now endorses a watershed management approach. Watershed advocacy assumes sustainable development is more likely to be achieved when policy decisions are based on a full accounting of the complex ecological and socio-economic interrelationships within a particular hydrographic unit." The EPA now advocates watershed management along the U.S.-Mexico border. Likewise, Mexico has endorsed watershed management through its river basin councils (*consejos de cuencas*) as mandated by Mexico's 1990 National Water Law. In his review of this subject, Mumme finds that:

> Such national initiatives are generating new opportunities on the border. These are seen in innovative efforts to coordinate inter-governmental planning within major river basins and tributary watersheds, to forge new partnerships with governmental and non-governmental stakeholders, to establish new advisory and attention groups, sometimes formalized as watershed councils, and to initiate studies within an ambit of public participation and stakeholder involvement. With the

support of foundations, universities, and NGOs, a number of important citizen based watershed initiatives have taken root (Mumme 2002).

What does all of this have to do with sustainability science? It falls under the rubric of what those advocating sustainability science call knowledge-action collaboratives. The NRC defines knowledge-action collaboratives as regional-scale "alliances of diverse and sector-specific groups jointly mobilized to design strategies and institutions that enable adaptive management and social learning for sustainable development" (NRC 1999: 7). The creation of such collaboratives presents opportunities for those advocating new regionalism/institutionalism to join efforts with scientists committed to linking science to society. The barriers and bridges to making this happen include both technical and social dimensions. Advances in the informational sciences have much to contribute along these lines.

## INFORMATIONAL SCIENCES, CYBERTOOLS, AND CYBERINFRASTRUCTURE

The National Science Foundation (NSF) has a Directorate for Computer and Information Science and Engineering which includes a Division of Information and Intelligent Systems.[4] This division has a grants program aimed at "Advancing Collaborative and Intelligent Systems and their Societal Implications" (NSF 2005). The NSF's request for applications in this grant category states: "Problems addressed by the Collaborative Systems area include storing, accessing and organizing, interpreting, protecting, summarizing, managing and using vast and growing quantities of IT-based data, information and knowledge that may be uncertain and incomplete." The NSF's emphasis on collaborative systems research is one of many new research frontiers opening up in the realm of informational

---

[4] The National Science Foundation is an independent federal agency with the mandate "to promote the progress of science; to advance the national health, prosperity, and welfare; to secure the national defense" (http://www.nsf.gov/about). The NSF funds approximately 20 percent of all federally supported basic research conducted by colleges and universities in the United States. It is the major federal source of funding for many fields, including computer science and the social sciences. Hence trends within this agency set the tone for broader shifts taking place in relationships of science to society.

science. The NSF's emphasis on building "next-generation cybertools" is indicative of a dramatic revolution taking place in applications of advanced information, communication, and visualization technologies. Cybertools enhance the analysis and visualization of scientific data. Such tools are being used in many ways (such as to improve computer processing power and to enhance data mining, data integration, information indexing, data confidentiality protection, and the interoperability of data from different sources). Cybertools are part of the NSF's broader thrust to develop "cyberinfrastructure" nationwide as well as internationally and globally.

A January 2003 report published by the NSF Blue Ribbon Advisory Panel on Cyberinfrastructure emphasizes how continuing progress in computing, information, and communication technologies has crossed a critical threshold. We are now in a position to create a comprehensive cyberinfrastructure "to address national and global priorities, such as understanding global climate change, protecting our natural environment, applying genomics-proteomics to human health, maintaining national security, mastering the world of nanotechnology, and predicting and protecting against natural and human disasters" (NSF Blue Ribbon Advisory Panel 2003: ES-1). Cyberinfrastructure (including integrated information, computing, and communications systems) is to the knowledge economy what highways, water systems, and power grids are to the industrial economy.[5] Every directorate within the NSF has funded or is exploring cyberinfrastructure-related projects.[6]

A U.S.-based "Internet2" consortium led by 207 universities in partnership with industry and government is developing and deploying advanced cyberinfrastructure nationally and globally. The Internet2's international thrust aims to facilitate global interoperability of advanced networking, as well as collaboration between U.S. researchers, faculty, and students and their overseas counterparts.[7] Throughout Latin America, Internet2 partner

---

[5] http://web.si.umich.edu/news/news-detail.cfm?NewsItemID=295.

[6] A whole new set of concepts, as well as subdisciplines, are emerging out of this thrust (for example, knowledge networking, digital government, federation of distributed intelligence, cybertrust, cybersecurity, networked infomechanical systems, e-science communities, grid communities, infocartography, and biological and environmental informatics).

[7] http://international.internet2.edu/index.cfm.

organizations can be found in Brazil (Rede Nacional de Ensino e Pesquisa, RNP), Chile (Red Universitaria Nacional, REUNA), Venezuela (Red Académica de Centros de Investigación y Universidades Nacionales de Alta Velocidad, REACCIUN2), and Mexico (Corporación Universitaria para el Desarrollo de Internet, CUDI). CUDI is made up of seventy-eight Mexican universities and research centers interconnected by Mexico's backbone network and linked to Internet2.[8]

The California Institute for Telecommunications and Information Technology (Calit2) is partnering with CUDI, the Corporation for Education Network Initiatives in California (CENIC), and the Center for Scientific Investigation and Higher Education of Ensenada (CICESE) to define a set of cross-border projects.[9] Given the so-called digital divide in Mexico, Latin America, and throughout the world, collaborative efforts of this sort are crucial. Unfortunately, "as the pace of network advances continues to accelerate, the gap between the technologically 'favored' regions and the rest of the world is, if anything, in danger of widening" (Alvarez and Ibarra 2003). Moreover, while profound opportunities exist for creating new research environments based upon cyberinfrastructure, the Blue Ribbon panel noted above found:

> [T]here are also real dangers of disappointing results and wasted investment for a variety of reasons including under funding in amount and duration, lack of understanding of technological futures, excessively redundant activities between science fields or between science fields and industry, lack of appreciation of social/cultural barriers, lack of appropriate organizational structures, inadequate related educational activities, and increased technological ("not invented here") balkanizations rather than interoperability among multiple disciplines (NSF Blue Ribbon Advisory Panel 2003: 4).

---

[8] http://www.cudi.edu.mx/index.html.

[9] Topics currently getting attention include intelligent buildings, applied physics, geophysics and information technology, oceanography and remote sensing, computer science, Internet2 development in Mexico, MEMS development, telecom research and development, and sensor networks.

Evidence for every single one of these points can be found limiting the prospects for building an integrated regional information system in the U.S.-Mexico borderlands, including in the San Diego–Tijuana city-region.

This is apparent in efforts to promote watershed management. In a report titled *New Strategies for America's Watersheds*, the NRC identified a series of "critical information gaps that hamper effective implementation of watershed management" (NRC et al. 1999). These gaps, which are evident in the watershed management initiatives along the U.S.-Mexico border, occur in the following areas:

- Linkages among watershed components (rivers, wetlands, groundwater, atmosphere, floodplains, upland areas).

- Integration across disciplines (especially biophysical and social sciences).

- Feedback among processes operating at different spatial and temporal scales.

- Inexpensive, useful indicators of watershed conditions and quantitative methods to evaluate land use and watershed management practices.

- Advanced watershed simulation models (especially models that link natural and social attributes) that are useful to and can be operated by managers who are not scientific experts; and understanding of risk and uncertainty in the decision-making process.

In view of these gaps, the authors of *New Strategies for America's Watersheds* make the case that good science is not enough. The accessibility and usefulness of watershed science are essential to successful watershed management; but as is the case with much basic science dealing with environmental problems, research translation is difficult. Authors of the report emphasize how the institutional and scientific complexity of watershed management makes it difficult to implement successfully:

> Watershed management without significant input of new scientific understanding, especially understanding of watershed processes and of the human dimensions, is doomed to inefficiency and eventual loss of credibility; research without

input from involved stakeholders and those with real management acumen will always prove less than useful (NRC et al. 1999).

This emphasis on involving stakeholders ties into the challenges of promoting environmental justice and social equity in the borderlands.

## ETHICS, SOCIAL EQUITY, AND CULTURE

The term "ethics" is generally defined as a set of moral principles or values (that is, moral philosophy that raises questions about how we define what is good and bad, and how we assign moral duty and obligation). "Equity" is generally understood in terms of fairness, impartiality, and justice. Ethics is a discipline that can help us shape normative theories about equity in development. This is important given that equity is one of the three Es of the sustainability challenge (equity, economy, and environment). In the United States, federal and state laws now require that social equity considerations (including environmental justice) be included in all regional planning programs. San Diego's Regional Comprehensive Plan has a chapter dedicated to the issue of social equity, which SANDAG defines, along with environmental justice, in terms outlined by the State of California:

> Environmental Justice and Social Equity is defined as the fair treatment of people of all races, cultures, and incomes with respect to the development, adoption, implementation, and enforcement of environmental laws, regulations, and policies (California Senate Bill 115 Statute of 1999).[10]

---

[10] California Senate Bill 115 is also known as the California Environmental Justice Act. As noted by authors of a legislative history of SB 115, the "California Environmental Justice Act requires the Office of Planning and Research, in consultation with State agencies, local agencies, and affected communities, to develop a State interagency environmental justice strategy that addresses any disproportionately high and adverse human and health or environmental effects of programs, policies, and activities on minority populations and low-income populations. In addition, the act requires each State agency to make the achievement of environmental justice part of its mission by identifying and addressing disproportionately high and adverse human health or environmental effects of its programs, policies, and activities on

In Mexico, the issue of social equity has made its way into how national security is conceptualized and into concerns about the relationship between society and nature. In 2001, for instance, Adolfo Aguilar Zinser (then Mexico's national security adviser, Office of the President) expressed concern that the lack of social equity in Mexico was leading to problems of national insecurity and vulnerability, and that prospects for improving social equity were undermined insofar as "deterioration of the environment creates tension between nature and the needs of the population" (Aguilar Zinser 2001).

The United Nations Human Settlements Programme (UN-Habitat) and many other international, national, and regional programs have begun to explicitly consider the prospects of sustainability in urban contexts. Cultural dimensions of urbanization and urban planning are often highlighted as essential to such efforts. This was certainly the case at the second session of the World Urban Forum on "Cities: Crossroads of Cultures, Inclusiveness and Integration?" in Barcelona in September 2004.[11] The UN-Habitat program released its annual report, *The State of the World's Cities 2004/2005: Globalization and Urban Culture*, at the World Urban Forum. John Friedmann helped prepare a section of the report on "globalization and the changing culture of planning," which lays out principles of an emerging planning culture that fits well with the integrative tasks of critical regional ecology. The case of Los Laureles Canyon in Tijuana provides a useful point of reference for the ethical and cultural challenges of critical regional ecology in cross-border settings.

---

minority populations and low-income populations in California" (http://www.ciwmb.ca.gov/Tires/FiveYearPlan/LegHistory.htm, accessed March 31, 2005).

[11] The Forum was held during the Universal Forum of Cultures, "an international event to celebrate cultural diversity, sustainable development and a culture of peace." A total of 4,400 delegates, representing national governments, local authorities, NGOs, and a range of Habitat Agenda partners participated. At the opening ceremony, world leaders and mayors warned that rapid urbanization was one of the greatest challenges facing humanity in the new millennium. See http://www.unhabitat.org/wuf/2004/documents/wuf_exec_summary.pdf.

## LOS LAURELES CANYON

The case of Los Laureles Canyon illustrates how problems of poverty and environmental systems intersect. Los Laureles Canyon is a 4.6-square-mile sub-watershed of the Tijuana River Watershed, which itself measures 1,735 square miles. Two-thirds of this watershed are south of the international border, and the Tijuana River flows through the Tijuana River Estuary to the ocean.

Los Laureles is one of five canyons that drain directly into the Tijuana River Estuary, an internationally recognized wetlands (recently designated as a Ramsar site)[12] which provides habitat for endangered and threatened bird, fish, and plant species. This sensitive ecosystem is being degraded by sediment, trash, and pollution flows that cross the border from Los Laureles Canyon into the United States during the rainy season. The rapidly growing urban population in Los Laureles Canyon (estimated at about 40,000) is also causing impacts south of the border in Tijuana. Irregular human settlement (in informal colonias or squatter settlements) on the canyon's steep and unstable hillsides is leading to deforestation; and with less groundcover, mudslides and flash floods are increasingly devastating. Roadways in the canyon are being extended to increase access for emergency vehicles. All of this has exacerbated the negative impacts on the Tijuana River National Estuarine Research Reserve (TRNERR),[13] especially Border Field State Park, whose salt marsh, trails, and access roads are peri-

---

[12] Ramsar is a city in Iran along the Caspian Sea where a global Convention on Wetlands was signed in 1971. The Rasmar Convention (an intergovernmental treaty that provides the framework for national action and international co-operation for the conservation and wise use of wetlands and their resources) calls for "the conservation and wise use of all wetlands through local, regional and national actions and international cooperation, as a contribution towards achieving sustainable development throughout the world" (Ramsar COP8, 2002). There are presently 144 contracting parties to the Convention, with 1,422 wetland sites totaling 123.9 million hectares designated as wetlands of international significance.

[13] The TRNERR was established in the United States in 1982 as a multi-agency management authority consisting of federal, state, county, city, and local agencies and organizations with a common interest in protecting the Tijuana River Estuary, an intertidal coastal estuary on the international border in the southernmost part of the San Diego metropolitan area.

odically covered with sediment and trash. Clearly the solution to this cross-border problem is going to require close collaboration between Mexican and U.S. counterparts.

Millions of dollars have been spent on "downstream solutions" on the U.S. side of the border, including building sedimentation basins in Goat Canyon (the U.S. portion of Los Laureles Canyon) to capture erosion-generated sediments flowing from Los Laureles into the United States. However, this reactive approach is expensive; more than thirty acres of salt marsh on the U.S. side of the border have been buried under sediments since the mid-1980s, and removing the sediments is costly.

U.S. and Mexican agencies and nonprofits have now begun to seek more proactive solutions. Oscar Romo is spearheading this effort through the National Oceanic and Atmospheric Administration's (NOAA) Coastal Training Program (CTP), based at the TRNERR. The CTP provides scientific information and skill-building opportunities to decision makers responsible for coastal management. Programs include seminars, hands-on skill training, participatory workshops, lectures, and technology demonstrations. The CTP has mobilized a cross-border campaign to address the problems facing Los Laureles Canyon, the Tijuana River Estuary, and other sub-basins of the Tijuana River Watershed. Through partnerships with the University of California, San Diego's Regional Workbench Consortium (RWBC), the California State Coastal Conservancy (CSCC), the International Community Foundation (ICF), Tijuana's IMPlan and Office of the Mayor, and other agencies in Mexico, the CTP has put together a community-based slope stabilization and erosion control project within Los Laureles Canyon. The aims of this project include:

- Stabilizing the slopes in Los Laureles Canyon with vegetative and structural means to prevent erosion within the canyon and the flow of sedimentation into the estuary.
- Building the capacity of the residents of Los Laureles Canyon to create a safer and healthier environment through means such as monitoring erosion, stabilizing slopes, and improving housing conditions while using existing and affordable resources.
- Managing solid waste and wastewater. Create a system to water the vegetative slope stabilization using wastewater.

- Developing strategies to improve the existing conditions of settlements in vulnerable areas through alternative, innovative, and comprehensive solutions.

- Pursuing financial and other support from public agencies (including agencies of the state and federal governments), community service groups, educational institutions, businesses, and individuals for the support of the projects (Regional Workbench).

- Consortium 2005: Los Laureles Canyon Project.

- Creation of pervious surfaces for roads (impervious surfaces exacerbate runoff and erosion).

- Establishing a community center.

- Constructing a sustainable model home.

The CTP is a good example of a program that uses environmental education and innovative projects to promote community-based ecological ethics (that is, an understanding and appreciation of how ecosystem integrity is essential to the well-being of all living beings, neighborhoods, cities, and the shared cross-border region). Culture change is as significant a part of this process as are politics, economics, engineering, science, and technology. The San Diego–based International Community Foundation has provided an important binational conduit for funding this effort. The ICF enabled the U.S.-based Coastal Conservancy to invest in the project (the Coastal Conservancy cannot directly manage/support projects in Mexico). Other sources of support include the EPA Border 2012 Program and in-kind contributions from the mayor of Tijuana. The cross-border nature of these partnerships is key. Oscar Romo and staff at the TRNERR and CTP work closely with Mexican NGOs and academics (such as, for example, Gaviotas, Universidad Iberoamericana, and Universidad Tecnológica de Tijuana) to improve water-quality monitoring and educational programs. In 2003, the TRNERR management authority expanded its membership to include the municipalities of Tijuana and Tecate, with their respective mayors as representatives. It is still too early in the process to predict whether the Los Laureles Canyon project will succeed as an innovative approach to watershed management, but the case does highlight new strategies that go beyond techno-fixes devised as stand-alone solutions divorced from the dynamics driving urban and regional development.

## CONCLUSION

The Los Laureles Canyon case offers a prism through which to briefly recap critical regional ecology's contributions to cross-border regionalism and sustainability. In terms of the new regionalism/institutionalism, the Los Laureles case clearly demonstrates the problems presented by scale and the fact that local development is always embedded in larger regional and global dynamics. Until there is more affordable housing available in Tijuana for low-income workers, it will be very difficult to stop the rapid, unsustainable development of irregular settlements in the canyon and elsewhere in Tijuana. Indeed, this is a major problem worldwide (see Davis 2004). Obviously, there need to be new regional and national approaches to urban-economic development and housing problems. What the new regionalist/institutionalist discourse suggests are ways to go about making this happen.

Binational institutional coordination on a watershed scale, living wages, corporate accountability, and regional governance are essential to improving both social equity and environmental stewardship in the border region. This is easier said than done. One major problem/constraint with the new regionalist discourse stems from its neoliberal bias in favor of export-led industrialization and strategies that seek to make city-regions more competitive in the global economy. The neoliberal development paradigm leaves little room for endogenous (including bioregional) approaches to development, as noted by Friedmann in this volume. This limits the options on the table, making social experiments in places like Los Laureles Canyon all the more important. The Los Laureles initiative, with its emphasis on creating greener, more sustainable approaches to community-based development (emphasizing fundamentals like recycling, landscape ecology, and appropriate technology), offers a platform for trying more endogenous approaches to improving quality of life and place.

For the sake of argument, let us assume the political will is in place to implement a new regionalist agenda with a serious commitment to social equity and environmental sustainability. This still leaves the challenge of producing the knowledge that can guide the process. This is where sustainability science comes into play. In the case of Los Laureles, the importance of the watershed as a hydrological unit of analysis has been made clear. As mentioned above, the Coastal Training Program has mobilized a cross-border campaign to address the problems facing Los Laureles Canyon and the Tijuana River Estuary. As one of the projects within the Regional Workbench Consortium, Los Laureles Canyon ties into a sustainability science network. One of the concrete benefits of this sustainability science network has come in the form of planning and decision-support tools, including solid terrain models of the Southern California and northern Baja California border region. Moreover, plans are under way—in partnership with San Diego Baykeeper—to apply toxicogenomics and biomolecular technologies to environmental monitoring, risk assessment, and bioremediation in those areas that are contaminated by toxicants. The aim, through university-based research translation and community outreach, is to apply the "new biology" to environmental policy and planning.[14] This linkage of science to society is increasingly crucial as fiscal crisis straps the state and as universities are being held closely accountable for their federal research dollars. Heightened pressure for accountability can be problematic in some respects, but it does create a fertile field for growing what some scientists call "ivory bridges" (Sonnert and Holton 2002).

To take the argument a bit further, let us assume that the political will is in place and that useful knowledge is being produced. This brings us to the challenge of knowledge integration and knowledge networking, including the need for cybertools and cyberinfrastructure. Unfortunately, while there is plenty of innovation taking place in informational systems geared to marketing and tracking such things as credit card usage, global control capability among distributed corporate enterprises, and a multitude of other profit-driven applications, the status of cybertools and cyberinfrastructure for integrated regionalism is in a primitive state. Part of the problem is that it is very difficult to raise funds or create a line item in budgets for knowledge management that involves multiple sectors, jurisdictions, and academic disciplines—especially when the problems involve envi-

---

[14] This work is funded by the National Institute of Environmental Health Sciences (NIEHS) through a Superfund Basic Research Program at the University of California, San Diego.

ronmental externalities and what can be characterized as the tragedy of the commons. Other impediments to developing robust regional information systems include, among others, the balkanization of research efforts, the wide-ranging diversity of knowledge ecologies, and the lack of data collection/sharing protocols. A number of crucial efforts are under way to deal with this situation, such as the San Diego–Tijuana Atlas project mentioned above. The establishment of the Regional Workbench Consortium in 1999—with labs led by Richard Marciano and Ilya Zaslavsky at the San Diego Supercomputer Center—is another important development.[15] These initiatives should prove useful for situating the Los Laureles Canyon project in its larger context while disseminating information about the case in ways that empower community-based participation and the co-production of scientific and technical solutions.

Finally, critical regional ecology would be incomplete if it only drew attention to new regionalism/institutionalism, sustainability science, and the informational sciences. Ethics and culture are equally important factors, and perhaps the most important in some respects. The Los Laureles case brings the unsustainability of uneven development into clear view—not just locally but also in the larger U.S.-Mexico borderlands and global contexts. There is nothing terribly new about this situation, except perhaps its magnitude. Lewis Mumford, a well-noted social critic, philosopher of culture and technics, and historian of cities, has drawn attention to this pattern of creative destruction going back to the earliest urban civilizations (Mumford 1961, 1972, 1997a, 1997b, 2000), blaming what he characterized as the urban displacement of nature:

> [T]he displacement of nature in the city rested, in part, upon an illusion—or, indeed, a series of illusions—as to the nature of man and his institutions: the illusions of self-sufficiency

---

[15] The RWBC is a collaborative network of university and community partners dedicated to enabling sustainable city-region development. It promotes multidisciplinary research and service learning aimed at understanding how problems of environment and development interrelate across local, regional, and global scales, focusing on the Southern California–northern Baja California transborder region, especially the San Diego–Tijuana city-region and coastal zone. See http://regionalworkbench.org/index.php.

and independence and the possibility of physical continuity without conscious renewal. Under the protective mantle of the city, seemingly so permanent, these illusions encouraged habits of predation or parasitism that eventually undermined the whole social and economic structure, after having worked ruin in the surrounding landscape and even in far-distant regions (Mumford 1972: 144).[16]

Efforts to promote sustainable urban development through local initiatives like the Los Laureles Canyon project, binational policy initiatives like the U.S.-Mexico Border 2012 Program, and global convocations like the World Urban Forums are attempts to rectify the kind of gross ecological ignorance that Mumford laments.[17] In this context, ethics draws attention to social equity while cultural theory helps us think through barriers and bridges to fostering progressive vision. Aldo Leopold's land ethic, for in-

---

[16] Mumford's sweeping indictment is an elegant oversimplification that continues to find support in the literature. For instance, Ponting (1993: 434) argues that "the story is repeated throughout human history and all over the globe, from Sumeria to ancient Egypt to pre-Columbian North America to tiny Easter Island: Human beings prosper by exploiting the earth's resources until those resources can no longer sustain the society's population, which leads to the decline and eventual collapse of that society." Despite the appeal of this line of argument, it is not at all certain that endogenous environmental changes due to human impact (such as aquifer depletion, soil salination, and erosion) are the main causal factor or driving force in the collapse of past societies. Richerson (1993) offers three other plausible hypotheses: "(1) exogenous environmental shocks or changes such as a series of dry years, long term climate deterioration, or the introduction of new diseases; (2) exogenous political or economic changes, such as the rise of pastoral nomad confederations or the shifting of critical trade systems; and (3) endogenous political or economic changes, such as a stress on ideological and political legitimacy when elite manipulation of the economy fails to keep up with population growth, or when the limits to imperial conquest lead to an inability to reward the military establishment" (p. 127). Diamond (2005) offers a more current overview of this issue.

[17] The U.S.-Mexico Border 2012 Program is a binational collaborative effort to protect the environment and public health in the U.S.-Mexico border region, consistent with the principles of sustainable development. For more information, see http://www.epa.gov/usmexicoborder.

stance, offers a meaningful view of human-nature relations. According to Leopold, we are "biotic citizens" sharing habitat with a larger biotic community—and our land-use planning should take that into account: "A thing is right when it tends to preserve the integrity, stability, and beauty of the biotic community. It is wrong when it tends otherwise" (Leopold 1987: 240). This sentiment on its own may be meaningless to people if they are malnourished, poorly housed, and lacking access to even the most rudimentary urban services and amenities. But if the land ethic, or ecological ethic, was to take root in the culture of organizations, markets, and institutions, then the basis of how we measure value may shift (Light and Rolston 2003). What does not get measured often does not get valued in a market system, and this is typically the case with many of the ecosystem services provided to us by stocks of natural capital (such as soil formation, waste assimilation by wetlands, pollination, renewable raw materials).

In the consumer culture of global capitalism, it is generally not known how much environmental quality is being given up in the name of development, nor how much development is being given up in the name of environmental protection. In an attempt to clarify such trade-offs at the national level, the World Bank did a pilot study in Mexico in the early 1990s to illustrate the potential magnitude of the adjustments required:

> When an adjustment was made for the depletion of oil, forests, and groundwater, Mexico's net national product was almost 7 percent lower. A further adjustment for the costs of avoiding environmental degradation, particularly air and water pollution and soil erosion, brought the national product down another 7 percent (World Bank 1992: 35–36).[18]

These figures draw attention to the real and potential problems stemming from counting the depletion of geological capital and ecological life-support systems as net current income. This begs the question: Is sustainable capitalism possible? Maybe, maybe not. Meanwhile, the least we can do is encourage social experimentation. Critical regional ecology draws attention to some promising frontiers for exploration along these lines.

---

[18] The report failed to mention the specific period covered by the study.

# References

Aguilar Zinser, Adolfo. 2001. "The New Government Responsibility: The War against Corruption, National Security, and Social Equity." Washington, D.C.: Inter-American Development Bank.

Alvarez, Heidi L., and Julio E. Ibarra. 2003. "Experiences with the Digital Divide in Latin America." In *2003 Round Table on Developing Countries' Access to Scientific Knowledge, The Abdus Salam ICTP*. Trieste, Italy.

Amin, Ash. 1999. "An Institutionalist Perspective on Regional Economic Development," *International Journal of Urban and Regional Research* 23.

Amin, Ash, N. J. Thrift, and ESF Programme on Regional and Urban Restructuring in Europe. 1994. *Globalization, Institutions, and Regional Development in Europe*. Oxford and New York: Oxford University Press.

Blatter, Joachim. 2002. "Emerging Cross-Border Regions as a Step towards Sustainable Development? Experiences and Considerations from Examples in Europe and North America," *International Journal of Economic Development* 2, no. 3: 402–39.

Bollman, Nick. 2002. "The New California Dream: Regional Solutions for 21st Century Challenges." Oakland: California Institute for County Government.

Browning-Aiken, A., H. Richter, D. C. Goodrich, B. Strain, and R. G. Varady. 2004. "The Upper San Pedro Basin: Fostering Collaborative Binational Watershed Management," *Water Resources Development* 20, no. 3: 353–67.

Calthorpe, Peter, and William B. Fulton. 2001. *The Regional City: Planning for the End of Sprawl*. Washington, D.C.: Island Press.

Cox, Millicent. 1999. "San Diego and Tijuana are One Metropolitan Area." Presentation at the Demographics Workshop, El Colegio de la Frontera Norte, October.

Davis, Mike. 2004. "Planet of Slums: Urban Involution of the Informal Proletariat," *New Left Review* 26: 5–34.

Diamond, Jared M. 2005. *Collapse: How Societies Choose to Fail or Succeed*. New York: Viking.

EPA (U.S. Environmental Protection Agency). 2005a. "U.S. Mexico Border," http://www.epa.gov/region09/border/feature.html, accessed March 31, 2005.

———. 2005b. "What Is a Watershed?" http://www.epa.gov/owow/watershed/whatis.html, accessed March 31, 2005.

Etzioni, Amitai. 2000. *The Third Way to a Good Society*. London: Demos.

Friedmann, John. 1992. *Empowerment: The Politics of Alternative Development*. Cambridge, Mass.: Blackwell.

Giddens, Anthony. 2003. *The Progressive Manifesto: New Ideas for the Centre-Left*. Cambridge and Malden, Mass.: Polity Press and Blackwell.

Herzog, Lawrence A. 1990. *Where North Meets South: Cities, Space, and Politics on the U.S.-Mexico Border*. Austin: Center for Mexican American Studies, University of Texas at Austin.

———. 1998. "Sustainability in the Transfrontier Metropolis," *Enfoque* (Center for U.S.-Mexican Studies, University of California, San Diego) 2: 11.

Herzog, Lawrence A., ed. 2000. *Shared Space: Rethinking the U.S.-Mexico Border Environment*. La Jolla: Center for U.S.-Mexican Studies, University of California, San Diego.

IDB (Inter-American Development Bank). 2004. "Social Equity Forum: Institutional Challenges for Sustainable and Equitable Social Policy in Latin America and the Caribbean." Washington, D.C., http://www.iadb.org/sds/doc/sixth_sef.pdf.

Kates, R. W., et al. 2001. "Environment and Development-Sustainability Science," *Science* 292: 641–42.

Katz, Bruce, ed. 2000. *Reflections on Regionalism*. Washington, D.C.: Brookings Institution Press.

Kipher, Stefan, and Karen Wirsig. 2004. "From Contradiction to Coherence? A Review Symposium on the US American 'New Regionalism,'" *Antipode* 36: 728–32.

Kiy, Richard, and Naoko Kada. 2004. "Blurred Borders: Transboundary Impacts and Solutions in the San Diego–Tijuana Region." San Diego: International Community Foundation.

Leopold, Aldo. 1987. *A Sand County Almanac, and Sketches Here and There*. New York: Oxford University Press.

Light, Andrew, and Holmes Rolston. 2003. *Environmental Ethics: An Anthology*. Malden, Mass.: Blackwell.

Mumford, Lewis. 1961. *The City in History: Its Origins, Its Transformations, and Its Prospects*. New York: Harcourt Brace Jovanovich.

———. 1972. "The Natural History of Urbanization." In *The Ecology of Man: An Ecosystem Approach*, ed. R. L. Smith. San Francisco: Harper and Row.

———. 1997a. *The Culture of Cities*. London: Routledge/Thoemmes.

———. 1997b. *The Myth of the Machine*. New York: MJF Books.

———. 2000. *Art and Technics*. New York: Columbia University Press.

Mumme, Stephen. 2002. "Watershed Management Holds Promise for U.S.-Mexican Border," *Arizona Water Resource* 10, no. 5.

NRC (National Research Council). 1999. *Our Common Journey: A Transition toward Sustainability*. Washington, D.C.: National Academy Press.

NRC, Committee on Watershed Management, Water Science and Technology Board, and Environment Commission on Geosciences and Resources. 1999. *New Strategies for America's Watersheds*. Washington, D.C.: National Academy Press.

NSF (National Science Foundation). 2005. "Program Solicitation NSF 05-551," Collaborative Systems, Universal Access, http://www.nsf.gov/pubs/2005/nsf05551/nsf05551.htm, accessed March 03, 2005.

NSF Blue Ribbon Advisory Panel on Cyberinfrastructure. 2003. "Revolutionizing Science and Engineering through Cyberinfrastructure." NSF.

Perloff, Harvey. 1981. "Editor's Introduction," *Journal of Planning Education and Research* 1, no. 1.

Pezzoli, Keith. n.d. "The Progressive Imagination: New Frontiers in Critical Regional Ecology." In progress.

Ponting, Clive. 1993. *A Green History of the World: The Environment and Collapse of Great Civilizations*. New York: Penguin.

Richerson, Peter J. 1993. "Humans as Components of the Lake Titicaca Ecosystem: A Model System for the Study of Environmental Deterioration." In *Humans as Components of Ecosystems: The Ecology of Subtle Human Effects and Populated Areas*, ed. Mark J. McDonnell and Steward T. A. Pickett. New York: Springer-Verlag.

SANDAG (San Diego Association of Governments). 2004. "Regional Comprehensive Plan for the San Diego Region." SANDAG.

———. 2005. "Borders Committee," http://www.sandag.org/index.asp?committeeid=54&fuseaction=committees.detail.

Schrèoder, Gerhard, Jèurgen Kocka, Friedhelm Neidhardt, and Wissenschaftszentrum Berlin fur Sozialforschung. 2002. *Progressive Governance for the XXI Century. Contribution to the Berlin Conference: Papers to the Experts' Conference*. New York: Kluwer Law International.

SDD (San Diego Dialogue). 2000. "The Global Engagement of San Diego/Baja California." La Jolla: Division of Extended Studies and Public Programs, University of California, San Diego

Sonnert, Gerhard, and Gerald James Holton. 2002. *Ivory Bridges: Connecting Science and Society*. Cambridge, Mass.: MIT Press.

Thayer, Robert L. 2003. *LifePlace: Bioregional Thought and Practice*. Berkeley: University of California Press.

UN-Habitat. 2001. *Cities in a Globalizing World: Global Report on Human Settlements 2001*. London: Earthscan.

Wheeler, Stephen. 2002. "The New Regionalism: Key Characteristics of an Emerging Movement," *Journal of the American Planning Association* 68, no. 3: 267–78.

World Bank. 1992. *World Development Report 1992: Development and the Environment*. New York: Oxford University Press.

Wright, Richard. 2005. "Tijuana River Watershed Atlas," http://www-rohan.sdsu.edu/dept/press/institute.html, accessed March 10, 2005.

Young, Oran R. 2002. *The Institutional Dimensions of Environmental Change: Fit, Interplay, and Scale*. Cambridge, Mass.: MIT Press.

PART III

Poverty, Vulnerability, and Environmental Management

# 6

# Urban Structure and Social Segregation in Tijuana

TITO ALEGRÍA

This chapter explores the relationship between the spatial structure of retail trade and services subcenters and the social-residential segregation of population groups by income level in a city. The data come from Tijuana, where market and institutional spatial mechanisms generate a specific systemic relationship between the economic-spatial structure and social segregation, and this relationship, in turn, generates a regressive income distribution in terms of the price of accessibility. In conceptual terms, the price of accessibility is a function of the distance between two locations: the residential areas where the city's inhabitants live and their city's commercial centers and employment opportunities. The mechanisms that underlie the distance measures are influenced by the location of the components of urban structure. Pahl has approached the question of location in his studies of public housing (1969, 1975), but relative location has not been examined in terms of the mechanisms that create commercial centers and subcenters, nor in terms of a relationship between the location of commercial centers and the spatial distribution of population groups by income level.

The present study attempts to address this shortcoming by examining the influence of urban structure on income redistribution through the spatial organization of jobs and services. The market mechanisms that lead to spatial concentrations of the service sector—understood to include both services and retail trade—have already been identified. In this study, the primary hypothesis is that market mechanisms locate commercial centers

---

This chapter has been submitted for publication in Spanish by El Colegio de la Frontera Norte–Monterrey. English translation by Sandra del Castillo.

close to residential areas with middle or high income levels and far from areas that house the city's poor. As a corollary, the price of accessibility is a direct function of the location of such centers and an indirect function of the location of residences. Further, the price of accessibility is greatest for the city's poorest residents.

Neighborhood-level data were used to test this hypothesis. In the following sections, I first operationalize the concepts of commercial center and segregation in statistical terms. I then discuss forms of socio-spatial segregation and propose a relative indicator of the price of accessibility. I then present the results of my analysis of centrality and segregation for the Tijuana case. And finally, I test the spatial relationship between them. Foremost among my conclusions are: (1) that the price of access to jobs and resources is highest for the poor, and (2) that the siting of urban resources is an important factor in the regressive redistribution of income.

## THE SPATIAL STRUCTURE OF URBAN RESOURCES AND EMPLOYMENT

The location of intra-urban resources explains much of the spatially driven regressive redistribution of income within a city. The remainder can be explained in terms of families' location. In this section, I discuss the mechanism that determines where shops and services are established (the services sector accounts for some 60 percent of local employment) and where manufacturing firms locate.

The decisions that determine the location of commercial centers do not appear in standard monocentric land-use theory, which posits a single "central business district," or CBD, which includes all types of activities and jobs. In this theory, the CBD location affects land prices as well as the location of residential areas within a city (Anas, Arnott, and Small 1998). However, this theory cannot represent today's large cities, with their multicentric and disperse urban structures (Gordon and Richardson 1996). Now, shops and services tend to locate in numerous concentrations within the urban space.

I propose to approach the topic of intra-urban multi-centrality with the aid of central place theory, originally developed for analyses of cities' location and sizes. According to this theory, market centers (cities) are distributed according to spatial distances and hierarchical functions (Berry and Parr 1988). Each good or service is viewed as a function that is offered in a market center. Each function has a market area that is specific to itself and different from all others. The market area encompasses the spaces where the consumers of a product reside. Consumers generally patronize the market centers closest to their homes in order to minimize their transportation costs. Typically, there is one center at the top of the hierarchy, which offers the full array of urban functions, and some of these functions will not be available in any other center because their market area is so extensive that it embraces the entire city. For centers that are lower in the hierarchy, their market shrinks in direct proportion to the reduction in the number of functions offered, until we reach the lowest level, that of the smaller urban locality.

We can draw five postulates from this theory that relate to the conformation of the intra-urban structure of market centers: (1) each activity has a surrounding market area from which it draws its customers; (2) market areas differ because the goods and services they offer have different minimum market areas; (3) the cost of transportation to a market center depends on its distance from one's home, and this will influence a consumer's choice of which center to patronize; (4) centers comprise a variety of activities, and their hierarchical ranking rises as the number of activities increases; and (5) centers are defined by the breadth of their supply of goods for final consumption, and not by the density of their employment. This last consideration means that the defining elements in market centers are commerce and services, not manufacturing.

Tests of central place theory in an inter-urban context have found that centers have more economic heft (in terms of employment) than the theory would predict. This reflects the fact that the same function serves more clients when it is located in a center that is higher in the hierarchy (Berry and Parr 1988: chap. 2). This also holds true when we turn to intra-urban centers, and it can be explained with the addition of a second argument: the use of economies of scale and scope by suppliers and consumers, which reduces the transaction costs for both seller and buyer (Stahl 1998). When a primary center offers goods high in the hierarchy—that is, products or services with a large market area—consumers who live at a distance can reduce their transportation costs by also purchasing goods that rank lower in the hierarchy at the same shopping center, a strategy that produces a concentration of consumption. Merchants in a market center can take advantage of a concentration of consumers by increasing the size and total number of functions in order to achieve economies of scale and scope, respectively. As a consequence of these strategies to reduce transaction costs, consumers spur large centers to grow ever larger, at the same time that smaller centers are forced to become smaller.

One way to operationalize the concept of "center," detect the presence of such centers, and determine their hierarchical standing is by measuring their "degree of centrality" (DC) to each neighborhood within a city. Following the argument presented above, an activity is central to a neighborhood (C = centrality index) if, after having served the neighborhood's residents, a shop also sells to persons coming from other neighborhoods. An activity is not considered central if it sells to only some of the neighborhood's inhabitants, while the remainder go to other neighborhoods where the activity is central. If we assume that the balance of trade in each activity in the city is in equilibrium, then we can assume that all persons employed in an activity serve all of the city's inhabitants, with each employee serving a determined number of inhabitants. If so, we can estimate an activity's centrality within a neighborhood by determining how many more times the activity serves consumers in that neighborhood over the citywide average for the same activity:

$$C_{ij} = \frac{(E_{ij}/P_j)}{(E_i/P)} \qquad (1)$$

where:
  $C_{ij}$ = centrality index for activity (sector) i in neighborhood j
  $E_{ij}$ = employees in activity i in neighborhood j
  $E_i$ = employees in activity i in the entire city
  $P_j$ = population of neighborhood j
  $P$ = total population of the city

An activity is central in a neighborhood when its centrality index is greater than 1 ($C_{ij} > 1$). A neighborhood is central when it has a central activity and its degree of centrality DC equals the number of central activities that it contains:

$$DC_j = \#(C_{ij} > 1) \qquad (2)$$

Central place theory postulates that the market areas of two centers with equal hierarchical standings will be the same in size; in fact, they generally differ. There are two possible explanations for this: first, differences in population density within and between the respective centers' areas of influence and, second, income differences between inhabitants of one area and the other.

The greater the (residential) population density of consumers in a center's market area, the smaller the market area. Consumers who patronize a center in a densely populated area occupy a small portion of the city's territory. This occurs in more consolidated areas and near the city's principal business district. Consumption among persons with higher incomes tends to be greater in quantity, diversity of products, and frequency, especially for goods and services with more income elasticity of demand. Such a situation can raise the hierarchical standing of the center that these customers patronize or cause the center's market area to contract—or some combination of both.

Given that distance between households and shopping areas adds new costs to the cost of consuming, people can be expected to patronize centers closer to their homes. High-income groups place a higher value on their travel time (opportunity costs) than do persons with lower incomes, for which reason they prefer to shop close to their places of residence. Businesses follow the consumers, offering their goods and services in densely concentrated zones near the residential areas of high-income groups. Thus market mechanisms produce a pattern in which high-hierarchy centers are spatially linked with high- and middle-income residential areas. Where incomes are lower, the centers' standing in the hierarchy will be lower and the market area of activities will be bigger. The poor must travel longer distances than the rich in order to consume the same good or service, and then they must pay more in transport or access costs for what is consumed. This is the way in which the structure of these centers generates accessibility prices that are regressive for society.

The centers' structure also supports the emergence of spatial monopolies or oligopolies, which facilitates the distribution of lower-quality goods and services at higher prices. Poor quality in a product or service is linked to lower levels of technology (less capital, more labor) and issues of quality control. The possibility of monopolizing a marketing venue allows a vendor to produce at maximum capacity (taking full advantage of economies of scale) using a level of technology that is below the citywide mean. Achieving this outcome is impossible in a more competitive commercial zone. Under such conditions, low productivity (the result of minimal technology) would force the vendor to increase prices in order to achieve a rate of return similar to that prevailing elsewhere in the city. The vendor can inflate the price even more at the point of sale in the absence of nearby competitors, up to the point where a balance is reached between the inflated price and the costs to the consumer of shifting to another commercial district.

This explains why prices for goods and services are higher in areas that house lower-income groups. Areas that encompass people with higher income levels display lower prices (primarily for standardized products) because of the increased sectoral competition that accompanies the decrease in spatial monopolies. In sum, the spatial mechanisms that influence the prices of goods and services generate regressive effects in the redistribution of income. These negative impacts are different from, and are added to, the price of accessibility, and together these factors create a pattern of unequal pricing throughout the urban area.

To summarize, personal incomes are generally viewed, from the perspective of demand for goods and services, as enabling consumption under two basic assumptions: (1) the costs of consumables are the same for all consumers, and (2) the costs of consumption are set in the marketplace. But as the preceding discussion illustrates, the costs of consumption vary by place, and prices are affected by forces outside of the marketplace, such as by the spatial organization of service-sector employment. Living costs are higher in some parts of the city than in others. Just as the costs of goods vary by location, so, too, do the real incomes of consumers. As we shall see in following sections, the real value of a peso is less for the poor than for higher-income individuals.

## TWO TYPES OF SEGREGATION

Setting aside for the moment the studies of daytime territorial segregation that have been conducted by urban geographers (see, for example, Peach 1975), segregation is defined in urban sociology as residential segregation. Under this definition, which prevails across all sociological currents, urban segregation is the territorial exclusion of any social group, and virtually all researchers have sought the causes of this segregation in the social structure, either as the ultimate causal factor or as a mechanism that mediates economic influences. Nevertheless, past studies of residential segregation share little else. They differ even in their construction of what segregation is. For some, it is the spatial exclusion of some social groups from an array of urban services. For others, it is the spatial separation between social groups. The former view can be called "segregation by location" and the latter, "segregation by differentiation" (Alegría 1998). In methodological terms, we can reduce this distinction by viewing researchers of location segregation as focusing on segregation *between* zones, and researchers of segregation by differentiation as being primarily interested in segregation *within* zones. In reality, both types of segregation exist.

**Segregation by Location**

Segregation by location is a condition of social and spatial exclusion vis-à-vis the advantages of urban life. Studies of this type of exclusion can be divided into two groups, depending on the context in which they were conducted. The first set of studies, which emerged in South America in the 1960s and 1970s, emphasized socioeconomic dualism, an expression of the economics of underdevelopment as the catalyst for social and spatial segregation—or marginalization—in cities. The second group of studies were conducted in England in the 1970s; these researchers emphasized the spatial distancing of some social groups from urban resources, viewing it as a regressive condition of the redistribution of wealth under capitalism. This essay adopts the latter approach.

From the perspective of the British studies, the city is composed of systems that distribute various types of rewards, among which space figures importantly. In the neo-Weberian version, an individual's life chances are affected by his or her relative access to both direct and indirect sources of income (Pahl 1969, 1975). People who live close to their jobs and to services and recreational centers have more advantages than those who live at a distance. The latter must spend more than the former to obtain the same urban resources, even when both groups receive the same salaries. The spatial distribution of urban resources and housing operates through two kinds of mechanisms: market mechanisms and institutional mechanisms.

Because urban resources are limited, they are not distributed evenly throughout the city. The distribution pattern of resources and housing constitutes a constraint for the people living under it, and it affects them independently of the restrictions imposed on them by the social hierarchy associated with the work environment.

When seeking a residential location (through market or institutional mechanisms) that is most advantageous in terms of its spatial relationship to resources, individuals at the base of the social hierarchy are at the greatest disadvantage. The competition for scarce local resources engenders urban conflicts, but it is also the source of residential segregation with respect to urban resources. Such segregation is an inevitable product of the distributive mechanisms for urban resources and housing—which negatively affect groups low in the social hierarchy—but it becomes an inherent element of these groups' living conditions given the regressive distribution of income that drives the process of spatial segregation. From this perspective, the regressive spatial distribution of income can be explained, first and foremost, by the mechanisms that govern the siting of urban housing.

Following the British current of neo-Marxism, location is also seen as a condition of segregation that causes income redistribution to be regressive (Harvey 1979). That is, the extraction of rent from urban land is the source of problems and conflicts within neighborhoods. As these conflicts unfold, neighborhood residents develop an awareness of themselves as a community differentiated from other communities. In and of itself, land's value renders a differentiation-segregation in social groups. At a different level of analysis, by creating new modes of consumption and new desires and needs, the urbanization process also brings into existence new groups defined by income levels or consumption patterns. These segments of society can crystallize as differentiated communities within the urban structure. Segregation between groups is the spatial result of the crystallization of such diverse communities. On the other hand, the location of these communities responds to mechanisms in the real estate market (as a consumer good) that are regulated by the logic of the financial sector and government, and are driven by the interests of property investors seeking to profit from housing needs in a given community.

Spatial segregation between housing and urban resources generates regressive impacts on income redistribution in two ways: through accessibility and through proximity. The former is expressed as the price of accessibility, and it encompasses the inconveniences encountered in getting to places offering employment opportunities and goods and services. These costs vary depending on the time and distance required to access these urban facilities; they also vary according to the individual's knowledge of his/her full range of choices and willingness to pursue them. In line with this perspective, the regressive redistribution of space is explained primarily by local, political, and real estate power mechanisms.

In Mexico's urban areas, the price of accessibility is an important factor in explaining the regressive redistribution of income, given the significant share of the family budget that poor households spend on transportation and the weak development of public transportation systems and urban roadways. The main accessibility costs are incurred in two spatial subsystems: transportation between home and work, and transportation from home to shops and services and back.

The logic that would lead an individual to live close to his or her workplace is frustrated by the constraints imposed by the real estate market. These constraints primarily affect the low-income population, whose income elasticity of demand for housing is minimal. Land invasions offer one informal means of increasing supply elasticity. These occur within cities or on their peripheries, on land that is not yet urbanized but is relatively accessible. Achieving the shortest distance between locations of employment and these informal settlements depends on a low level of interest in the land on the part of commercial, industrial, and real estate capital, and on a generally propitious political atmosphere. The most common products of the land invasion process are large extensions on the urban periphery inhabited by low-income individuals housed at a substantial distance from their places of work. This distance carries high accessibility costs, cutting into these workers' real incomes, which are already low. Approximately 37 percent of trips made in Tijuana are to work (PDUE 1993). The proportion is much lower in cities with higher average incomes; for example, trips to work account for only 25 percent of total trips made in Los Angeles (Richardson and Bae 1993). This supports the hypothesis that low-income workers' commutes to work account for even more than the average of 37 percent, increasing the importance of transportation costs in the household budgets of these workers' families.

The spatial subsystem of home/shops and services governs the relationship of households to goods, services, and recreation. Many goods and services are only available at certain locations within the city. This is owing to the logic of central location (for personal and professional goods and services) or to the lack of attention on the part of local government (regarding public services such as water, sewerage, and so on). These services are scarcest in low-income neighborhoods, where water offers a glaring example of the price of accessibility. Families in low-income neighborhoods pay five times more for a cubic meter of water from a tanker truck than wealthy families pay for the same amount of water delivered via water lines into their homes.

Two indices were developed for estimating the price of accessibility from each neighborhood in Tijuana: one for accessibility to places of employment, the other for accessibility to shops and services:

$$P_j^C = \sum_k DC_k \Big/ d_{jk}^2 \qquad (3)$$

and

$$P_j^E = \sum_k E_k \Big/ d_{jk}^2 \qquad (4)$$

where:
- $PC_j$ = accessibility index from neighborhood j to the areas of shops and services
- $PE_j$ = accessibility index from neighborhood j to places of employment
- $DC_k$ = degree of centrality of neighborhood k
- $E_k$ = total employment in neighborhood k
- $d_{jk}$ = lineal distance from neighborhood j to neighborhood k

The first index measures a neighborhood's potential to access all centers of commerce and services within the city, taking into account the hierarchical status of the center at each distance measure from the neighborhood. The second measures a neighborhood's potential to access all places of employment in the city, taking into account the number of jobs at each distance measure from the neighborhood.

## Segregation by Differentiation

In general terms, segregation by differentiation refers to the spatial exclusion between social groups. Early studies of this type of exclusion by Duncan and Duncan (1955a) looked at the relationship between social stratification and spatial distribution, relating an ecological view of the city with the Weberian notion of social class. These authors understood urban segregation as the spatial distance between social groups and as a process that was in opposition to social integration. They designed a "dissimilarity index" to measure this distance—the degree to which the distribution of one group differs from that of another across basic geostatistical areas. These authors' segregation index is similar, but with one difference: the group to be compared includes all of the remaining working population. The equation yields a segregation value for a city, which is the percentage of all members of a social group who would have to relocate in order to make their distribution similar to that of the remainder of the working population with which their group is being compared (Duncan and Duncan 1955b). The simplicity and utility of this approach have put it at the methodological center of studies of segregation over recent decades, whether they follow the method, use it comparatively, or criticize it (Cadwallader 1985; Wong 1993; Farley 1984; Smith 1991). Paradoxically, this index does not measure distance at all; it merely expresses the average proportion by which two distributions differ from one another. Apart from the usual (minor) criticisms of indices that employ geographic units of aggregation (a change in extension changes the index value), this index is unidimensional, with no application to bidimensional space. Moreover, this index can provide no information on the social composition of an urban neighborhood (or basic geostatistical area), making it of no value for calculating changes in a neighborhood over time.

Although Duncan and Duncan's primary objective was to investigate residential segregation—or the absence of spatial integration—among occupational groups, their results led them to note the importance of considering class and status (in the Weberian sense) separately in future studies (Duncan and Duncan 1955a), a task they themselves did not pursue. For Weber, class is merely a concept employed in sociological analysis or an idea "by which groups of individuals, who share approximately similar life possibilities, direct their actions" (Weber 1968, cited in Saunders 1984).

According to this view, society can be broken down in many ways, and all of these classifications are based on people's ability to participate in markets. The most relevant are the owners of businesses and real estate. Individuals whose life chances are similar belong to the same class—in any of these classifications—whereas status groups are defined by their members' specific patterns of consumption. Each class holds a position on a hierarchical structure that reflects the capacity (of groups and the individuals in them) vis-à-vis the market, not between classes.

In fact, sociological analysis equated urban segregation with spatial separation between occupational groups. Studies in the United States have demonstrated that spatial separation between racial groups becomes a question of social segregation because it engenders cumulative causal processes that negatively affect nonwhites (Massey and Denton 1996).

The use of professional or occupational categories for analyses of segregation relies on two weak assumptions. The first is that occupational category is a good measure of the markets for labor and goods—and thus of the housing market as well. Spatial distance by occupation would be the consequence of the "invisible hand" of economic competition. One could infer the magnitude of spatial distance from the income differentials between occupational categories. Nevertheless, a multitude of studies confirm that occupation is only one of many determinants of income differentials, and it is not necessarily the most important one. Others include education, age, ethnicity, gender, and economic sector (Berndt 1996; Heller 1987; Ihlanfeldt 1992), as well as social class in the Marxist sense of position in the system of production (Wright 1979). These studies cast doubt on the usefulness of occupational class in explaining segregation by differentiation; the explanatory variable that remains is status. It follows, then, that people differentiate themselves within an area by appropriating the symbols of status as just one more form of social distinction. Yet this esthetic view of segregation is incompatible with the way in which people legitimate their symbols: the distinction is more the result than the cause of status (Bourdieu 1990).

The second assumption is that the same mechanism of spatial differentiation is operating for all professional groups. This supposition was quickly called into question in analyses of segregation. Feldman and Tilly (1960) demonstrated that the spatial distribution of a set of occupational categories is determined primarily by education and, to a lesser degree, by income. Their most important conclusion was that education is more powerful for explaining the distribution of white-collar workers, while income has more explanatory value regarding blue-collar workers. These results confirm that there is no single mechanism underlying spatial distribution, and there may be more than two; but above all, they reveal that the reasons for spatial differentiation are different at the two extremes of the social scale. Among elites—the group most able to self-segregate—cultural stratum is determinant, whereas for the lower classes—who are forced into segregation—economic stratum is more important. This suggests that economic rationality governs residential choice most strongly when resources are at their lowest.

I have suggested elsewhere that segregation by differentiation comes into play in the process of accessing housing, a process that depends on the household head's knowledge and income level (Alegría 1994). Knowledge is a complex factor comprising both empirical and practical aspects (Thrift 1985). This argument, which was confirmed for segregation between income groups, will not be developed here. Rather, I suggest that this kind of segregation is not spatially linked to either the centrality or the distribution of employment, which eliminates it as an explanatory factor in the regressive redistribution of income that results from the spatial organization of the city. An opposing view can be found in the work of Massey and Denton (1996), who posit that racial segregation is one of the causes of social conflict (violence, crime, and so on) and of the loss of a fiscal base and, hence, of public investment. Nevertheless, these authors do not specify that this kind of segregation exerts its negative impacts through the redistribution of income.

## RESULTS AND ANALYSIS

As Tijuana has grown, this border city of 1.3 million inhabitants has not followed the pattern of a declining old city center, nor has it substantially modified the locational pattern of social groups. Tijuana's social zones are arranged in nearly concentric circles, with the wealthiest areas in the middle and social rankings dropping the further one moves from this core. The mechanism for assigning residential location to the wealthy areas has two variants. In the first variant, the traditional wealthy areas benefit from their long-established and continuous identification as prestigious neighborhoods. This identity prevented their decay and provided the vitality to redevelop the adjacent old city center, something that has not occurred in other cities. These wealthy areas bordering the old city center acted as a key economic factor in the revitalization of the urban core because they ensured the income-generating capacity of shopping areas aimed at mid- and high-level consumers. In the second variant, the emergence of a limited number of new high-income neighborhoods primarily reflects residential segregation as a practice of high-end consumption. Social distinction, premised on what Bourdieu calls *habitus*, arises from this practice of consumption operating in a spatial dimension and materializing as residential segregation.

In the competition for the best business locations, the hierarchy of retail and service centers has been the axis organizing urban economic space. These businesses, which provide the foundation for the centers, have long formed the dominant sector in Mexico's northern border cities. Tijuana's tertiary activities, most of which are related to tourism, were established near the international border crossing, the area with the best accessibility to the United States. Over time, other activities moved into the area, including many that are central to the functioning of any Mexican city, transforming the zone into the functional city center. Infrastructural efforts taken in tandem converted this downtown area into the best-supplied and most accessible zone from any point in the city. Achieving this level of accessibility for the downtown came about through the efforts of economically powerful local groups—service-sector entrepreneurs—who pressured incumbent politicians to invest in the required infrastructure. The result was (until fairly recently) a radiocentric system of streets and public transit routes, which meant reduced access to areas on the periphery where most industries were located. The opening of a new border crossing east of Tijuana in the 1980s facilitated a regional blooming of export-producing industries. More recently, new plants have become more dispersed throughout the city as companies have tried to locate near the zones where their workers live, in the process reducing the price of access to the workplace.

Tijuana's tertiary centers—the areas where retail and service activities are concentrated—were traditionally also the areas with the highest employment density. But this spatial pattern has shifted with the rapid expansion of manufacturing in recent decades, leading to the establishment of zones on the periphery of Tijuana that have increasingly dense employment.

The accessibility between home and place of employment in the context of urban expansion has been the subject of much discussion, especially the question of whether the location of jobs follows the location of workers' households or vice versa. Studies conducted in the United States lead to the conclusion that most employment in the service sector follows the residential location of the workers, but there is a lack of consensus whether the same sequence holds for manufacturing jobs (Steinnes 1977; Cooke 1978; Thurston and Yezer 1994).

One can derive a similar conclusion regarding service-sector employment in Tijuana based on tests of sequential correlations over time. The hypothesis would state that higher residents' salaries in a given area attract tertiary-sector jobs. A complementary hypothesis would postulate that tertiary-sector employment in an area does not attract higher salaries. If the former hypothesis is valid, then jobs would appear in an area some time after the appearance of residents with high incomes. This time lapse could be between two and three years, during which merchants identify sales opportunities, invest in commercial spaces, and begin operations.

To test this hypothesis, I calculated the correlation by neighborhood between residents in 1990 and service-sector employment in 1993. To confirm that jobs do not attract residents, I calculated the correlation by neighborhood between service-sector employment in 1988 and residents in 1990. The data are organized by census tract; they correspond to the Tijuana urban area and are taken from the population and economic censuses of 1988, 1990, and 1993. The results, presented in table 6.1, support the hypothesis of sequentiality, although not at a statistically significant level. The correlation for the population-employment sequence is stronger than that for the employment-population sequence, and the former is stronger for services than for commerce. Further, as expected, the correlations are negative for low-income residents and positive for those with higher incomes.

One additional measure was taken to test whether the location of tertiary centers can be explained by their spatial association with income groups. I ran three regression models in which the dependent variable was

Table 6.1. Correlation by Census Tract

|  | EMP93 COM[a] | EMP93 SER[b] | EMP87 COM[a] | EMP87 SER[b] | MW_0–2[c] | MW_2–5[d] | MW_5+[e] |
|---|---|---|---|---|---|---|---|
| EMP93COM | 1.000 | .854 | .839 | .773 | -.155 | -.146 | .213 |
| Sig. (2-tailed) |  | .000 | .000 | .000 | .037 | .050 | .004 |
| EMP93SER | .854 | 1.000 | .836 | .926 | -.227 | -.308 | .364 |
| Sig. (2-tailed) | .000 |  | .000 | .000 | .002 | .000 | .000 |
| EMP87COM | .839 | .836 | 1.000 | .883 | -.156 | -.105 | .191 |
| Sig. (2-tailed) | .000 | .000 |  | .000 | .036 | .159 | .010 |
| EMP87SER | .773 | .926 | .883 | 1.000 | -.168 | -.224 | .267 |
| Sig. (2-tailed) | .000 | .000 | .000 |  | .024 | .002 | .000 |
| MW_0–2 | -.155 | -.227 | -.156 | -.168 | 1.000 | -.039 | -.831 |
| Sig. (2-tailed) | .037 | .002 | .036 | .024 |  | .599 | .000 |
| MW_2–5 | -.146 | -.308 | -.105 | -.224 | -.039 | 1.000 | -.523 |
| Sig. (2-tailed) | .050 | .000 | .159 | .002 | .599 |  | .000 |
| MW_5+ | .213 | .364 | .191 | .267 | -.831 | -.523 | 1.000 |
| Sig. (2-tailed) | .004 | .000 | .010 | .000 | .000 | .000 |  |
| N | 181 | 181 | 181 | 181 | 181 | 181 | 181 |

*Sources*: Mexico's Economic Census, 1988 and 1994; Population Census, 1990.

[a] EMP87COM and EMP93COM: employment in the commercial sector, 1993 and 1987.
[b] EMP87SER and EMP93SER: employment in the service sector, 1993 and 1987.
[c] MW_0–2: percentage of resident workers who receive between 0 and 2 times the minimum wage, 1990.
[d] MW_2–5: percentage of resident workers who receive between 2 and 5 times the minimum wage, 1990.
[e] MW_5+: percentage of resident workers who receive more than 5 times the minimum wage, 1990.

the degree of centrality DC, defined in equation 2 (see figure 6.1). The first model used the value of the neighborhood itself. For the second model, the value was the highest value of DC found in a circle whose radius measured 1 kilometer and whose center is the geographic centroid of the neighborhood. In model 3, the value of DC was obtained as in model 2, but using a circle whose radius measured 1.5 kilometers.

The independent variables were: (1) number of residents in the neighborhood who earn less than two times the minimum wage, and (2) the number of neighborhood residents who earn more than five times the minimum (figures 6.2a, 6.2b). In 1993, Tijuana's urban area measured 21,750 hectares and encompassed 312 neighborhoods (census tracts) which averaged 70 hectares each, or the equivalent of a circle with a radius of approximately one-half kilometer. A circle with a radius of 1 kilometer covers four neighborhoods on average, and one whose radius is 1.5 kilometers will encompass an average of nine neighborhoods. The results of this analysis, presented in table 6.2, indicate that the regression models offer an acceptable representation of the data and that the independent variables are significant. The rise in R-squared as the radius increased confirms that higher-income families are indeed determining the proximity of higher-level commercial centers, even when these are located in an adjacent neighborhood. This supports the hypothesis that the spatial structure of tertiary centers in urban space depends, in terms of demand, on where high-income consumers reside.

Two tests were devised to determine whether the spatial organization of tertiary centers and jobs has a regressive effect on the redistribution of income within the city. We estimated the indices of accessibility to centers and to jobs following equations 3 and 4.

For the case of access to centers, two measures employed the index of accessibility to centers as the dependent variable. In the first regression, we used the average salary of the residents of each neighborhood as the independent variable. The results, presented in figure 6.3, confirm that lower-income neighborhoods have less accessibility to these centers. In the second test, we calculated two linear accessibility functions: one for the poorest and one for the wealthiest residents of each neighborhood. The result (figure 6.4) reveals that neighborhoods with higher percentages of poor residents or a lower percentage of more wealthy ones are concentrated in

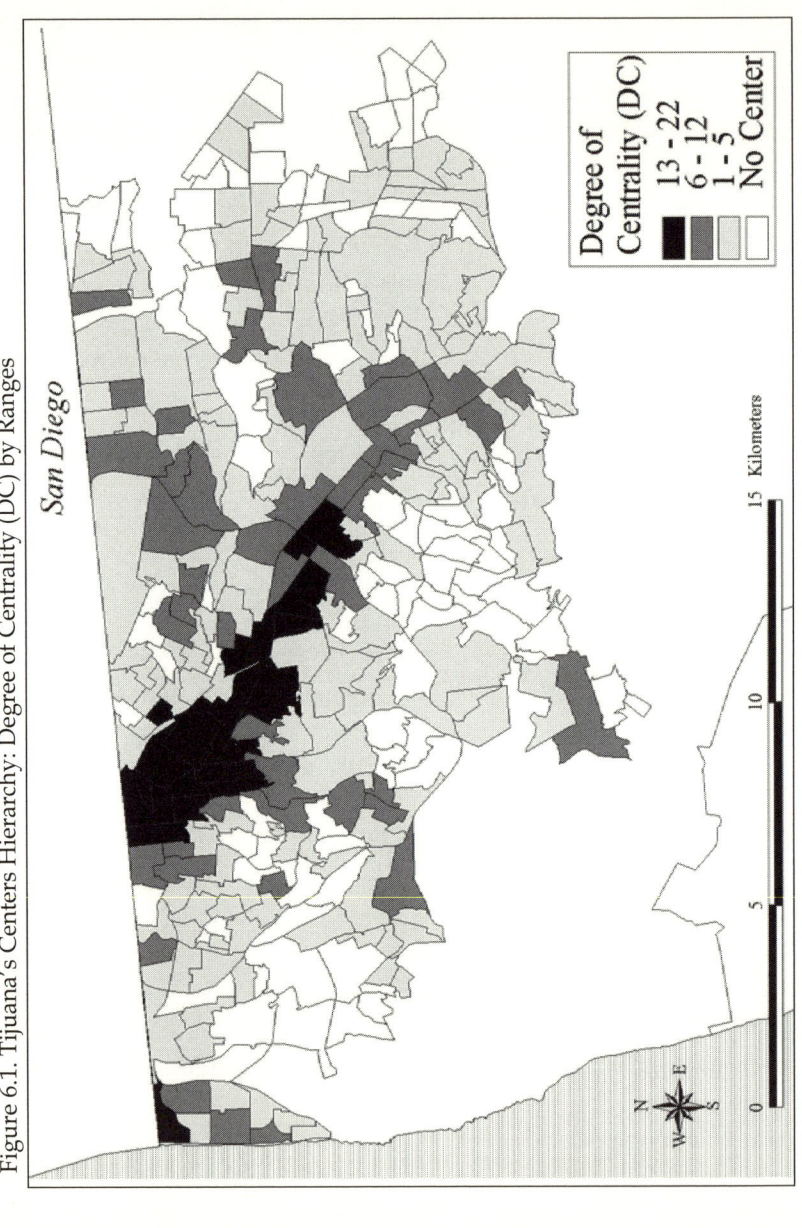
Figure 6.1. Tijuana's Centers Hierarchy: Degree of Centrality (DC) by Ranges

Table 6.2. Regression Analyses, with Degree of Centrality as the Dependent Variable

| Variables | Model 1 Neighborhood's Degree of Centrality | | Model 2 Higher Degree of Centrality Given a Radius of 1 km | | Model 3 Higher Degree of Centrality Given a Radius of 1.5 km | |
|---|---|---|---|---|---|---|
| | Coefficient | Sig. | Coefficient | Sig. | Coefficient | Sig. |
| (Constant) | 2.874 | 0.00 | 4.882 | 0.00 | 7.152 | 0.00 |
| MW0–2[a] | −6.353E-03 | 0.00 | −4.428E-03 | 0.01 | −3.459E-03 | 0.05 |
| MW5+[b] | 2.574E-02 | 0.00 | 3.529E-02 | 0.00 | 3.872E-02 | 0.00 |
| R | 0.453 | | 0.526 | | 0.575 | |
| R-squared | 0.205 | | 0.276 | | 0.331 | |
| (*) Neighborhood average[c] | 1 | | 4 | | 9 | |

[a] MW0–2: workers who receive 2 times the minimum wage or less.
[b] MW5+: workers who receive more than 5 times the minimum wage.
[c] (*) Number of neighborhoods included when selecting for higher degree of centrality.

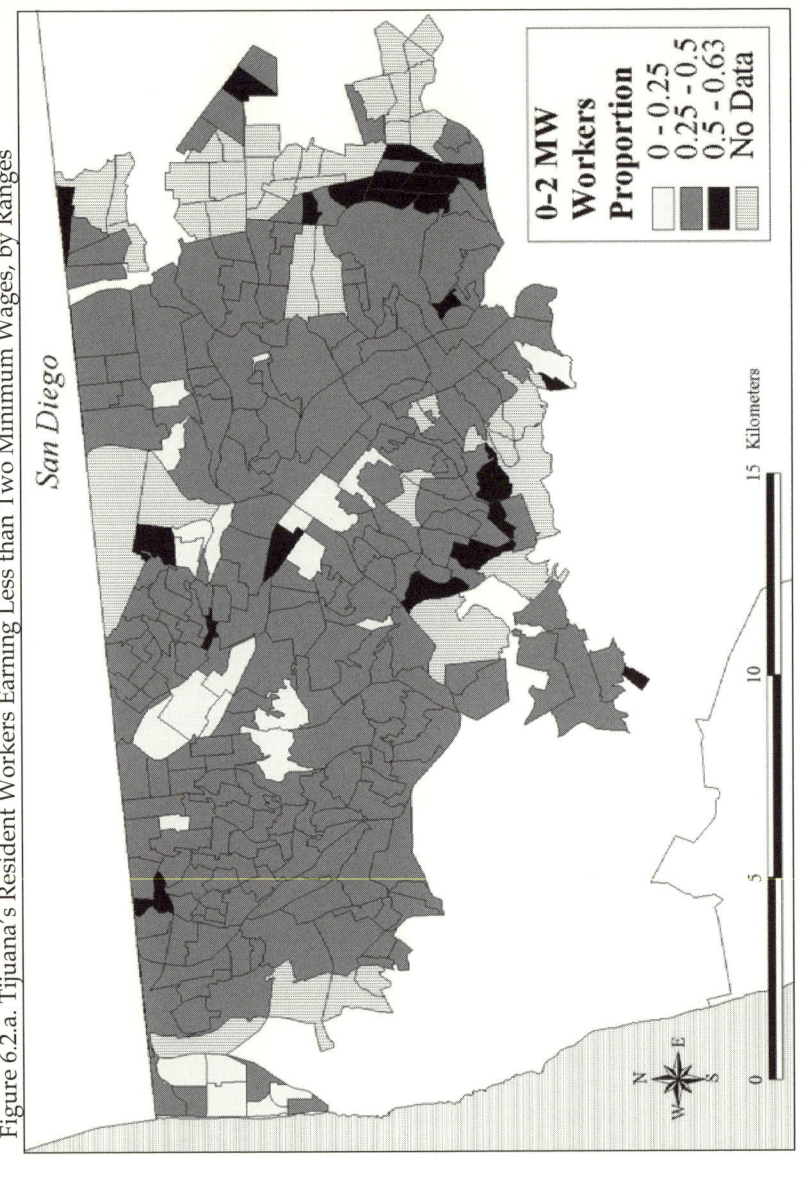
Figure 6.2.a. Tijuana's Resident Workers Earning Less than Two Minimum Wages, by Ranges

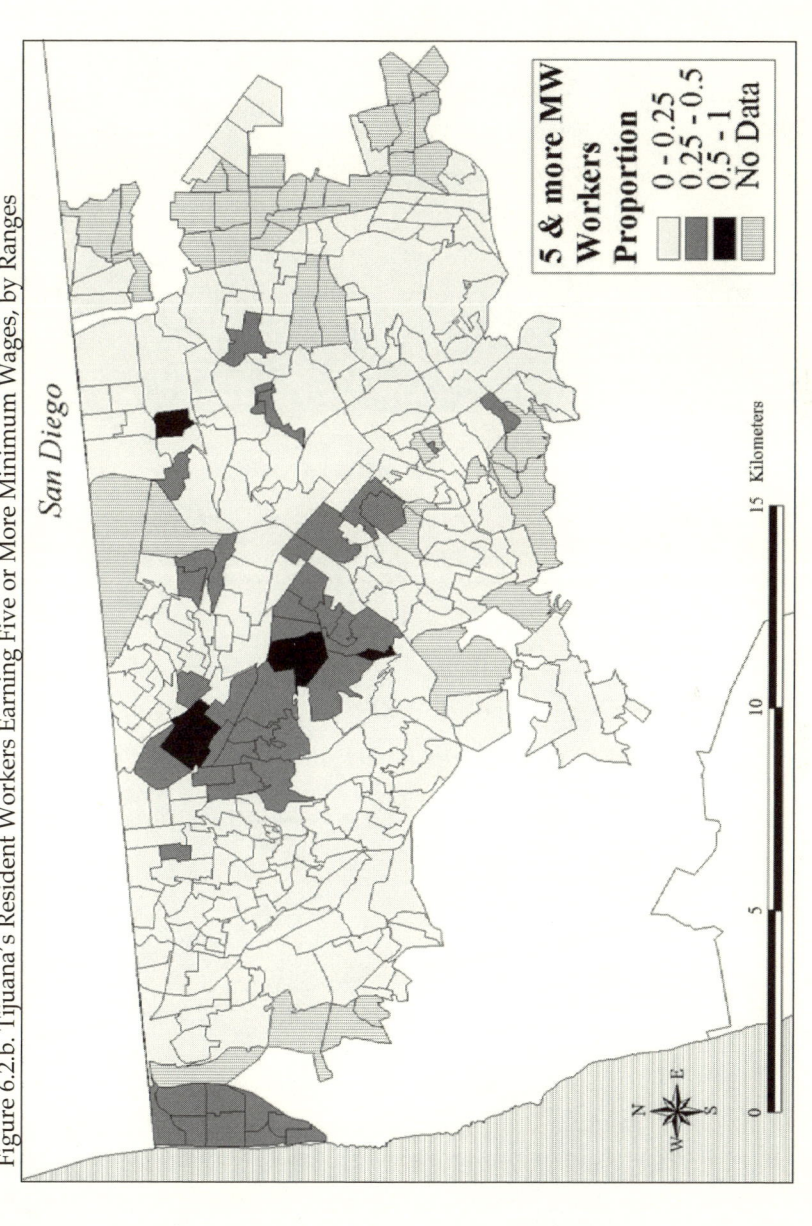
Figure 6.2.b. Tijuana's Resident Workers Earning Five or More Minimum Wages, by Ranges

Figure 6.3.

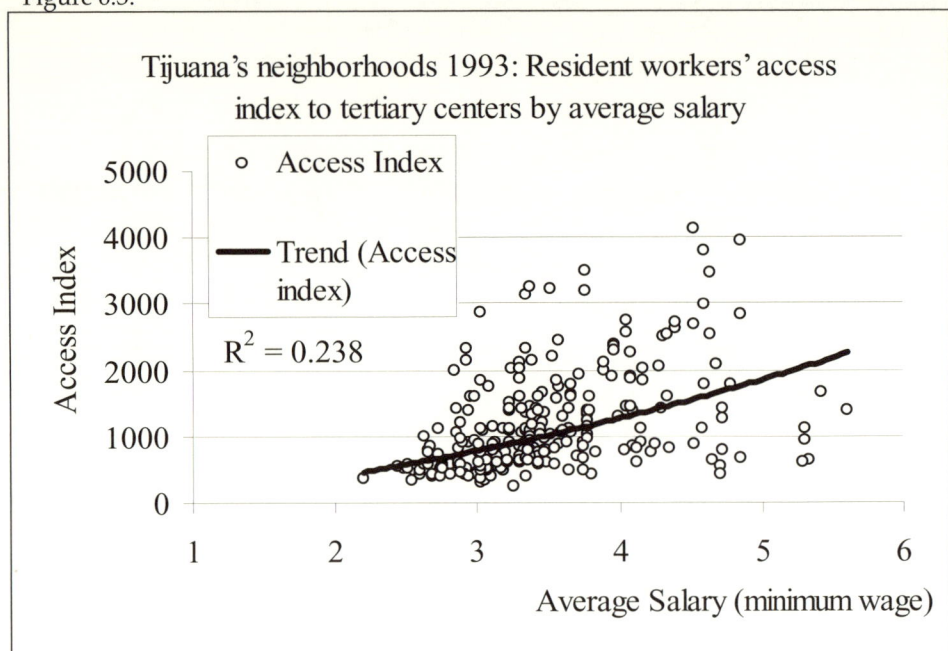

Figure 6.4.

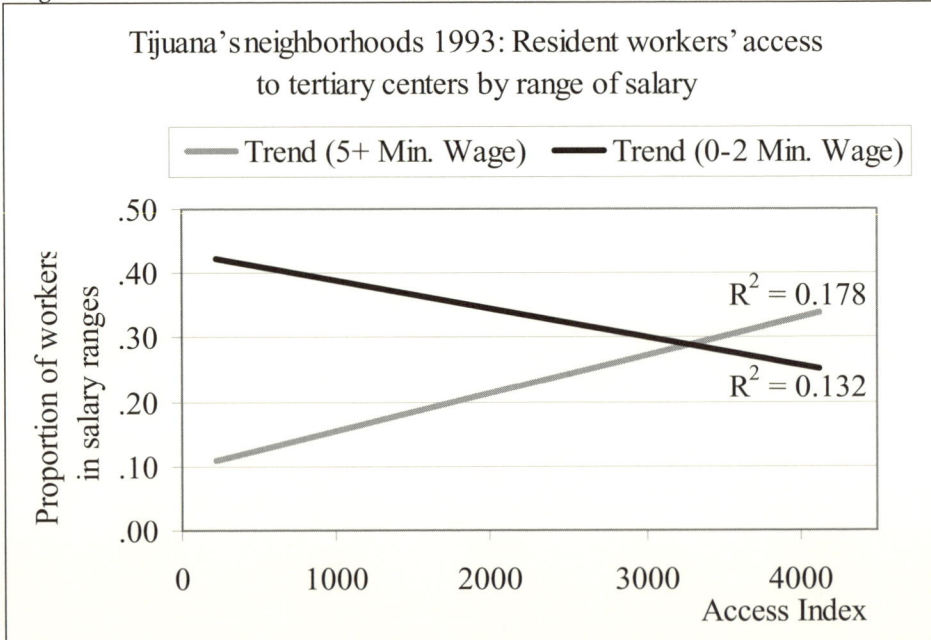

Figure 6.5.

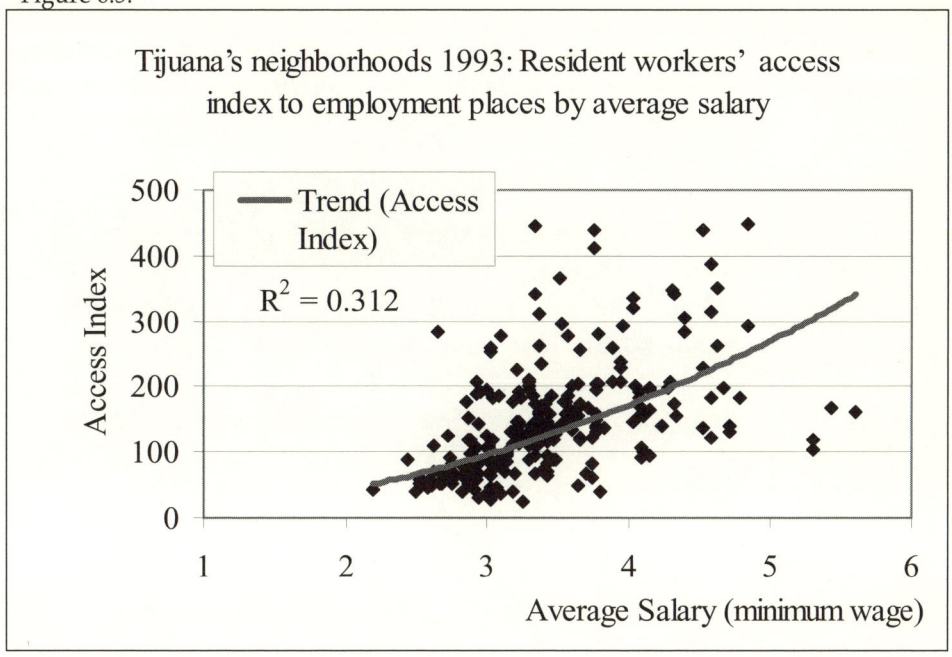

Figure 6.6.

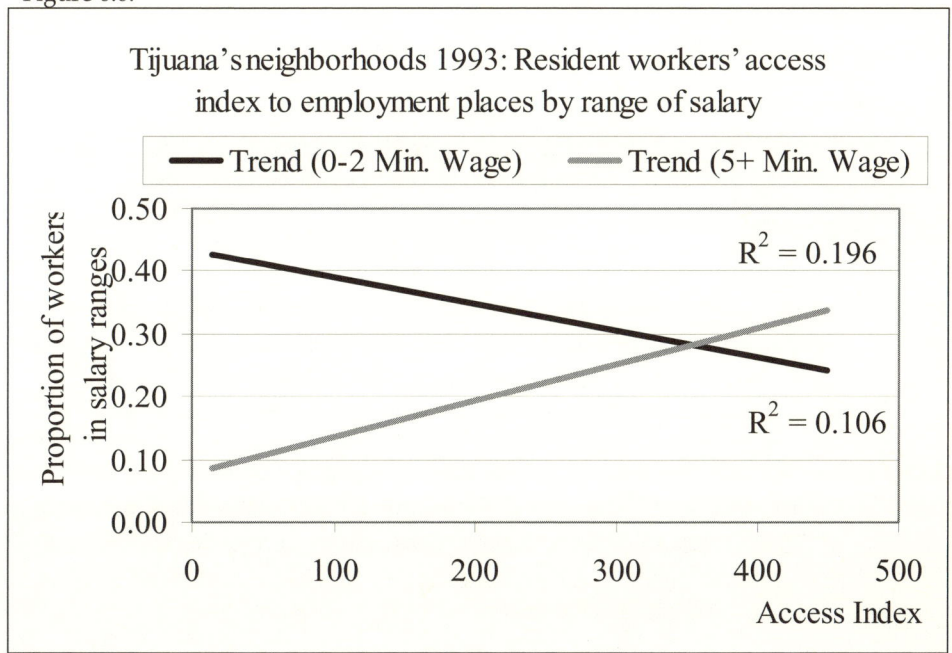

the areas with the lowest levels of access to centers. That is, the spatial tendency is as follows: as neighborhoods have higher proportions of higher-income residents, they will also have better access to commercial centers.

The second set of tests was similar to the first, but it looked at the index of accessibility from residential locations to those areas with jobs. The number of jobs includes those in the commercial, services, and manufacturing sectors. The results of the first test (figure 6.5) reveal that accessibility to places of employment increases with higher average neighborhood incomes. The results of the second test (figure 6.6) show that neighborhoods with higher proportions of poor residents or lower proportions of residents who are relatively better off concentrate at the lowest levels in terms of access to places of employment. The spatial tendency is that as neighborhoods have higher proportions of wealthier inhabitants, they will have better access to employment zones.

These four calculations demonstrate that the spatial organization of tertiary centers and jobs generates a regressive redistribution of income within the city, since the poor reside in areas with less access to both types of urban resources while the city's wealthier residents tend to reside in areas with higher levels of accessibility.

## CONCLUSIONS

This chapter has demonstrated that the redistribution of income is regressive because of the way in which resources are organized in urban space. The key conclusions are the following:

- Tertiary-sector activities—trade and services—tend to locate near residential areas with high-income inhabitants. This process of adaptive localization takes time; although this study did not attempt to define the period involved in this process, its effects are clearly visible after three years of residence in an area.

- The spatial arrangement of commerce and services is driven by market mechanisms and is expressed as groupings of these activities in centers in different urban neighborhoods. These centers are ordered hierarchically, á la Christaller. The present study has demonstrated this from the demand side.

- The price of accessibility to urban resources (tertiary centers and employment), as discussed by Harvey, is *potentially* higher for the lower-income segments of the population and lower for those at upper income levels. This study confirmed this potential, though no data were available with which to determine the share of the population whose spatial behavior reflects this potential. If this held true for the majority of the population, it would confirm that the spatial organization of these urban resources is one of the causes of regressive income redistribution. The other spatial explanation for the regressive redistribution of income lies in the mechanisms for siting residential areas, a factor not examined in this study.

- The price of accessibility operates on the basis of segregation by location, which involves the isolation of certain social groups with respect to urban resources. Segregation by differentiation, which is segregation between social groups, appears not to generate direct regressive effects on income redistribution.

- Additionally, the fact that the price of accessibility to jobs is higher among low-income groups is erecting socially regressive barriers within the labor market. This price of accessibility decreases one's likelihood of finding employment because transportation services and routes serve marginal areas less efficiently than they service areas of dense employment and because distance hinders the flows of information, further benefiting job-rich areas and disadvantaging the areas on the urban periphery where low-income workers and would-be workers tend to reside. Periods of unemployment lengthen on par with the length of the job search, and the latter correlates with the distance between one's residence and the areas where jobs are concentrated, as has been demonstrated for other urban areas (Vipond 1984).

## References

Alegría, Tito. 1994. "Segregación socioespacial urbana: el ejemplo de Tijuana," *Estudios Demográficos y Urbanos* 9, no. 2 (May–August).

———. 1998. "Segregación socio-espacial urbana: crítica de enfoques." Presented at the seminar "Ciudades y Desarrollo Regional en México," CIESAS-Golfo, Xalapa, Veracruz, August 27–29.

Anas, Alex, Richard Arnott, and Kenneth A. Small. 1998. "Urban Spatial Structure," *Journal of Economic Literature* 36, no. 3.

Berndt, Ernst. 1996. *The Practice of Econometrics*. Reading, Mass.: Addison-Wesley.

Berry, Brian, and John Parr. 1988. *Market Centers and Retail Location*. Englewood Cliffs; N.J. Prentice Hall.

Bourdieu, Pierre. 1990. *Sociología y cultura*. Mexico: Grijalbo and CONACULTA.

Cadwallader, Martin. 1985. *Analytical Urban Geography*. Englewood Cliffs, N.J.: Prentice-Hall.

Cooke, Timothy. 1978. "Causality Reconsidered: A Note," *Journal of Urban Economics* 5: 538–42.

Duncan, O. D., and B. Duncan. 1955a. "Residential Distribution and Occupational Stratification," *American Journal of Sociology* 60, no. 5.

———. 1955b. "A Methodological Analysis of Segregation Indexes," *American Sociological Review* 20.

Farley, John. 1984. "P* Segregation Indices: What Can They Tell Us about Housing Segregation in 1980?" *Urban Studies* 21, no. 3.

Feldman, A. S., and C. Tilly. 1960. "The Inter-action of Social and Physical Space," *American Sociological Review* 25, no. 6.

Gordon, Peter, and Harry Richardson. 1996. "Beyond Polycentricity: The Dispersed Metropolis, Los Angeles 1970–1990," *Journal of the American Planning Association* 62, no. 3.

Harvey, David. 1979. *Urbanismo y desigualdad social*. Mexico City: Siglo Veintiuno.

Heller, Celia, ed. 1987. *Structured Social Inequality*. New York: Macmillan.

Ihlanfeldt, Keith. 1992. "Intraurban Wage Gradients: Evidence by Race, Gender, Occupational Class, and Sector," *Journal of Urban Economics* 32: 70–91.

Massey, Douglas, and N. Denton. 1996. *American Apartheid*. Cambridge, Mass.: Harvard University Press.

Pahl, R. 1969. "Urban Social Theory and Research," *Environment and Planning* 1: 143–54.

———. 1975. *Whose City?* London: Penguin.

PDUE (Planeación del Desarrollo Urbano y Ecología). 1993. *Programa de desarrollo urbano del centro de población Tijuana*. Tijuana: Dirección de Planeación del Desarrollo Urbano y Ecología, Gobierno Municipal.

Peach, Ceri, ed. 1975. *Urban Social Segregation*. London: Longman.

Richardson, Harry, and C. H.-C. Bae. 1993. "Brown Sky Blues: Are Transportation RxS a Cure?" Los Angeles: School of Urban and Regional Planning, University of Southern California.

Saunders, Peter. 1984. *Social Theory and the Urban Question*. London: Hutchinson and Co.

Smith, Richard. 1991. "The Measurement of Segregation Change through Integration and Deconcentration, 1970–1980," *Urban Affairs* 26, no. 4.

Stahl. Konrad. 1998. "Theories of Urban Business Location." In *Handbook of Regional and Urban Economics*, vol. 2, ed. Edwin S. Mills. Amsterdam and New York: North-Holland.

Steinnes, Donald. 1977. "Causality and Intraurban Location," *Journal of Urban Economics* 4: 69–79.

Thrift, Nigel. 1985. "Flies and Germs: A Geography of Knowledge." In *Social Relations and Spatial Structure*, ed. Derek Gregory and John Urry. New York: St. Martin's Press.

Thurston, L., and A. Yezer. 1994. "Causality in the Suburbanization of Population and Employment," *Journal of Urban Economics* 35: 105–18.

Vipond, Joan. 1984. "The Intra-urban Unemployment Gradient: The Influence of Location on Unemployment," *Urban Studies* 21, no. 4.

Weber, Max. 1968. *Economy and Society*. New York: Bedminster Press.

Wong, David. 1993. "Spatial Indices of Segregation," *Urban Studies* 30, no. 3.

Wright, Erik. 1979. *Class Structure and Income Determination*. New York: Academic Press.

# 7

## Counting the Environment In: Considerations of the Risk of Hazardous *Maquiladora* Waste

KATHRYN KOPINAK

There have been many stages in the scholarly research on Mexican *maquiladoras* since the mid-1960s, when the Mexican government passed the first legislation allowing foreign companies to import materials and equipment for duty-free processing and export the products paying tax only on the value added. Plants doing the processing in Mexico have been called in-bond plants, export processors, and maquiladoras, or simply maquilas. Researchers studying them have recently become known in Spanish as *maquiladorólogos/as*, indicating a specialized area of study. The area is important heuristically as a new contribution to knowledge on globalization and cross-border regional development. Another reason for increased attention to this area of study is the fact that maquiladora industries are now the dominant industrial type in Mexico, as opposed to domestically owned industries producing for the internal market, which had been the norm since the 1940s. They also constitute the main base of the economy at the northern border and in other regions such as the Yucatán Peninsula in southeastern Mexico.

Maquiladora industries have undergone boom periods and cyclical recessions throughout their history. Most recently, from 2000 to 2004, more maquila jobs were lost than ever before; this was due to the downturn in the U.S. economy as well as the flight of companies to Central America and

---

While the contents of this essay are the sole responsibility of the author, thanks are due to Cirila Quintero, Ricardo Santés, and Ted Schrecker for their comments on an earlier draft.

China. However, in 2005 the maquiladoras began to grow again, and in February of that year they employed 1,148,266 people in Mexico, according to INEGI (*Frontera* 2005). Although this was not as high as the employment level of 2000, companies were once again competing for workers (Ortiz 2005). More jobs were created in Tijuana in 2004 than in any other municipality in the country.

The subject of this essay—the social and especially environmental costs of industrial growth—was a central part of the early maquiladora literature (Carrillo and Jasís 1983; Carrillo 1986; Arenal 1986; Iglesias 1985; Valdez-Villalva 1985). Roberto Sánchez's (1990a) ground-breaking work on hazardous waste generated by maquiladoras was published at the start of the maquiladora boom of the 1990s. Analyzing data on imports to Mexicali, Baja California, by maquiladora, he found that these factories generated significant amounts of hazardous waste. However, very little was shipped back to the United States, as required by Mexican law. Sánchez concluded that most of the maquiladora-generated hazardous waste was left in Mexico and had not been treated to render it nonhazardous. This author also noted that attention to these problems was urgently required.

However, throughout the 1990s there was less, not more, attention to the environmental costs of industrial growth by researchers within Mexico, who arguably do most basic scientific investigation of maquiladora industrialization. The environmental costs issue last appeared in the literature in a debate between George Baker and Ellwyn Stoddard, published in the first two issues of the journal *Río Bravo*, in 1991 and 1992. A new agenda for research on equity and the environment, which is the subject of this book, should reconsider the costs of industrial growth and suggest measures to reduce the inequality that has been a part of polarized labor markets in maquiladora cities (Hualde 2002).

This essay opens up a conceptual framework that has become hegemonic in the maquiladora research literature over the last decade in order to suggest ways in which we might better understand the environmental risks involved in rapid industrial growth. The focus is on Tijuana because, between 1986 and 1999, it was the city from which the most hazardous waste entered the United States—15,225.5 tons out of a total of 42,165.5 (Kopinak 2002: 101), almost all of it generated by maquiladora industries. We do not know how much hazardous waste generated by maquiladoras was not exported, as required by law, but Tijuana's high level of exports is assumed to be an indicator that it is the Mexican city, or one of the Mexican cities, in which the most hazardous waste is generated.

Research during the 1990s turned its focus away from social costs to investigate a promising new kind of maquiladora—represented by a small number of large capital-intensive plants that used advanced technology and hired more highly skilled labor for lean production processes; these were called second- and third-generation maquilas (Carrillo and Hualde 1998).[1] First-generation plants, which were the norm from 1966 to the late 1970s, hired women to do simple, low-skilled assembly, especially in the garment and electronic sectors. The goal of firms that subcontract work to first-generation maquilas is cost reduction, making these types of plants "cash cows" (Gerber 2002). Second-generation plants include more manufacturing, especially in the automotive and electronic sectors, and hire more men, particularly in skilled positions. A few third-generation plants emerged in the 1990s in the same sectors that did some design and research, and they hired more Mexican male engineers and managers. It was predicted that with greater investment due to trade promotion under the North American Free Trade Agreement (NAFTA), second- and third-generation plants would become the new norm and stimulate greater production of supplies in Mexico, which on average had never accounted for more than approximately 2 percent of all inputs. The majority of maquiladora industries in Mexico would supposedly no longer do unskilled assembly, which adds little value. Instead, this activity would move to Central America and the Caribbean (Gereffi 1992). Some first-generation plants were expected to remain, however, to supply second- and third-generation plants, forming production systems that are regionally based. Researchers focusing on the "new maquila" (another name for second-generation plants) argued that more advanced manufacturing work would bring the development of clustered production systems, which would transfer more advanced technology from the global to the local scene and bring more highly skilled and better-paid jobs.

---

[1] Exceptions to this trend of ignoring the social costs of industrial growth during the 1990s were more likely to be published outside of Mexico, such as Ganster and Hamson's (1995) work on child care and family planning services in the maquiladora industry.

Researchers conceptualizing their investigations in terms of the three-generation typology of maquilas have not yet looked at the environmental implications of the maquilization of Mexico. A partial exception is Humberto García (1998), whose work is strongly influenced by both Sánchez and the three-generation typology. García assessed how the productive level of an electronics maquiladora influences its environmental management practices. Smaller assembly firms, those considered first-generation and making up the majority of factories in the Tijuana region, were found to only adopt environmental management systems and separate substances in response to greater regulation, such as more inspections after NAFTA. Maquilas that began as assemblers but later added some manufacturing—that is, second-generation plants—tend to adopt the environmental policies and equipment demanded by the market and by their parent companies. When the client only buys from companies using specific environmental policies, the maquila will adopt those policies. For example, Philips Electronics, with one maquiladora in Tijuana, thirteen in Ciudad Juárez, and one in Matamoros, has been a pioneer in environmental management and has instituted more stringent environmental goals within their plants than required by law (Pizzorusso 1998). On the other hand, García found that some second-generation plants may have no corporate environmental policy at all.

## CRITICALLY REVIEWING AND RECONCEPTUALIZING CORE CONCEPTS IN RECENT MAQUILADORA RESEARCH

The focus of *maquiladorólogos/as* on the advantages and potential of the new maquila is the manifestation in the academy of the effects of the state-led opening of the Mexican economy to world markets. Although business groups paid lip service to the fact that workers' falling wages could hardly contribute much to the dynamism of the Mexican economy (Rodríguez 1997), the large research projects on maquiladora industries during the 1990s focused on topics more generally of interest to business. Carrillo and Santibáñez's (1993) study on the high turnover rates among maquiladora employees, cosponsored and copublished by Mexico's Labor Ministry (STPS) and El Colegio de la Frontera Norte, represents the turning point of the literature in this direction. As Barbara Adam notes, "knowledge is always mediated, be this through visual representation, stories, metaphors or perspectives" (1998: 43). The mediation of scientific data and other information on maquiladora industrialization by the three-generation typology illuminates some aspects of industrial growth while ignoring others, as do most mediations. The explanation of why environmental considerations would be omitted comes from environmental sociology's concept of the treadmill of production. When capital-intensive investment creates ecological problems, state managers are constrained from invoking policies that would prevent this from occurring, due to the state's role of supporting accumulation in capitalist societies.

As a form of discourse, the three-generation typology is part of the Mexican version of the cult of management whereby government, and the research institutions within its jurisdiction, were urged to become more like business, adopting values esteemed by the private sector (Mintzberg 1996: 83). Since business is less concerned with environmental costs than is the larger society, it is not surprising that research with this focus was deemphasized during the 1990s. However, this leaves Mexico with a long way still to go in order to reach the objective of sustainable development, which Urquidi (1999: 32) emphasizes has equity as a fundamental goal. If maquiladora industries are to contribute more to sustainability, their pay structures must facilitate greater equality in income, more employment security, and access to social benefits. Urquidi also notes that if development were sustainable, people would suffer fewer disadvantages from the administrative acts of government and behaviors of business. An example of this is the replacement of Mexican-owned autoparts makers in the 1990s by foreign-owned maquiladoras, due to the fact that Mexico's Ministry of Commerce (SECOFI) ignored the legal obligation of auto assemblers in Mexico to use a certain proportion of parts produced by domestically owned companies, a requirement established under the 1989 Decree of the Development and Modernization of the Auto Industry (Kopinak 1996: 179, 180). Domestic autoparts makers had employed more Mexicans and paid higher wages than was the case in the autoparts maquiladoras.

Elsewhere I have presented a thorough critique of the three-generation typology and argued for the inclusion of a social costs perspective to broaden the scope of maquiladora research (Kopinak 2004). Interest in the social costs of industrial growth has been renewed by the spread of maquiladoras as the predominant form of industry throughout Mexico and into

Central America, as well as the onset in 2000 of the worst economic crisis in Mexican maquiladora history. The decreased diversity within the Mexican economy, and the dependence of growing portions of the labor force on the maquiladora sector for jobs, mean that when there is a downturn in that sector, there are few other sources of work. This is no longer a concern only for the U.S.-Mexico border region. When maquiladoras expand southward, most of the jobs they bring are not the more highly skilled ones of the third-generation plants, but the lower-paid and lower-skilled ones characteristic of first-generation plants.

In addition, the unemployment inherent in industrial dispersion and crisis indicates that the question posed by those using the three-generation typology as to whether maquiladora industrialization leads to development or social problems (see, for example, Alonso, Carrillo, and Contreras 2002) is inappropriately framed. The issue is not, as Stoddard (1987) put it, whether the maquiladora industry is *either* a calamity *or* a catalyst, but how, in fact, it is *both*. Framing the question in either/or terms inevitably leads to a one-sided view, which might be avoided by recognizing that this industry is both a calamity and a catalyst. Environmental sociology explains this in terms of the societal-environmental dialectic, whereby economic growth requires an increased use of natural resources, creating environmental problems which, in turn, can threaten future economic growth (Schnailberg 1980; Schnailberg and Gould 1994). In terms of the focus of this essay, maquiladora-generated hazardous waste will, if not properly handled, end up in the rivers that drain the Tijuana watershed. The largest number of maquiladoras in this area produce electronic goods, which require large quantities of high-quality water in their production processes.

Using the concept of social costs analytically, researchers are more likely to understand how environmental problems are predictable outcomes of the kind of industrialization represented by maquilization; that is, they are outcomes of a particular political economy. William Kapp's seminal work, *The Social Costs of Private Enterprise*, argued that it is particularly harmful to the social sciences' search for truth to compartmentalize social, economic, and political reality, and that economic studies must be broadened to include social costs, social values, and social returns, which would then transform economics into a deeper form of political economy (1971: 251, 261). He insisted that the concepts of wealth and production needed to be expanded to include the things produced that are not exchanged in markets.

> Such a broadening of the fundamental concepts of economic science would also open the way for a genuinely economic theory of public revenues and expenditures. Indeed, taxes would be clearly recognized as outlays for production. This is easily understood in the case of taxes levied for the purpose of remedying the losses caused by air and water pollution, erosion, deforestation, unemployment, etc. (Kapp 1971: 254).

This discussion now turns to a focus on environmental costs, showing how the research agenda may be broadened to include them. In seeking to bring environmental considerations back into the mainstream of maquiladora research, we go back to a prediction that Sánchez made over a dozen years ago (1990b: 323). He suggested that the 1990s would see many discoveries of clandestine, illegally dumped hazardous wastes in northern Mexico. However, due to the lack of a Superfund, such as that provided in the United States under EPA legislation, the cost of cleaning up these sites would be paid by the larger Mexican society. With Sánchez's appointment to head the North American Commission for Environmental Cooperation in 1994, his work was reoriented to a more continental level of analysis (Sánchez-Rodríguez et al. 1998).

A social costs perspective can revive this line of research initiated in the early 1990s. Kapp (1971: 67) argued that while social costs have long been recognized in terms of the impairment of labor force participants (as, for example, through industrial accidents and diseases), environmental costs have been less well understood as social costs of industrial activity, because the causal relation between environmental degradation and productive activities is not as visible. However, environmental costs of industrialization may be more important because they are experienced by a larger, more heterogeneous group of people than just those making up the industrial labor force. The research on health and safety risks in Mexican maquilas is small but growing (Denman 1990; Quintero and Romo 2001), but research on environmental hazards is less well developed.

Mexico introduced new environmental legislation in 1988 that is very similar to U.S. environmental legislation, but it has insufficient resources to enforce its laws. This allows maquiladoras, especially those abandoning hazardous waste in Mexico, "to use the border as a shield against legal action," according to the Commission for Environmental Cooperation (CEC 2002: 42) in its report on the worst case of abandoned hazardous waste on the border. Companies can move production to Mexico in order to avoid paying environmental costs, not only because of the different government structures and vastly unequal amounts of public money available for enforcement on either side of the border, but also because border communities have historically been alienated from the central parts of their respective countries. They have less status and power, making it easier for the violators of environmental law to act with impunity.

Tijuana has been the location of the worst cases of abandoned hazardous waste by maquiladora companies, creating dangerous brownfield sites at the former location of the Alco Pacífico and Metales y Derivados factories. While the Alco Pacífico site has undergone some remediation, local experts argue that the cleanup was not done properly and that the site remains unsafe.[2] Dust picked up at the site by summer winds exposes workers in nearby maquiladoras and is blown into the Alamar River. The Alamar carries it to the Río Tijuana, which, in turn, carries it across the border into the Tijuana River Estuary and the Pacific Ocean. Approximately 8,500 tons of poisonous lead and other toxins remained at the location of the former Metales y Derivados plant in the decade between 1984 and 1994, though the site was partially cleaned at the time of writing. This company was a repeat offender, and in 1987 Mexico's Office of the Attorney General for Environmental Protection (PROFEPA) forced it to remove "the piles of lead oxide and lead slag" it had dumped into Alamar Creek (CEC 2002: 36). In his study of both cases, Santés Álvarez (2004: 30) shows how government environmental institutions and their bureaucracies have put international business and trade before the health of the population and its environment.

Obee's (1997) modeling of air pollution suggests that both poor and middle-class Tijuana residents suffer negative impacts due to the chaotic

---

[2] Personal communication with Oscar Romo, coastal training program coordinator at the Tijuana River National Estuarine Research Reserve, June 28, 2005. See the Tijuana River Estuary Web site at http://www.tijuanaestuary.com/education.asp.

growth of the city and the resulting low degree of residential segregation by class. Many middle-class *fraccionamientos* in the center of the city are very close to maquiladoras, since zoning laws regulating the location of industry have not been well enforced and industries prefer to locate in areas with good infrastructure, which middle-class communities tend to have. In a study of the spatial relationship between Tijuana maquiladora plants and their workers' homes, Barajas and Kopinak (2003: 24) found that although 27 percent of the respondents were employed in plants located in middle-class *fraccionamientos*, none of them lived in these relatively upscale areas. Even though there are obvious class differences in the quality of housing and transportation with which Mexicans of means can protect themselves from environmental hazards, the inequality that is created by the socializing of industrial environmental costs in Mexico may well not be as great among Mexicans as it is between them and their U.S. neighbors. That is, middle-class Mexicans cannot evade the negative environmental impacts of industrialization to as great an extent as can the middle class north of the border. It should be noted that the use of the border as a shield against the enforcement of environmental regulations can also have negative repercussions on those who live close to the international line on the U.S. side, as evidenced by the high number of births of children with neural tube defects at the eastern end of the border in Texas (Hendricks, Simpson, and Larsen 1999).

## CONSTRUCTING AN INDEX OF RISK FOR HAZARDOUS MATERIALS

Recent scholarly publications demonstrate quite clearly that industrial growth at Mexico's northern border has contributed substantially to the environmental risks there (Méndez Mungaray 1995; Ashur et al. 1997). However, my interviews with environmental activists in Tijuana indicate that this awareness of risk may not be present outside of scientific circles. This is especially true in maquiladora cities, where many residents are recently arrived migrants seeking work and setting up new households. Thus the lack of information on the maquiladoras' environmental risks—which reflects the newness of Mexico's environmental legislation and the insufficiency of resources for its implementation—converges with a local population too concerned with subsistence and shelter issues to worry about the dangers of industrial hazardous waste that may not be immediately obvious. This is hardly restricted to Mexico or even to the developing world; it is reflective of and inseparable from the political economy of private industrial production. Considering Tijuana specifically, Galicot (2002: 10-B) says that many of the sixty-five thousand immigrants the city receives every year remain attached to their hometowns and develop little identification with their new home. Pushed out of their communities by unemployment, they are attracted to Tijuana because of its relatively plentiful maquiladora jobs, and perhaps for its reputation as a crossing point to the United States. However, there is little public-spirited integration of these newcomers, leading to negative behavior and attitudes on their part, such as throwing garbage in the streets and failing to support reforestation and cleanup campaigns.

There is evidence, however, that this is changing with the emergence of dynamic nongovernmental organizations (NGOs) such as Colectivo Chilpancingo Pro Justicia Ambiental, which is a member of the Environmental Health Coalition in San Diego. The three-generation maquila typology throws light on the production of goods but seldom acknowledges the concomitant production of waste that is an integral part of the process. NGO spokespersons are challenging its exponents to widen the purview. Forum Fronterizo recently held a meeting in San Diego on "The Future of Manufacturing in Baja California" to respond to concerns of approximately three hundred attendees about the long-run viability of Mexican maquiladoras at the western tip of the U.S.-Mexico border.[3] This meeting provided a good example of the cult of management, with academic researchers and government leaders all introduced by the governor of Baja California. The academics presented results on industrial upgrading, the challenges facing maquiladora industries during the current economic

---

[3] The meeting was sponsored by the San Diego Dialogue on July 18, 2002. The Dialogue is a self-funded public policy organization whose goal is to "advance solutions to this cross-border region's long-term challenges in economy, environment and equity," http://www.sddialogue.org/about.htm. Attended by leaders from business, government, and academia, the Forum's luncheon series focuses on the Dialogue's mission to support cross-border development. It has been highly successful "in catalyzing local, state and federal collaboration on binational concerns and launching new cross-border initiatives" (http://www.sddialogue.org/cross.htm).

recession, and the state government's plan for a comprehensive industrial policy. The final question came from a representative of a local NGO, the Environmental Health Coalition, who asked a government representative to expand on something he had said about improving the quality of life. The latter responded by asking what the questioner meant by quality of life. She replied that the low maquiladora wages and the high cost of living makes it difficult for most maquiladora workers to enjoy a good quality of life. She added that workers' quality of life had been threatened for eight years by the brownfield site at the Metales y Derivados former maquiladora. This kind of public dialogue signals that it is no longer acceptable to consider economic and environmental dimensions of industrialization in separate and divorced contexts; they must be addressed together.

The Environmental Health Coalition is only one example of the robust grassroots environmental movement that has arisen in Mexico in the last decade (see Cohen and Méndez 2000). Another was the Playas de Tijuana Housewives Association, which was pivotal in mobilizing area residents and U.S. environmental groups to successfully oppose the siting of a hazardous waste incinerator in their suburb (Estrada Orihuela and Kiy 1998). These groups have built up their organizational strength at the border via annual meetings of Encuentro Fronterizo (five since 1998), described as "broad border-wide events geared toward the training, education, and networking needs [of] community organizations, activists and border citizens in general" (http://sbs.arizona.edu/laac/border/significance.html). By introducing questions of environmental risk into government and business agendas, these groups may be moving Mexico in the direction of a risk society, which some argue has been the pattern in many more developed countries such as Germany. Beck (1999: 72) argues that as part of the dynamic of modernization, both Western and non-Western societies move in two stages from a focus on the industrial production of goods and wealth to an awareness of environmental risk as a central feature of industrial growth.

One of the difficulties of rounding out the agenda has been a lack of reliable information about the kinds of hazards present in border communities. To help fill this gap in information and work toward developing an educational program to inform people of the dangers, I collected data on hazardous waste in Baja California, constructed an index of risk to code its

Table 7.1. Criteria Used to Construct an Index of Risk for Hazardous Waste

| Levels | Environmental Risk CRETIB Criteria[1] | Workplace Risk CPT, CCT, P[2] | Health Risk $DL_{50}$, $CL_{50}$[3] | Response Risk ID, Safety, Hazards, Actions[4] |
|---|---|---|---|---|
| Minimal | 1 criterion | Low | Acute short-term effects | Rapid and efficient response |
| Moderate | 2–3 criteria | Moderate | Acute long-term effects | Slow but efficient response |
| High | 4 criteria | High | Chronic medium-term effects | Slow and inefficient response |
| Very high | 5 or more criteria | Very high | Chronic long-term effects | Very slow and inefficient response |

[1] Corrosive, Reactive, Explosive, Toxic, Inflammable, Biologically Infectious (NOM-052-ECOL/93).

[2] Weighted average concentration over time (CPT), Concentration for short-term exposure (CCT), and Peak Concentration (P), which is the concentration that should not be exceeded at any time in the workplace (NOM-010-STPS-1994).

[3] Refers to the toxicity and dosage. $DL_{50}$ is the quantity that is lethal to half of a homogeneous group of experimental animals exposed to a toxic substance. $CL_{50}$ is the average lethal concentration if the toxic substance is inhaled (NOM-114-STPS/1994).

[4] *Guía Norteamericana de Respuesta en Caso de Emergencia*, published by the U.S. Transportation Department, Transport Canada, and the Secretaría de Comunicaciones y Transportes, 1996.

dangers, and mapped it for the *municipio* of Tijuana.[4] The data on environmental hazards are from official reports by companies to SEMARNAP and the EPA for 1998, and must be considered an underestimate since they do not include what fails to be reported. However, these data do permit us to begin to sketch a picture of where the riskiest wastes are produced and who may be exposed nearby.

Beck (1999: 8) identifies risk as "the distribution of 'bads,'" logically connected to the distribution of "goods." Risk is further measured by a multiplication of probability with the intensity (the seriousness of the "bads") and scope (that is, the number of people affected) of the distribution of "bads" (van Loon 2000: 166). The index of risk constructed to analyze the data on hazardous wastes in this work takes into account the following negative characteristics: environmental danger, workplace risk, health, and the ease of response to emergencies, each of which are elaborated in a separate column in table 7.1. The environmental risk criteria are broken down in the second column as those that are deemed hazardous under Mexican law: substances that are corrosive, reactive, explosive, toxic, flammable, and biologically infectious (known by the Spanish acronym CRETIB). Risk at work, shown in the third column, reflects van Loon's notion of intensity noted above. It is defined under Mexican law as particular threats to safety and health in the workplace, and includes the specification of the concentration of particular substances that are dangerous to the workers' health and safety in the long term, short term, or for any amount of time at all. The third criterion also refers to intensity by evaluating whether the results of exposure on health might be short-term acute, long-term acute, medium-term chronic, or long-term chronic. The final criterion is the type of risk introduced by the possible reactions to emergency exposure: a rapid and efficient response, an efficient but slow response, a slow and inefficient response, or a very slow and inefficient response.[5] Each of these criteria was taken into account in evaluating the productive process at a plant and deciding on a level of risk that would reflect all four factors.

---

[4] Early results were published in Kopinak 2002 and Kopinak and Barajas 2002.

[5] This was adopted from the 1996 *Guía Norteamericana de Respuesta en Caso de Emergencia*, published by the U.S. Transportation Department, Transport Canada, and the Secretaría de Comunicaciones y Transportes.

This index has four levels of risk—minimal, moderate, high, very high—which were used to code data that industries reported to SEMARNAP and the EPA for 1998. For example, a hazardous waste report was assessed as having minimal risk if it had only one danger (out of the six possible CRETIB), a low level of concentration in the workplace, acute short-term effects on health caused by exposure, and a rapid and efficient response in case of emergency. The risk index was assessed as very high if there were five or more dangers (of the six possible CRETIB), a very high concentration in the workplace, chronic long-term effects on health that are caused by exposure, and a slow and inefficient response in case of emergency.

Whether or not these risks are realized depends on the management of hazardous wastes, something that is beyond the scope of this essay. However, there are several reasons to pay attention to such risks even before considering research on the management of waste. First, although maquiladora generators of hazardous materials are legally bound to return them to the country of origin, they are also legally permitted to store them on site for unspecified periods. The Good Neighbor Environmental Board—an independent federal advisory committee on environment and infrastructure needs comprising representatives of the U.S. states contiguous with Mexico—has recommended that Mexican authorities be encouraged to revise their hazardous waste laws to establish finite and enforceable time limits for storage at generator facilities, recycling facilities, and transport and treatment facilities (GNEB 2001: 43). However, until this occurs, waste can be stored on site indefinitely. Winckell et al. (2000: 41) argue that an earthquake at the level of 6.5 can realistically be expected in Tijuana, and they rate most of the buildings housing maquiladoras as incapable of withstanding such a quake, which suggests the likelihood of spills and exposure of nearby populations.

## WASTE DISTRIBUTION IN RELATION TO POPULATION: RECOGNIZING NEW KINDS OF CLUSTERS

Only about 11 percent of the hazardous wastes generated in Tijuana in 1998 were found to have high or very high levels of risk. However, they were generated in the factories with the biggest average labor forces, putting these wastes in close proximity to large numbers of workers daily. It was also found that the riskiest wastes were located in a few very concentrated areas of the city, very close to densely populated residential neighborhoods and the highest concentrations of children under fourteen years of age (see Kopinak and Barajas 2002), with the greatest concentrations appearing in the northeast section of the city.

Ciudad Industrial, in northeast Tijuana, had the largest concentration of hazardous waste at high and very high risk levels, with 24 percent of all kilograms reported as generated at the two highest levels. It is also the location of the Metales y Derivados brownfield in the industrial park atop Mesa de Otay, which was designed and built as an export platform during the 1970s. Plants here tend to be large and produce capital and intermediate goods for export, and also for people living in the densely populated colonias surrounding these parks. Nueva Tijuana, for example, to the northwest of Ciudad Industrial and between it and Frontera Business Park, is a residential community for people who work in the industrial parks.

Parque Industrial Pacífico, with 15 percent of total waste at the high and very high risk levels, is the location with the second-largest concentration. This industrial park is very close to highly populated residential areas, and some people live within a few hundred feet of plants in the park.

Other plants generating almost 29,000 kilograms of high-risk and very-high-risk hazardous waste are located right across the street from the State University of Baja California (UABC), on the eastern edge of the Parque Internacional Tijuana. There was a great deal of opposition to building this industrial park adjacent to the university, and the generation of high-risk hazardous waste on the side facing the school remains cause for concern.

The "spine" of Tijuana, the wide roads paralleling the canalized Río Tijuana, contains two additional very-high-risk hazardous-waste generators, two high-risk generators, and several moderate-risk and minimal-risk generators. If waste is dumped in this location, it is likely to end up in the Tijuana River, which carries it across the border, where it settles in land on the U.S. side and drains into the Pacific Ocean.

The location pattern of plants generating the riskiest hazardous waste can be seen as a logical result of the emergence of what those working with the three-generation typology have called clusters.

> Local specialization, forms of vertical integration, and horizontal coordination have given way to the formation of *clus-*

> *ters*.... These processes of industrial agglomeration have derived from a productive-territorial specialization, and have had a strong impact on local educational systems to stimulate the formation of technical and administrative teams. In this respect, the two best-known cases are the so-called *Television Capital* in Tijuana and *Harness Valley* in Ciudad Juárez in Chihuahua (Alonso, Carrillo, and Contreras 2002: 50; emphasis in the original).

What these authors do not say about clusters in the preceding quotation is that the highly skilled maquila employees who take part in technical and administrative teams are partly responsible not only for the increase in skill level in the labor force, but also for the proximity of schools to hazardous-waste generators. A small group of male engineers, educated in the same local public schools, established themselves in a few plants in the early 1980s, before Tijuana maquiladoras boomed. In the early years of Tijuana's industrialization, they taught engineering classes in the technical school and maintained close ties with other nearby public schools and many new educational institutions that trained maquiladora personnel. This small, tightly knit network participated in both education and maquiladora production, which resulted in the close spatial relationship now observed between the educational and production systems. As Hualde (2002: 136) notes, "This physical proximity helps in the daily interaction and mutual understanding of the individuals who participate in each one of the systems."

Maquiladora workers are also partly responsible for the proximity, but we only realize this when we include them in our sources of information and look at both the costs and benefits of their choice of where to live. Barajas and Kopinak (2003) found that the majority of Tijuana maquila workers expressed a preference for living close to their workplace. However, workers with better jobs and those who had lived the longest at their current address reported living farther away from their workplace than those with the most basic jobs, indicating that when they have a choice, maquila employees prefer to live farther away. Interestingly, those who live close to work were found to have better infrastructure, with higher rates of running water in the home, household connections to sewer lines, and public telephones in their colonia, probably reflecting the fact that cities like Tijuana provide good infrastructure to industrial clients, which nearby residents then enjoy by proximity.

## CONCLUSION

This chapter assesses one of the most commonly used conceptual frameworks to study maquiladora industries in the 1990s, the notion of three different productive levels or generations of plants. It shows why this framework must be—and how it can be—broadened to include a focus on equity by integrating a social costs analysis, with particular consideration of environmental costs. As a result of this exercise, at least four specific types of inequality, or unfairness in regard to the environment, have been highlighted.

One is social inequity, which occurs with the relocation of hazardous-waste generators to low-income or unregulated areas (Fletcher 2003: 67). Although Tijuana residents have higher average incomes and lower unemployment rates than many other urban Mexicans, they certainly earn less than residents north of the border, where most of Tijuana's maquiladoras originate. The very rapid growth of industries generating substantial amounts of risky hazardous waste decreases the possibility that residents can use their relatively greater earning ability to protect themselves from suffering due to these risks. Coming as new migrants from nonindustrial areas, they may be unfamiliar with the risks involved. This social inequality is compounded by the fact that administrative positions in municipal government turn over every three years, so there is no institutional memory or continuity that would help make local government more proactive in dealing with the risks presented (Guillén López 2004). As Schrecker (2002: 48) argues, environmental quality *can* be provided selectively; and although areas contingent to both sides of the U.S.-Mexico border share some environmental hazards, the study of maquiladora industries demonstrates that they present more dangers in Mexico than in the United States.

The second type of inequality involves intergenerational equity, as "when past or present decision makers set policies which unnecessarily transfer risk to future generations" (Fletcher 2003: 67). The proximity of the generators of hazardous waste to densely populated residential districts with high numbers of children under age fourteen is evidence of intergenerational inequality in the environmental sphere. So is the proximity of schools to industrial parks that generate the riskiest hazardous waste. Children and students are more likely to be exposed to such risky hazardous wastes because there are very few public green spaces where they can play and because zoning laws have not been enforced to keep industries out of residential neighborhoods.

The third form of inequality is spatial, occurring when communities with very slight ties to industries that generate or use toxic substances in large quantities are expected to bear the burden of the waste (Fletcher 2003: 67). Mexican maquiladoras produce for export, and it is well known that, on average, only 2 percent of their inputs are made in Mexico. Many analysts have concluded from this that maquiladoras constitute an economic enclave, with few ties to the larger Mexican economy. The value added in Mexico comes almost entirely in the form of wages paid to workers, who, we have seen, often live in densely populated residential communities next door to the generators of the greatest amounts of highest-risk hazardous waste. Mexican laws that allow on-site storage for indefinite periods can cancel out other laws that require export of hazardous materials to their country of origin.

The fourth type of inequality is procedural. It occurs when decision-making processes show preferences for industrial interests over community or environmental interests (Fletcher 2003: 67). The fact that the two worst brownfields on the border are in Tijuana and that they were not efficiently or effectively cleaned up for over a decade shows that environmental authorities only went partway in demonstrating procedural equity. They closed both companies due to their violation of environmental law, but they were not very successful in remediation, which would have better protected local populations.

While it has been shown that some maquiladoras moved to Tijuana to reduce the environmental costs of their businesses, there is no information on how knowledgeable the people living closest to high-risk hazardous waste are about the latent dangers represented by these nearby clusters of risky hazardous wastes. Local residents cannot make informed decisions on where to live without knowing the risks involved. Based on the findings of this research, a survey is proposed of residents closest to the generators of the riskiest hazardous waste in Ciudad Industrial and the area near the UABC. The goals of the survey would be twofold: education and mobilization. As Beck (1999: 16) argues, one of the positive aspects of sharing the risks that cross borders is that it can become a powerful basis of community. Constructing a "community of risk" with participatory research methods encourages the taking of responsibility.

The research instrument should be designed not only to find out how much residents know about the risks their industrial neighbors pose, but also to educate them about the dangers. For example, almost all maquiladoras in Tijuana, and especially those in the electric and electronics sectors, use organic solvents and heavy metals. Organic solvents are carcinogenic and have negative effects on the nervous system, the blood, liver, kidneys, and the cardiovascular system (Gerr and Letz 1998). Exposure to heavy metals can lead to skin disorders, lung cancer, acute gastrointestinal symptoms, osteoporosis, respiratory disorders, and other problems (Fischbein 1998). The degree of damage is dependent on the toxicity of a hazardous substance, the form and duration of exposure, and the dose and concentration to which one is exposed.

While this essay has focused on only one maquiladora city, Tijuana, there is reason to believe that future research might find similar clustering of the generators of hazardous waste near dense population groupings in other Mexican cities. Mexicali, which is part of the same industrial corridor as Tijuana and has many of the same kinds of industries, began its industrial growth much later and for many years had plants better spatially organized in industrial parks. As the number of companies has increased, however, and labor has become scarce, companies have begun to follow the same strategy for dealing with high turnover among workers as they do in Tijuana—relocation out of industrial parks and into residential neighborhoods to be closer to workers. It is also quite easy to find cities attempting to lure investors by boasting that their newly built industrial parks are very close to highly skilled labor. This is the case for Escobedo, Nuevo León, just north of Monterrey. The city's Web site touts the 29.5-hectare Parque Industrial Nexxus XXI as part of an industrial corridor close to residential areas that can provide the industrial complex with highly qualified workers (http://www.escobedo.gob.mx/economia.html). This confirms that the same kind of urban planning that put the Nueva Tijuana residential neighborhood right next to Ciudad Industrial in the 1970s still predominates in newly industrializing parts of Mexico.

## References

Adam, Barbara. 1998. *Timescapes of Modernity: The Environment and Invisible Hazards.* London: Routledge.
Alonso, Jorge, Jorge Carrillo, and Óscar Contreras. 2002. "Aprendizaje tecnológico en las maquiladoras de México," *Frontera Norte* 14: 43–82.
Arenal, Sandra. 1986. *Sangre joven: la maquiladora por dentro.* Mexico: Nuestro Tiempo.
Ashur, Suleiman, M. Hadi Baaj, K. David Pijawka, and Dear Serhan. 1997. "Environmental Impact Assessment of Transporting Hazardous Waste Generated by Maquiladora Industry in U.S. Mexico Border Region," *Transportation Research Record* 1602: 84–92.
Baker, George. 1989. "Costos sociales e ingresos de la industria maquildora," *Comercio Exterior* 39, no. 10: 893–906.
———. 1991. "Mexican Labor Is Not Cheap," *Río Bravo* 1: 7–21.
Barajas, Rocío, and Kathryn Kopinak. 2003. "La fuerza de trabajo en la maquiladora: ubicación de sus espacios laborales y de reproducción en Tijuana," *Región y Sociedad* 15, no. 26: 3–48.
Beck, Ulrich. 1999. *World Risk Society.* Cambridge: Polity Press.
Carrillo, Jorge. 1986. "Maquiladoras: industrialización fronteriza y riesgos de trabajo. El caso de Baja California." In *Reestructuración industrial: maquiladoras en la frontera México–Estados Unidos,* ed. Jorge Carrillo. Mexico: Conaculta and COLEF.
Carrillo, Jorge, and Alfredo Hualde. 1998. "Third Generation Maquiladoras?" *Journal of Borderlands Studies* 13, no. 1: 79–97.
Carrillo, Jorge, and Mónica Jasís. 1983. "La salud y la mujer obrera en las plantas maquiladoras: el caso de Tijuana." Tijuana: Cefnomex. Mimeo.
Carrillo, Jorge, and Jorge Santibáñez. 1993. *Rotación de personal en las maquiladoras de exportación en Tijuana.* Tijuana: Secretaría de Trabajo y Previsión Social and El Colegio de la Frontera Norte.
CEC (Commission for Environmental Cooperation of North America). 2002. *Metales y Derivados Final Factual Record.* North American Environmental Law and Policy Series, vol. 8. Montreal: Editions Yvon Blais.
Cohen, Miriam, and Luis Méndez. 2000. *Maquila y movimientos ambientalistas: examen de un riesgo compartido.* Mexico: Grupo Editorial Eón.
Denman, Catalina. 1990. "Tiempos modernos: trabajar y morir." In *Modernización y legislación laboral en el noroeste de México,* ed. F. Mora and V. Reynoso. Hermosillo, Mexico: El Colegio de Sonora.
Estrada Orihuela, Sergio, and Richard Kiy. 1998. "The Handling of Hazardous Industrial Waste on the U.S.-Mexico Border: A Case Study of Titisa." In *Environmental Management on North America's Borders,* ed. Richard Kiy and John Wirth. College Station: Texas A&M University Press.

Fischbein, Alf. 1998. "Occupational and Environmental Exposure to Lead." In *Environmental and Occupational Medicine*, ed. William N. Rom. 3d ed. Philadelphia, Penn.: Kippincott-Raven.

Fletcher, Thomas. 2003. *From Love Canal to Environmental Justice: The Politics of Hazardous Waste on the Canada-U.S. Border*. Peterborough, Ont.: Broadview Press.

*Frontera* (Tijuana). 2005. "Crece empleo 9.2% en maquila de BC," April 29, http://www.frontera.info/buscar/traernotanew.asp?NumNota=322435, accessed May 2, 2005.

Galicot, José. 2002. "Imagen de Tijuana," *Zeta*, May 31.

Ganster, Paul, and Dana V. Hamson. 1995. *A Resource Guide for Child Care and Family Planning Services in the Maquiladora Industry*. San Diego: Institute for Regional Studies of the Californias.

García, Humberto. 1998. "Trayectorias productivas y tecnología ambiental en la industria maquiladora electrónica de Tijuana." Master's thesis, El Colegio de la Frontera Norte.

Gerber, James. 2002. Presentation on "The Future of Manufacturing in Baja California," Forum Fronterizo, San Diego, July 18.

Gereffi, Gary. 1992. "Mexico's Maquiladora Industries and North American Integration." In *North America without Borders? Integrating Canada, the United States and Mexico*, ed. S. J. Randall, with H. Konrad and S. Silverman. Calgary: University of Calgary Press.

Gerr, Redric, and Richard Letz. 1998. "Organic Solvents." In *Environmental and Occupational Medicine*, ed. William N. Rom. 3d ed. Philadelphia, Penn.: Kippincott-Raven.

GNEB (Good Neighbor Environmental Board). 2001. *Fifth Report of the Good Neighbor Environmental Board to the President and Congress of the United States*. San Diego: California EPA.

Guillén López, Tonatiuh. 2004. "Tijuana, ciudad frágil," *Frontera* (Tijuana), February 23.

Hendricks, Katherine A., J. Scott Simpson, and Russell D. Larsen. 1999. "Neural Tube Defects along the Texas-Mexico Border, 1993–1995," *American Journal of Epidemiology* 149: 1119–27.

Hualde, Alfredo. 2002. "Todos los rostros de la industrialización." In *Globalización, trabajo, y maquilas*, ed. M. de la O and C. Quintero. Mexico: Friedrich Ebert.

Iglesias, Norma. 1985. *La flor más bella de la maquiladora*. Mexico: Secretaría de Educación Pública and Centro de Estudios Fronterizos.

Kapp, K. William. 1971. *The Social Costs of Private Enterprise*. New York: Schoken.

Kopinak, Kathryn. 1996. *Desert Capitalism: Maquiladoras in North America's Western Industrial Corridor*. Tucson: University of Arizona Press.

———. 2002. "Environmental Implications of New Mexican Industrial Investment: The Rise of Asian Origin Maquiladoras as Generators of Hazardous Waste," *Asian Journal of Latin American Studies* 15, no. 1: 91–120.

———. 2004. "Accounts Payable: An Introduction." In *The Social Costs of Industrial Growth in Northern Mexico*. La Jolla: Center for U.S.-Mexican Studies, University of California, San Diego.

Kopinak, Kathryn, and Ma. del Rocío Barajas. 2002. "Too Close for Comfort? The Proximity of Industrial Hazardous Wastes to Local Populations in Tijuana, Baja California," *Journal of Environment and Development* 11, no. 3: 215–46.

Méndez Mungaray, Elizabeth. 1995. "La industria maquiladora en Tijuana: riesgo ambiental y calidad de vida," *Comercio Exterior* 45, no. 2: 159–63.

Mintzberg, Henry. 1996. "Managing Government. Governing Management," *Harvard Business Review*, May–June, pp. 75–83.

Obee, Anne. 1997. "Environmental Degradation: Industrialization, Population, and Urban Structure." Master's thesis, San Diego State University.

Ortiz, Alfredo. 2005. "Encabeza la maquila empleos," *Frontera* (Tijuana), April 22, http://www.frontera.info/buscar/traernotanew.asp?NumNota=320808, accessed May 3, 2005.

Pizzorusso, Ann. 1998. "The Maquiladoras and the Environment." In *Environmental Management on North America's Borders*, ed. Richard Kiy and John Wirth. College Station: Texas A&M University Press.

Quintero, Cirila, and María de Lourdes Romo. 2001. "Riesgos laborales en la maquiladora: la experiencia tamaulipeca," *Frontera Norte* 13, no. 2: 11–46.

Rodríguez, Leticia. 1997. "Apertura de mercado sin sacrificio social: Coparmex," *El Financiero*, September 18.

Sánchez, Roberto. 1990a. "Health and Environmental Risks of the Maquiladora in Mexicali," *Natural Resources Journal* 30: 163–86.

———. 1990b. "Contaminación industrial en la frontera norte: algunas consideraciones para la década de los noventa," *Estudios Sociológicos* 7, no. 23: 305–30.

Sánchez-Rodríguez, Roberto, Konrad Von Moltke, Stephen Mumme, John Kirton, and Donald Munton. 1998. "The Dynamics of Transboundary Environmental Agreements in North America: Discussion of Preliminary Findings." In *Environmental Management on North America's Borders*, ed. Richard Kiy and John Wirth. College Station: Texas A&M University Press.

Santés Álvarez, Ricardo. 2004. "Gobernación ambiental en México en el marco del TLCAN (1993–2003): el desafío de los residuos industriales peligrosos," *Región y Sociedad* 16, no. 31: 3–37.

Schnailberg, Allan. 1980. *The Environment: From Surplus to Scarcity*. New York: Oxford University Press.

Schnailberg, Allan, and Kenneth Gould. 1994. *Environment and Society: The Enduring Conflict*. New York: St. Martin's.

Schrecker, Ted. 2002. "Place, Class and the Privatized Environment." In *Toxic Criminology: Environment, Law and the State in Canada*, ed. S. Boyd, D. E. Chunn, and R. Menzies. Halifax: Fernwood.

Stoddard, Ellwyn. 1987. *Maquila: Assembly Plants in Northern Mexico*. El Paso: Texas Western Press.

———. 1992. "George Baker's 'Mexican Labor is Not Cheap': A Rejoinder and Critical Commentary," *Río Bravo* 1, no. 2: 107–25.

Urquidi, Víctor. 1999. "Globalización, medio ambiente y desarrollo sustentable." In *Desarrollo sustentable, medio ambiente y población: a cinco años de Rio*, ed. Haydea Izazola. Zinacantepec, Mexico: El Colegio Mexiquense.

van Loon, Joost. 2000. "Virtual Risks in an Age of Cybernetic Reproduction." In *The Risk Society and Beyond: Critical Issues for Social Theory*, ed. Barbara Adam, Ulrich Beck, and Joost van Loon. London: Sage.

Valdez-Villalva, Guillermina. 1985. "New Policies and Strategies of Multinational Corporations during the Mexican National Crisis 1982–1983." In *The U.S. and Mexico: Borderland Development and the National Economies*, ed. Lay James Gibson and Alfonso Corona Rentería. Boulder, Colo.: Westview.

Winckell, Alain, Michel Le Page, Gerardo Chávez, Rafael Vela, Roberto Castañeda, and Carlos González. 2000. *¿Y si un terremoto de magnitud 6.5 se produjera en la falla de La Nación? Aportes para un escenario sísmico en Tijuana*. Tijuana: El Colegio de la Frontera Norte and Institut de Recherche pour Développement.

# 8

## Social Vulnerability and Disaster Risk in Tijuana: Preliminary Findings

NORA L. BRINGAS RÁBAGO AND ROBERTO SÁNCHEZ R.

The catastrophic tsunami that hit south Asia in December 2004 underscored the close linkages between poverty, environment, and development, as well as the marginal attention that developing countries have given to risk prevention and management. The increasing frequency of what are incorrectly labeled "natural disasters" and their tremendous impact on the poorest countries confirm that these disasters continue to be one of development's "unresolved problems."

Despite discussions and declarations by well-intentioned international organizations, the struggle against poverty seems to be failing worldwide, and the devastation wreaked by nearly every natural disaster can be traced back to poverty (World Bank Group 2003). So widespread is global concern with environmental deterioration and the "sustainability" of development that, following the Johannesburg Summit in 2002, the United Nations launched the World Disaster Reduction Awareness Campaign. In so doing,

---

Much of the work presented in this chapter is the result of a project entitled "Reducing the Negative Consequences of Climate Variability through the Use of Forecast and Vulnerability Analysis in Cities: The Case of Tijuana, Mexico" (hereinafter, the "Reducing Negative Consequences" project). The project is a collaboration among the University of California, Santa Cruz, El Colegio de la Frontera Norte (COLEF), Centro de Investigación Científica y de Educación Superior de Ensenada (CICESE), Dirección de Protección Civil, and Consejo Planeación Municipal of Tijuana. The project receives support from the National Oceanic and Atmospheric Administration (NOAA). Translation by Sandra del Castillo.

the UN was spurred by the fact that three times as many disasters occurred in the 1990s as in the 1960s—despite the fact that the 1990s had been declared the International Decade for Natural Disaster Reduction.

Although the disasters of the 1990s took place throughout the world, the majority of their victims were in developing countries, from which we can infer that the same type of disaster will produce different impacts depending on whether the affected country is developed or still an aspirant to development. And this difference is tied to differential access to resources, the ways in which social groups structure their lives, and inappropriate land use patterns, which, in turn, produce varying degrees of impact on a country's economic, social, and political sectors (Miño 1998).

Nature is continuously subjected to a dynamic process of formation and transformation, which has led to the adoption of "natural" as a modifier for the sinister aftereffects of natural phenomena such as earthquakes, tsunamis, hurricanes, droughts, and floods. But what in fact determines a population's susceptibility to these aftereffects is human activity. As Maskrey (1993) noted, natural phenomena do not necessarily cause disasters. Rather, "natural" disasters are the result of human intervention; when humankind modifies the landscape in an irresponsible manner, this can generate adverse conditions that raise the population's vulnerability to disaster risk.

Climate change, deforestation, unceasing population growth, and uncontrolled urban sprawl have made today's societies more vulnerable to natural threats. These factors have prompted increases in both the number and frequency of such risks. The same is true of certain human activities that, by exacerbating social vulnerability to natural threats—such as the torrential rains spawned by El Niño—transform these events into true disasters (EIRD 2003). As the chronology of natural disasters illustrates, certain regions of Asia, Latin America, and the Caribbean are the most severely affected by these kinds of catastrophes (Lavell 2000; UNDP 2002; Vargas 2002; CEPAL-BID 2000; CEPAL 2003; PNUD 2004).

In recent years, climate change has provoked a dramatic rise in the number of natural events that have brought death and destruction to developing countries. Between 1980 and 2000, 75 percent of the world's population was exposed to at least one natural disaster, including earthquakes, hurricanes, flooding, and drought (PNUD 2004). Unfortunately, the trend suggests that these phenomena will become incrementally more frequent and more dangerous due to the conditions of marginality and environmental degradation that exist in developing countries, which engender new risks and increase the vulnerability of populations that are hard pressed to recover from these extreme events (UNDP 2002: 1; World Bank Group 2003). Even more worrisome is that fact that development will accelerate the risks even more (PNUD 2004).

Disasters that are linked to climatic factors in urban areas around the world underscore the need to improve the use of forecasting and to more thoroughly analyze the vulnerability of specific, generally less protected social groups. Certain features of Latin American cities—rapid growth, incomplete urbanization, insufficient urban planning, severe and continuous economic crisis—mean that they are particularly exposed to the deleterious impacts of climatic variation.

Poverty and population growth exacerbate the costs of natural threats because they are progressively pushing people into ever more vulnerable areas. We offer the case of Tijuana to illustrate this trend. This city's urbanization process and its interwoven urban, social, and environmental problems linked to climatic events like El Niño are representative of the conditions that prevail in many cities in Latin America (Herzer 2004; Cohen 2003; De Mattos 2002). This chapter examines Tijuana's urban area in order to identify zones that are highly vulnerable to the disastrous impacts of natural phenomena such as heavy rainfall. We divide the chapter into three sections. The first describes the general context within which such disasters occur worldwide. The second offers a theoretical framework for our study. And the third section details the methodological and geographic techniques used in this study and presents some preliminary findings.

## VULNERABILITY AND DISASTER RISK

### The Origin of Disasters

Physical, chemical, and biological processes have always transformed ecosystems. However, the irresponsible actions of the human community over the last four decades have set in motion a cascade of pernicious processes that are affecting climate change. These include desertification, the loss of biodiversity, and deforestation. When combined with the socioeconomic features of countries in development, they intensify the frequency and magnitude of "natural" disasters.

In past decades there was much discussion of the weakening of humankind's link to nature as a factor in environmental problems, a detachment that began with the Industrial Revolution. Today we see that many societies have been complicit in their own environmental degradation, but this is not true of all societies and certainly not to the same degree. Industrialized countries are principally responsible for current environmental woes. The development model these countries have followed pays no heed to its deleterious impacts in the environment, as evidenced in the buildup of greenhouse gases and the indiscriminate destruction of natural resources. Yet those who suffer these perverse effects are overwhelmingly the residents of countries in development, and this is the case because developing countries are those with the most vulnerable populations (PNUD 2004).

Climate change is an indisputable outcome of a failure to address the impacts of development. It represents a latent threat for everyone, not only because of its origins but also because of its medium- and long-term impacts. These can already be seen in natural events that, because of human action, are transformed into true disasters, taking lives and inflicting huge social, economic, and environmental costs, and widening still further the gap between poverty rates in developed and underdeveloped countries.

Blaikie and colleagues (1996) suggest that "the crucial point to understanding why disasters occur is that they are not caused only by natural events. They are also the product of the political and economic environment, due to the way in which different groups of people structure their lives." Thus we cannot understand disasters unless we analyze the social context in which these occur.

Natural hazards can present a very serious threat to human development, but the level of risk does not depend so much on the event as on the level of vulnerability of the people who are affected (Maskrey 1993). Among the factors in the social context that increase a population's vulnerability are low incomes, high unemployment, limited or no access to urbanizable land, and unsound use of natural resources. Political and economic factors also play a role in how natural events affect populations; these include the prevailing economic model, spatial and economic segregation, rapid and unplanned urban growth, and access to basic public services. Such considerations can compel people to settle on hillsides and in flood zones, putting themselves at risk simply because they lack any alternative to such precarious living conditions.

### The Impacts of Natural Disasters

A report by the United Nations Environment Programme on reducing the risks from natural disasters notes that about 184 people around the world die every day as the result of disasters driven by natural events (PNUD 2004: 1). The same study reports that about 75 percent of the world's population reside in areas that in 1980–2000 were hit by a natural event such as a hurricane, earthquake, or flood. Alarmingly, about 53 percent of the deaths that result from such phenomena occur in countries that rank low on the human development index, even though these countries account for only 11 percent of the total at-risk population. The study estimates that for each death attributable to disaster, some three thousand persons are at risk.

As distressing as these numbers are, they underestimate the true magnitude of the problem, because they exclude events with localized impacts in developing countries. And further, there is a lack of reliable data on the human and economic losses attributable to disasters.

A review of natural disasters from 1950 to 1999 reveals a substantial increase, especially over the 1990s. In the 1990s, 4,777 natural catastrophes were recorded, which together accounted for 880,000 deaths and serious impacts on the health and sustenance of another 1.88 billion (*Boletín ONU* 2002). In 1999 alone, there were over 700 major disasters, which together caused economic losses totaling over US$100 billion (ONU 2000).

Over the course of the 1990s, many countries implemented meaningful efforts to reduce the impacts of natural disasters which, in addition to taking human lives, undercut populations' means of subsistence and damaged public infrastructure. Yet economic losses still totaled US$783.8 billion between 1991 and 2000, with 51.1 percent of these occurring in Asia and 26.1 percent in Latin America.[1] Economic losses due to catastrophes between 1994 and 2004 were seven times the level of losses in the 1960s

---

[1] These data were drawn from EM-DAT, an international data base on disasters compiled by the Katholieke Universiteit Leuven, available at www.em.-dat.net.

(Munich Re 2005). The substantial losses recorded in the 1990s made this decade one of the worst ever for "unnatural" disasters, catastrophes provoked more by human action than by nature. The greater danger, of course, is that this trend toward more frequent and severe extreme climatic events will continue into the future (Abramovitz 2001).

Natural disasters of the magnitude of the tsunami that hit south Asia in late December 2004 obviously constitute an obstacle to efforts to address extreme poverty, as outlined in the Millennium Development Goals (BID 2004), and reducing poverty rates in the medium term seems an unattainable objective. The unequal income distribution within and between nations, the absence of policies to prevent and mitigate risk, and the failure to implement minimal norms in newly urbanizing areas are just some of the elements that exacerbate the destruction wrought by natural events.

**Defining Social Vulnerability**

To understand how a threatening event in the natural world becomes a true catastrophe—bringing death, destroying infrastructure, and wiping out populations' means of subsistence—we should begin by focusing on the vulnerability of people residing in areas that have been affected by such events.

Until the 1970s, disasters were equated with natural phenomena. Earthquakes, droughts, or hurricanes were seen as acts of god. Disasters, it was thought, had no cause outside of themselves, and social factors were never considered (Romero and Maskrey 1993; Cardona 1993, 2001; Lavell 2004; PNUD 2004). Beginning in the 1970s, however, observers began to note that the same kind of physical threat produced very different outcomes depending on the affected area's urban structure. These observations spurred interest in designing buildings, bridges, roadways, and so on, that could withstand natural phenomena and thus mitigate their impacts (PNUD 2004; Lavell 2004; Cardona 1993).

In the 1980s social scientists further advanced their understanding of the differential impacts of natural events when they noted the importance of affected populations' ability to weather such events and recover from the associated losses in life and material goods. From that point forward, reducing social vulnerability was seen as a way to minimize the effects of catastrophes, and natural phenomena were no longer equated with natural disasters (PNUD 2004).

Hugely significant advances in understanding catastrophes were made beginning in the 1990s, when researchers began to view the development process itself as the source of various forms of vulnerability, because development exacerbates or transforms threats originating in the natural world. Experts began to study a disaster as a historically constructed "process" in which social and natural conditions hold equal importance in structuring risk[2] and together create the context within which disasters take place (Lavell 2004).

The literature on disasters is also relevant for the study of the interactions between city and climate (Blaikie et al. 1996; Bocco, Sánchez, and Riemann 1993; Herzer 2004). Most important are studies that emphasize the processes that create vulnerability, over and above poverty and the disasters themselves (Blaikie et al. 1996; Bohle, Downing, and Watts 1994; Chambers 1989; Adger 1999). Equally important for understanding vulnerability are studies that focus on class structure, income disparities, and the disaggregation of power structures (Bohle, Downing, and Watts 1994).

Within the context of risks in nature, vulnerability comprises "the characteristics of a person or group regarding their capacity to anticipate, confront, resist, and recover from the impact of a natural risk" (Blaikie et al. 1996). In this sense, vulnerability involves a combination of factors that determine the degree to which an individual's life and means of survival are put at risk by a discrete, identifiable event in nature or society. Vulnerability is also an expression of risk and stress and the difficulty of coping with them. This suggests two aspects of vulnerability. The first is external—the risks and stressors to which an individual or his/her means of support are subjected. The other is internal and involves the individual's inability to respond, given the lack of means with which to act to prevent

---

[2] Risk is expressed as "the probability of surpassing a threshold in economic, social, or environmental consequences in a specific place during a specific period of time" (Cardona 2001). According to CEPAL-BID (2000: 5), "Risk begins as a product of the function that relates threat and vulnerability a priori, and is considered intrinsic and latent within society, with one reservation: its level, the degree to which it is perceived, and measures to deal with it all depend on the directives laid out by the society itself."

harm (Chambers 1989). In a context of climate change and food insecurity, vulnerability can be viewed as "a multidimensional social space defined by the particular political, economic, and institutional capacities available to people in specific places at specific times" (Bohle, Downing, and Watts 1994).

Borrowing from the aforementioned definitions of vulnerability, the present study identifies a group's vulnerability as the dynamic balance between the external (the event or disturbance) and the internal (the spectrum of social and economic relations that determine access to the resources needed to minimize the event's prejudicial impacts). This definition assumes a dynamic approach to vulnerability in which the focus extends beyond the disasters themselves to emphasize processes.

## VULNERABILITY AND DISASTER RISK IN TIJUANA
### Key Attributes of the Physical Environment

Tijuana sits at the northwestern edge of Mexico's border with the United States, just south of San Diego, California. Its topography consists primarily of low hills and small valleys. Sixty-five percent of the inhabited area is on moderate slopes of up to 10 percent, inclines that are deemed suitable for most urban land uses; these are located primarily in the urban area's westernmost sections. However, about 25 percent of the urban area is on 10 to 20 percent slopes, which are unsuitable for urban use because of the high cost of providing them with basic services. The remaining 10 percent of the urban area consists of slopes so steep (over 20 percent) that their inhabitants are highly vulnerable to natural events. These steep slopes are found in Tijuana's southern, southeastern, and southwestern sectors. Another feature of Tijuana is the network of streambeds which, in the rainy season, carry water into the Tijuana River and eventually across the border into California (Piñera and Ortiz Figueroa 1985).

### Tijuana's Population and Urban Structure

At the beginning of the twentieth century, Tijuana had only 242 inhabitants; by 2000 its residents numbered 1,148,681, nearly half of the total population of the state of Baja California. Much of Tijuana's demographic and economic dynamism is due to the city's character as a border town and its geographic isolation from Mexico's economic and political center. Tijuana's early economy, until the 1950s, rested on tourism and trade, which benefited from Prohibition and from the United States' involvement in two World Wars and conflicts in Korea and Vietnam (Bringas R. 1991).

International migration began to play a role in Tijuana's population dynamic beginning with the Bracero Program, which brought Mexican farmworkers to the United States beginning in 1942. When the Bracero Program ended in 1964, many returning migrants stayed in Tijuana, adding to the pool of job seekers and augmenting existing urban problems. Construction of the rail link between Sonora and Baja California in 1948 also brought international migrants to the area (Küsel 1988: 15).

Hoping to create jobs and spur tourism in the border region, as well as to promote the border's economic integration with the rest of Mexico, the Mexican government implemented the National Border Program (PRONAF) in 1961. PRONAF was replaced in 1965 by the Border Industrialization Program (BIP), which aimed to diversify the economy through the introduction of in-bond manufacturing plants, or *maquiladoras* (Barrera Bassols 1987). The introduction of this new industrial subsector unleashed a torrent of in-migration to Tijuana from all areas of Mexico, and this influx continues today, with strong repercussions on Tijuana's urbanization.

As the city and its economy have grown, so, too, has the demand for land and housing. Unfortunately, Tijuana's historical lag in providing urban infrastructure has also become increasingly notable over time. Even though incomes and employment rates in Tijuana exceed national averages, the city continues to suffer serious shortages in water, housing, and public transportation (Ayuntamiento de Tijuana 1999, 2002), all of which have repercussions on the local population's quality of life.

Tijuana's urban problems have worsened in recent years, exacerbated by the lack of land suitable for urbanization. The constant influx of migrants to the city has accentuated these shortfalls, at the same time that it has driven growth in peripheral areas, where it is doubly hard to promote and implement any urban or territorial standards. Indeed, some observers suggest that a substantial share of Tijuana's urban development is the product of irregular claims to property, with irregular settlements accounting for 43 percent of Tijuana's land area, concentrating 53 percent of its population, and containing 52 percent of its family dwellings (Alegría and Ordóñez 2005: 121).

Table 8.1. Historical Growth of Tijuana's Urban Area

| | Surface Area (hectares) | Years since Prior Measure | Increase since Prior Measure (hectares) | Annual Increase (hectares) | Daily Increase (hectares) | Average Growth Period | Average Growth Percent |
|---|---|---|---|---|---|---|---|
| 1935 | 1159.00 | | | | | | |
| 1950 | 1744.00 | 15 | 585.00 | 39 | 0.11 | 1935–1950 | 3.4 |
| 1972 | 7,789.00 | 22 | 6,045.00 | 275 | 0.75 | 1950–1972 | 15.8 |
| 1989 | 16,087.00 | 17 | 8,298.00 | 488.12 | 1.34 | 1972–1989 | 6.3 |
| 1994 | 25,653.53 | 5 | 9,566.53 | 1,913.31 | 5.24 | 1989–1994 | 11.9 |
| 2000 | 26,046.69 | 6 | 393.16 | 65.53 | 0.18 | 1994–2000 | 0.3 |
| 1972–2000 | 18,257.69 | 28 | 18,257.69 | 652.06 | 1.79 | 1972–2000 | 8.4 |
| 1935–2000 | 24,887.69 | 65 | 24,887.69 | 382.89 | 1.05 | 1935–2000 | 33.0 |

*Sources*: Aguilar Méndez 1992 (for 1935 and 1950) and "Reducing Negative Consequences" project.

Tijuana's broken topography is spotlighted by wayward urban growth in canyons and up hillsides, problems of land ownership, inadequate housing supply, poor-quality housing, and chronic lack of water. All of these factors accentuate the inequalities between the modern Tijuana of the Zona Río and the Tijuana of the squatter settlements that push the city further to the east, south, southeast, and southwest, reaching toward a conurbation with Tecate to the east and Playas de Rosarito to the southwest.

## Expansion of the Urban Area

In 1935, Tijuana covered only 1,159 hectares, concentrated in what is now the city center and areas, such as Colonia Libertad, adjacent to the international border. But from that point forward it grew in all directions, reaching an area of 26,046 hectares in 2000 (see table 8.1, figure 8.1). This explosive growth was fed by an influx of migrants whose settlement added an average of 1.3 hectares per day to the city's urban area between 1972 and 1989. This growth was dispersed and unplanned, extending into flood-prone lowlands and up slopes with inclines of up to 40 percent (see table 8.2). Such areas typically pose special technical difficulties and present high costs in terms of the introduction of public services.

Table 8.2. Annual Percent Increase in Tijuana's Urbanized Area, by Incline, 1972–2000

| Percent Incline | Percent Increase in Area | | | |
|---|---|---|---|---|
| | 1972–1989 | 1989–1994 | 1994–2000 | 1972–2000 |
| 0–10 | 5.26 | 8.94 | 0.21 | 6.33 |
| 10–20 | 7.91 | 12.93 | 0.17 | 10.36 |
| 20–30 | 16.54 | 18.65 | 0.06 | 22.83 |
| 30–40 | 13.45 | 33.82 | 0.08 | 28.16 |
| 40–50 | 8.45 | 20.16 | 1.00 | 14.95 |

Source: "Reducing Negative Consequences" project; see first (unnumbered) note at the beginning of this chapter.

In table 8.2, we note a progressive pattern in urban growth by incline. That is, in 1972–1989, most growth took place on inclines of 20 to 30 percent; in 1989–1994, we find most growth on inclines of 30 to 40 percent, and by 1994–2000, new settlements are being established on inclines of between 40 and 50 percent. All of these are inappropriate for urban development,

Figure 8.1. Urbanization in Tijuana, 1972–2000

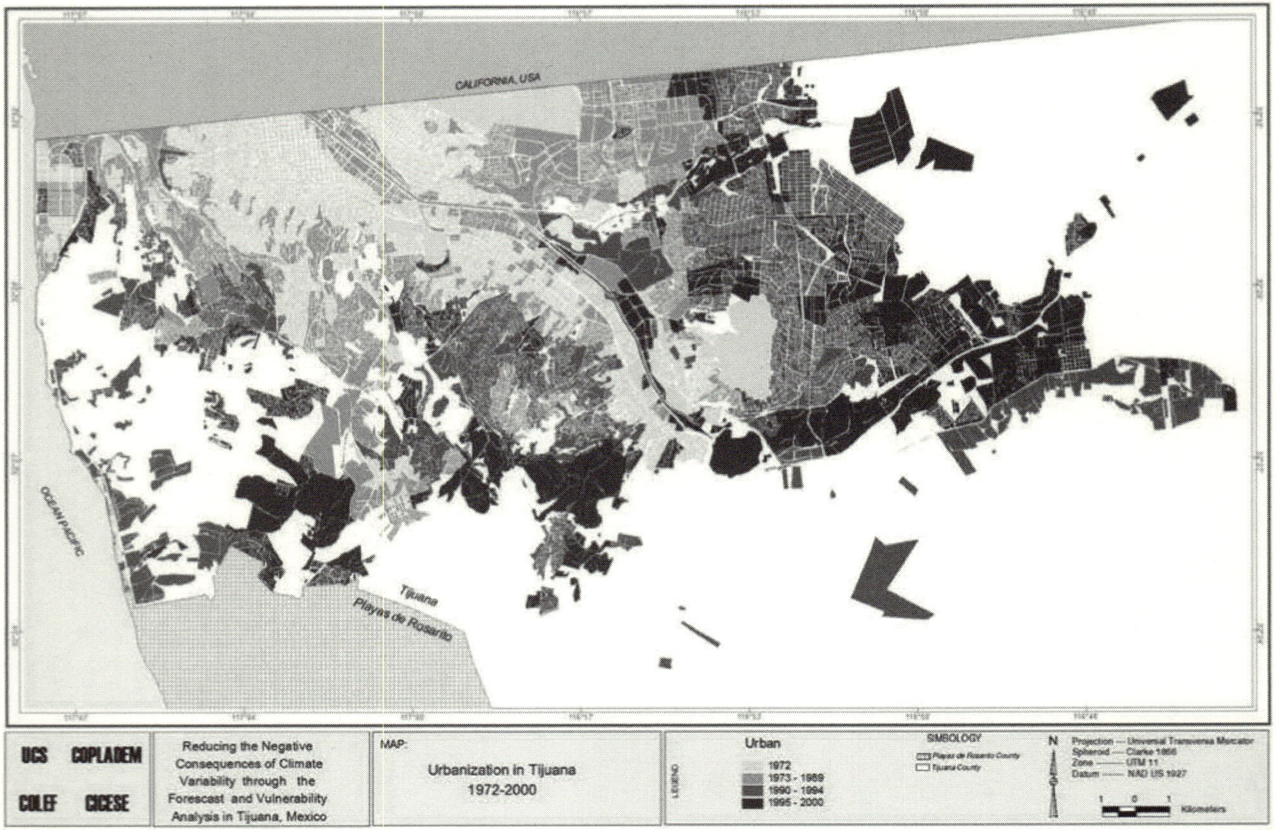

but it is very clear that, over time, poor residents have been pressed into areas that pose higher and higher degrees of disaster risk.

Tijuana's precipitous and haphazard expansion into zones not suited for urbanization and extreme alterations to the local landscape have aggravated the risks to which various social groups are exposed. In upcoming years, Tijuana could well have to deal with the negative repercussions of these shortsighted actions, especially given that risk is a historically created process. Distressingly, all of the threads that can turn a natural threat into a true catastrophe are becoming entwined in Tijuana.

## MAPPING VULNERABILITY

The El Niño phenomenon, which generated torrential rains in the winter of 1992–1993, killed thirty-six people in Tijuana. It also laid waste to 1,960 hectares, 10 percent of the urban area; this damage was due to erosion and mudslides in canyons and on hillsides (57 percent); to soil deposits in low areas, especially along the Tijuana River channel (20 percent); and to oversaturation of hilltops (Bocco, Sánchez, and Riemann 1993).

Besides the loss in human life, there were immeasurable economic costs. The city was paralyzed for two weeks as damaged or destroyed transport routes prevented people from reaching their places of work. Industry, commerce, and services were immobilized, and the city's population was isolated in a fragmented city. An unanticipated outcome of the disaster was the discovery that local officials were totally unprepared for anything of this scale and that there was no forecasting capacity that might have helped lower the risks to the population. Much of the destruction caused by the 1992–1993 storms can be attributed to structural elements in Tijuana's growth—how the landscape was altered and where the population settled—that created conditions of vulnerability.

### Creating a GIS to Study Vulnerability

New technologies (remote sensing and geographic information systems) are essential tools in policymaking for disaster prevention.[3] On one hand,

---

[3] Geographic Information Systems (GIS) are a valuable tool for decision makers. They help them construct and analyze spatial models, which is especially useful to policymakers responsible for regulating urban growth, preventing and managing risk, and doing regional planning.

they help in weather forecasting, and on the other, they aid in identifying zones particularly vulnerable to the risks of nature, thus allowing for steps to lower the disaster risk or to respond more rapidly when disasters occur.

We approached the issue of vulnerability using a variety of methodological tools. In addition to a literature review, we did an exhaustive review of newspaper coverage of major climatic events in Tijuana and the damage they caused between 1970 and early 2001. We consulted more than 20,000 issues of the state's major newspapers (*El Heraldo de Baja California*, *El Mexicano*, and *Frontera*). We also reviewed master's theses on this subject (Aragón Arreola 1994; Montalvo Arrieta 1996; Romo Aguilar 1996; Pérez Cerón 2002; Zavala 2002). We organized this information in a database constructed of four modules: events, damage, consequences, and action responses by local authorities. Given our interest in presenting the information visually, we linked the database to mapping software to facilitate construction of a GIS that would give the data a spatial dimension.

### Climatic Events and Their Consequences in Tijuana, 1970–2001

In our review of newspaper archives, we identified 349 rainfall-related events in Tijuana between 1970 and 2001. Rainfall, whether torrential or not, caused flooding, landslides, and mudslides, with flooding being the most frequent result. The 1990s included two strong El Niños, in 1992–1993 and in 1997–1998, which increased the risks of landslides and mudslides, as evidenced by the data in table 8.3 (also see figure 8.2 for damage wrought).

The problems that rainfall brings to Tijuana are compounded by the city's urban development pattern, which has included housing construction in low-lying areas along riverbeds and in canyons and ravines. Rains also impact roadways, causing bottlenecks and collisions.

Flooding results because of the city's inadequate and inefficient network of storm drains, which have been installed in only 60 percent of the urban area (mostly in the Zona Río, downtown, and parts of Playas de Tijuana). Even where drainage is available, it is often blocked with trash, which ranges from old furniture to dead animals and abandoned cars.[4]

---

[4] Héctor Moreno Navarro, director of Tijuana's Municipal Urbanization Unit, reported that the annual budget for storm drains is 20 million pesos. Of this amount, 6 million go to keeping drains clear of debris (San 2003).

Table 8.3. Incidence of Various Climate-Linked Events in Tijuana, 1970–2001

|           | Floods | Landslides | Mudslides | Total |
|-----------|--------|------------|-----------|-------|
| 1970s     | 63     | 4          | 19        | 86    |
| 1980s     | 13     |            | 1         | 14    |
| 1990s     | 102    | 58         | 44        | 204   |
| 2000–2001 | 40     |            | 5         | 45    |
| Total     | 218    | 62         | 69        | 349   |

Source: "Reducing Negative Consequences" project.

A substantial share of the landslides and rockslides that occur in Tijuana are induced by torrents of water that carry accumulated trash down hillsides and into low-lying areas. These slides cover the streets, rendering them impassible to both pedestrian and vehicular traffic. And any roadways that have been carved into the hillsides are gutted or even carried away. Mudslides are another common result of the urbanization of the foothills around Tijuana, as seasonal rains carry newly exposed soil downhill and into homes, roadways, and municipal drainage systems.

Table 8.4. Incidence of Various Kinds of Damage Caused by Climatic Events in Tijuana, 1970–2001

|           | Houses Damaged | People Left Homeless | Deaths | Single Persons Relocated | Families Relocated |
|-----------|----------------|----------------------|--------|--------------------------|--------------------|
| 1970s     | 1,743          | 84,200               | 17     | 110                      | 830                |
| 1980s     | 600            | 3,542                | 1      | 20,000                   |                    |
| 1990s     | 353            | 14                   | 50     | 241                      | 29                 |
| 2000–2001 | 154            |                      |        |                          | 150                |

Source: "Reducing Negative Consequences" project.

These climatic events bring high costs to Tijuana residents in terms of lost lives and possessions, and high economic costs to city officials in terms of damaged infrastructure and equipment. (See table 8.4 for the costs in lives, damaged homes, persons made homeless, and forced evacuations between 1970 and 2001.) For example, flooding affected 1,017 hectares in Tijuana in 2000, and this area now includes nearly 114,000 homes. Another 9,661 hectares and 90,600 at-risk homes were hit by landslides, and nearly 3,000 hectares, with 4,624 homes, felt the impacts of mudslides (figure 8.3).

Figure 8.2. Types of Damage in Urban Area of Tijuana, 2000

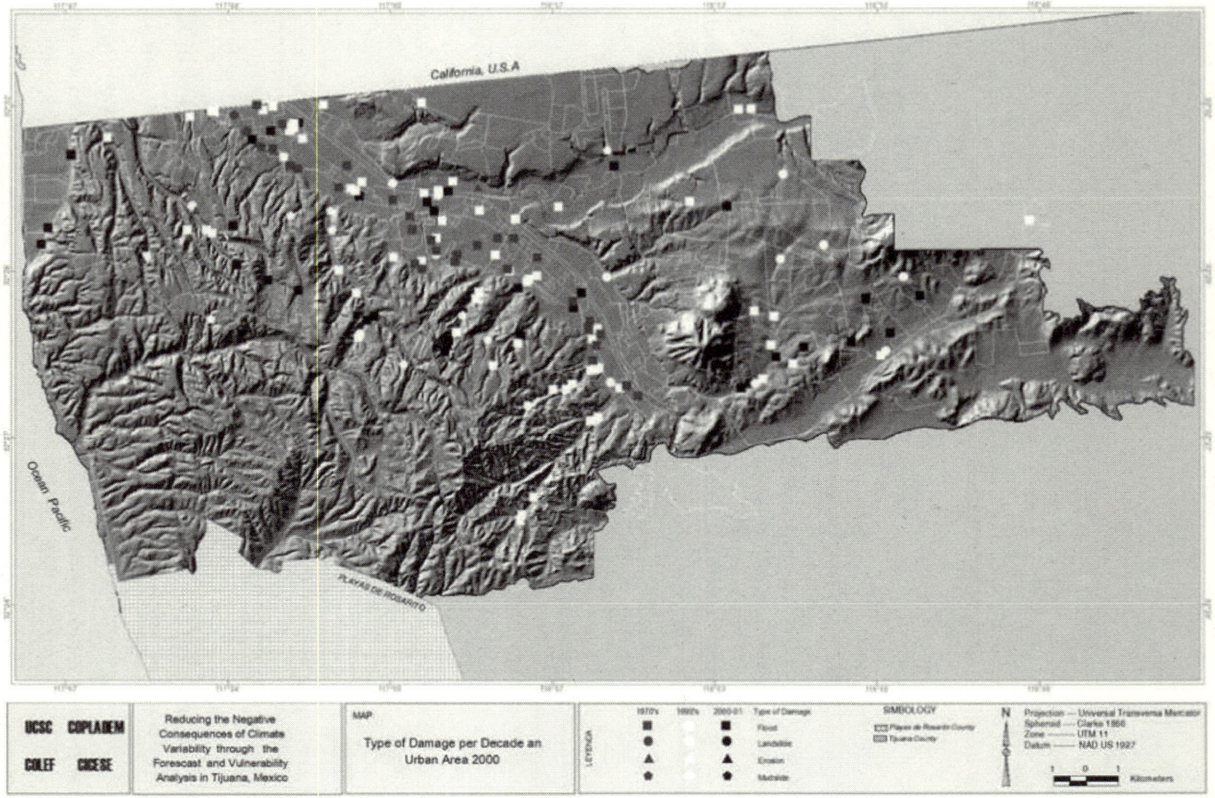

Figure 8.3. At-Risk Areas of Tijuana, 2000

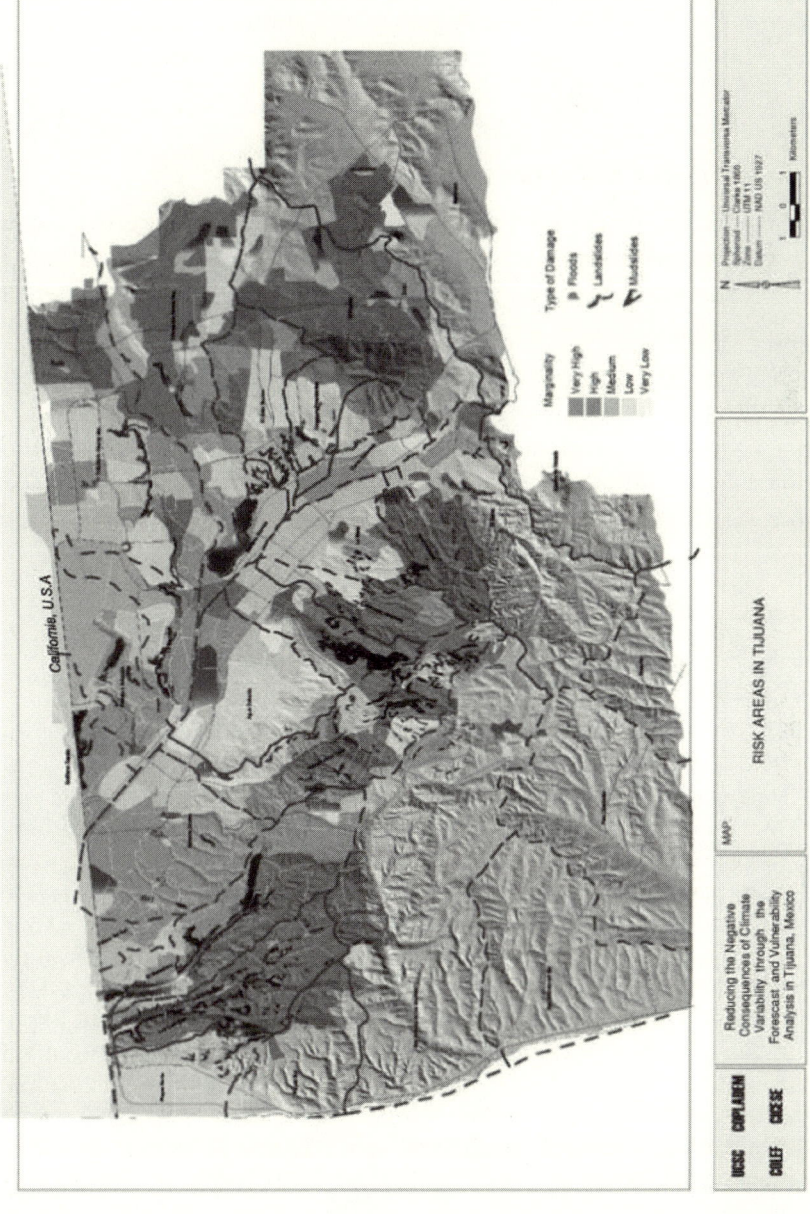

Most of the land areas and people who suffered the impacts of the 2000 floods were in zones ranked medium or high in terms of marginality, underscoring the close links between poverty and these groups' vulnerability to climatic disasters. It is clearly the poorest populations who are most seriously affected by these disasters.

## MARGINALITY AND AREAS OF RISK

Tijuana's headlong population growth and uncontrolled urban expansion have exacerbated the socioeconomic inequality between population groups as well as their spatial segregation from one another within the city. Lacking alternatives, the poor are forced to live in high-risk zones, where each natural event, even the less severe, leaves the population in increasingly fragile conditions and less able to weather the next threat of nature.

To identify marginal zones in Tijuana in 2000, we looked at data from the Baja California Program for Urban Development and Management (Bringas R. 2003), which includes thirty-two variables[5] that can be used to

---

[5] These variables are: population 65 years and older; dependent status; population without health care; disabled population; population born outside the state; illiterate population 15 years and older; population of children aged 6 to 14 not in school; population 15 years and older with no post-elementary education; average years of education; number of live births among women 12 years and older; unemployed population; population employed in the secondary sector; population employed in the service sector; population employed in the primary sector; population working as day laborers; employed population working up to 32 hours in a given workweek; employed population that receives no income from work; employed population that receives up to two minimum wages; dwellings with roofs constructed of light-weight, natural, and nonresistant materials; dwellings with walls of light-weight, natural, and nonresistant materials; one-room houses; houses without piped water or sewerage; houses without piped water, sewerage, or electricity; rented houses; households without a car or truck; households without a television; households without a refrigerator; households without a telephone; households without services; average number of persons per room in the home; female-headed households; and total population in female-headed households.

develop a marginality index for the urban area when used jointly with census tract data on population and housing. This research revealed a rather even distribution of marginality in Tijuana, with 36 percent of the population living at high and very high levels of marginalization, 32 percent at low and very low levels of marginalization, and 31 percent at levels in between.[6]

Of Tijuana's total 2000 population of over one million, the impacts of the flooding that followed upon that year's torrential rains were felt disproportionately by population groups in zones ranked as midlevel or high on the marginality scale. Landslides and mudslides produced their most dramatic impacts on populations in areas ranked midlevel and low in terms of marginality (see table 8.5).

The land areas most affected by landslides were areas of medium and high levels of marginality, and the same is true for areas that experienced mudslides (see table 8.6, figure 8.3).

The preceding demonstrates that high marginality is a key factor in the social vulnerability of various population groups. This conclusion is based on the fact that natural events affect all areas, but differences appear among social groups in terms of their capacity to respond to these events and the resources they have at their disposal for undertaking such a response.

**FINAL THOUGHTS**

In Tijuana, as in many other cities in developing countries, the poverty that structures the daily existence of many city inhabitants forces them to live in areas that are prone to risk. Many of these areas are particularly vulnerable to the flooding, landslides, and mudslides that accompany torrential rains, and local residents are defenseless against the aftermath. Furthermore, the threats are intensified by the lack of appropriate urban planning and the failure to comply with existing regulations.

---

[6] The marginality index employed by Mexico's National Population Council (CONAPO), which uses regional-level data, indicates a very low degree of marginality for the Tijuana *municipio* overall, in sharp contrast to the situation within the *municipio*'s urbanized area.

Table 8.5. Population Exposed to Disaster Risk, by Type of Risk and Degree of Marginalization, 2000

| Degree of Marginalization | Flooding | | Landslides | | Mudslides | |
|---|---|---|---|---|---|---|
| | People (N) | % | People (N) | % | People (N) | % |
| Very high | 8,703 | 12.03 | 3,634 | 8.21 | 132 | 0.50 |
| High | 18,654 | 25.79 | 7,110 | 16.05 | 995 | 3.74 |
| Medium | 27,161 | 37.55 | 18,607 | 42.01 | 10,838 | 40.79 |
| Low | 15,433 | 21.34 | 11,972 | 27.03 | 14,185 | 53.39 |
| Very low | 2,375 | 3.28 | 2,965 | 6.69 | 420 | 1.58 |
| Total | 72,326 | 100.00 | 44,288 | 100.00 | 26,570 | 100.00 |

Source: "Reducing Negative Consequences" project.

Table 8.6. Land Area (in square meters) at Risk by Type of Risk and Degree of Marginalization

| Degree of Marginalization | Flooding | | Mudslides | | Landslides | |
|---|---|---|---|---|---|---|
| | Area | % | Area | % | Area | % |
| Very high | 465,755m² | 4.45 | 1,048,830m² | 10.87 | 40,911m² | 1.38 |
| High | 2,258,990 | 21.57 | 2,486,998 | 25.76 | 1,858,348 | 62.91 |
| Medium | 3,190,622 | 30.46 | 3,204,597 | 33.20 | 916,515 | 31.03 |
| Low | 3,697,834 | 35.31 | 2,051,605 | 21.25 | 124,976 | 4.23 |
| Very low | 974,343 | 9.30 | 594,390 | 6.16 | 13,339 | 0.45 |
| Total | 10,587,544 | 100.00 | 9,386,420 | 100.00 | 2,954,089 | 100.00 |

Source: "Reducing Negative Consequences" project.

Studies of vulnerability allow us to analyze the social factors that put populations at ever-increasing levels of risk. These factors include poverty, population growth, precipitous urbanization, social exclusion, an unjust distribution of land, the loss of ground cover, environmental degradation, and the lax enforcement of laws and regulations, among others. Natural phenomena need not automatically cause human tragedies. The adverse conditions that can turn a natural event into a disaster include the number of people at risk and how they are inserted into the urban system. Poverty raises vulnerability to disasters, and disasters perpetuate poverty.

To better understand the process by which natural phenomena evolve into disasters, we must, as Herzer (2004) noted, "seek the causes of natural disaster in the forms and types of urban growth and infrastructure, in urban politics, and in the lack of true understanding that the various social actors possess." The factors that influence the structuring of urban space help explain why people settle in high-risk areas, making it essential to understand these factors and determine how they are shaping this urban space of vulnerability. It is also necessary to identify the linkages between these social processes and geographic distribution variables. Perhaps then we can fully comprehend that many disasters are not the result solely of natural causes. Indeed, by looking instead at social processes, we can determine how risk has developed over time.

The concept of vulnerability adds to our understanding of the human dimension of global climate change, but its study requires an integrated perspective that connects social processes with natural ones. An analysis of vulnerability must look at both its external aspects (impacts) and its internal ones (responses). Vulnerability's internal dimension comprises a wide range of social and economic relations that determine access to the resources needed to minimize damage.

In the case of Tijuana, these social and economic relations are created through transnational and local processes that are the forces driving rapid urban growth. The structural conditions of social inequity create a segregated urban space characterized by a severe lack of urban planning at the same time that they put pressure on low-income groups to settle in high-risk areas.

Important elements for reducing disaster risk in the future are state-of-the-art weather forecasting technology and an early-warning system to alert people to climate threats and the catastrophes that can result from them. As important and urgent as this last element is, it will not be sufficient. The population of Tijuana, like those of other cities in developing countries, often will not act even when forewarned of a natural event, reflecting their limited capacity to offer an effective response. In fact, they may respond in the opposite manner, refusing to evacuate for fear of losing not only their homes and belongings but also their claim to the land.

This concern is paramount for people in areas that began as irregular settlements, beyond the bounds of urban control. This population knows that if they abandon their homes, they will probably not be allowed to return; as a result, they develop different responses to natural disasters. As for the authorities, their responses to natural disasters tend to be technical ones implemented after the fact—aiding victims and repairing infrastructure—but this assistance tends to drop off quickly and the underlying problems are forgotten until the next climatic event occurs.

It is clear that the population that is affected by disasters should take a more active role in the search for ways to confront and eliminate the factors that augment disaster risk. And no matter how much effort goes into finding solutions or how promising these solutions appear, they will prove futile if the population groups exposed to risk refuse to act.

The results of our research have allowed us to sketch a preliminary guide to understanding the complexity of urban systems and the interplay between environmental change and urban space—in its social, economic, political, cultural, and biophysical dimensions. What is needed is to advance our understanding of these interactions and avoid fragmented perspectives on complex realities. Analyzing vulnerability is a useful tool in this regard. Our results can also contribute to the application of other concepts (such as socio-ecological resilience and maintenance) that together yield integrated approaches to populations' adaptations to so-called natural disasters.

## References

Abramovitz, Janet N. 2001. "Unnatural Disasters." Worldwatch Institute Paper No. 158.

Adger, W. Nail. 1999. "Social Vulnerability to Climate Change and Extremes in Coastal Vietnam," *World Development* 27, no. 2: 249–69.

Aguilar Méndez, Fernando Antonio. 1990. "La expansión territorial de las ciudades de México." Mexico City: Universidad Autónoma Metropolitana–Xochimilco. Manuscript.

Alegría, Tito, and Gerardo Ordóñez. 2005. *Legalizando la ciudad: asentamientos informales y procesos de regularización en Tijuana.* Tijuana: El Colegio de la Frontera Norte.

Aragón Arreola, Manuel de Jesús. 1994. "Evaluación del riesgo geológico debido a movimientos de ladera en la ciudad de Tijuana, B.C., México." Master's thesis, Centro de Investigación Científica y de Educación Superior de Ensenada.

Ayuntamiento de Tijuana. 1999. *Plan Municipal de Desarrollo 1998–2001.* Tijuana, B.C.: H. XVI Ayuntamiento de Tijuana.

———. 2002. *Plan Municipal de Desarrollo 2002–2004.* Tijuana, B.C.: H. XVII Ayuntamiento de Tijuana.

Barrera Bassols, Dalia. 1987. *Condiciones de vida de los trabajadores de Tijuana. 1970–1978.* Mexico City: Instituto Nacional de Antropología e Historia and Secretaría de Educación Pública.

BID (Banco Interamericano de Desarrollo). 2004. *Los Objetivos de Desarrollo del Milenio en América Latina y el Caribe: retos, acciones y compromisos.* Washington, D.C.: Inter-American Development Bank.

Blaikie, Piers, Terry Cannon, Ian Davis, and Benjamin Wisner. 1996. *Vulnerabilidad: el entorno social, político y económico de los desastres.* Red de Estudios Sociales en Prevención de Desastres en América Latina. Bogotá, Colombia: LA RED/ITDG.

Bocco, Gerardo, Roberto Sánchez, and Hugo Riemann. 1993. "Evaluación del impacto de las inundaciones en Tijuana (enero de 1993): uso integrado de percepción remota y sistemas de información geográfica," *Frontera Norte* 5, no. 10: 53–84.

Bohle, Hans G., Thomas E. Downing, and Michael J. Watts. 1994. "Climate Change and Social Vulnerability: Toward a Sociology and Geography of Food Insecurity," *Global Environmental Change* 4 (March): 37–48.

Bringas R., Nora L. 1991. "Diagnóstico del sector turístico en Tijuana." In *Grupos de visitantes y actividades turísticas en Tijuana,* ed. Nora L. Bringas R. and Jorge Carrillo V. Tijuana: El Colegio de la Frontera Norte.

Bringas R., Nora L., ed. 2003. "Programa de desarrollo urbano y ordenamiento territorial para el estado de B.C." Research Report. Tijuana: El Colegio de la Frontera Norte and Secretaría de Asentamientos Humanos y Obras Públicas del Estado de Baja California.

Cardona, Omar Darío. 1993. "Evaluación de la amenaza, la vulnerabilidad y el riesgo." In *Los desastres no son naturales,* ed. Andrew Maskrey. Bogotá, Colombia: LA RED.

———. 2001. "La necesidad de repensar de manera holística los conceptos de vulnerabilidad y riesgo: una crítica y una revisión necesaria para la gestión." Prepared for the conference "Vulnerability in Disaster Theory and Practice," Wageningen, Holland, June 29–30.

CEPAL (Comisión Económica para América Latina y el Caribe). 2003. *Manual para la estimación de los efectos socio-económicos y ambientales de los desastres.* CEPAL/World Bank.

CEPAL-BID (Comisión Económica para América Latina y el Caribe–Banco Interamericano de Desarrollo). 2000. *Un tema de desarrollo: la reducción de la vulnerabilidad frente a los desastres.* Document prepared for the seminar "Enfrentando desastres naturales: una cuestión del desarrollo," New Orleans, March 25–26.

Chambers, R. 1989. "Vulnerability, Coping and Policy," *IDS Bulletin* 20, no. 2.

Cohen, Barney. 2003. "Urban Growth in Developing Countries: A Review of Current Trends and a Caution Regarding Existing Forecasts," *World Development* 32, no. 1: 23–51.

De Mattos, Carlos A. 2002. "Redes, nodos y ciudades: transformación de la metrópoli latinoamericana." Presented at the VII Seminario Internacional de la Red Iberoamericana de Investigadores sobre Globalización y Territorio, Camagüey, Cuba, November 27–29.

EIRD (Estrategia Internacional para la Reducción de los Desastres). 2002. "Los desastres naturales y el desarrollo sostenible: considerando los vínculos entre el desarrollo, el medio ambiente y los desastres naturales." Document No. 5, second preparatory session, January 28–February 8.

———. 2003. *Vivir con el riesgo.* World Campaign for Disaster Prevention, EIRD.

Herzer, Hilda María. 2004. "Riesgo, inundación y gestión en la ciudad de Buenos Aires." Taller IAI, Mexico City, October–November.

Küsel, Corina. 1988. "Tijuana: ¿una ciudad dónde fluyen leche y miel? Desarrollo de la economía y de las condiciones de reproducción." In *Tijuana, cambio social y migración*, ed. Víctor Klagsbrunn. Tijuana: El Colegio de la Frontera Norte.

Lavell, Allan. 2000. "Desastres durante una década: lecciones y avances conceptuales y prácticos en América Latina (1990–1999)." In *Anuario político y social de América Latina*, no. 3. FLACSO–LA RED.

———. 2004. "La red de estudios sociales en prevención de desastres en América Latina, La RED: antecedentes, formación y contribución al desarrollo de los conceptos, estudios y la práctica en el tema de los riesgos y desastres en América Latina: 1980–2004." Unpublished.

Maskrey, Andrew, ed. 1993. *Los desastres no son naturales.* Bogotá, Colombia: LA RED.

Miño, Hilda María. 1998. *La vulnerabilidad y el desarrollo económico.* Nicaragua: Programa Nacional de Competitividad.

Montalvo Arrieta, Juan Carlos. 1996. "Deslizamientos de laderas inducidos por terremotos en la ciudad de Tijuana, B.C., México." Master's thesis, Centro de Investigación Científica y de Educación Superior de Ensenada.

Munich RE. 2005. *Topics: Annual Review, Natural Catastrophes 2004*. Knowledge Series. Munich.

ONU (Organización de las Naciones Unidas). 2000. "Establecimiento de un sistema de gestión de desastres naturales mundial, integrado y basado en el espacio." Report A/AC.105/758, by the Asamblea General, Comisión sobre la Utilización de Espacio Ultraterrestre con Fines Pacíficos.

Pérez Cerón, Rosalbina. 2002. "Evaluación de la gestión del riesgo en Tijuana, B.C. México, entre 1993 y 2001." Master's thesis, El Colegio de la Frontera Norte/Centro de Investigación Científica y de Educación Superior de Ensenada.

Piñera, David, and Jesús Ortiz Figueroa. 1985. "El medio geográfico." In *Historia de Tijuana. Semblanza general*, ed. David Piñera. Tijuana: Instituto de Investigaciones Históricas, Universidad Nacional Autónoma de México and Universidad Autónoma de Baja California.

PNUD (Programa de las Naciones Unidas para el Desarrollo). 2004. *La reducción de riesgos de desastres: un desafío para el desarrollo*. Dirección de Prevención de Crisis y de Recuperación.

Romero, Gilberto, and Andrew Maskrey. 1993. "Como entender los desastres naturales." In *Los desastres no son naturales*, ed. Andrew Maskrey. Bogotá, Colombia: LA RED.

Romo Aguilar, María de Lourdes. 1996. "Riesgo y vulnerabilidad social en la zona urbana de Tijuana, B.C." Master's thesis, El Colegio de la Frontera Norte and Centro de Investigación Científica y de Educación Superior de Ensenada.

San, Luis Adolfo. 2003. "Es insuficiente el drenaje pluvial," *Frontera*, http://www.frontera.info/edicionenlinea/notas/Noticias/20031117/33499.asp.

UNDP (United Nations Development Programme). 2002. "Climate Risk Management Approach to Disaster Reduction and Adaptation to Climate Change." Draft summary of the UNDP Expert Group Meeting on Integrating Disaster Reduction with Adaptation to Climate Change, Havana, June 19–21.

Vargas, Jorge Enrique. 2002. "Políticas públicas para la reducción de la vulnerabilidad frente a los desastres naturales y socio-naturales." Serie Medio Ambiente y Desarrollo, no. 50. Santiago de Chile: División de Medio Ambiente y Asentamientos Humanos, CEPAL, April.

World Bank Group. 2003. *Poverty and Climate Change: Reducing the Vulnerability of the Poor through Adaptation*. Washington, D.C.: World Bank.

Zavala, Luis Enrique. 2002. "Zonas de riesgo en Tijuana, B.C.: El caso de la Colonia Tres de Octubre." Master's thesis, El Colegio de la Frontera Norte.

# 9

## Environment, Poverty, and Gender: Using and Managing Environmental Resources in a Tijuana Colonia

RUTH GAXIOLA ALDAMA

Achieving a sustainable environment is a priority goal shared by nations around the world. The United Nations has supported a multitude of projects and convened many world summits in pursuit of sustainable development, yet the record for involving local communities in this process has been quite poor. Recently, however, there has been increasing awareness that sustainable development goes beyond ecological considerations and a recognition that social considerations are also indispensable for its attainment. Hence the urgency to promote the equitable incorporation of all social actors into the process. This must begin at the micro level of rural and urban communities, which, in the last instance, are the actors who must deal most directly with the impacts of environmental degradation and that currently have the weakest voice in decision making.

Few studies of Tijuana have incorporated environmental issues. Instead, they generally focus on the provision of services and infrastructure, women's social participation, and so on, at the regional or local level. This gap in the research argues for the need to examine, at the micro level of the household, the relationship between residents of an urban community and their environmental milieu, along with the factors that impinge on this relationship.

The present study defines a sustainable environment as one in which access to and use of natural resources follows an equitable pattern that allows for the preservation or restoration, if needed, of the array of natural

---

Translation by Sandra del Castillo.

resources and that ensures acceptable standards of living for the local population and a fair distribution of the benefits derived from the exploitation of their environment. Attaining this ideal of a sustainable environment presents a formidable challenge given the lack of significant progress in formulating appropriate political frameworks at the municipal level. Discussions at recent summits sponsored by the United Nations—the Rio Summit in 1992; Global Forum 94: Cities and Sustainable Development, held in Manchester, England, in 1994; and the second United Nations Conference on Human Settlements (Habitat II) in Istanbul in 1996—have highlighted the importance of embedding sustainable development policies within the local arena (Cárdenas 1998; Guzmán 2000).

The central argument underpinning the present research is that the relationship between residents of Colonia La Esperanza in Tijuana and their environment is operationalized through their customary use and management of resources, and that these practices are determined by factors that operate at both the macro and micro levels (see figure 9.1).

Figure 9.1. Factors Operating in a Sustainable Environment

**SOCIETY** ↔ **ENVIRONMENT**

↓

**Practices of resource use and management within the household and in the community**

**Micro-level factors**
- Sociocultural features
- Socioeconomic features (income level and access to basic services)
- Sociodemographic features (gender, age, place of birth)

**Macro-level factors**
Physical features
 - Orography

Public policies:
 - Urban development
 - Provision of public services
 - Environmental policies

↓

**Sustainable Environment**

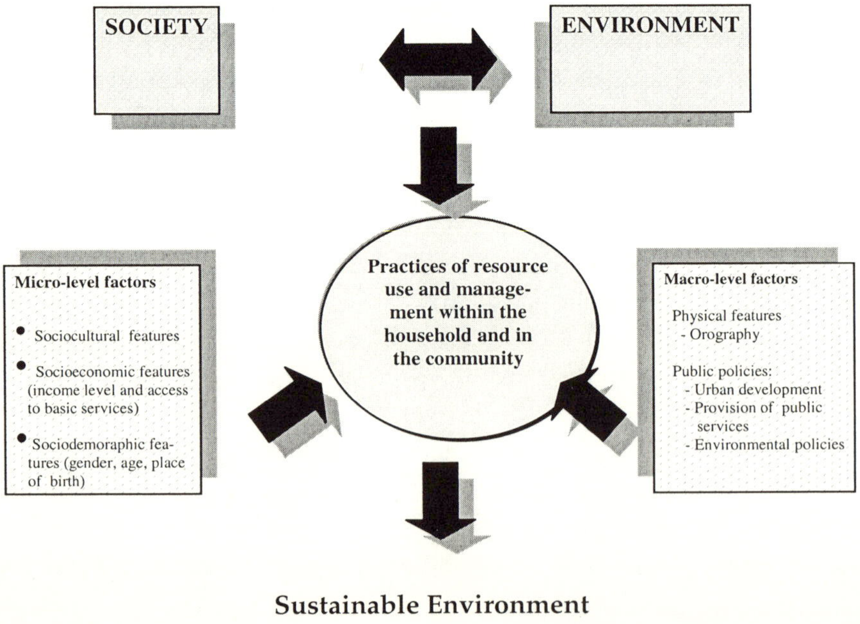

Macro-level factors[1] include physical features, such as the orographical characteristics of the terrain, as well as public policies. Both influence residents' practices of resource use and management. Because macro-level factors are external and beyond the control of the colonia's inhabitants, the present research looks instead at micro-level factors[2]—households' sociocultural, socioeconomic, and sociodemographic features—and how these features determine the customary forms of resource use and management and how they affect the colonia's environmental sustainability.

Households provide an optimal level at which to analyze the relationship between people and environment. According to Martínez and Salles (1996), the household is the space most susceptible to the effects of environmental deterioration; conditions within the home determine the incidence of disease and the quality of life of the household's members.

These authors define the household along two dimensions: a spatial dimension that encompasses the dwelling and its surroundings, and a relational dimension that involves the ways in which household members relate to one another. This conceptualization allows us to determine the impacts of the structural characteristics of a dwelling and its surroundings on the individuals who compose the household and, vice versa, how the household's activities generate effects in the spatial dimension.

In the case of La Esperanza, the spatial dimension of the households' environmental context is affected by a larger encompassing context of a degraded environment, with polluted air, water, and soil and with severe problems of erosion and depleted groundcover (figure 9.2). But it is also subject to the effects of an internal context shaped by the characteristics of the households themselves in terms of their infrastructure and their homes' fitness as dwellings.

Responding to the environmental problems affecting these households involves a series of actions to diminish the impacts of the environmental risk factors that arise from both the external and internal contexts. These include the deteriorating conditions of the homes and their lack of basic public services, and these are the result, in turn, of the poverty that prevails

---

[1] Macro-level factors are structural, large-scale, and generally beyond the control of the people they affect.

[2] Micro-level factors operate on a smaller scale, such as at the household level, and they are more easily controlled.

among colonia residents, which can increase the deleterious impacts of environmental degradation and/or limit the inhabitants' efforts to lessen the impact of environmental degradation on their quality of life.

Figure 9.2. The Spatial Dimension of Households' Environmental Context

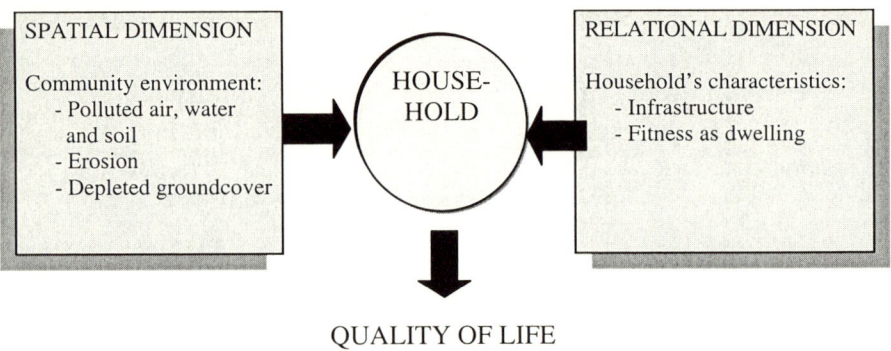

QUALITY OF LIFE

The household serves a mediating function between its members and its external and internal environmental contexts. It is within the household that family members develop actions to improve the quality of their lives and limit the effects of an environment in decline on their health and well-being (Martínez and Salles 1996).

The impacts that a degraded environment generate within households, and within urban communities more generally, include environmental risk factors (pathogens and contaminants in the air, water, soil, and food) and the environmental degradation itself (overexploitation of renewable and nonrenewable resources, generation of large quantities of biodegradable and nonbiodegradable waste) (Mena 1996; Vega 1996; PNUD-CE 1999).

These considerations confirm the need for household-level and community-level studies to identify the practices of resource use and maintenance that local residents employ to reduce environmental risks and to determine how these practices are related to economic factors, such as income level and access to basic services, as well as to sociocultural factors like gender, age, education, and the practices followed in the residents' places of origin. Such an approach would also open a window on the current environmental problematic which reflects in part the environmental management policies of local governments, and it would promote the inclusion of colonia residents, along with local authorities, in the search for solutions. Such collaboration is particularly appropriate given that these typically low-income colonia residents shoulder a disproportionate share of the negative impacts of environmental degradation.

The principal hypothesis of the present study is that the practices of resource use and management and the measures that colonia residents take to mitigate environmental impacts within the household depend on socioeconomic factors such as income level and access to basic services, and to sociocultural factors such as gender, education, age, place of origin, and employment status.

## THE STUDY AREA

The Colonia La Esperanza, in the southern portion of Tijuana, began as an irregular settlement in 1982, at a time when Tijuana was expanding southward into canyons and up hillsides. Because of the area's challenging topography, it was not provided with basic infrastructure for another ten years. The broken topography forces a structural asymmetry in the colonia's appearance, a feature it shares with the majority of irregular settlements that have been established in southern and southeastern Tijuana. It covers about one-half square kilometer, and it includes hillside slopes of over 30 degrees, though some homes in the southern portion of the colonia are on level plots.

These topographic features place the colonia among Tijuana's high-risk areas (Ruiz and Aceves 1998),[3] with houses constructed in a zone inappropriate for urban development. Tijuana's Office of Civil Protection has identified areas within the colonia that show signs of previous flooding and mudslides. Although the colonia has no appropriate spaces for future expansion, families continue to build more irregular housing there, often in riverbeds and on hillsides. These areas are considered federal land and are reserved for use as green belts, one more reason that these types of settlements typically lack basic services.

---

[3] High-risk areas are prone to flooding, landslides, and mudslides. These zones are generally in canyons or riverbeds, or on hillsides.

According to the 1998 property registry, Colonia La Esperanza had a population of 5,386 inhabitants in 1,193 dwellings. The residents' average age was twenty years. Population density within the colonia was 10,049 people per square kilometer, much higher than the Tijuana average of 3,261 per square kilometer. Of the households, 55.4 percent had between 2 and 7 persons per room, which ranks them as overcrowded. The average for the colonia overall was 5.2 people per dwelling.

The colonia is highly representative of the housing problems in Tijuana, particularly with regard to the quality of the materials used in construction. Forty percent of houses in Tijuana have been identified as in poor condition for habitation (COPLADEM 1995). In La Esperanza, most roofs (69.5 percent) are made of wood; only 27.7 percent are concrete. Wood is also the most common material for walls (59.3 percent of the homes); 38.6 percent have walls of brick or concrete block. Most of the homes (75.9 percent) have cement floors, but 16.8 percent have dirt floors, which are often covered with rugs or carpeting to keep down the dust. The quality of materials varies. For example, among the wood used in homes, one finds pallets covered with cloth, scrap lumber, doors, and recycled lumber brought from the United States.

Service provision is a major problem throughout Tijuana, primarily in zones that began as irregular settlements, and the lag in providing basic services to La Esperanza is a direct consequence of its origins as an irregular settlement. According to the 1998 property registry, which compares the provision of potable water, sewerage, and power in the colonias and Tijuana, coverage in La Esperanza ranks low for all three services, which is attributed to the colonia's topography and to its residents' limited economic resources with which to pay for such services (see table 9.1).

Table 9.1. Provision of Services in La Esperanza in Comparative Perspective

| Service | La Esperanza | Neighboring Colonias[a] | Tijuana | Difference |
|---|---|---|---|---|
| Electricity | 94% | 96% | 95% | Minimal |
| Potable Water | 59% | 74% | 74% | Significant |
| Sewerage | 47% | 68% | 71% | Significant |

Source: Tijuana property registry, March 1998.
[a] Neighboring colonias include Sánchez Taboada, Reforma, Infonavit Latinos y Cachanillas, Anexo Sánchez Taboada, and Sirak M. Baloyán.

Trash collection is also linked to the topography in the colonia, where narrow and steep streets prohibit the entry of garbage trucks to certain areas, undermining any regularity in trash collection schedules. Given the intermittent nature of trash collection, many colonia residents resort to practices that are bad for the environment, such as burning their trash or creating ad hoc trash dumps in canyons, streets, and riverbeds, contributing to Tijuana's soil contamination problems.

Most of La Esperanza's roads are secondary ones that cannot handle vehicular traffic, and because they are not paved they are not even fit for foot traffic during the rainy season, further limiting access to and within the colonia. The only areas with paved roads are in the colonia's southern section. And as occurs throughout Tijuana but especially in the areas that are most lacking in basic infrastructure, emissions of particulate matter from unpaved roads, erosion, and open-air trash dumps add to air pollution problems and threaten the health of colonia inhabitants.

In addition to the basic services discussed above, Colonia La Esperanza lacks grocery stores, a central marketplace, recreational facilities, children's playgrounds, day-care centers, health and sports centers, and some 6,000 square meters of recommended green space.

## ENVIRONMENTAL CONCERNS

La Esperanza's environmental problems vary by zone within the colonia (figure 9.3). The classification of areas in the colonia was developed in an earlier study (Gaxiola et al. 2001) which identified management units using a method developed by the Nature Conservancy to define environmental units and analyze their impacts (Andrade, Morales, and Hernández 1999). The methodology involves selecting homogenous sections by vegetation or land use. Given that land use in La Esperanza is predominantly urban, we identified land sections based on the area's homogenous characteristics, described below.

Because the colonia's consolidated urban area is near secondary roads and is situated on land that is suited to urban development, this portion of the colonia has the best infrastructure. Urban services, primarily street paving and sewerage, provide a semblance of ordered and organized urban living. The unconsolidated urban area, however, lacks both infrastructure and urban services. Settlement in areas of harsh terrain and a random urban structure account for most of the land area in the colonia. Hillsides are the most difficult areas on which to build, and these are the zones with the fewest homes. No households have constructed homes in the riverbed.

Figure 9.3. Management Units in La Esperanza

The colonia's dominant environmental problems are: (1) contamination of water sources caused by wastewater flows down canyons and through river channels, as well as seepage from septic tanks and latrines; (2) air contamination due to emissions of particulate matter from unpaved streets, open-air defecation, and erosion as groundcover is removed to make way for residential construction; and (3) soil contamination caused by disposal of trash and wastewater in riverbeds, roadways, and canyons. The most severe challenges occur on the slopes and in the unconsolidated area, where public services are scarcest and where living conditions are far worse than in the consolidated area.

This environmental situation has repercussions on colonia inhabitants by increasing their vulnerability to disease, especially respiratory illnesses; by threatening their physical well-being in poorly constructed dwellings built on slopes and in areas prone to mudslides, landslides, and flooding; and through the deterioration of access routes to and from the colonia.

In an effort to address their environmental problems, along with other challenges stemming from poverty and lack of resources, some households in La Esperanza have undertaken a series of practices for sustainable resource use and management, along with environmental management techniques aimed at reducing the deleterious impacts of environmental degradation on their households. Other households in the colonia have not adopted these sustainable practices.

## SUSTAINABLE PRACTICES FOR RESOURCE USE AND MANAGEMENT

The term "practices for sustainable resource use and management" refers to activities that promote the equitable access to and use of environmental resources (table 9.2). By employing such practices, residents are contributing to sustainable development, avoiding further environmental damage, reducing environmental risks associated with inappropriate resource use, and achieving a fair distribution of environment-related tasks and benefits. By contrast, nonsustainable practices of resource use and management are all activities pursued by households that increase environmental degradation, exhaust natural resources such as water, foster inequitable access to and use of resources, and do not fairly distribute the tasks and benefits associated with resource exploitation, given that women shoulder most of the related responsibilities while all family members reap the benefits.

Table 9.2. Resource Use and Management Practices

| Resource | Sustainable Practice | Nonsustainable Practices |
|---|---|---|
| Water | Using gray water to irrigate plants and wash patios, and for reuse in bathrooms | Disposing of gray water in the street or down hillsides and in canyons |
| Trash, separating by type | Separating trash into organics and inorganics, including food scraps, fruit and vegetable peelings, bottles and cardboard, glass, cans, plastics, and paper | No separating of trash |
| Trash, recycling and reuse | Composting trash for plant fertilizer, using trash as animal feed, and selling or otherwise recycling aluminum and cardboard | Burning plastic and paper, burying glass and cans |
| Trash, disposing of uncollected trash | Transporting uncollected trash to sites with regular trash pickup; depositing trash in designated trash containers | Burning or burying trash, or disposing of it in streets or canyons |

*Source*: Based on results of a survey conducted in Colonia La Esperanza, April 2002.

Classifying households based on the number of sustainable practices followed yields five groups, ranging from households that follow no sustainable practices to those that employ all four (see table 9.3, figure 9.4).

Differences in households' incorporation of sustainable practices can be attributed largely to households' access to services. The lack of services substantially increases a household's vulnerability to environmental risks. This accords with Schteingart's finding in Mexico City that access to basic services was more important than other factors, including income level, in explaining neighborhoods' environmental conditions (Schteingart 1996). Similar studies in urban areas in Chile and Ecuador also found a direct relationship between the lack of urban services and an increase in environmental risks. Households with lower environmental risks were those that took measures to manage their environment (Mena 1996; Vega 1996).

Environment, Poverty, and Gender 185

Table 9.3. Household Distribution by Number of Sustainable Practices Employed

| Number of Sustainable Practices | Number of Households | Percent of Households |
|---|---|---|
| 0 | 56 | 43.1 |
| 1 | 24 | 18.5 |
| 2 | 34 | 26.2 |
| 3 | 15 | 11.5 |
| 4 | 1 | 0.8 |
| Total | 130 | 100 |

*Source*: Based on results of a survey in Colonia La Esperanza, April 2002.

Figure 9.4. Household Distribution by Practices Employed

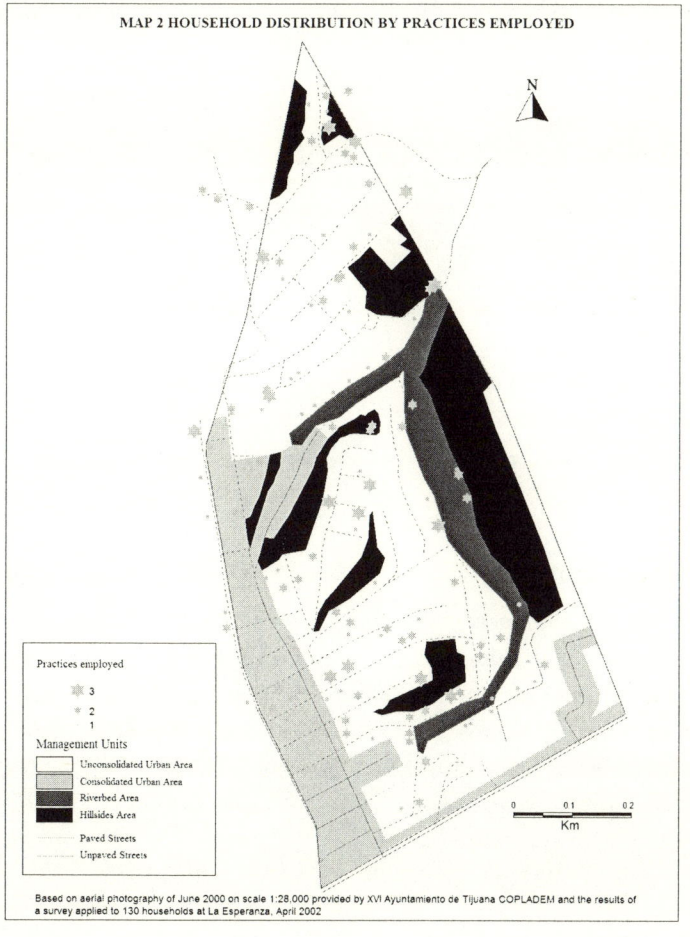

The most common practices in the use and management of environmental resources in La Esperanza involve trash disposal (in 37.6 percent of households) and recycling and the use of recycled materials (33.3 percent of households). These were followed by disposal of uncollected trash (14.9 percent) and disposal of gray water (14.2 percent).

Colonia residents also took additional steps within their households to mitigate deleterious environmental impacts; I refer to those as environmental management practices (see table 9.4). These were not included with the practices of resource use and management because they relate more to elements that influence environmental quality. They are divided into two groups: "good management" when they reduce the impacts of environmental risks within the household, and "poor management" when the household fails to act and, as a result, suffers higher levels of environmental risk.

Table 9.4. Environmental Management Practices in Colonia La Esperanza Households

| Practice | Good Management | Poor Management |
|---|---|---|
| Care of water containers | 88.5% | 11.5% |
| Trash and garbage disposal | 99.1% | 0.9% |
| Dust control around the home | 90.5% | 9.5% |
| Dust control within the home | 97.5% | 2.5% |

*Source:* Survey conducted with 130 La Esperanza households, April 2002.

## PRINCIPAL FINDINGS

A key finding of this research is that the residents of La Esperanza (primarily the women residents) employ a range of practices for sustainable resource use and management. Among the households surveyed, 56.9 percent employ measures that are environmentally beneficial. The principal factors accounting for households' incorporation of sustainable practices and good resource management measures were gender and access to basic services.

## Women as the Primary Actors in Sustainable Resource Use and Management

When analyzing the differential participation of women in resource use and management, it is important to recall the differential access to and use of resources by gender overall. All family members use environmental resources and whatever basic services are available; all generate trash and wastewater. However, those who take measures to care for the environment, who act to mitigate the environmental risks that result from all family members' use of and access to resources, are overwhelmingly women. This fact speaks to the inequitable distribution of responsibilities in the area of environmental management.

In Colonia La Esperanza, the adult woman in the household is responsible for implementing sustainable practices in the use and management of resources, although other family members can contribute in this area as they assist in general household tasks. For example, the mother generally washes the clothes and prepares the meals; the former task can incorporate environmentally beneficial disposal/use of gray water, and the latter, trash separation and recycling. Because older daughters typically help with housecleaning, they also help control dust inside and outside of the house. Fathers and sons tend to be more involved in disposing of trash and handling the water that is purchased or otherwise obtained for household use (see table 9.5). Men's relatively higher contribution to trash removal reflects the fact that they carry bags of household trash with them when they leave for work, depositing these bags in trash bins elsewhere in the neighborhood or at their workplaces. Alternately, for households lacking access to nearby trash collection points, older sons can transport the family's trash bins to the closest pickup point on days that trash collection is scheduled.

The role of women in the use and management of environmental resources falls within their broader socioculturally assigned role in social reproduction, encompassing all of the responsibilities associated with the care of home and family. These responsibilities are independent of whether the woman is economically active, substantially increasing the task load for working women by effectively compelling them to work the equivalent of double or even triple shifts. Scholars have noted that such workloads, which reduce or eliminate time for rest and relaxation, generate health problems among women (Boltvinik 2002; Mena 1996; Rico 1996; Vega 1996).

Table 9.5. The Use of Sustainable Practices in the Home, by Gender

| Sustainable Practice | Women | | Men | | Men and Women | |
|---|---|---|---|---|---|---|
| | Frequency | % | Frequency | % | Frequency | % |
| Reusing water | 29 | 90.6 | 0 | 0.0 | 3 | 9.4 |
| Trash disposal | 33 | 67.4 | 8 | 16.3 | 8 | 16.3 |
| Separating trash | 41 | 87.2 | 3 | 6.4 | 3 | 6.4 |

*Source*: Survey conducted with 130 La Esperanza households, April 2002.

Because measures to address households' environmental risks are being taken by women within the household, they tend to become invisible or devalued, as has happened more generally for tasks involved in social reproduction. Some scholars (see, for example, Jackson 1998a, 1998b; Agarwal 1998) view women as key actors, capable of transforming their surroundings through the steps they take to improve and manage their environment. The present research has confirmed the importance of women's participation in such activities and the outcomes that result. However, the full array of responsibilities should not fall solely to women; efforts must be made to encourage the participation of other family members in order to realize a fairer distribution of these tasks.

A salient feature of the studies in Mexico City and Latin America, and in the present research as well, is that all adopt the household as the unit of analysis and view it as an entity inserted between individuals and society. This perspective increases the visibility of measures for sustainable resource use that otherwise would remain hidden within the private household domain.

## Access to Public Services

Access to services—drinking water, sewerage, street paving, power, and trash collection—affects the number of practices for sustainable resource use and management that a household will employ. That is, the more services to which households have access, the fewer will be the practices for sustainable resource use and management (figure 9.5). And access to public services is determined, in turn, by topographical conditions, by residents' income levels, and by the patterns of land ownership.

Figure 9.5. Sustainable Practices in Households by Access to Public Services

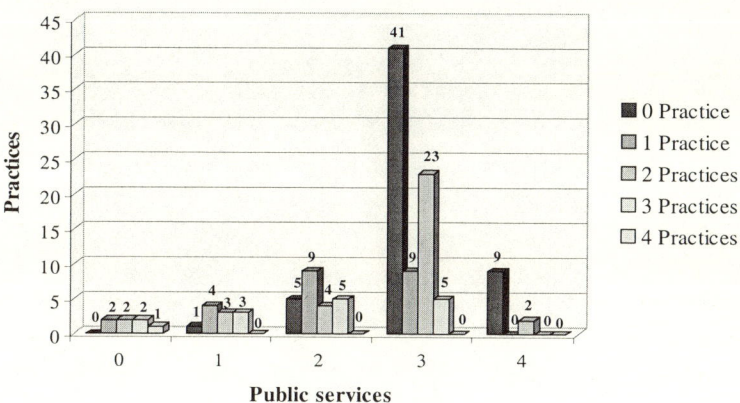

A contingency table test for Chi-squared was run to determine whether the number of services is independent of the sustainable practices employed within households. The test yielded a result of 53.64, above the critical value for $X^2_{(0.05,\ 12)}$, or 26.296. From this, we can discard the null hypothesis and conclude that the number of services does indeed determine the number of sustainable practices that households employ. That is, the two variables are not independent of one another.

The distribution of households by access to public services shows concentrations on hillsides and in the unconsolidated urban area (figures 9.6–9.9). In these zones we find the dwellings that are most precarious in terms of suitability for habitation and most susceptible to environmental threats. Other researchers have reported similar findings elsewhere (Schteingart 1996; Vega 1996; Mena 1996; Martínez and Salles 1996). This suggests that, in addition to environmental circumstances, the relationship between residents and the surrounding environment also reflects the physical condition of the homes, with residents taking steps to decrease environmental risk factors that affect their health. Nevertheless, these same households also display nonsustainable practices, such as burning their trash in order to reduce the health risks of mounds of garbage.

Figure 9.6. Household Distribution by Practices Employed

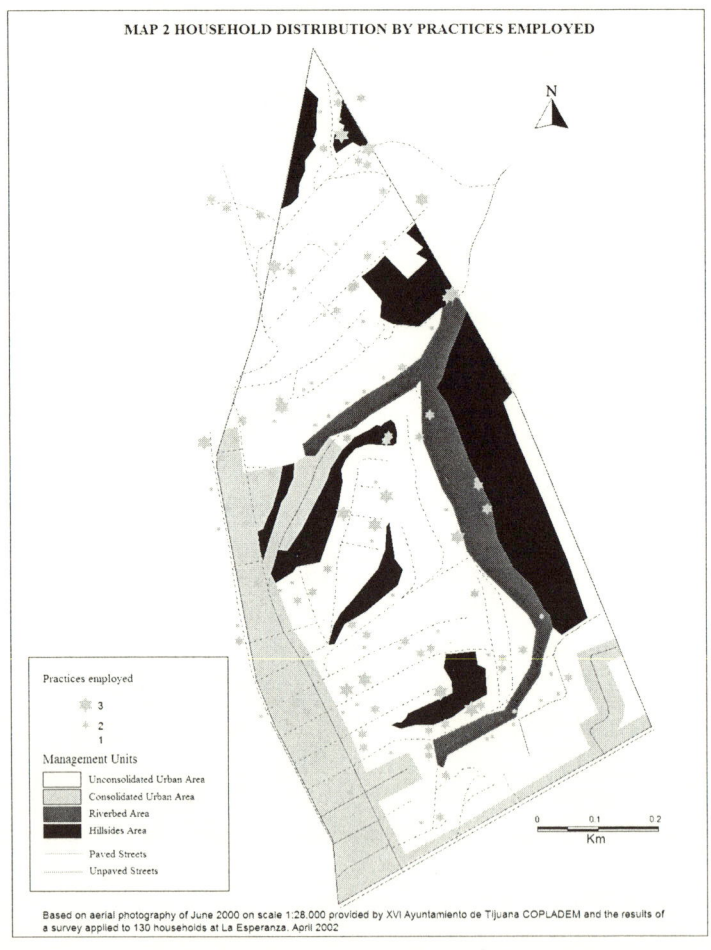

The measures that La Esperanza residents are taking to counteract the effects of a deteriorating environment can be separated into those that are

*Environment, Poverty, and Gender* 191

preventive and those that are mitigative (table 9.6). Preventive measures aim to reduce the incidence of illness within the family, while mitigative measures address the lack of public services and natural resources—or they may derive from a culture of environmental awareness. However, the fact that the latter are spurred by the lack of resources and emerge as a kind of intra-household survival strategy suggests that they are probably not the result of heightened environmental awareness.

Figure 9.7. Household Distribution by Management Practices Employed

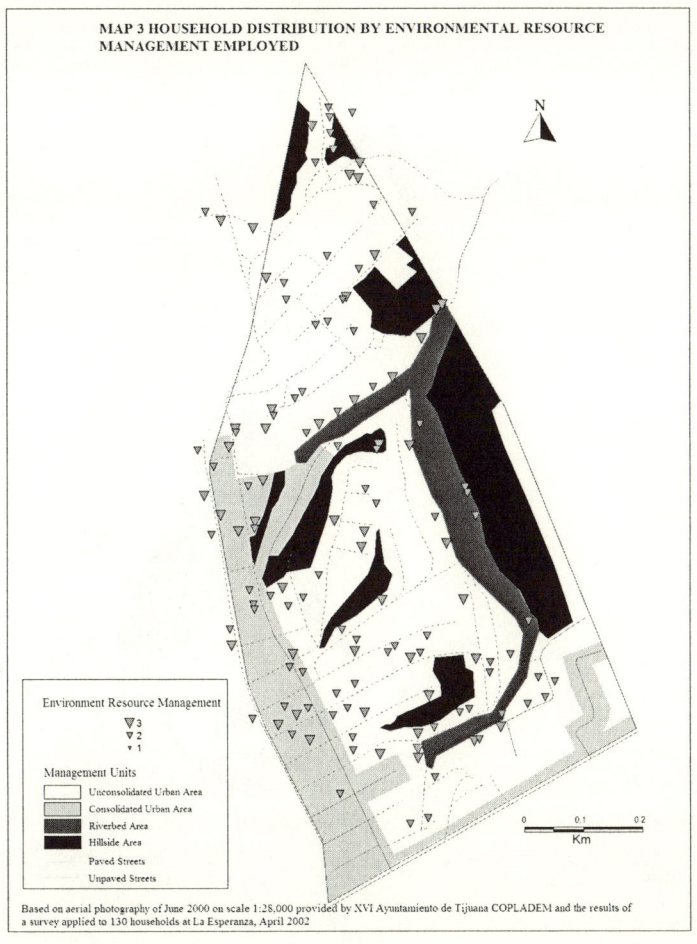

The use of gray water in bathrooms and to irrigate vegetation is considered a preventive mechanism because it is the absence of water lines and sewerage in these homes—attributable to the high costs and access problems involved in providing these services to the neighborhoods—that accounts for the inhabitants' recycling efforts. Thus the recycling is basically an economic strategy to reduce the costs of obtaining water for household use. A heightened environmental awareness internalized in their places of origin may play a secondary role in some households.

Figure 9.8. Household Distribution by Access to Clean Water

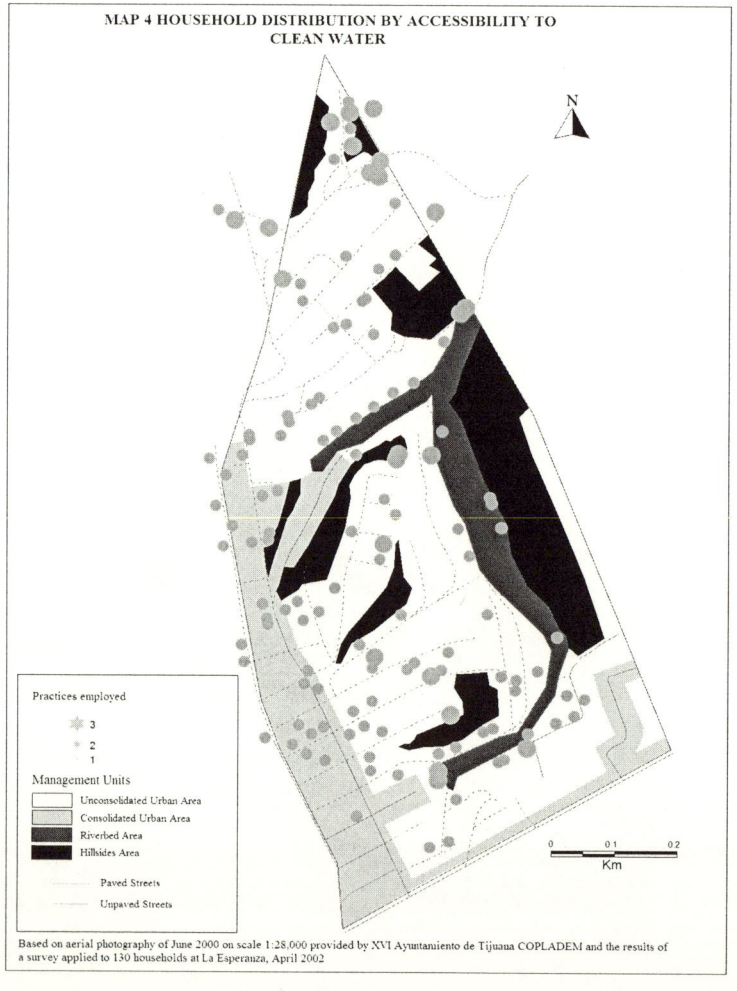

Figure 9.9. Household Distribution by Access to Sewerage Systems

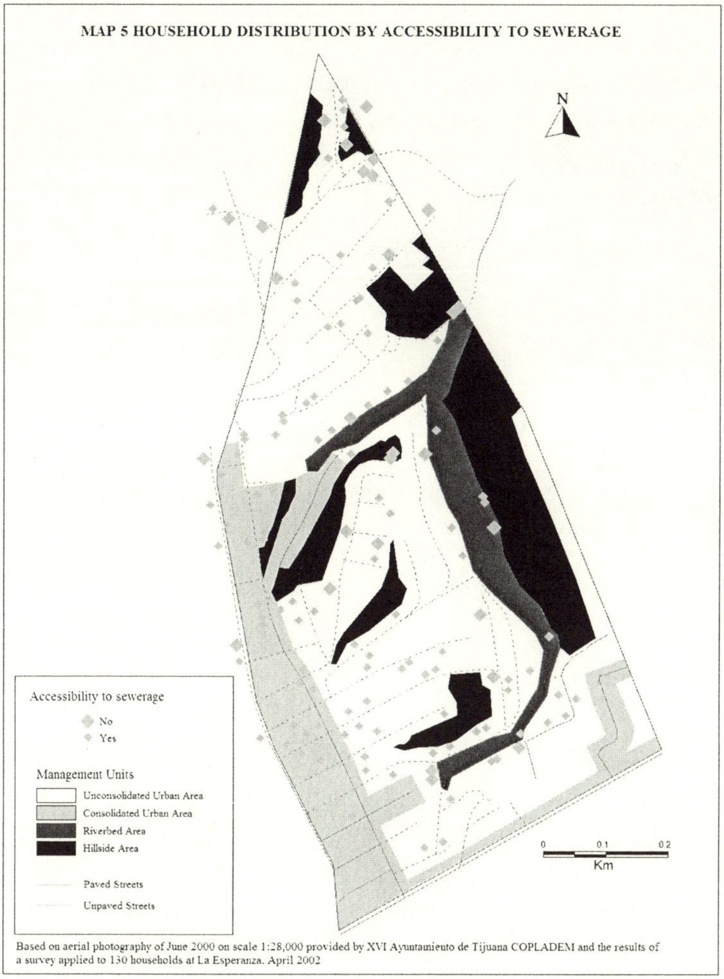

Measures for managing trash are considered to be both preventive and mitigative. Separating trash into organic and inorganic matter is largely mitigative since it responds to the lack of a collection service for solid wastes, but it is also encouraged by a cultural mind-set that stresses recycling. Organic wastes are used as feed for domestic animals and in compost, uses that are common in residents' areas of origin, where they are engrained in local culture. On the other hand, aluminum, cardboard, and paper are recycled for cash, which provides an additional source of household income. When households deal with their trash in a sustainable manner because they lack access to trash collection services, they are engaging in a preventive strategy; their aim is to avoid the spread of disease vectors, such as mosquitoes, that can bring illness to the entire family. By avoiding trash buildups, they are also improving the physical appearance of their homes and neighborhoods.

Table 9.6. Categorization of Resource Use and Management Practices by Type of Action and Incentive

| Resource Used and Managed | Type of Action | Incentive for Action |
|---|---|---|
| Water: reused in bathrooms and used to irrigate plants and clean patios | Mitigative Preventive | Water scarcity<br>Lack of sewerage<br>Economic savings<br>Culture of environmental awareness |
| Trash: separation into organics and inorganics | Mitigative | Lack of collection service<br>Culture of environmental awareness |
| Trash: recycling and reuse of separated material | Mitigative | Culture of environmental awareness<br>Recycling of materials as additional source of household income |
| Trash: disposing of uncollected trash | Preventive | Prevent gastrointestinal diseases<br>Culture of environmental awareness |

Households pursue other preventive measures to safeguard family members' health by reducing the environmental risks that come from contaminated air and water. Since these environmental threats arise due to the lack of street paving, the lack of trash collection, and erosion processes, they are also considered mitigative (see table 9.7).

Table 9.7. Categorization of Environmental Management Practices by Type of Action and Incentive

| Environmental Management Practice | Type of Action | Incentive |
|---|---|---|
| Care of drinking water<br>  Wash containers and keep covered<br>  Add purifying agent | Preventive | Prevent illness in the family |
| Dispose of trash through trash collection services<br>  Store trash in large bags or containers | Preventive | Prevent illness in the family |
| Control dust within the home<br>  Dust, sweep, mop<br>  Close doors and windows | Preventive | Prevent illness in the family<br>Address lack of street paving and improve living conditions in the home |
| Control dust outside the home<br>  Wet down the street and patio | Preventive | Prevent illness in the family<br>Address the lack of street paving and existing sources of erosion |

Another consideration is that the impoverished conditions of households in La Esperanza are reflected in their homes and in the ways that residents relate to their environment. Lacking the economic resources with which to obtain basic services or improve their homes, they must seek other alternatives to resolve the problems arising from their lack of drinking water and their generation of solid waste and gray and wastewater. Some of their strategies—such as burning trash, dumping wastewater into canyons and streambeds—are not sustainable and, in fact, exacerbate existing environmental problems. This sets up a vicious circle in which residents' actions further degrade the environment, and the deteriorating environment increasingly threatens the residents' health and quality of life.

By employing particular resource use and management practices in their homes and combining these with other environmental management measures, the inhabitants of Colonia La Esperanza are responding to the deteriorated conditions of their internal and external environments, conditions that reflect the spatial and relational dimensions of their households. From this we can conclude that environmental sustainability at the household level reflects a range of degrees and shadings that vary depending on access to resources, their distribution and use by household members, and the rationale that first gave rise to the practices of environmental use and management.

**References**

Agarwal, B. 1998. "El debate sobre género y medio ambiente: lecciones de la India." In *Género y medio ambiente*. Cuernavaca, Mexico: Cidhal Centro para Mujeres.

Andrade, M., G. Morales, and A. Hernández. 1999. "Guía de análisis de impactos y sus fuentes en áreas naturales." Mexico: The Nature Conservancy.

Boltvinik, J. 2002. "Pobreza de tiempo," *La Jornada Virtual*, April 19 and 26, www.jornada.unam.com.

Cárdenas, L. A. 1998. "Definición de un marco teórico para comprender el concepto de desarrollo sustentable." Boletín 33. Santiago, Chile: Instituto de la Vivienda, Facultad de Arquitectura y Urbanismo, Universidad de Chile.

COPLADEM (Comité de Planeación para el Desarrollo Municipal). 1995. *Plan Estratégico de Tijuana*. Tijuana, B.C.: XIV Ayuntamiento de Tijuana and COPLADEM.

Gaxiola, R., M. Luna, R. Pérez, P. Rivera, and C. Villeda. 2001. "Plan de manejo ambiental para la Colonia La Esperanza." Tijuana: El Colegio de la Frontera Norte.

Guzmán, S. 2000. "Los dilemas del desarrollo sustentable: limitantes para alcanzar el desarrollo sustentable en Tijuana," *El Bordo* (Universidad Iberoamericana Noroeste), año 3, vol. III, no. 5.

Jackson, C. 1998a. "Análisis de género y ambientalismos." In *Género y medio ambiente*. Cuernavaca, Mexico: Cidhal Centro para Mujeres.

———. 1998b. "Las mujeres y el medio ambiente en el desarrollo: ¿hacer lo que resulte natural?" In *Género y medio ambiente*. Cuernavaca, Mexico: Cidhal Centro para Mujeres.

Martínez, C., and V. Salles. 1996. "La imposibilidad de vivir de otra manera: hogares en contextos de deterioro ambiental." In *Género y ambiente en América Latina*, ed. M. Velázquez. Cuernavaca, Mexico: Centro Regional de Investigaciones Multidisciplinarias, Universidad Nacional Autónoma de México.

Mena, N. 1996. "Interrelaciones entre población, mujer y medio ambiente: metodología de la investigación." In *Género y ambiente en América Latina*, ed. M. Velázquez. Cuernavaca, Mexico: Centro Regional de Investigaciones Multidisciplinarias, Universidad Nacional Autónoma de México.

PNUD-CE (Programa de las Naciones Unidas para el Desarrollo–Comisión Europea). 1999. "Combatir la pobreza y mejorar al mismo tiempo el medio ambiente: opciones óptimas," www.undp.org/seed/pei.

Rico, M. N. 1996. "Género, ambiente y pobreza: un estudio exploratorio en el medio ambiente urbano popular de Santiago de Chile." In *Género y ambiente en América Latina*, ed. M. Velázquez. Cuernavaca, Mexico: Centro Regional de Investigaciones Multidisciplinarias, Universidad Nacional Autónoma de México.

Ruiz, B., and P. Aceves. 1998. "Pobreza y desigualdad social en Tijuana," *El Bordo* (Universidad Iberoamericana Noroeste) 1, no. 2.

Schteingart, M. 1996. "Pobreza, mujer y medio ambiente en la ciudad de México." In *Género y ambiente en América Latina*, ed. M. Velázquez. Cuernavaca, Mexico: Centro Regional de Investigaciones Multidisciplinarias, Universidad Nacional Autónoma de México.

Vega, S. 1996. "Hogares urbanos y medio ambiente: comportamientos ambientales y salud familiar." In *Género y ambiente en América Latina*, ed. M. Velázquez. Cuernavaca, Mexico: Centro Regional de Investigaciones Multidisciplinarias, Universidad Nacional Autónoma de México.

PART IV

Civil Society in Action in the Border Region

# 10
## Acquiring Knowledge and Improving Environmental Policy: A Binational Agency for Civic Organizations

BASILIO VERDUZCO CHÁVEZ

This chapter addresses the issue of knowledge acquisition among civic organizations, a topic that has gained relevance in recent years as a core element in decision making in both the public and private arenas (Klabbers 2000; Busemberg 2001; Beech et al. 2002; Popper and Lipshitz 2002). Borrowing elements from organization theory and political science, I analyze prevailing perspectives on the development of a binational agenda among organizations supporting better regional environmental policies. I explore how events such as the Johannesburg Summit affect civic organizations' knowledge acquisition[1] and, in particular, whether they have an impact on the construction of a binational agenda.

Three primary factors can influence how a society—or a region, such as the border region—makes the link between knowledge acquisition and improving environmental policy: (1) the general characteristics of civic organizations and their previous mobilization experience; (2) the level of consensus within organizations about the importance of using knowledge to improve public policy; and (3) the organizations' capacity to overcome structural problems and take advantage of the opportunities associated with changing contexts or focal events.

---

Translation by Sandra del Castillo.

[1] Organizations' acquisition of knowledge and organizational learning are used interchangeably in this essay. However, the two can be used to refer to distinct processes. For example, knowledge acquisition can be considered part of broader and more complex processes of organizational learning.

Some scholars argue that events or outcomes that affect broad sectors of society can shape learning processes at both individual and organizational levels (Strange and Leung 1999; Garrett 2001). Following this perspective, focal events attract public attention and demonstrate the need to introduce changes in action strategies and in the network of relations among actors who participate in the public debate (Busemberg 2001). Because of the way it views the relationship between actors and structure, this perspective lends itself to a study of how diverse organizations participate in improving environmental policy in the border region and what impact a particular event might have.

This essay, whose objective is to explore the relationship between events and organizational learning, is divided into four sections. The first presents an analysis of the relationship between acquiring knowledge and improving environmental policy. The second reviews the major recommendations accorded at Johannesburg and their implications for organizational learning among civic groups on the border. The third section discusses the experiences of civic organizations on the border and the ways in which these experiences stimulate learning processes throughout the region. And the fourth offers some conclusions about the options available to civic organizations for advancing a binational agenda designed to improve their knowledge acquisition and enhance their involvement in the design and implementation of environmental policies.

## KNOWLEDGE ACQUISITION AND ENVIRONMENTAL POLICY

The idea that knowledge can be brought to bear to improve public policy is deeply rooted in society, and it has given rise to broad planning currents, each with its own perspective.[2] Of course, this idea has not been exempt from criticism for its marked modernizing bias, which assumes the supremacy of a rationalism based on "expert knowledge" and its disdain for the alternative or popular knowledge held within communities.[3] The de-

---

[2] For example, see Friedmann 1987 on the rise of four major schools of thought on planning.

[3] Notable here is the work of Scott (1998), who illustrates how science has produced innumerable failures which can only be explained by the excessive emphasis placed on the knowledge of experts as the basis for achieving order and development.

bate surrounding the use of knowledge as a means of improving public policy is particularly relevant given the existing inequality in access to knowledge and the increasing complexity of the problems to be addressed by decision makers.

Some currents within this debate have suggested that the question is not whether the knowledge used in policy design comes from experts or from the community at large, but rather how the information has been selected and how it has been processed by organizations within the society. Civic organizations have a key role to play in these activities by linking local communities and scientific institutions (Shrum 2000).

According to organization theory and a good deal of political science theory, there is a multitude of circumstances than can either favor or hinder the acquisition of knowledge. Some of the most studied are: organizations' characteristics and prior mobilization experience, consensus about the need to use knowledge to improve public policy, organizational capacity to take advantage of opportunities, involvement in various institutional contexts, and the building of organizational networks (Schott 2001). The issue at the heart of network building has been to determine what kinds of opportunities open the most space for improving organizational learning and how these opportunities have been exploited by the organizations or by individuals within a society. One of the most provocative proposals to be examined in this line of research is that focal events influence the processes of organizational learning, and this, in turn, enables organizations to alter the way that they are able to influence the public policy agenda.

In this regard, organizational learning is of primary importance because of organizations' capacity to generate, coordinate, and maintain complex techno-scientific systems, as well as their impact on how complex information is transmitted, stored, and utilized (Vaughan 1999). Organizational learning is particularly important for public policy design because of the limited capacity of individuals to influence policy design in an informed manner. Some key points in support of this argument are the following:

- First, some events focus policy and public attention on a specific issue. These focal events can serve as symbols that elevate the issue to governmental agendas and provide the impetus for policy reforms and new institutional arrangements that can shape future decision making in a specific policy sphere.

- Second, the processes of knowledge acquisition are determined by institutional arrangements in which the learning occurs, and these institutional arrangements explain why and how individuals learn. Organizations help create analysis teams that are accepted by social groups, and they propose solutions that align with the interests of the groups they represent. The role of organizations becomes crucial when dealing with complex issues. This is the case because individuals are limited in their capacity to apply, or even access, the full range of relevant information, especially when the issue in question requires ongoing monitoring to determine its evolution or when it involves an international border, where clearly differentiated traditions of information generation and dissemination prevail. The organizational role becomes critical when individuals are unable to comprehend all of the information that is relevant for a particular decision; in this case, their ability to influence the decision-making process is shaped through a learning process.

- Third, in light of the preceding points, civic organizations—and cooperative efforts between organizations—can facilitate learning among individuals by functioning as information processors and as generators of causal stories that use available information to contextualize issues. In so doing, they reduce the exclusion that has been noted when policy design is predicated on an intensive use of technical knowledge (Sosa Elízaga 2002).

- Fourth, advances achieved regionally and nationally in the area of organized participation in environmental policy design confirm that network building is a viable option for supporting knowledge acquisition processes and for carrying newly acquired knowledge into the policy-making arena. Experts in organization theory have highlighted the role of "communities of practice" (Ayas and Zeniuk 2001; Tsoukas 2002; Swan, Scarbrough, and Robertson 2002). These "communities" enable their members to share and exchange preferences, inclinations, and perspectives, thereby adding new experiences and knowledge—and, hence, modes of effective action—to their repertoires.

In sum, we can confirm that learning remains central to improving public policy and that organizations play a very important role in facilitating the acquisition of knowledge and in applying it toward the goal of bettering environmental policy.

What is needed, however, is empirical confirmation of the assertion that focal events are catalysts in this process. Observers of this phenomenon do not hesitate to affirm that this relationship does indeed exist, and they point to supporting evidence. For example, they note that spectacular successes and natural or technological disasters, as well as radical changes in the rules governing social, economic, or political relations, cause organizations to reexamine their store of knowledge and to revise their internal action strategies and their relationships with other organizations working on the same issues. Another example that supports the solidity of our assertion is the U.S. government's creation of the Department of Homeland Security—in record time and without major opposition from any interest group—following the terrorist attacks of September 11, 2001.

From the various studies in this area, we can deduce that the impact of focal events on learning processes is determined by both the characteristics of the event and the public policy context in which we detect empirical evidence of change. Despite the apparent strength of the connection between focal events and the acquisition of knowledge, we are lacking empirical studies that allow us to observe the differentiation processes of this relationship in detail.

After studying a number of organizations that were obliged to expand their knowledge base in order to formulate alternative environmental policy proposals within their area of influence, I find the following hypothesis increasingly convincing: not only is there a marked differentiation among the impacts that a focal event engenders, but institutional contexts play an important role in explaining the advances that result. In the following section, I analyze certain features of the Johannesburg Summit that make it an interesting case for analysis of the impacts on learning processes of regional civic organizations.

## LEARNING FROM JOHANNESBURG

The achievements of the Johannesburg Summit on Sustainable Development as a focal event and the summit's impacts on the processes of knowledge acquisition and environmental policy design in the Mexico-U.S. border region are not immediately apparent. On the one hand, the summit can be classified as a focal event because it displays the following characteristics:

- Various organizations from around the world participated in its preparation.
- It addresses themes of public interest about which there is a great deal of uncertainty.
- The preparation of summit documents required regional-level analyses, which awakened the interest of a multitude of actors.
- It encouraged debate on the implications of development and economic growth for the well-being and sustainability of various regions of the planet.
- It helped promote convergence about the key topics in environmental policy.

Nevertheless, in order to understand the summit's full impacts, we must keep in mind the preexisting experiences and structures of regional and worldwide environmental organizations and the ways in which they have managed the border-area institutional context. Above all, it is crucial to consider the contributions of binational networks to the definition of environmental problems on the border. These transnational networks have been shown to play a significant role in constructing identity representations for local inhabitants and the ideas that are linked to these identities (Mato 2000).

In recent decades, the debates emerging at the regional level about topics of worldwide interest have followed two notably different paths. The first is the path of regional-level counterparts of the large environmental organizations that operate internationally. These regional chapters typically work to implement actions in their own area that are consistent with the key agenda themes of the parent organization, and they can serve as interlocutors in their region when issues under debate fall within these agenda themes or when regional-level discussions involve an issue that is of more general interest for the organization. For organizations of this type, world summits offer the opportunity to expand the resources dedicated to analyzing a small number of problems or to increase public awareness of a specific issue.

A second way that global environmental policy is grounded at the regional level is through local or regional organizations. These organizations typically focus on problems that are regional in nature, and they generally originate in response to projects, programs, or trends present in the regional context. For organizations on this path to addressing environmental issues, world meetings like the Johannesburg Summit have relevance because the problems these groups confront are tied to international agreements accorded between countries.

Given the existence of these two trajectories, it is to be expected that events such as the Johannesburg Summit will have differential impacts on the learning processes of both kinds of organization. This explains why the activism of the two types of organization before, during, and after the summit differed so notably. While organizations operating at the national or global level established a strong presence in Johannesburg and offered discussion points for the meeting's agenda, regional organizations displayed little enthusiasm for achieving a similar level of participation.

This suggests that although the World Summit for Sustainable Development is a key event, one that broadens opportunities for debating ways to improve environmental policy, there are limits on its capacity to influence organizational learning at the regional level. My hypothesis is that the impacts of Johannesburg within the Mexico-U.S. border region are constrained by a series of factors, including the following:

- Events like the Johannesburg Summit do not solve some basic problems noted in the learning processes of civic organizations, such as the asymmetry in resources and capacity between these groups and other public and private organizations that also participate in policy making.

- Such events foment an unequal convergence of interests which becomes visible at the regional level in organizational strategies to facilitate selection processes (identification of priority issues to be addressed) and in the emergence of actors who are crucial to the consensus-building process on which environmental policy depends (unequal opportunities for leadership creation).

Although there is insufficient evidence to put this hypothesis to the test, my observations of organizational experiences in the region suggest that this is the direction in which the summit's impacts lie.

First, if one reviews the declarations appearing in the media or aired in open forums, it becomes clear that the summit's achievements did not generate a great deal of enthusiasm among regional civic organizations. At the very least, we can note the huge gap between the discourse surrounding the summit and the heated debates that accompanied negotiations of the North American Free Trade Agreement (NAFTA), which spurred an extensive mobilization of civil society and the formation of networks to address key points of the trade agreement.

The gap between the global and the regional or local cannot be ignored, and it was acknowledged to a certain degree in Johannesburg. In reviewing some key points in the summit's Plan of Implementation, we see substantial interest in bringing the main global actors closer together with the regional or local actors who experience local environmental problems firsthand. These agenda points outline a scenario in which civic organizations intensify their efforts to join the global with the local.

The implementation plan that emerged from the Johannesburg Summit sketches out a task for civil society: the co-production of knowledge and information. Moreover, civil society groups are encouraged to channel popular experience and autochthonous knowledge as a complement to the technical analyses required in the formulation of environmental policy (WSSD 2002). A few activities that the Plan of Implementation suggests be undertaken by civil society are particularly notable:

- Improve technology transfer at the regional and bilateral levels, especially through actions aimed at enhancing interaction and collaboration among stakeholders and through the development and strengthening of networks and the establishment of consortiums to develop technologies and knowledge and to utilize those already present in the public domain.

- Create more capacity in the areas of science and technology with actions directed at promoting collaboration and partnerships among various actors, including nongovernmental organizations (NGOs) and networks of academics and scientists.

- Improve policy and decision making via collaboration among people working in the natural and social sciences, and between scientists and decision makers. This would include efforts to increase the application of scientific knowledge and the beneficial use of local popular knowledge, to rely increasingly on comprehensive evaluations, to sustain support for international scientific assessments, and to improve scientific and technological policies.

- Establish linkages between scientists and institutional actors, and support the involvement of councils of scientists in decision making. Promote information-based decisions and reaffirm the precautionary principle.
- Establish regular channels of communication between decision makers and scientists, and strengthen network formation.
- Explore issues of global interest through open workshops. Support NGO involvement in establishing transparent information systems, developing clear and fair procedures for including community representatives, collaborating in the design and introduction of educational and capacity-building programs for decision making, and implementing educational practices that emphasize sustainable development.

The preceding points suggest that, although the Johannesburg Summit can influence organizational learning at the level of regions, for civic organizations to gain a voice in improving environmental policy, they must follow a path of cooperation, seeking partnerships and promoting a division of tasks.

Given this agenda, it merits examining the extent to which prior experiences on the border can empower organizations to take advantage of the opportunities that arise out of events such as the Johannesburg Summit.

## CIVIC MOBILIZATION ON THE BORDER: KNOWLEDGE AND INFLUENCE

Civil society's prior mobilization experience around environmental issues constitutes a significant factor to consider in analyses of how knowledge acquisition processes unfold in a region and the resulting impacts on improving environmental policy—or, as in the present case, in an analysis of the impacts of focal events like the Johannesburg Summit on this process. A key function of civic organizations is to frame the issues and create alternative discourses that spur citizens to take action in a particular direction (Laraña 2001).

In many ways, the prior experiences of civic organizations in the border region give little cause for optimism in terms of any positive impacts to be expected from the Johannesburg Summit. Among the aspects that could limit any gains are the following:

- A serious problem exists on the border with regard to capacity building and strengthening among civic organizations that would allow them to improve their processes of knowledge acquisition and insert the acquired knowledge into the decision-making process. Evidence of this fact is found in these organizations' poor technical capacity and—because they are unable to conduct their own research—their need to rely on secondary sources. For example, a study of NGOs in Tijuana found that only 13 percent of them premise their activities on scientific findings; 7 percent of these rely on results of research that they themselves conduct, and 6 percent use data from studies carried out by other institutions (Ruiz Vargas 2002).

- There is no broad consensus regarding the value of scholarship in improving environmental policy. This is a divisive point in the environmental community, and traces of the questioning of science's value can even be found among the organizations that are the strongest proponents of the benefits that science and technology can offer for addressing environmental degradation. In my study of hundreds of environmental conflicts along the entire length of the Mexico-U.S. border, I found substantial evidence of such a perspective. On the one hand, I found that opposition to polluting industries was based on perceptions that had little scientific support. On the other hand, although the more experienced organizations made good use of technical information in framing environmental problems, the vast majority of small organizations were less committed to acquiring new information and made do with small "information points" that emerged in debates. Some of my informants even suggested that accumulating supporting evidence was of little value, given that these groups had no means of analyzing any data they collected.

- Within the spaces that exist for citizen participation, groups generally do not reach the point of implementing program objectives. The mechanisms that support the public's input of ideas and suggestions are limited to sessions designated ex profeso, annual meetings of working groups, or conferences open to the public.

- NGO representatives and members of the general public can comment during the annual meetings, but there are no resources earmarked for knowledge acquisition. This problem—the lack of financial resources that would enable civic organizations to undertake their own research on environmental problems or to underwrite independent research conducted by experts—affects these venues to a greater or lesser degree.

- The overwhelming majority of civic organizations have a short life cycle. Many of the mobilization efforts seen in civil society focus on specific events or circumstances, and they tend to fade away once there has been some resolution on that respective issue that is accepted by the community. Estimates suggest that only a fifth of civic organizations continue in existence for more than fifteen years.

- Multilateral cooperation offers a number of advantages, though cooperative undertakings have been limited thus far. There are, nevertheless, some successful examples, such as the Paso del Norte Air Quality Task Force and cross-border collaboration to halt the construction of projects that pose a threat to the environment. But cooperation in the production and acquisition of knowledge is not among the top priorities of such binational collaboration efforts.

On the other hand, one must recognize that the border region has witnessed substantial citizen mobilization and that several organizations active in this area have clearly demonstrated their capacity to exploit the information base extensively in the interest of producing better environmental policy. In particular, some of these groups, including organizations active in environmental health issues, have adopted the optimal strategy of not relying solely on purely technical reports authored by experts; they have taken the extra step of developing their own information sources and participatory strategies in an effort to upgrade their learning processes. It is this combination of experiences that will define civic organizations' capacity and determine which issues are included on the binational agenda.

## LEARNING AND ENVIRONMENTAL POLICY: TOWARD A BINATIONAL AGENDA

The preceding discussion confirms that building a knowledge base is a systematic task that requires resources and collaboration. And the environmental behaviors of the actors involved in such collaborations will be subject to the impacts of their own social contexts (Olli, Grendstad, and Wollebaek 2001). That is, the social context creates spaces that condition how actors relate to one another as they work to support or defend a given environmental cause.

Given the mobilization trajectory that exists in the border region, efforts to construct a binational agenda whose objective is to improve environmental policies by improving the learning processes of civic organizations should focus on building strength on two fronts. The first is to build consensus on the need to draw on existing knowledge in the process of developing better environmental policy. The second is to reach agreement on the optimal mechanisms for acquiring knowledge and employing it to influence public policy making. Adopting this perspective, we can identify the following as the salient actions for advancing the binational agenda:

- Develop mechanisms that enable cooperation despite the problems of asymmetry between organizations. This does not mean homogenizing their capacities, but rather strengthening the division of labor and forming specialized teams to address specific issues. These work teams can specialize both by region and by topic.

- Encourage dialogue about the validity and relevance of incorporating scientific findings when developing regional environmental policies. Notable here is the fact that, despite the organizations' varying degrees of willingness to adopt scientific evidence when addressing environmental problems, there has been no open debate on this variability, leading some organizational members to assume that all of their counterparts hold the same position.

- Design cooperative strategies that empower environmental groups to increase the resources they devote to building a knowledge base and ensure that they make optimal use of existing information resources.

- Improve communication channels on key aspects of environmental policy (risk, vulnerability) where problems are proliferating.

- Increase the participation of representatives from communities and civic organizations in the scientific and technical committees that meet to study regional environmental problems.

Despite the interest that focal events such as the Johannesburg Summit awaken among all organizations involved in the pursuit of better environmental policy at both the regional and global levels, it is nevertheless clear that much remains to be learned about such events' implications for organizational learning. This gap can only be lessened through empirical studies that demonstrate how learning occurs within organizations and the differences that exist in this process across organizations. And further, especially for areas like the Mexico-U.S. border region, such studies must undertake detailed analyses of international cooperative efforts in order to understand how institutional contexts will shape the regional impacts of these focal events.

**References**

Ayas, Karen, and Nick Zeniuk. 2001. "Project-based Learning: Building Communities of Reflective Practitioners," *Management Learning* 32, no. 1: 61–76.

Beech, Nic, Robert MacIntosh, Donald MacLean, Jill Shepherd, and John Stokes. 2002. "Exploring Constraints on Developing Knowledge on the Need for Conflict," *Management Learning* 33, no. 4: 459–75.

Busemberg, George J. 2001. "Learning in Organizations and Public Policy," *Journal of Public Policy* 21, no. 2: 173–89.

Friedmann, John. 1987. *Planning in the Public Domain: From Knowledge to Action.* Princeton, N.J.: Princeton University Press.

Garrett, Terence M. 2001. "The Waco, Texas, ATF raid and Challenger Launch Decision: Management, Judgment, and the Knowledge Analytic," *American Review of Public Administration* 31, no. 1: 66–86.

Klabbers, Jan H. G. 2000. "Learning as Acquisition and Learning as Interaction," *Simulation & Gaming* 31, no. 3: 380–406.

Laraña, Enrique, 2001. "Reflexivity, Risk and Collective Action over Waste Management: A Constructive Proposal," *Current Sociology* 49, no. 1: 23–48.

Mato, Daniel. 2000. "Transnational Networking and the Social Production of Representations of Identities by Indigenous Peoples' Organizations of Latin America," *International Sociology* 15, no. 2: 343–60.

Olli, Eero, Gunnar Grendstad, and Dag Wollebaek. 2001. "Correlates of Environmental Behaviors: Bringing Back Social Context," *Environment and Behavior* 33, no. 2: 181–208.

Popper, Micha, and Raanan Lipshitz. 2002. "Organizational Learning Mechanisms, Culture, and Feasibility," *Management Learning* 31, no. 2: 181–96.

Ruiz Vargas, Benedicto. 2002. "Las ONG en Tijuana: un perfil general," http://www.tij.uia.mx/elbordo/vol04/bordo4_ong_2a.html, accessed November 2002.

Schott, Thomas. 2001. "Knowledge Networks: Global Webs of Knowledge Education, Science, and Technology," *American Behavioral Scientist* 44, no. 10: 1740–51.

Scott, James C. 1998. *Seeing Like a State: How Certain Schemes to Improve the Human Condition Have Failed*. New Haven, Conn.: Yale University Press.

Shrum, Wesley. 2000. "Science and Story in Development: The Emergence of Non-Governmental Organizations in Agricultural Research," *Social Studies of Science* 30, no. 1: 95–124.

Sosa Elízaga, Raquel. 2002. "Social Exclusion and Knowledge," *Current Sociology* 50, no. 1: 89–98.

Strange, Jeffrey J., and Cynthia C. Leung. 1999. "How Anecdotal Accounts in News and in Fiction Can Influence Judgments of a Social Problem's Urgency, Causes, and Cures," *Personality and Social Psychology Bulletin* 25, no. 4: 436–49.

Swan, Jacky, Harry Scarbrough, and Maxine Robertson. 2002. "The Construction of 'Communities of Practice' in the Management of Innovation," *Management Learning* 33, no. 4: 477–96.

Tsoukas, Haridimos. 2002. "Knowledge-based Perspectives on Organizations: Situated Knowledge, Novelty, and Communities of Practice," *Management Learning* 33, no. 4: 419–26.

Vaughan, Diane. 1999. "The Role of the Organization in the Production of Techno-Scientific Knowledge," *Social Studies of Science* 29, no. 6: 913–43.

WSSD (World Summit on Sustainable Development). 2002. "World Summit on Sustainable Development Plan of Implementation," http://www.johannesburgsummit.org/html/documents/summit_docs/2309_planfinal.htm, accessed November 2002.

# 11

## Environmental Justice and Border Tribes: The Case of San Diego County

MICHAEL CONNOLLY MISKWISH

There are approximately twenty-five U.S. Indian tribes with reservations in the U.S.-Mexico border area.[1] About seventeen of these are located in San Diego County, California. Both because of their unique status as Indian tribes and as a result of their proximity to the border, these communities face a multitude of geopolitical challenges. Many of these challenges are based on tribes' history as both adversaries and allies to the Spanish, Mexican, and American nations. Other bases for these challenges include the political and legal framework applicable to Indian tribes in the United States and conflicts over land and resources that continue between tribal and non-Indian communities. Added to these is the existence of the border itself, which cleaved communities that preexisted it and serves to restrict access to community and traditional territory.

On the one hand, this has resulted in disparate impacts on tribal environmental, natural, and cultural resources; on the other hand, the situation

---

The author would like to thank Marta J. Burg, J.D. for her valuable comments and review of legal content, and Dr. Jay Jones for his review and edits related to the references to hydrogeology.

[1] "Reservation" refers to a defined area of land initially held by the U.S. government for the use and benefit of a tribe. Within the boundaries of many reservations today, different types of landholdings may be found, including land held by the United States for a tribe (tribal trust land); land held by the United States for individual Indians and/or their heirs (allotments); and non-Indian land owned in fee. For further discussion, see the section dealing with the history of reservations.

has produced a series of social, economic, and environmental constraints to prosperity for tribal communities. It is only recently that some of the roadblocks to both environmental and natural/cultural resource protection and prosperity have been overcome through legislation and litigation. However, tribes are still unfairly subjected to double standards, resulting in inequitable environmental and cultural harms and in financial or jurisdictional concessions to state or local demands that hinder tribal economic development.

The tribes in the border area, and in San Diego County in particular, face a variety of environmental challenges. Some—such as air and water pollution, lack of sanitation facilities, and threats from hazardous and solid waste transportation and illegal disposal—are problems the tribes share with non-Indian border communities. Others—such as lack of access to culturally necessary sacred sites and natural resources, either because of their location on the other side of the border or due to environmental degradation—are arguably unique tribal environmental challenges.

At the same time, the tribes suffer inequities in their efforts to generate revenue for the betterment of their people. For instance, tribes are seldom recognized for their contributions to the county infrastructure and tax base. Instead, perceived fiscal impacts of tribal operations and development are fodder for political demagoguery and false assertions. Tribes are held to a higher standard of environmental protection for on-reservation development than was imposed upon previous off-reservation development—development that has already caused significant environmental impacts in the border area in general and on tribal communities in particular. There is increasing pressure on tribal communities to maintain what is sometimes the last clean environment, although the tribes have not contributed to the pollution or natural resource impacts that now require conservation efforts, open space reserves, or market trading to minimize further harms.

Environmental justice associated with the dual challenges of tribal environmental and natural resource protection and sustainable tribal economic development cannot be addressed without a comprehensive look at the overarching sources of conflict and inequity. The most pronounced of these are discussed in this chapter.

## HISTORY

To understand the current conditions of native nations in San Diego County, one must look to the early history of the area; the conditions of entry by the Indian people of what is today San Diego County into the United States; and the subsequent development of the tribal relationship with various other levels of government in the United States.

### Indian Control of San Diego County prior to the Mexican-American War

Indigenous Indian tribes of San Diego County include the Kumeyaay (Diegueño), Luiseño, Cupa, and Cahuilla.[2] There are currently twelve bands of Kumeyaay Indians living on different reservations in the county; three Luiseño reservations, one Cupa and Luiseño reservation, and one Cahuilla reservation.[3] Because the Kumeyaay inhabit the areas of San Diego County that are closest to the border (see figures 11.1 and 11.2), this discussion focuses on their history.

The Kumeyaay are known to have inhabited what is now San Diego County for at least three thousand years and most likely merged with pre-existing cultures going back over ten thousand years. Some estimates place approximately twenty thousand Kumeyaay in the area before the arrival of Europeans. The Kumeyaay were seasonal hunters and gatherers organized into clans called "Sh'mull," which governed territories from year-round coastal villages to seasonal camps in the mountains and desert. Each self-governing band, which may have included from two hundred to a thousand members, would have had access to all resources in its territory. The Kumeyaay are known to have been accomplished horticulturists who grew grains, grasses, beans, squash, perennials, shrubs, oaks, cactus, and, in the historic period, wheat and corn. They used their knowledge of astronomy to determine when to plant and harvest their crops.

---

[2] For general information regarding the history of these and other tribes, see Smithsonian 1978–; Kroeber 1976. Unless otherwise stated, source materials for the balance of this History section include the following: Shipek 1987; Carrico 1987; and http://kumeyaay.com/history.

[3] Several additional reservations in Riverside County, California, are home to other bands of Cahuilla and Luiseño.

Figure 11.1. Tribal Lands in the San Diego Region

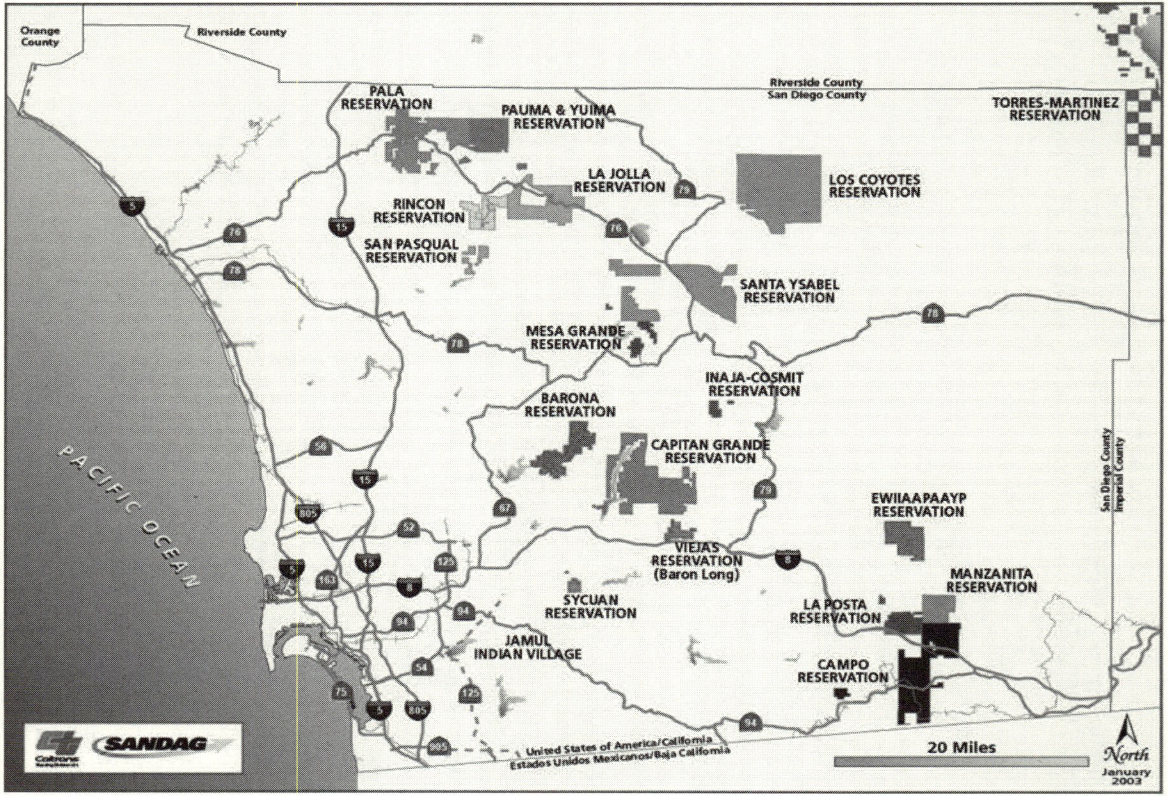

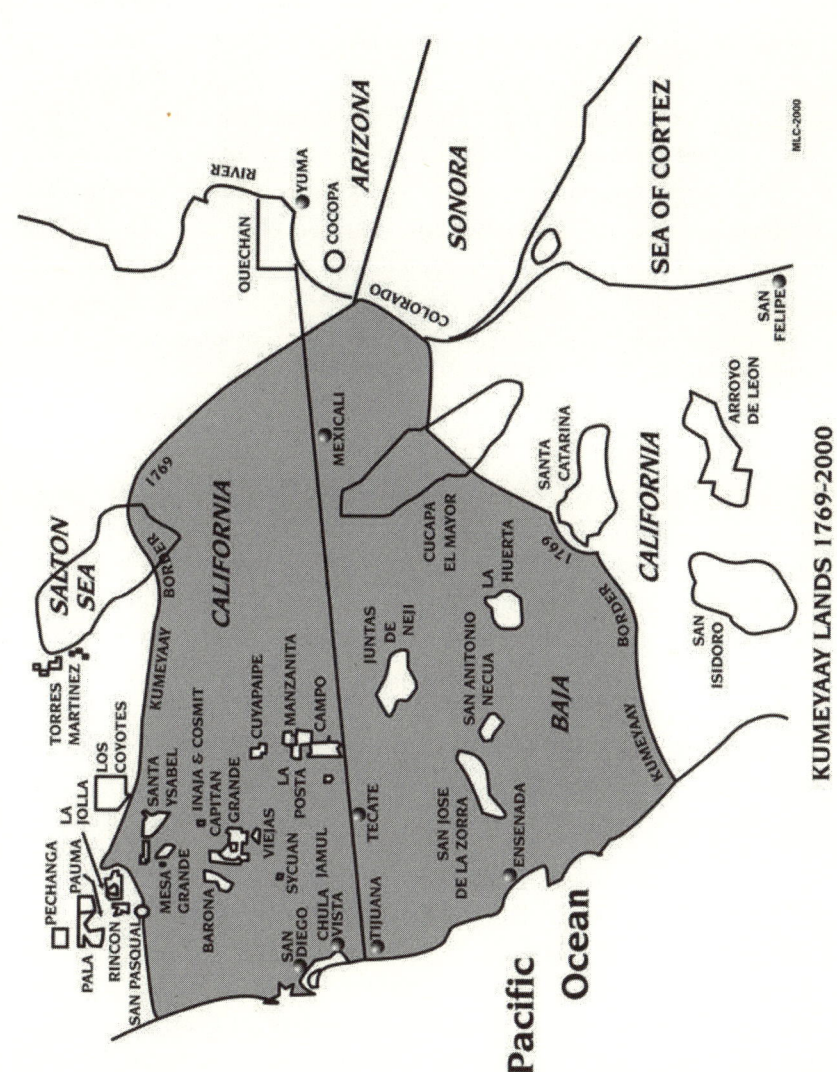

Figure 11.2. Kumeyaay Lands, 1769-2000

From the onset of the Spanish period, which began with the establishment in 1769 of the first mission in Alta California, European influence in the territory of the Kumeyaay people had a drastic effect on traditional life. The Kumeyaay were captured by settlers, converted to Christianity, and used for slave labor. The tribes located in what is now the southeastern portion of San Diego County, however, widely escaped enslavement because of their remote location, far from the presidio and the Mission San Diego de Alcalá, and their willingness to mount defensive (and sometimes offensive) operations against superior Spanish weaponry. They did, however, lose the ability to utilize their coastal resources in the traditional manner.

The Kumeyaay were universally affected by displacement as first the Spanish and then the Mexicans moved into and occupied traditional coastal territory. The Indians most directly affected by this intrusion were joined by Kumeyaay from outlying areas to defend their homeland, their people, and their way of life. Tribal attacks on the Spanish, and then on the Mexicans, reached all the way to the main coastal highway, El Camino Real. In the 1830s, the Mexican government secularized lands and created large ranchos throughout the San Diego area. Many of these lands had been promised to Christian Kumeyaay, who responded by rebelling and joining with the Kumeyaay of the interior. By the 1830s, Indian raiders began to drive the Mexican occupiers from their lands, forcing the closure of ranchos. By the 1840s, the tribal campaign had forced the abandonment of all the rancho operations within present San Diego County. Kumeyaay were launching attacks directly against the city of San Diego by 1842.

### The Mexican-American War and the Treaty of Guadalupe Hidalgo

After over seventy years of conflict with Mexico and Spain, the free Kumeyaay welcomed the United States' entry into the Mexican-American War. A contingent of Kumeyaay met with General Kearney on his march into San Diego and offered their allegiance and assistance. Kearney declined the assistance but promised fairness to the Indians under the U.S. government.

The Treaty of Guadalupe Hidalgo between the United States and Mexico to secure the peace and resolve the Mexican-American War (1846–1848) had several significant effects on the Indian people in the border area. Primarily, it ceded jurisdiction of lands, including what is now San Diego County, to the United States, and it fixed a permanent border between the two countries (Article V).[4] This border split existing tribal communities, making Indian people in the area subject to two different governments and legal regimes. This circumstance continues to present a variety of challenges to the border tribes today.

In addition, under the treaty the United States agreed to honor existing land rights of Mexicans residing in the territory ceded to Mexico (Article VIII). Therefore, despite the fact that tribal occupation predated the establishment of the ranchos and the fact that the Indians controlled most of San Diego County prior to the war, the paper land rights associated with the ranchos were given preeminence over Indian land claims.

The treaty also provided Mexicans in the new U.S. territory the opportunity to become citizens of the United States if they so chose (Article IX). By contrast, the Indian people were not afforded the rights of citizenship until 1924.

Finally, the treaty put the Indian people under the "exclusive control" of the U.S. government, provided for their "forcible restraint" from incursions on either side of the border, and contemplated their removal from the new U.S. territory to allow settlement by citizens (Article XI).

### The Treaty of Santa Ysabel and Indian Land Concessions

In 1852, the Kumeyaay of San Diego County negotiated the Treaty of Santa Ysabel with federal representatives.[5] In return for the surrender of property claims to the east (from the desert foothills to the dunes of Imperial County) and west (from the Cuyamaca Mountains to the coast), an 1100-square-mile reservation was to be created in San Diego County, with additional land in Imperial County (see figure 11.3). This treaty, along with sixteen others in California, was not ratified by the U.S. Senate, which illegally and unethically placed the action under seal, hiding the result from

---

[4] For the full text of the treaty, see www.yale.edu/lawweb/avalon/diplomacy/mexico/guadhida.htm.

[5] The Treaty of Temecula, negotiated in the same period, covered a smaller portion of northern San Diego County for the Luiseño, Cahuilla, and Cupeño tribes.

# Figure 11.3. Reservation Negotiated in the Treaty of Santa Ysabel

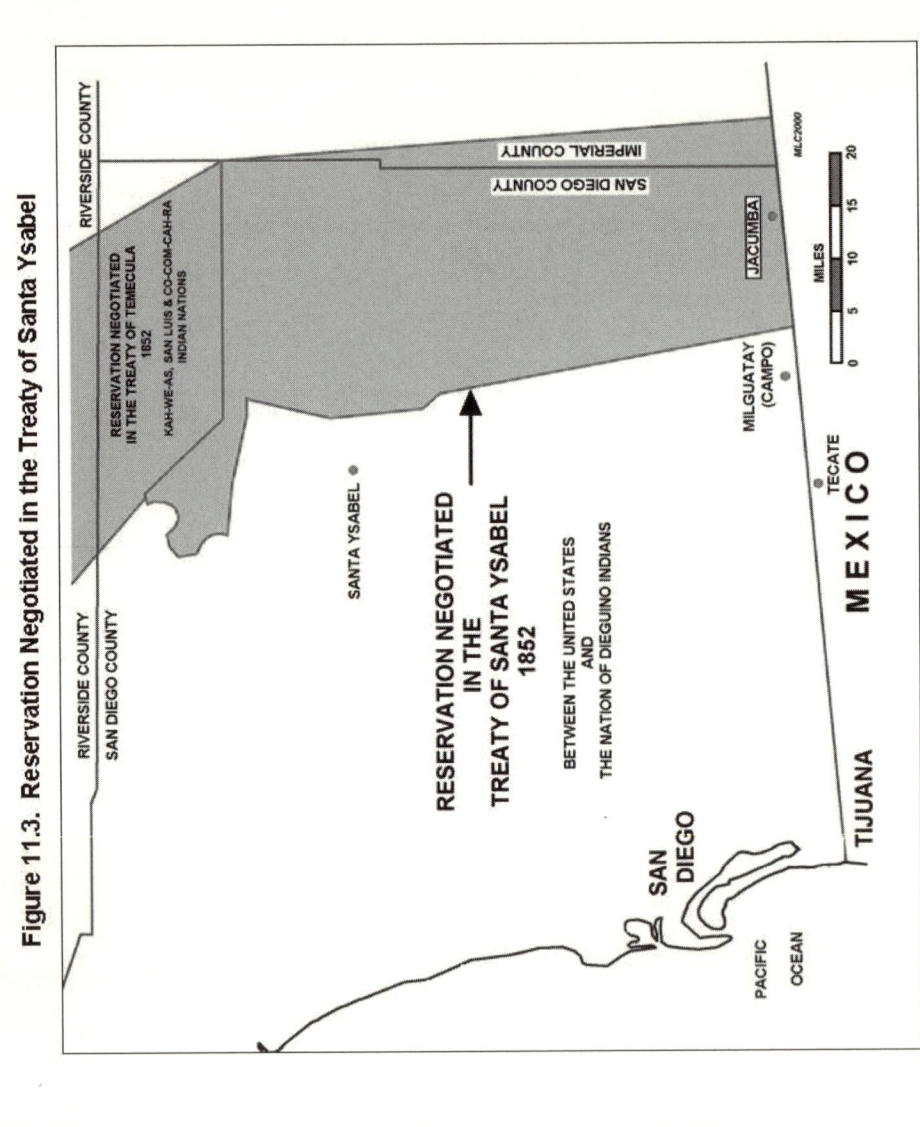

the Indians until after 1900.[6] This was followed by state-sponsored extermination programs (under the guise of militia actions), forced servitude under vagrancy laws, and the forced removal of women and children from their homes (Johnston-Dodds 2002)—actions that resulted in the destruction of 90 percent of the California Indian population between 1850 and 1860.[7]

At this same time and continuing through 1893, the San Diego tribes found themselves in legal limbo as they labored within the cattle and agriculture industry and built the beginnings of the transportation and communications infrastructure of San Diego County. Kumeyaay saw lands they themselves had improved sold out from under them as supposed "treaty lands" were carved up for homesteaders. Lacking citizenship, Kumeyaay were not allowed to file homesteads themselves and were even prevented from gaining citizenship through the naturalization process because they lacked a "country of origin."

## The Reservations

The first reservations in San Diego County were created from 1875 to 1893 through congressional acts and executive orders. Through these authorities, lands were set aside and held in trust by the United States for the sole use and benefit of the Indian tribes and their members. In the 1920s the United States opened the nation to suit for land claims by aggrieved Indian tribes. The courts found that the actions of the United States regarding the California treaties had, in fact, been illegal. However, under settlements negotiated by the State of California on behalf of the Indian people, little compensation would come to the California Indian people.

In the 1950s, in an effort to force the assimilation of Indian people into the general population, the U.S. Congress enacted laws to terminate Indian lands[8] and to give police authority over tribal lands in California and other

---

[6] See Cohen 1982: chap. 2, sec. B, notes 297–305 and accompanying text.

[7] See the sources cited in note 2.

[8] See House Concurrent Resolution 108 (1953), implemented by Acts of Congress terminating individual Indian tribes, discussed in Cohen 1982: chap. 2, sec. E, in particular, notes 204–253 and accompanying text. None of the implementing legislation specifically applied to any of the tribes in the border area.

states.[9] This taking of tribal authority further eroded tribal self-governance capability and forced many tribal citizens to abandon their lands for jobs in the cities or to rely on government welfare and food surplus programs. Indian children were taken from schools by county child-welfare officials and adopted into non-Indian families without the permission of the Indian parents. The Indian Self-Determination Act of 1975[10] provided the basis for a renewed support of self-governance and Indian control of economic development on tribal lands.

Today, the tribes in San Diego County, as elsewhere in the United States, have reservations that are a fraction of the size of their traditional territories[11] and that are surrounded by land controlled by federal or state agencies or private parties. These fragmented tribal lands are for the most part located in remote, desolate areas on which traditional subsistence activities are limited or impossible and on which modern economic endeavors are only minimally feasible due to limited size of lands, challenging terrain, and remoteness from urban areas. Although set aside as a

---

[9] See Pub. L. No. 83-280, August 15, 1953 (codified at 18 U.S.C. § 1162; 25 U.S.C. §§ 1321–1326; 28 U.S.C. § 1360). This law, commonly known as PL-280, gave general criminal jurisdiction over Indian Country to several specified states, including California. It also applied the civil law of those states to Indian Country and gave the courts of those states authority to hear cases arising in Indian Country under those laws. As originally applied, the tribes within the states that were granted jurisdiction were not afforded an opportunity to approve or disapprove; the law was subsequently amended to require tribal approval. This law remains in effect. Although states can seek to retrocede the jurisdiction granted to them, California has not done so.

[10] Pub. L. No. 93-638, January 4, 1975 (codified at 25 U.S.C. §§ 13a, 450–450n, 455–457, 458–458e, and so on).

[11] Tribal lands were further diminished by implementation of the General Allotment Act of 1887, pursuant to which many reservations were divided into farm-sized plots (allotments) and assigned to individual Indian families, and opened in part for homesteading by non-Indians. See Act of February 8, 1887 (codified at 25 U.S.C. §§ 331–334, 339, 341–342, 348–349, 354, 381). While the division and unrestricted sale of Indian lands were halted by subsequent legislation (see Indian Reorganization Act of 1934, codified as amended at 25 U.S.C. §§ 461–479), allotment activities resulted in a checkerboarding phenomenon, whereby non-Indians came to own lands in fee within the interior boundaries of certain reservations.

homeland for the use, benefit, and subsistence of the Indian people, most reservation lands do not afford the necessary opportunities. Tribal communities now struggle to protect their environments and natural resources from harm caused by off-reservation activities while at the same time searching for ways to provide for their people through generation of revenue from regulatory and economic development activities. The following discussion addresses how tribes experience and deal with each of these goals, as well as the tensions between them.

## ENVIRONMENTAL PROTECTION, NATURAL RESOURCES, AND LAND-USE ISSUES

### Overview of Legal and Political Framework in U.S. Indian Country

The ability to enact and enforce civil regulatory laws is one of the fundamental powers of government. In the United States, this power is jealously guarded by state and local governments who have constitutional parameters to protect their roles. For Indian tribes, however, the powers of civil regulatory authority are not powers created by the Constitution; instead, tribal civil regulatory authority is part of the inherent power that tribes retained despite their absorption into the United States. Given the constitutional establishment of congressional authority over Indian tribes and the subsequent Supreme Court definition of tribes as "domestic dependent nations,"[12] Indian tribes operate in a manner similar to states on many levels, with some of the aspects of independent nationhood still legally applied.

In particular, through their inherent sovereignty and right of self-government, tribal governments generally have jurisdiction over the activities of Indians in Indian Country; this includes the authority to regulate Indian people and lands and to have disputes resolved in tribal courts or other dispute resolution arenas.[13] However, Indian people and lands may be subject to federal laws and courts as well, where Congress has expressed a clear intent to so apply those laws. On the other hand, absent an

---

[12] See *Cherokee Nation v. Georgia*, 30 U.S. (5 Pet.) 1, 17 (1831).

[13] See, for example, *Santa Clara Pueblo v. Martinez*, 436 U.S. 49, 59–60 (1978); *U.S. v. Mazurie*, 419 U.S. 544, 557 (1975).

express delegation of such authority from Congress, states generally have no civil or regulatory jurisdiction over Indian people in Indian Country.[14]

Tribal governments may also regulate activities of non-Indians in Indian Country in certain circumstances, such as where a consensual relationship exists or where the non-Indian's conduct threatens or has a direct effect on the political integrity, economic security, or health or welfare of the tribe.[15] States, too, may regulate non-Indians in Indian Country in certain circumstances, depending upon the character of the reservation (that is, the predominance of non-Indians within the reservation's exterior borders) or where state regulation does not interfere with tribal sovereignty and self-government.[16] The issue of whether a state or a tribe has jurisdiction over particular persons or activities within the boundaries of a reservation has been one of the areas of great controversy between states and tribes in the United States in modern times.

**Environmental Regulation**

The U.S. Congress has occupied the field of environmental regulation with comprehensive statutory schemes addressing the nation's air, land, and water pollution and natural resource management.[17] These statutes are generally civil and regulatory in nature, and vest authority in a federal agency, such as the Environmental Protection Agency, to implement and enforce their provisions. Some provide for states to assume authority in lieu of the federal program, and some specifically contemplate states and regional authorities taking a leading role. It is important to note, however, that state environmental programs generally do not apply in Indian Coun-

---

[14] See, for example, *California v. Cabazon Band of Mission Indians*, 480 U.S. 202, 206 (1987), and note that more recent U.S. Supreme Court decisions are serving to erode tribal sovereign authority in favor of state jurisdiction in certain circumstances.

[15] See, for example, *Montana v. United States*, 450 U.S. 544, 565–66 (1981); but see note 13 above.

[16] See, for example, *Brendale v. Yakima Indian Nation*, 492 U.S. 408 (1989).

[17] See, for example, Clean Air Act, 42 U.S.C. § 7401, et seq.; Federal Water Pollution Control Act, 33 U.S.C. § 1521, et seq.; Safe Drinking Water Act, 42 U.S.C. § 300f et seq.; Solid Waste Disposal Act, 42 U.S.C. § 6901, et seq.; Endangered Species Act, 16 U.S.C. § 1532, et seq.

try, so the federal government has been left to enforce environmental laws on tribal lands. Since the mid-1980s, several federal environmental statutes have expressly articulated a role for tribal governments to assume program authority as well. Thus tribes now share many of the same authorities under federal environmental law that applies to the states. Tribes also possess a significant amount of internal authority over environmental control based on the inherent sovereign authority they possess over their land as "sovereign domestic nations."

## Impacts of Off-Reservation Development

Tribal lands management has not substantially contributed to current environmental impairment in the border area or elsewhere, yet Indian people have historically been subjected to significant negative health and quality-of-life impacts resulting from off-reservation commercial and industrial development and the corresponding increase in pollution. While having to endure such impacts, tribal communities have not received commensurate health care, social services, or other economic benefits that non-tribal communities derive from revenues generated by such developments. Instead, tribes are more likely to bear additional costs of off-reservation resource mismanagement in areas as wide-ranging as air pollution control and endangered species protection.

For instance, tribes can find themselves in non-attainment under the Clean Air Act[18] due to their proximity to significant upwind off-reservation pollution sources. This can create a requirement for tribes to purchase air pollution offsets before engaging in businesses with emission potential. In effect, the tribes must pay the pollution sources because of conditions those sources created. In some cases, this "buy in" may be sufficient to discourage potential development on tribal lands. Tribes must still deal with the health, environmental, and social costs of the off-reservation pollution while realizing none of the revenue streams those sources provide to the state and local governments.

In recent years, market-trading programs have been proposed for wide-ranging issues such as global warming. Under this scheme, the tribes, just

---

[18] See 42 U.S.C. § 7501(2).

as developing nations throughout the world, would be unfairly penalized for having a lack of pollution to generate market-trading assets.

Another example involves protecting habitat for sensitive species under the Endangered Species Act[19] or the Clean Water Act.[20] A recent mechanism for wildlife preservation is habitat mitigation banking, a program by which lands purchased outside of a development area can be "banked" for use to offset or mitigate the removal of habitat by development elsewhere. Wetlands in particular may be subject to mitigation banking. Tribes could once again be forced to "buy in" to programs, rewarding those industries or jurisdictions that created the conditions resulting in scarce wetland areas. The presence of wetlands on tribal lands is not rewarded or compensated and, in fact, may penalize a tribe by restricting or preventing use of scarce tribal lands.

Increasingly, tribal communities find themselves being looked to as offset areas for the environmental degradation of the off-reservation environment. For tribes just starting to develop their economic base, this is a particularly onerous and inequitable burden. Tribal lands are often viewed as "rural, undeveloped lands," with state and county land-use planners and environmentalists seeking to "preserve" the land as open space or endangered species habitat. Little regard is placed on the tribes' own land-use plans, long-term intentions, or needs.

It is virtually impossible to get a full accounting of the economic impacts and social costs of these off-reservation views regarding tribal lands. As a case in point, in San Diego County the Multiple Species Conservation Plan was held up as a model of intergovernmental cooperation, yet no tribal government or land-use planning designations were incorporated in the plan. When tribal activities require an environmental assessment under the National Environmental Policy Act (NEPA),[21] consideration must be made regarding the adjacent land uses. If the adjacent land use is incom-

---

[19] See, generally, 16 U.S.C. § 1532, et seq.

[20] See, for example, 33 U.S.C. § 1344 and implementing regulations (protecting wetlands, among other things).

[21] 42 U.S.C. § 4321 et seq. The NEPA environmental review process, which applies to "federal actions," will often be triggered by development on reservation land if a federal approval (such as a permit or lease approval) is required.

patible with the proposed tribal use, the tribe is the party asked to accede in the process. As the county grows, the cost to convert urbanized land into suitable habitat will continue to rise. This will increase the pressure to force tribal and other rural lands into offsets for urban growth. Yet, as discussed further below, tribal governments (unlike off-reservation rural jurisdictions) are not beneficiaries of the revenue stream derived from the urban lands. If the lack of development on tribal lands is to be considered an offset for urban residential and industrial development, then any restriction on development of tribal lands should be accompanied by a corresponding sharing of the revenues derived from the associated off-reservation lands.

**Shared Resources: Groundwater**

Indian tribes with encroaching development on both sides of the U.S.-Mexico border share a common problem of increasing pressure on a crucial resource: groundwater. Generally, regulators and resource managers treat ground and surface water separately, yet the two are intricately linked. In addition to increasing use, long-term depletions of the aquifers create conditions that can also deteriorate the quality of water through increased concentration of dissolved solids and metals, and they increase the likelihood of cross-contamination from pollution sources such as livestock and sewage septic systems.

In the United States, tribes are increasingly accused of impacting off-reservation drinking water wells, yet the most wasteful resource management practices occur in the off-reservation community. To enable an understanding of the current situation, some basics of the border aquifer system are presented below.

*Groundwater and Geology.* The border aquifer system is dominated by the Southern California batholith, a large complex of granitic rock. Water occurs within the fractures of the granitic bedrock and within the pore space of overlying materials. In many areas, the fractured bedrock is overlain by a transitional layer of decomposed granite of variable thickness. In the center of the valleys are varying quantities of granular material (typically sand and silt) that occurs in alluvial channels within existing stream channels and valleys. Because the border area has never had glaciation, the geological deposits are the result of long-term erosion and weathering from the original mountain-building period thirty million years ago.

With the exception of a few areas near water-supply reservoirs that are used to store and export water to the city of San Diego or to Tijuana, the border area is dependent upon groundwater. Flows in many of the area's streams and creeks are limited primarily to storm flows or following winters with above-normal rainfall. Both surface water and groundwater are strongly influenced by the above-normal rainfall seasons that occur approximately every five to ten years in association with the "El Niño" phenomenon.

Water storage within the rock and soils provides for seasonal storage of winter rainfall. Long-term water production generally increases if the amount of available subsurface storage increases. Border-area water storage rates can be described in terms of the amount of water that can be stored in the subsurface. The granitic bedrock offers the lowest amount of storage—on the order of 0.1 percent by volume (that is, 1,000 acre-feet of rock will hold one acre-foot of water). Decomposed granite offers better storage—on the order of 5 percent by volume. Water storage within the alluvial materials within the valleys is typically on the order of 25 percent by volume; however, the extent of these materials is quite limited.

Occasionally, especially in active fault areas, bedrock fractures can hold large amounts of water in storage or can serve as drains over a wide area. It is generally the fractures in the bedrock that provide the conduit for water to drinking water wells and the overburden of decomposed granite that provides the long-term storage.

The long-term availability of water (also termed the sustainable or safe yield) is determined based on water balance methods that account for the amount of water that enters and is stored in the subsurface on a seasonal basis. By including runoff (the amount of water that flows along the ground surface), soil moisture capacity (the soil's ability to allow water to pass into the ground), meteorological data (primarily rainfall), and evapotranspiration rate (water lost from the soil due to evaporation and plant use), we can make a conservative estimate of the maximum storage capacity of an individual basin. This technique is currently used by San Diego County's Department of Planning and Land Use (DPLU) to determine the suitability of specific sites for residential development in accordance with the county's Groundwater Ordinance.[22] However, this method is only used for projects that require DPLU approval. Agricultural uses, which represent some of the most intense water demands, are specifically exempt from the Groundwater Ordinance. As a result, a significant portion of water use in the rural border region is unconstrained.

*Comparative Land Uses.* In the history of both U.S. and Mexican Indian people, the lands most suited to farming and ranching were sequestered for non-Indian usage. In many cases, tribal communities ended up with rocky, steep-sloped lands with few productive water sources. As development progressed in the coastal areas, water needs were increasingly met with imported water. Yet most tribal communities are located in areas that lack access to imported water.

Both the United States and Mexico have laws regarding water usage that favor agricultural users. In addition, marginal grazing lands can be devastated by poor range management practices. Long-term leases of public lands in the United States for grazing have resulted in the loss of thousands of acre-feet of water storage due to the erosion and deforestation of riparian areas. The hundreds of thousands of dollars directed to habitat restoration have corrected only a tiny portion of the damage. The true cost of these practices will be orders of magnitude in excess of any commercial benefit to the consumers of these practices. The combined effect is that land management in the off-reservation area is skewed to favor wasteful and unsustainable agricultural and livestock usage while residential and/or commercial usages on tribal lands are increasingly targeted for restriction or regulation.

*Impacts to Tribal Communities.* For Indian communities in the border zone, attempts to regulate water usage create inequities, with significant impacts to the tribal economies. In the United States, county regulators increasingly seek to regulate water usage on reservation lands, ostensibly to protect water resources. Yet agricultural usage is exempted from any control, and range management has little or no oversight from off-reservation regula-

---

[22] See San Diego County Code, Title 6, Division 7, Chapter 7, at www.co.san-diego.ca.us/dplu/Resource/docs/3~pdf/GROUNDWATER-ORD.pdf.

tors. In Mexico, attempts to regulate water usage have resulted in laws requiring the metering of new drinking water wells; yet, as in the United States, agricultural wells are exempted. This has presented a quandary for Mexico's Indian communities, who only now are capable of upgrading their water systems to provide adequate public health protection. If they include new wells in their systems, they could very well find themselves subject to additional costs for the same level of water usage, since any new wells would require meters. Coastal communities are also supplementing their surface water (both imported and local) with large-scale groundwater pumping. In the case of the Los Coyotes Reservation in San Diego County, over forty production wells situated just outside the reservation boundary pump large quantities of water for coastal communities, with no mechanism for protecting the Indian community from overdrafts.

*Courses of Action.* To maintain water quality for the mountain areas of the border zone, water quantity issues must be incorporated into the discussion. Any fair discussion of land uses must include wastewater disposal, agriculture, and livestock. There must be balance between the beneficiaries of the resources and the cost of equity.

A bill is currently under review in the U.S. Congress to characterize the transboundary aquifer.[23] This study should be supplemented and expanded to give a solid technical and economic baseline that can be incorporated into state and reservation land-use planning activities for both sides of the border.

**Cultural Impacts**

Off-reservation development activities have also meant increased cultural costs for tribal people by impinging on their ability to access religious sites, use water resources for traditional and religious purposes, and use traditional plants as food and medicines. Tribal cultures, as most cultures, carried with them the tools to deal with issues of violence, substance abuse, health living, and care for children and the elderly. When practice of a culture is constrained, a void is created. Most tribal people have found it

---

[23] See H.R. 469, at www.theorator.com/bills109/hr469.html, and S. 1957, at www.theorator.com/bills/108/s1957.html.

hard or impossible to fill this void; and when they have filled it, it has often been with socially destructive elements. Cultural and religious impacts are felt doubly in the border area, where tribal people have restricted access, if any, to members of their traditional communities who now live on the other side of the border, and to plants and other natural materials used for traditional activities, rituals, and ceremonies.

**The Myth of CEQA Equity**

The lack of recognition accorded to tribal governments continually brings the issue of California Environmental Quality Act (CEQA)[24] compliance into discussions regarding environmental impacts associated with activities both on and off the reservation. CEQA is a California process law that brings state-recognized planning and regulatory agencies into the decision-making process. When tribes are asked to comply with CEQA, it is rarely a request for compliance with specific environmental standards. Rather, it is an attempt to circumvent the tribe's land-use planning decision through procedural actions. Since tribal land-use planning and regulatory agencies are not recognized in the CEQA process, off-reservation designations of open space, scenic highways, community character, or species conservation plans all guide the CEQA process, without requirements for compliance with tribal plans. This can put off-reservation designations completely at odds with the reservation community's criteria for development or conservation. This state process has never acknowledged the disparities inherent in the existing system, where a community such as a reservation can only derive governmental revenue from its land base.

Absent any recognition of the unique status of Indian lands in California, CEQA will continue to be used as a political tool for inequity in dealing with tribes by making tribal planning and designation processes subservient to the state. As discussed below, not only are tribal governments deprived of the land-based revenues afforded the state, but state and local regulatory agencies and governments that seek to challenge tribal authority and jurisdiction are partially funded by revenues from those very tribal communities.

---

[24] Cal. Pub. Resources Code § 21000 et seq., at ceres.ca.gov/ceqa.

## THE ECONOMICS OF ENVIRONMENTAL PROTECTION AND LAND OWNERSHIP

While tribal governments have the authority and responsibility to protect the reservation environment in accordance with their own policies for the welfare of their communities, they lack the revenue streams to support such governmental activities that are available to off-reservation governmental authorities.

For example, the state and county regularly use their total acreage, including Indian reservation lands, in formulas to secure federal funding. They also use total population, stream and river miles, surface water acreage, and so on, even if the state or county has no regulatory jurisdiction over the tribal lands included in the total. More importantly, the portion of funding derived from tribal figures is not shared with tribal governments; instead, it is allocated to the state or county. Additionally, tribal tax dollars are used to build state regulatory programs, in that a portion of the tax dollars derived from reservations supplements funding from the federal government in the implementation of environmental regulatory programs under the major environmental acts. Tribes, too, can access the federal disbursements, but they do not share in a return of revenues drawn from reservation lands by the state.

Moreover, as a result of the status of reservation lands (see the section on the history of the reservations, above), many tribes have had to acquire additional land to ensure the social and economic viability of their communities. When doing so, they have come under attack by county groups and governments for depriving the off-reservation community of the associated tax base or of appropriating lands designated for agriculture or open space. From the tribal perspective, these lands are being returned after having been illegally removed from tribal jurisdiction. A more appropriate external response would be to acknowledge the original illegality and to incorporate into county land-use planning the ultimate restoration of the treaty land base of 1,100 square miles.

Further, allotted land within reservations may be sold to non-Indians under existing law.[25] When this happens, county taxes and planning jurisdiction are immediately imposed upon the transfer of title. Yet when tribes

---

[25] See note 10 above.

seek to acquire additional lands, they must negotiate a series of hurdles aimed to delay, hinder, or force economic concessions prior to the transfer of the land. Many times, environmental laws are used as smokescreens to hinder the transfer process.

## TAXATION

One of the most important tools that communities use to attract business development and expand their economies is their tax base. Across the United States, tax breaks for particular industries or commercial activities are also used to help define the character of a community. As their economies develop, well-managed communities use their revenue to build their infrastructure and ensure that the business community is provided with basic governmental services. Imagine the constraints on economic development if another jurisdiction had the authority to draw this entire tax base without any obligation to share it with local government! Imagine if the tax rates for the local community were always set by another jurisdiction, one that had no obligation or interest in seeing the local community thrive! This is the situation for tribal communities in San Diego County and across California.

### Sales, Property, Income, and Highway Taxes

Tribes face a different situation than do states with regard to taxation of businesses and individuals. When owned by non-Indians, on-reservation businesses are subject to state taxation. For individuals working within a tribal setting, salaries are subject to state taxation if the employees are non-Indians or non-member Indians, even if they are residents of the reservation and are provided services by the tribe. Indian people living on the reservation but working off the reservation are also subject to state taxation. States have been able to extract sales tax on purchases made by non-Indians on tribal lands. None of these taxes derived from tribal lands are shared with the tribal governments. This means that a tribal government—while responsible for protecting its residents and the environment and creating an infrastructure that makes business operations feasible and consistent—must put business at a profit disadvantage through double taxation or forgo tax revenues in order to create a level playing field. In cases where Indians may have a good case for challenging the assessment of sales tax on tribal lands—such as retail gasoline sales—the state of California has subverted tribal authority by requiring the collection of sales tax by the wholesalers, once again creating a situation where the tribal community must put itself under double taxation or forgo taxes to create a level playing field. Petroleum vendors are threatened with the loss of the ability to sell in the state if they do not collect the taxes. Taxes collected on gasoline sales are not shared with tribal governments, yet state/county road construction, which is partially funded from tribal revenues, does not fund reservation projects.

Should a tribe decide to use real estate development to build its economy, it may still find itself subject to external taxation. Counties impose possessory interest taxes on long-term leases to non-Indians for housing on tribal lands, in effect creating an artificial property tax. This tax may be imposed regardless of the county's legal standing to provide governmental services or infrastructure to the property owner.[26]

**Opportunity Costs**

Opportunity costs can be a difficult concept to quantify, yet they are a reality that may have the greatest impact on a community's long-term quality of life. For decades, state and county governments have used reservation tax dollars to build the economic engine of San Diego County. Indian tax revenue has been used to build the harbor infrastructure, coastal highways, industrial zones, the commercial Golden Triangle zone, and manufacturing and international commerce. The county has benefited from the increases in revenues derived from these commercial activities and has shared none of the revenue with the tribal governments. One potential alternative would be the sharing of urban industrial zones with tribal governments. Yet county authorities jealously guard their industrial tax zones, thereby forcing tribes to look within the reservation boundaries for commensurate revenue sources.

Training and education have been central to maintaining a high level of professional proficiency in developing the infrastructure of governmental

---

[26] See *Agua Caliente Band of Cahuilla Indians v. Riverside County*, 442 F.2d 1184 (9th Cir. 1971), cert denied, 405 U.S. 933 (1972).

administration. Tribal governments are disadvantaged by the loss of tax revenues that could assist with these needs within the tribal communities. The long-term effect has been the loss of skilled staff to off-reservation jurisdictions, which have the resources to provide adequate compensation.

Tribes are forced into governmental ownership as the only way to approach economic survival and ensure that discretionary revenues are directed within the tribal community.

**Other Revenue Sources**

The state and other off-reservation governments derive revenue from additional sources that impact reservation resources. For instance, in many parts of the United States, including California, the U.S. Forest Service shares locally derived revenue with local governments for roads and schools, including a portion that passes through the local government to area tribes. However, San Diego County does not have a program for disbursal of the tribal share of this revenue.

Many federal programs still do not have provisions for appropriation of federal dollars to tribal communities. In the area of environmental protection, the Solid Waste Disposal Act is the most significant.[27] The result is the lack of a direct funding mechanism to support tribal solid and hazardous waste programs. Yet reservation residents are responsible for paying federal income tax at the same rate as other citizens.

**INDIAN GAMING**

Several border tribes—including Barona, Campo, Sycuan, and Viejas—operate casinos, and others, such as La Posta and Santa Ysabel, are in the process of developing such facilities. Indian gaming (tribal operation of facilities offering bingo, "Las Vegas–style" gambling, and other games of chance) is thus an important part of any discussion regarding tribal economic and environmental justice in the border area. Indian gaming has unique characteristics that partially separate it from other equity considerations. However, tribal communities must continually deal with a steady stream of misinformation in the general public.

---

[27] See 42 U.S.C. 6901, et seq.

Indian gaming has its roots in the traditional games of most tribes in California. It was introduced as a commercial enterprise to Californians in the early 1980s. In *California vs. Cabazon Band*,[28] the U.S. Supreme Court held that the state cannot prohibit tribes from engaging in forms of gaming that are not prohibited by the state. Therefore, while full casinos were not authorized, gambling that resembled the state lottery was. This resulted in the establishment of a limited number of bingo halls and card rooms on reservations located mostly in areas with a large population base.

Gaming on U.S. Indian reservations was officially regulated at the federal level after Congress passed the Indian Gaming Regulatory Act (IGRA) in 1988.[29] This legislation allows tribes to operate casinos if they have compacts with their respective state governments specifying the quantity and types of regulated gaming permitted on reservation lands.

In 2001, California voters approved Proposition 1A, which authorized the governor of California to negotiate compacts with federally recognized tribes for slot machines, lottery games, and other forms of gambling on Indian lands. This was followed by a period of rapid growth of Indian gaming and casinos, especially in southern California. All existing compacts are valid until 2020. However, Governor Arnold Schwarzenegger has begun to renegotiate existing compacts to extract more money from gaming tribes in order to help address California's budget deficit.

Section 10.8.1 of the compacts requires that, prior to development of a casino, a tribe "shall adopt an ordinance providing for the preparation, circulation, and consideration by the tribe of environmental impact reports concerning potential off-Reservation environmental impacts." In drafting the ordinance, the tribe is "to make a good faith effort to incorporate the policies and purposes of the National Environmental Policy Act (NEPA) and the California Environmental Quality Act (CEQA) consistent with the tribe's governmental interests."

Gaming is a government enterprise; as such, it is heavily taxed and regulated. Under the Indian Gaming Regulatory Act, tribes must use funds for governmental, economic, charitable, and general welfare purposes. Second, revenues must be distributed in accordance with a federally ap-

---

[28] 480 U.S. 202 (1987).

[29] Codified at 25 U.S.C. § 2701, et seq.

proved "Revenue Allocation Plan" that prioritizes social and governmental needs over distributions to individual tribal members. Third, for most non-Indian communities, governmental operations will derive revenue both from the industry and from the employees of that industry.[30] However, while tribal governmental operations may be funded out of gaming revenue, 100 percent of non-Indian employee taxes go to the state. Fourth, pursuant to the tribal-state compacts in effect in California, the state gets additional impact revenue from the tribes for the cost of governmental services associated with gaming, such as law enforcement. Another provision in certain of the compacts provides local government impact aid out of gaming revenues. The only reason gaming can exist at all, in the present regulatory climate, is that the profit margins are high enough to overcome disparities that would destroy any other economic venture subjected to similar demands. The fact that profits are still possible does not negate the fact that additional profits that should be going to the tribal community under any rational concept of fairness are diverted off-reservation.

When tribal businesses (including gaming) are compared to other types of business operating within the state, there is an added consideration related to tribal contributions to the state economy. Profits from tribal gaming are split between governmental operations (a government tax, in effect) and individual "per capita" distributions.[31] The bulk of spending by tribal governments and individual tribal members is within the state. Even when tribal casinos are under management agreements with out-of-state companies, most of the derived revenue is immediately reinvested in the state economy. This results in a "churning" or multiple turnover of transactions, which generates significant tax revenue to local and state government. Yet foreign corporations can operate throughout the state and divert most or all of their earnings out of state. Even an out-of-state U.S. corporation may

---

[30] A tribe may enact an income or sales tax, but this is seldom done because of the competition for employees. Given that a tribal tax would reduce take-home wages, it would exacerbate the competition for workers. A sales tax becomes a double tax since it does not supplant the existing state sales tax.

[31] In the initial phases of a casino or other highly capitalized enterprise, most or all profit may go to investors who do not reside locally. Generally, this situation reverses within a ten-year period.

contribute little or nothing in profit to the California tax base. The benefit of having an industry that keeps earnings within the state is significant when compared to foreign or out-of-state corporations. Yet tribal economies are singled out for fair-share arguments as if money going into tribal economies is a loss to the state.

**THE BORDER**

The border has a long history of influence on many tribal communities in the borderlands. Except for a brief period during World War II, the border was generally open to travel until about thirty years ago. Ranchers, workers, and Indian people regularly used many informal crossing areas to visit relatives and attend cultural activities. Many Indian people used the border as a life-saving refuge from murderous ranchers in the mid-1800s. Other Indians found a livelihood in the shadow economy of smuggling, an unfortunate lure to some people to this day. With the advent of environmental regulatory programs and international trade treaties, the transboundary environment has become of increasing concern, further highlighted by recent terrorist events.

Tribes in the border area are on the front lines of a confusing, disjointed U.S. immigration policy. Constant aircraft overflights are supplemented by roadway checkpoints that intrude into the daily life of all border residents. Major routes for undocumented alien traffic go through tribal lands, and poor transient sanitation and health is a ticking time bomb for exotic illnesses to sweep the tribal and border communities. Key concerns include direct contact with individuals affected by highly infectious diseases, such as tuberculosis, and the impact of fecal-borne pathogens that can enter the groundwater supply. Informal discussions with U.S. Border Patrol agents indicate that, on an annual basis, approximately 100,000 undocumented aliens (roughly 300 per day) pass through the Campo area alone.

Tribal members constantly deal with undocumented immigrants passing through the reservation. Tribal members have also been challenged and detained by the U.S. Border Patrol while simply walking through their own lands. Foot traffic, U.S. Border Patrol traffic, and litter threaten sensitive marshlands and riparian zones. Unauthorized roads have opened areas of the reservations to traffic where no traffic existed before. Some casino clients and reservation residents have succumbed to the lure of the easy money to be made transporting undocumented aliens, and some have spent time in jail as a result. The United States' failed immigration policy will never be overcome solely through the brute force of barriers, patrols, and technology, yet tribal resources to deal with the current impacts are almost nonexistent. Even the new Department of Homeland Security does not appropriate money to tribal communities.

The Kumeyaay of San Diego County are among the binational tribes along the U.S.-Mexico border. This adds another element to equity issues in the border zone. Relatives of the San Diego Kumeyaay who reside in Mexico have long been subjected to a much lower quality of life than that of Mexican citizens in general. Kumeyaay in the United States have worked hard to assist their cultural counterparts in Mexico to improve their sanitation, environment, resource management, and communications. Because transboundary cultural activities have been severely impacted by the elevated restrictions on travel, the Kumeyaay have worked with the Mexican and U.S. governments to provide an expedited process for temporary transboundary cultural contacts. Kumeyaay and other border tribes have worked with the tribal people of Mexico and with nongovernmental organizations to improve drinking water and sanitation facilities, health care, education, nutrition, and communications.

**CONCLUSION**

Environmental justice or environmental equity can have a variety of meanings depending on the community affected. In many ways, environmental justice on Indian lands means the ability of the majority to make their own decisions. In other ways, it is having an equal place at the table when making regional, national, or international decisions that affect the quality of life for the tribal community.

Environmental justice for tribal communities cannot be properly understood without looking at the big picture of history, resources, tradition, economics, and culture. Participation by tribes in the Good Neighbor Environmental Board, Border 2012, and other transboundary groups is helping to bring the scope and magnitude of tribal issues to the attention of both U.S. and Mexican officials. Some of the initial successes of the last decade are being supplemented through the hard work and dedication of the many people on both sides of the border who work on tribal issues, but much still needs to be done. With adequate resources and authority, tribes on both sides of the border have the possibility to achieve parity with the non-tribal communities.

**References**

Carrico, Richard L. 1987. *Strangers in a Stolen Land: American Indians in San Diego, 1850–1880*. Sacramento, Calif.: Sierra Oaks Publishing Company.

Cohen, Felix S. 1982. *Felix S. Cohen's Handbook of Federal Indian Law*. 3d ed. Charlottesville, Vir.: Bobbs-Merrill.

Johnston-Dodds, Kimberly. 2002. *Early California Laws and Policies Related to California Indians*. CRB-02-014. Sacramento: California Research Bureau.

Kroeber, A. L. 1976. *Handbook of the Indians of California*. New York: Dover.

Shipek, Florence Connolly. 1987. *Pushed into the Rocks: Southern California Indian Land Tenure, 1769–1986*. Lincoln: University of Nebraska Press.

Smithsonian Institution. 1978–. *Handbook of North American Indians*. Washington, D.C.: Smithsonian Institution.

# 12

## Youth and Education for Sustainability on the Border: Imagining the Future Citizens of Baja California

ALEJANDRO MONSIVÁIS CARRILLO AND LAURA SILVÁN

Environmental education alone will never suffice to reverse the devastation done to our environment nor to drive a shift toward sustainable development. On the other hand, environmental education is a prerequisite for achieving both of these goals. Along the border separating California and Baja California, environmental education is an increasingly relevant field for promoting a strengthening of citizen networks and citizen action. Because this border region is home to intense and accelerated sociocultural convergence and intersection, if offers a space in which environmental education can promote new valuations and practices within civil society that will generate a thoughtful and sustainable interaction with the natural surroundings.

Rather than testing an array of hypotheses, this chapter attempts to imagine possible future scenarios by presenting some thoughts about building citizen capacity based on the intersection of education for sustainability and socialization of the region's youths. Our starting point is that educating for sustainability—including the idea of environmental education—can constitute a space for empowering citizen action, especially cross-border, insurgent citizen action by groups of young people.

Our assertion is based on three observations. The first is the increasing importance of civil society's participation in public debates. At issue is the

---

The authors thank Jane Clough-Riquelme and the anonymous readers who provided valuable comments on an earlier draft of this essay. Translation by Sandra del Castillo.

need to spur citizen initiatives in support of education for sustainability, especially given the current context in which political, economic, social, and environmental problems far outstrip the management capacity of local government and, at the same time, cannot be dealt with efficiently through political responses at the national level. The second observation involves an obvious yet highly relevant need: the need to create institutional and social mechanisms through which upcoming generations can gain the experience and skills needed to develop an integral relationship with their natural and built environment. The third arises from a concrete empirical tendency: Baja California's young people are well positioned to develop their life trajectories, but the lack of institutional credibility, as well as the instability inherent in the border dynamic, may limit the number of channels these youths can employ to resolve the various problems in their environment.

Maintaining our focus on education for sustainability as a space for empowering action among groups of young people, we have divided the following discussion into four sections plus conclusions. One might argue that the information and thematic organization presented here are somewhat contingent. Therefore, we reiterate that this essay reflects a desire to provide information for subsequent discussion and development. The first section below considers the concepts of education for sustainability and insurgent citizenship and briefly reviews the definition of youths as subject. The second section outlines some attributes of the youth citizen culture in Baja California. The third provides an overview of the various examples of environmental education in the border region. And the fourth lists some key points for interpreting the scenarios within which border youths are receiving their political socialization and environmental education.

## EDUCATION FOR SUSTAINABILITY, CITIZEN EMPOWERMENT, AND YOUTH ACTION

Environmental education—or, as it is now called, education for sustainable development—is a new field, having entered international political agendas about thirty years ago. Its mission has grown increasingly complex over time, and today its goal is to project an interconnected view of reality that is not limited to environmental questions. Indeed, the difference between environmental education and education for sustainable development (or for sustainability) lies in the importance given to environmental themes within the broader social, political, and economic context. For Paden (2000), environmental education portrays environmental values against the background of political, social, and economic issues. In a subtle but transcendental shift, education for sustainability seeks to educate equally on environmental issues and on the means to attain social equity and economic prosperity. That is, sustainability envisions a close link between economic well-being, social justice, and the dynamic preservation of the natural environment. This essay is guided by the perspective of education in sustainable development, and when we use the term environmental education we are referring to education in the ecological principles of sustainability.

Much of the discussion and a large share of the projects dealing with education for sustainability involve the development of curricula, teaching approaches, and meaningful learning experiences. In this essay we want to highlight a different dimension of education for sustainability: the dimension that converts it into a means for citizen empowerment. Education for sustainable development holds the potential to disseminate, along the entire Mexican border with the United States, the idea of insurgent citizenship.

According to Friedmann, insurgent citizenship is a form of active participation in (temporary, deterritorialized, and transnational) social movements in defense of existing democratic principles and the creation of new rights. The primary characteristic of this form of citizenship is that it seeks, in a time of globalization and varied cross-border flows, to expand the spaces for democracy (Friedmann 2002: 77). Notable among the normative principles of insurgent citizenship are the following: actions are focused on specific groups whose life opportunities are being undermined by structural forces expressed in concrete forms of power and control; the various insurgent efforts by citizens are interconnected via flexible networks and solidarity groups, and they range from community mobilization to nongovernmental organizations, churches, students, academics, international agencies, private foundations, and so on; and their endeavors are aimed at resolving interrelated problems of varying degrees of complexity and ranging from the micro-local to the global (Friedmann 2002: 83–84).

The linking of citizen efforts in support of sustainability in the California–Baja California border region can help create cross-border enclaves with social and political influence. The ultimate objective is to strengthen public discussion based on a coordination of transitional efforts between social and governmental actors and among social actors. Indeed, this is a potential testing ground for new, deliberative forms of democracy able to transcend human dimensions to reach environmental dimensions (cf. Dryzek 2000: 140–61).

Young people constitute a strategic population sector for education in sustainability. In this sense, the design of institutional spaces and educational programs is of key importance. But youths' participation—as insurgent citizens and as both recipients and disseminators of environmental education and sustainability—is of even greater salience. For the youth of Baja California, as is demonstrated below, contact with the environmental networks taking shape in civil society can empower them as citizens. Before discussing this topic in detail, we must identify the specific characteristics of these youths and consider the evolving way in which they are viewed from a policy perspective.

Studies of youth identities, lifestyles, and culture have demonstrated that the situation of young people in today's society is a specific sociocultural phenomenon (see Feixa 1998; Furlong and Cartmel 1997; Miles 2000; Reguillo 2000, 2002; Valenzuela Arce 1997; Wyn and White 1993). Youth as a life stage does not refer only to the transition from childhood to adulthood; it is also a setting for working out new subjectivities. Despite differences in gender, ethnicity, nationality, or socioeconomic status, youths share preferences and identities, dilemmas and tensions. Their identities, lifestyles, and group formations become a metaphor for social change because they represent what it means to actively appropriate the varied trends of a reflexive modernity.

To understand youth as something more than a transitional period implies reconceptualizing the role of young people as social subjects. In this regard, the discussion has direct impacts in the sphere of public policy. Various organizations and authors have emphasized that rising poverty rates and deteriorating living conditions for the populations of Latin America constitute mechanisms for exclusion and segregation of young people (CELADE 2000; CEPAL 2000; Rodríguez 2000). The vista of a future with the possibility of progress and social mobility has collapsed for many young Latin Americans in recent decades. Therefore, according to the Centro Latinoamericano de Demografía (CELADE 2000) and the Economic Commission for Latin America and the Caribbean (CEPAL 2000), policy design should focus on youths as strategic actors in development. The point here is that, despite premising this goal on a participatory approach to youths' inclusion, it is insufficient for addressing problems of segregation and exclusion if it is limited to the realm of economic rationality. To speak of including young people, of making them participants in controlling their own destinies, the focus must also extend to cultural and political dimensions. In this sense, the notion of citizenship is a substantive framework for considering youths' inclusion from another angle (Krauskopf 2000; Reguillo 2000; Wallace 2001).[1] That is, it is necessary to envision young people as sociocultural actors and as subjects within a democracy.

## YOUTH ON THE BAJA CALIFORNIA BORDER

Baja California ranks high among Mexican states in terms of its economic and social development.[2] Of a statewide population of just under 2.5 million, nearly a third (32.7 percent) are between the ages of twelve and twenty-nine. The state's relatively high levels of development and well-being are due in large part to its border location and character. Over the course of the twentieth century, Baja California's population grew and urbanized at an accelerated pace.[3] In the economic sphere, Baja California

---

[1] Citizenship is a position of subject, universal in nature, which confers rights and obligations within the political community. As formally defined, it constitutes a field of representation open to multicultural integration. It is on this plane that citizenship, regardless of the age at which one acquires full rights, can be envisioned as a space of empowerment for the young population. For a full discussion of this topic, see Monsiváis Carrillo 2002.

[2] Mexico's National Population Council (CONAPO) ranks the state fourth nationally on the human development index (see the section on "Desarrollo humano en México," in CONAPO 2000), while the National Institute of Statistics, Geography, and Informatics places it within the second stratum of states in terms of the well-being of its residents (INEGI 2001).

[3] The population expansion is reflected in the growth rates registered in the 1990s, when population growth measured 4.2 percent, compared to 1.9 percent for Mexico as a whole. Urbanization increased on par. Of the national

exhibits a broad and diversified mix of tourism, commerce, and financial and other services. The service sector employs 65.4 percent of the economically active population (EAP), the manufacturing sector accounts for 28.3 percent, and the remaining 6.3 percent are in agriculture. The state's economically active population includes 55.28 percent of people over the age of twelve, and young people between the ages of twelve and twenty-nine account for 43.9 percent of the total EAP.

These figures are intended to provide the general socioeconomic profile of Baja California. Yet despite the indicators on well-being in the state, there are wide disparities within the population. Internal and international migration, as well as labor market conditions that lower production costs by hiring low-skilled workers, are among the factors that give rise to a context that is dynamic and flexible, but also unstable and unequal.

Baja California's youth form part of a dynamic and plural society, whose peculiarities facilitate young people's emergence as salient social actors. Nevertheless, this same dynamism and the presence of rapid sociocultural exchanges seem to create uncertainties and instabilities that limit young people's ability to assume their citizenship rights. According to data from the 2000 National Youth Survey (Encuesta Nacional de Juventud 2000),[4] three phenomena are associated with this situation: a tendency to actively promote stability in the private sphere, an increasing lack of trust of and respect for government institutions, and an atmosphere of uncertainty regarding citizen action and participation. In the following pages, we describe how these phenomena manifest themselves.

---

population, 60.9 percent reside in urban areas; but in Baja California, 77.3 percent live in cites with more than 100,000 inhabitants and 91.6 percent live in cities or towns with more than 2,500 inhabitants. The state's population is concentrated in three of the state's five municipal areas (*municipios*): Tijuana, with 1,210,820 inhabitants; Mexicali, with 764,602; and Ensenada, with 370,730 (INEGI 2001).

[4] The 2000 National Youth Survey, which covered populations at both the national and state levels, was designed by the Center for Research and Studies on Youth (CIEJ) at the Mexican Youth Institute (IMJ). Its data base includes 59,608 cases that, when expanded statistically, represent 33,634,860 youths throughout the country. In Baja California, 1,634 youths were interviewed, representing 860,712 young people. The tables included in the Youth Survey's final report give the case counts in expanded form. See ENJ 2002.

An element to note at the outset is the relevance that symbolic capital and cultural consumption acquire in the border context. In the field of education, for example, average years of schooling in Baja California exceed the national average (8.2 years versus 7.2 years nationwide). Literacy rates diverge even more; 96.3 percent of the Baja California population over the age of fifteen is literate, compared to 90.5 percent of the national population. These indicators demonstrate that the state's population is well positioned to understand and address the region's problems.

A factor that is even more important than the state's relatively high education levels is the population's cultural attributes. The robust consumer culture of the border region exerts a strong influence on the formation of values, identities, and lifestyles among the population. Baja California youth have a multitude of access channels to the flows of merchandise on both sides of the border, including new and used clothing, household appliances, music, cars, and so on.

Table 12.1 compares access in Mexico and in Baja California to various consumer goods: radios, CD players, televisions, cable TV, camcorders, video game playstations, telephones, computers, cars, and the Internet. This table demonstrates the exclusive use young people make of these products—that is, they are the owners and users—and that ownership levels are higher in Baja California than in the country as a whole. Baja California shows widespread use of video games, phones, computers, the Internet, and vehicles (cars and trucks) at levels above national averages. Having sole use of such items as important symbolic elements in social behavior is a notable attribute of young people in the state. This access to and use of such consumer goods, when added to the state's socioeconomic indicators and sociopolitical profile, offer elements that can help us understand the negotiation of subjective well-being among the youth population.

Table 12.2 shows that young people's future expectations center on forming new households. Notably, these expectations displace those that would emerge under conditions of economic precariousness and still others linked to different forms of self-realization. The data in this table indicate that, for young people, what is most important is to marry, have children, and have a home of their own.

In table 12.3, we can see that youth and gender are the dominant forms of self-identification among Baja California's young people. As their second

Table. 12.1. Cultural Attributes: Access to Consumer Goods among Youths Aged 12 to 29 (percentages)

| | Type of Use | Video Games | Telephone | Personal Computer | Internet | Vehicle |
|---|---|---|---|---|---|---|
| Baja California | General | 21.6% | 48.4% | 20.7% | 7.1% | 48.6% |
| (n = 860,712) | Exclusive | 5.6 | 11.3 | 7.0 | 2.3 | 15.3 |
| All of Mexico | General | 14.2 | 34.0 | 10.4 | 4.8 | 27.1 |
| (n = 33,634,860) | Exclusive | 4.0 | 4.6 | 2.5 | 1.3 | 4.3 |

*Source:* ENJ 2002.

Table 12.2. Expectations of Baja Californian Youths Aged 12 to 29, by Gender (percentages)

| Expectations | First Priority (n = 697,879) | | Second Priority (n = 626,517) | | Third Priority (n = 576,864) | |
|---|---|---|---|---|---|---|
| | *Males* | *Females* | *Males* | *Females* | *Males* | *Females* |
| Marry | 31.5% | 35.6% | 12.4% | 10.8% | 9.1% | 10.5% |
| Have children | 5.7 | 8.5 | 26.1 | 29.7 | 11.4 | 12.6 |
| Own a business | 21.3 | 16.5 | 11.8 | 10.5 | 14.4 | 11.9 |
| Have a good job | 23.4 | 15.6 | 18.5 | 21.8 | 10.7 | 9.9 |
| Work abroad | 2.3 | 0.9 | 9.4 | 3.1 | 6.6 | 3.4 |
| Have own home | 7.2 | 9.4 | 16.9 | 19.5 | 26.4 | 32.0 |
| Help others | 2.8 | 3.3 | 2.7 | 3.5 | 12.2 | 8.5 |
| Travel | 0.8 | 0.4 | 1.4 | 0.5 | 8.4 | 11.1 |
| No response | 5.1 | 9.7 | 0.8 | 0.6 | 0.9 | 0.2 |
| Total | 100 | 100 | 100 | 100 | 100 | 100 |

*Source:* ENJ 2002.

Table 12.3. Self-Identifiers among Baja California Youths Aged 15 to 29, by Gender (percentages)

| Referent | First Choice (n = 697,879) | | Second Choice (n = 627,674) | | Third Choice (n = 589,894) | |
|---|---|---|---|---|---|---|
| | Males | Females | Males | Females | Males | Females |
| Young | 62.9% | 47.1% | 4.2% | 5.3% | 4.0% | 5.1% |
| Gender | 8.0 | 24.6 | 12.8 | 30.7 | 4.4 | 3.7 |
| Student | 4.1 | 3.8 | 21.6 | 15.7 | 4.1 | 8.4 |
| Worker | 6.8 | 3.0 | 32.8 | 19.8 | 15.1 | 13.8 |
| Mexican | 7.1 | 1.8 | 14.5 | 10.0 | 28.3 | 21.9 |
| Citizen | 1.8 | 0.4 | 7.1 | 3.7 | 15.2 | 5.9 |
| Son or daughter | 1.6 | 4.4 | 4.0 | 5.7 | 19.6 | 21.1 |
| Mother or father | 1.3 | 5.7 | 2.9 | 8.7 | 8.5 | 18.8 |
| None | 6.1 | 8.6 | | 0.2 | 0.8 | 0.8 |
| No response | 0.3 | 0.6 | 0.1 | 0.2 | 0 | 0.5 |
| Total | 100 | 100 | 100 | 100 | 100 | 100 |

*Source*: ENJ 2002.

identity marker, young people generally offer worker, student, or Mexican. And as their third identifier, they list Mexican, son/daughter, and worker. What is of note here is that responses regarding identity markers differ by gender. Young men see themselves as youths, workers, students, and Mexicans, whereas gender is the primary referent among young women. This difference is also expressed in the way young women tend to distance themselves more from identities, such as citizen, that are linked to the public arena. Even though this identity marker is not common among youths in general, it is even rarer in the identity repertoire of young women.

Without going into detail about the socioeconomic differences or the polarization of educational and employment opportunities in Baja California, it is essential to note that the border region offers a number of ways to think about subjective well-being. The region's young people have access to various markets for consumer goods, and they are absorbed in reproducing and enjoying their lifestyle. On the other hand, their emphasis on stability in the private sphere is accompanied by their marked withdrawal from public space. In other words, the aspects of citizenship that favor social well-being open up possibilities for creating relatively stable private contexts but, as will be discussed below, they seem not to spur proactive attitudes in the public sphere.

A notable feature of the relationship that Baja Californians maintain with referents of the public/political sphere is a combination of distancing, suspicion, and ambiguity. For Baja Californians, political issues have little relevance in daily life, and state and government agencies have minimal credibility. Table 12.4 displays the degrees of trust young people have in government, political parties, Congress, labor unions, church, NGOs, the army, media, the family, and schools. The young people surveyed were given the opportunity to name their top three choices. The most frequent top choices were church and family. As a second choice in terms of level of trust, the leading response was the family, followed by the schools, church, and the media. In third place we find schools and the family. Political parties, the national Congress, labor unions, and civic organizations garnered lower degrees of trust; even the army scored higher than some. It is clear in these data that the institutions in which young people expressed trust are those of the private sphere: the family, church, and school.

Table 12.4. Institutions That Inspire Trust among Youths Aged 15 to 29 (percentages)

|  | First Choice (n = 697,879) | Second Choice (n = 575,376) | Third Choice (n = 508,376) |
|---|---|---|---|
| Government | 9.6% | 2.8% | 1.96% |
| Political parties | 1.0 | 2.4 | 0.4 |
| Congress | 1.4 | 1.4 | 0.9 |
| Labor unions | 2.3 | 1.3 | 0.9 |
| Church | 34.7 | 13.2 | 10 |
| Civic organizations | 0.9 | 2 | 2.7 |
| Army | 4.5 | 5.9 | 3.7 |
| Media | 3.4 | 10.8 | 9.0 |
| Family | 29.4 | 42.2 | 20.2 |
| School | 2.9 | 17.6 | 47.5 |
| None | 2.2 | 0.6 | 2.5 |
| No response | 7.9 | 0 | 0.2 |
| Total | 100 | 100 | 100 |

Source: ENJ 2002.

The same can be said about the representatives of various social institutions. Table 12.5 reveals respondents' levels of trust in such institutions through three response options: trust, little trust, and no trust. Among the social actors who ranked highest in terms of young Baja Californians' trust were teachers, doctors, and priests. Among the least trusted were politicians, local and federal police, and labor leaders. The trust placed in priests, teachers, and doctors may be based on respect for a specific way of asserting authority. Independent of the behavior of specific teachers, priests, and doctors, these positions are associated with a style of charismatic leadership that is exercised in a paternal or authoritarian way. On the other hand, the mid-range levels of trust in defenders of human rights, civic organizations, and businesspeople suggest the gradual emergence of new channels of self-identification.

Another observation merits mention here. When comparing responses from local youths with those obtained at the national level, it becomes apparent that a higher proportion of Baja Californian young people take an intermediate viewpoint, neither totally in favor nor totally opposed. For

Table. 12.5. Levels of Trust in Social Institutions among Youths Aged 15 to 29 (percentages)

| | Trust | | Little Trust | | No Trust | |
|---|---|---|---|---|---|---|
| | Baja California (n = 697,879) | Mexico (n = 26,913,981) | Baja California | Mexico | Baja California | Mexico |
| Politicians | 7.1% | 6.5% | 40.1% | 38.6% | 44.3% | 52.2% |
| Judges | 15.7 | 15.4 | 46.8 | 44.7 | 28.9 | 37.2 |
| Teachers | 52.6 | 65.4 | 31.9 | 26.7 | 7.1 | 5.3 |
| Doctors | 52.1 | 70.1 | 32.9 | 22.1 | 6.1 | 5.1 |
| Police | 7.5 | 11.6 | 45.3 | 37.7 | 38.8 | 48.0 |
| Businessmen | 16.5 | 16.8 | 46.2 | 44.8 | 28.5 | 35.6 |
| Military | 22.0 | 29.0 | 43.8 | 37.4 | 25.8 | 30.7 |
| Labor leaders | 9.5 | 12.1 | 43.3 | 35.4 | 38.3 | 49.6 |
| Priests | 42.7 | 58.6 | 34.3 | 22.9 | 14.2 | 15.8 |
| Federal police | 8.3 | 12.1 | 39.3 | 30.5 | 43.4 | 54.6 |
| Defenders of human rights | 32.4 | 46.6 | 45.0 | 36.3 | 13.6 | 14.3 |
| Members of civic organizations | 17.8 | 28.1 | 48.9 | 42.5 | 24.0 | 26.2 |

*Source*: ENJ 2002.

example, in table 12.5 the percentages tallied for the "little trust" response are consistently higher for the Baja California population. In the majority of cases where a Baja Californian respondent does not select the "trust" response, he or she chooses "little trust" rather than expressing a total lack of trust. These young people are taking a stance that does not commit them firmly to one position or another, suggesting that they lack well-defined categories for framing their experiences.

These results convey a sense of mistrust and caution. The institutions and actors who are the least trusted by young people are those that form part of the structure of the public sphere and that intervene in civil society's interactions with the state. This gap between those who are trusted and those who are not reflects the crisis in Mexico's institutional spaces and the precariousness of the bridges constructed to connect youth identities and political participation.

In terms of electoral participation, which is the exercise of one facet of the political rights of citizenship, more young people claim to have a voter identification card than actually do.[5] Table 12.6 suggests that over 80 percent of young people in Baja California have voter ID cards. However, Martínez Caballero (2002: 156, 159) found that the population between the ages of eighteen and twenty-five is underrepresented in both the pool of potential voters and on the list of registered voters.[6]

Survey responses related to social and political participation suggest a tendency toward apathy and distancing. Baja California's youth show a reduced level of involvement in any kind of social, political, or cultural

---

[5] Baja California was the first Mexican state to implement voter ID cards with the voter's photograph. The administration of Governor Ernesto Ruffo introduced the photo voter ID in 1992 as a means of combating electoral fraud, and the federal government adopted it in 1994. Since then, two separate election agencies—one federal and one state-level—have dispensed their own voter cards in Baja California, based on the same voter list. In the summer of 2002 it was suggested that the state abandon its voter card in the interests of reducing costs, but the state responded by suggesting that the federal voter ID be discontinued instead. The discussions stalled, and the issue of duplicate cards remains to be addressed at a future date.

[6] The under-registration of young people is even more significant when we consider that a key problem in the voter registry in Baja California is an overall under-registration of voters.

participation, and they are less willing to participate in various kinds of activities than is true among youth at the national level. Table 12.7 confirms that these young people have low levels of membership in social organizations, that few have participated in collective mobilizations, and that they tend to build alternative group identities. Among those who have participated in some kind of group, most were involved in religious, student, or sports organizations.

Table 12.6. Electoral Participation among Youths Aged 18 to 29 (percentages)

|  | Youths with Voter ID (n = 544,458) | Youths Who Have Voted (n = 544,458) | Youths Who Voted in 2000 (n = 544,458) |
|---|---|---|---|
| Yes | 83.4% | 80.7% | 66.7% |
| No | 12.7 | 14.8 | 28.3 |
| Not specified | 3.9 | 4.4 | 5.0 |
| Total | 100 | 100 | 100 |

*Source*: ENJ 2002.

Table 12.7. Social and Political Participation among Youths (percentages)

|  | Participate in Social Organizations (n = 859,755; ages 12–29) | Participate in Political Demonstrations (n = 697,879; ages 15–29) | Produce Posters, Graffiti, or Fanzines (n = 697,879; ages 15–29) |
|---|---|---|---|
| Yes | 12.7% | 2.8% | 1.8% |
| No | 86.6 | 87.2 | 86.8 |
| Not specified | 0.6 | 10 | 11.3 |
| Total | 100 | 100 | 100 |

*Source*: ENJ 2002.

There are, however, some groups toward which Baja California youth are favorably disposed in terms of participation: those groups that address environmental protection, crime control and security, peace, defense of indigenous rights, human rights, and defense of the rights of people with

HIV/AIDS. This set of areas of concern suggests that youths give priority to currently salient issues linked with quality of life and respect for human dignity (table 12.8).

There are two additional findings that merit mention. First, a higher proportion of Baja California youths is willing to take part in actions in support of homosexual and abortion rights than is found nationwide. Approximately a third of the state's young people seem to be questioning androcentric views of sexuality and women's rights over their bodies. Second, despite greater support on these topics, overall willingness to participate still remains lower than at the national level, suggesting that large sectors of Baja Californians are not moved to act on these issues.

Young people's tendency to distance themselves from the public arena is also visible in their symbolic representation of citizen action. Table 12.9 presents the characteristics that Baja California youth attribute to a "good citizen." The most frequent, given by about a third of the respondents, is "know what's going on." This was followed by "be committed to addressing the country's problems" and "don't get involved." Other answers that ranked relatively high were "no response" and "follow the norms of the majority." Apparently, for young Baja Californians, the exercise of good citizenship consists basically of keeping abreast of events but not getting overly involved.

## ENVIRONMENTAL EDUCATION ON THE BORDER: A GROWTH FIELD

Education for sustainability has gained importance in Mexico in recent years, initially in the form of environmental education. Environmental education entered the school curriculum in 1986 through the presidential decree that created the National Environmental Education Program (PRONEA), and environmental topics are now prominent in preschool, elementary, and secondary school texts. Nevertheless, obstacles remain that prevent a full implementation of this educational policy in practice. For example, despite a few notable exceptions, there is an overall shortage of teachers with appropriate training to present a pro-environment curriculum, and this dilutes the impacts produced in the students' education. At an institutional level, it is hoped that the Training Center for Sustainable Development (CECADESU) will facilitate better linkages between environmental policy and the Education Ministry. One program that shows

Table 12.8. Issue Areas in Which Youths Aged 15 to 29 Are Willing to Become Active (percentages)

| | Willing to Participate | | Not Willing to Participate | |
|---|---|---|---|---|
| | Baja California (n = 697,879) | Mexico (n = 26,713,184) | Baja California | Mexico |
| Political parties | 21.9% | 23.8% | 68.7% | 73.3% |
| Peace | 67.3 | 83.9 | 23.5 | 13.2 |
| Human rights | 63.4 | 83.9 | 27.4 | 13.2 |
| Civic protests | 39.8 | 44.9 | 51.0 | 52.2 |
| Homosexual rights | 29.0 | 25.5 | 61.4 | 71.6 |
| Abortion rights | 24.4 | 18.1 | 66.2 | 79.0 |
| HIV/AIDS | 54.7 | 67.1 | 35.5 | 29.9 |
| Indigenous rights | 65.7 | 85.9 | 25.0 | 11.2 |
| Environmental defense | 69.9 | 86.1 | 20.9 | 10.9 |
| Crime control and security | 69.0 | 81.8 | 21.8 | 15.2 |

Source: ENJ 2002.

promise for promoting such linkages and joint actions is the Environmental Program for Youth 2000–2006 (Programa Ambiental para la Juventud 2000–2006), which involves a large number of federal-level public institutions.

Table 12.9. Characteristics That Youths Aged 15 to 29 Attribute to a "Good Citizen" (percentages)

| Characteristic | Total (n = 697,657) |
|---|---|
| Awareness of current events | 33.8% |
| Commitment to resolving the country's problems | 15.6 |
| Follow the norms of the majority society | 9.2 |
| Don't get involved | 16.0 |
| Speak your mind, regardless of the consequences | 4.8 |
| Help others | 7.4 |
| Not specified | 13.2 |
| Total | 100 |

Source: ENJ 2002.

Environmental education and education for sustainability in Baja California are very visible in certain universities and academic areas. Examples include the Tijuana Technological Institute (Instituto Tecnológico de Tijuana), which offers a degree program in environmental engineering; the Mexicali campus of the National Teachers University (Universidad Pedagógica Nacional), which awards a master's degree in environmental education; and El Colegio de la Frontera Norte (COLEF), which, in collaboration with the Center for Scientific Research and Higher Education of Ensenada (CICESE), supports a master's program in integrated environmental management. Several other institutions of higher learning give courses on environmental systems and train their faculty to conduct activities such as water quality monitoring.

Many other environmental education efforts take place in Baja California but outside of the academic arena. These are sponsored by federal, state, and municipal authorities, often in collaboration with academic institutions, and they involve environmental fairs, exhibits, campaigns, and specialized materials. Thus, for example, since 1996 the Ecology Office (Dirección de Ecología General) has organized Expoambiente for children and youths, and Tijuana has held ongoing workshops, forestation campaigns, and environmental education programs in Parque Estatal Morales.

Another dynamic area of education on environmental topics is found within civil society. Civic organizations working on environmental issues in the border region are involved in a wide range of activities that include, among others: training teachers in environmental education; training community outreach "promoters" (residents of working-class neighborhoods); developing educational and teaching materials; holding conferences that bring organizational representatives together with academics from regional institutions; producing audiovisual materials for the general public; staging temporary and permanent art exhibits with educational content; organizing educational fieldtrips for student groups; advising the educational sector on the design and development of teaching programs; and sponsoring forums and inter-institutional networks, many of them binational.

There are a number of civil society groups in Baja California that work on educating for sustainability. The following are among them: the Border Environmental Education Project (PFEA) supports networking among organizations dedicated to environmental education on Mexico's northern border; the Biregional Environmental Education Project (PROBEA A.C.) trains Baja California teachers and professors; Ecology Village (Aldea Ecológica) promotes workshops on reuse and recycling of waste materials; Ecoparque, a COLEF initiative, offers tours and workshops at its installations; Foundation Hope (Fundación Esperanza) provides an informational program on appropriate water uses through community promoters in Tijuana; the Community Services Center at the Universidad Iberoamericana offers workshops on water use and recycling for community promoters; the Working Group of Thermoelectric Engineers of the Border (Grupo de Trabajo de Termoeléctricas Fronterizas) gives workshops on developing sustainable policies for building new thermoelectric plants in the border region; the Children's Foundation (Fundación Los Niños) trains community outreach volunteers in promoting consumption of organic food products, recycling, and composting; Tecate's Citizen Participation and Defense

Committee (Comité de Participación y Defensa Ciudadana) offers environmental education classes for adults; Tecate's "Las Piedras" Environmental Education Center (Centro de Educación Ambiental "Las Piedras") trains students and teachers; CUNA's Indigenous Center for Environmental Information Management (Centro Indígena de Manejo de Información Ambiental) is active in Ensenada; and Pro Esteros promotes the conservation of wetlands and natural resources among children, adolescents, and fishermen. Still other organizations involved in environmental education activities are Ecosol-Cultura Ecológica, the Boy Scouts, and Gaviotas, among others. A number of the aforementioned groups have links and influence with organizations on the U.S. side of the border.

Notable among the groups engaged in cross-border collaboration are the Biregional Environmental Education Project (PROBEA) and the Environmental Education Council for the Californias (EECC/CEAC), both established after 1998. PROBEA also collaborates with U.S. groups and institutions, including the San Diego Natural History Museum, Daedalus, the Alliance for Environmental Education, Sistemas Bilingües, the Border Environmental Educational Project, Tijuana River National Estuarine Research Reserve, Los Niños, Olas Limpias, Pro Esteros, San Diego County Water Authority, and the Sistema Educativo Estatal (Baja California), among others. The EECC, for its part, defines itself as a binational network of environmental organizations for community research, policy, dissemination, and advocacy that are involved or interested in environmental education. It comprises more than thirty organizations, which come from both sides of the border.

The preceding discussion sketched out the current situation of environmental education as promoted by citizen groups. What we have found certainly suggests that social organizations in the California–Baja California border zone have made significant steps in environmental education through programs that adopt a range of perspectives and that operate cross-nationally.

## MAPPING UNCERTAINTY: REFLECTIONS ON THE POLITICAL-CULTURAL BORDER SCENARIO

At this point we must consider the broader political-cultural context in which political socialization and environmental education programs unfold among the border region's youth. This discussion considers the impact that sociocultural processes on the border produce on the forms of civic and social participation of the region's citizens.

Tijuana–San Diego is a place of dynamic processes of sociocultural exchange. García Canclini (1990) and Valenzuela Arce (1998, 2000) have highlighted the hybrid and syncretic nature of social processes on the border between Tijuana and the United States, emphasizing that these processes are crosscut by power relationships that generate inequality and confrontation. Nevertheless, there has been little note of the influence these sociocultural processes exert on the tensions that permeate citizen participation in the area. Below, we focus on the effects that sociocultural tensions produce on the Mexican side of the border, identifying three interlinked processes that shape border actors' choices for citizen participation.

### Indeterminate Sociability Structures

The first element to consider is what we call "indeterminate sociability structures," which have their roots in the historical character of the border region. Given the region's short history of just over a hundred years and its mere four decades of modernization, the structures that underlie the area's social relations are not yet securely embedded, and they offer unstable referents to guide the processes of socialization and the negotiation of social identities. Related factors here include the population mobility associated with migration flows; accelerated and unplanned urban growth which unintentionally contributes to segmenting and polarizing access to basic urban services; the nascent consolidation of civil society institutions and actors (universities, political parties, labor organizations, church groups, and so on); a labor market that is flexible and expanding, but also volatile and unstable; and the recent transformation of state institutions. This last point merits special note: the transformation of public debate in Baja California during the 1990s illustrates the obstacles that exist to the creation of new institutional referents. In particular, as discussed further below, the construction of spaces and referents for socialization in a culture of democracy still encounters areas that lag behind.

Beginning with the election of opposition candidate Ernesto Ruffo of the National Action Party (PAN) to the governorship in 1989, Baja California has consolidated an institutional apparatus that guarantees transparency and equity in electoral processes, achieved balance between the three branches of state power, and reformed the structure of public administration at both the state and municipal levels in the interest of making more efficient the design and implementation of public policies (Espinoza Valle 1998, 2000; Guillén López 1993, 2001; Rodríguez and Ward 1994). Among political actors, the PAN has consolidated as the primary political force, even though, as Hernández Vicencio (2001) has observed, there are still some areas in need of better institutionalization. The party has gained in overall strength despite intense infighting, and its gains are thanks in no small measure to the fragmentation that emerged over the same period in the state-level organizations of the other two main parties, the Institutional Revolutionary Party (PRI) and Party of the Democratic Revolution (PRD).

Ironically, despite these advances, the area that most suffers from the lack of citizen involvement is that of political representation. The abstention rate for the 2001 local elections was 64 percent, and in the 2003 midterm elections it soared even higher, to 70 percent. These numbers can be read as an expression of the distancing between political actors and Baja California society. Further, they suggest that, even though the state's political parties (basically the PAN and the PRI) compete for positions of popular representation, both have evolved toward a model of low citizen participation.

Moreover, the channels for linking the citizenry and government remain undeveloped and precarious. According to various analysts (see Guillén López 2001; Ruiz Vargas 2001), the alternating administrations, and particularly the PAN administrations, have had little success in building new links with civil society or in democratically incorporating citizen participation in public debate. Among other things, this means that the citizenry still finds few channels or referents in the political arena through which it can expect concrete responses to the dilemmas of daily life.

## Symbolic Uncertainty

"Symbolic uncertainty" is the second important sociocultural process we have identified. Given the region's indeterminate sociability structures, exchanges between the distinct symbolic codes that exist in the border region produce unstable and ambiguous semantic reinscription on the Mexican side of the border. Not only do the conjunctures of traditions, binational referents, technologies, and cultural industries create hybridizations; at the same time, they also question certainties and make knowledge relative. The importance of this process lies in the fact that the reconstruction of social meanings is not always achieved through what we might call inclusionary dialogue. Quite the contrary; they tend to contribute to conflict among social actors. In this way, nationality, ethnicity, skin color, and accent are all elements that, in combination, determine various kinds of discordances in public space. For example, with regard to relations between what is "American" and what is "Latino-Mexicano," the cultural mixes and exchanges—typified by the combined use of English and Spanish—serve simultaneously to establish hierarchies of varying reach, which range from the merely colloquial ("the most attractive feature of Tijuana is San Diego") to a legitimization of violence, as observed in the racist attitudes toward Latinos and the persecution of so-called illegal aliens.

**Strategic Interventions**

The third process we call "strategic interventions." The instabilities, confrontations, and potentialities that are reproduced in multiple areas of life on the border oblige individuals to develop tactics that ensure some continuity in their daily surroundings. On the Mexican side of the border, these tactics tend to be instrumental and particularistic in nature. On the one hand, the aim is to maximize overall conditions of well-being given an unstable socioeconomic context. On the other, the deployment of these strategies works to protect each actor's specific interests. These two features are best understood from a historical perspective: Mexico's northern border has long been viewed as an area where anyone with the will and determination can succeed—regardless of whether success comes from legitimate or illegal endeavors. On the other hand, Mexico's corporatist and clientelistic tradition in social negotiation is less embedded in the border region than in other areas of the country.

The notion of "strategic interventions" refers to a series of measures actors can employ to benefit from the border region's symbolic and material resources. The border's particular pattern of economic development, a tax structure that permits the controlled but relatively easy importation of U.S. products, and regional consumers' pragmatic outlook present border residents with a multitude of opportunities. In this sense, "strategic interventions" have a highly salient cultural dimension; they develop in parallel with the model lifestyles of Southern California—which, on a symbolic plane, represent the pinnacle of the "American way of life"—through transborder flows of media content, people, and merchandise.

These measures—and the full set of sociocultural processes mentioned previously—produce ambivalence in terms of empowering border actors. On one hand, they are reproducing a way of life that resolves border life's uncertainty and instability in particularistic terms. A key point here is that private life on the border is highly vulnerable. Transnational organized crime networks, rising public insecurity (kidnappings, car theft, burglaries), and a poorly developed justice system all undermine individuals' ability to retain control over their persons and belongings. When we add the instabilities that derive from the border's economic development model, it is not difficult to understand why people's priorities turn on building certainty and continuity in their private lives. On the other hand, the use of strategic interventions links with the reconstruction of social meanings through the consumption and idealization of Southern Californian lifestyles, meaning that the forms of youths' citizen empowerment are largely focused on stability in private life and subjective well-being.

Nevertheless, the border's sociocultural dynamics and concomitant dilemmas can produce other outcomes. Based on their concrete daily experiences, border actors have articulated various social action projects. These projects vary by objective, duration, and mobilizing capacity. Many are targeted actions by small groups to benefit charitable works. Others aim to preserve cultural patterns, protect human rights, or promote sustainable development. And these projects—regardless of whether their action arena is the neighborhood, the municipality, or the transborder region—together are creating new forms of civil society action in the Tijuana area. Although these undertakings may be dispersed, uneven, or short-term, they are bringing to the regional civic arena a sense of citizen capacity to intervene and participate in issues of shared concern. It remains to more precisely evaluate the durability and impacts of these social groupings and movements. But, as we noted at the beginning of this essay, our aim is to point out that this social action space represents an arena with a plethora of opportunities for citizen empowerment.

## FINAL REFLECTIONS

Above, we suggested that education for sustainability in the California–Baja California border region offers an arena for the citizen empowerment of border youths. We provided a series of arguments, based on a variety of sources, to suggest points for review and reflection. We indicated the need to view this population from new angles that may hold answers for transforming the region's young people into key actors in a sustainable society. Based on data from the National Youth Survey, we analyzed the current situation of Baja California youths, a population with more uncertainty than certainty, working to build stability into their private lives. This does not make them passive actors; rather, it imbues their actions with more social meanings. We also briefly reviewed the regional development of environmental education and education for sustainability, identifying some of the social organizations that are active on this front.

Seeking to provide some keys to understanding the logics of the youthful population's political culture and the dynamic of the social organizations that educate them about sustainability, we have outlined three sociocultural processes that are shaping social action in the Tijuana border region. These processes—which we call indeterminate sociability structures, symbolic uncertainties, and strategic interventions—are some of the factors defining the conditions for individual choices of privatistic action strategies distanced from the common interest, but they are also driving various forms of participation and cross-border social action.

Given these circumstances, what is needed is to purposefully create social spaces capable of linking these individuals' life trajectories with projects that advance sustainability. We want to emphasize the need to build bridges between actions for sustainability and the spaces of youths' socialization. The border is, without question, a region that experiences intense sociocultural confrontations and uncertainties; but social action to promote an integral and sustainable relationship with the environment can give new meanings to sociability.

In sum, there is an urgent need to encourage research and education on and for sustainability, citizen action, and the involvement of young people in these endeavors. We are convinced that this region's future will depend in large part on how well these tasks can be made to resonate with one another.

## References

CELADE (Centro Latinoamericano y Caribeño de Demografía). 2000. *Juventud, población y desarrollo: problemas, posibilidades y desafíos*. Santiago de Chile: CELADE.

CEPAL (Comisión Económica para América Latina y el Caribe). 2000. *Adolescencia y juventud en América Latina y el Caribe: problemas, oportunidades y desafíos en el comienzo de un nuevo siglo*. Santiago de Chile: CEPAL.

CONAPO (Consejo Nacional de Población). 2000. *La situación demográfica de México*. Mexico City: CONAPO.

Dryzek, John. 2000. *Deliberative Democracy and Beyond*. Oxford: Oxford University Press.

ENJ (Encuesta Nacional de Juventud 2000). 2002. *Jóvenes mexicanos del siglo XXI. Encuesta Nacional de Juventud 2000*. Mexico: Secretaría de Educación Pública and Centro de Investigación y Estudios sobre Juventud, Instituto Mexicano de la Juventud.

Espinoza Valle, Víctor A. 1998. *Alternancia política y gestión pública: el Partido Acción Nacional en el gobierno de Baja California*. Tijuana: El Colegio de la Frontera Norte.

———. 2000. "El segundo gobierno de oposición en Baja California (1995–1998)." In *Alternancia y transición política*, ed. Víctor Espinoza Valle. Mexico: El Colegio de la Frontera Norte and Plaza y Valdés.

Feixa, Carles. 1998. *El reloj de arena: culturas juveniles en México*. Mexico: Secretaría de Educación Pública and Centro de Investigación y Estudios sobre Juventud, Instituto Mexicano de la Juventud.

Friedmann, John. 2002. *The Prospect of Cities*. Minneapolis: University of Minnesota Press.

Furlong, Andy, and Fred Cartmel. 1997. *Young People and Social Change. Individualization and Risk in Late Modernity*. Buckingham: Open University Press.

García Canclini, Néstor. 1990. *Culturas híbridas: estrategias para entrar y salir de la modernidad*. Mexico: Grijalbo.

Guillén López, Tonatiuh. 1993. *Baja California 1989–1992: alternancia política y transición democrática*. Mexico: El Colegio de la Frontera Norte and CIIH, Universidad Nacional Autónoma de México.

———. 2001. "Democratic Transitions in Baja California: Stages and Actors." In *Party Politics and the Struggle for Democracy in Mexico*, ed. Kevin J. Middlebrook. La Jolla: Center for U.S.-Mexican Studies, University of California, San Diego.

Hernández Vicencio, Tania. 2001. *De la oposición al poder: el PAN en Baja California, 1986–2000*. Mexico: El Colegio de la Frontera Norte.

INEGI (Instituto Nacional de Estadística, Geografía e Informática). 2001. *Tabulados Básicos. Estados Unidos Mexicanos. XII Censo General de Población y Vivienda 2000*. Mexico: INEGI.

Krauskopf, Dina. 2000. "Cambio de paradigmas y participación política," *JÓVENes, Revista de Estudios sobre Juventud* 4, no. 11 (April–June): 142–57.

Martínez Caballero, Graciela. 2002. "Migración-mortalidad—sobre registro en el padrón electoral: el caso de Baja California 1995–2001." Master's thesis, El Colegio de la Frontera Norte.

Miles, Steven. 2000. *Youth Lifestyles in a Changing World*. Buckingham and Philadelphia: Open University Press.

Monsiváis Carrillo, Alejandro. 2002. "Ciudadanía y juventud: elementos para una articulación conceptual," *Perfiles Latinoamericanos* 20: 157–76.

Paden, Mary. 2000. "Education for Sustainability and Environmental Education." In *Education for a Sustainable Future*, ed. Keith A. Wheeler and Anne Perraca Bijur. New York: Kluwer Academic/Plenum.

Reguillo, Rossana. 2000. *Emergencia de culturas juveniles: estrategias del desencanto*. Buenos Aires: Norma.

———. 2002. "Cuerpos juveniles, políticas de identidad." In *Movimientos juveniles en América Latina: pachucos, malandros, punketos*, ed. Carles Feixa, Fidel Molina, and Carles Alsinet. Spain: Ariel.

Rodríguez, Ernesto. 2000. "Políticas públicas de juventud y reforma del Estado en América Latina: un vínculo a construir." In *El lugar de las organizaciones civiles en las políticas públicas de juventud*, ed. Héctor Morales Gil de la Torre. Mexico: Secretaría de Educación Pública and Centro de Investigación y Estudios sobre Juventud, Instituto Mexicano de la Juventud.

Rodríguez, Victoria E., and Peter M. Ward. 1994. *Political Change in Baja California*. La Jolla: Center for U.S.-Mexican Studies, University of California, San Diego.

Ruiz Vargas, Benedicto. 2001. "La relación gobierno-sociedad en Baja California." In *La experiencia de PAN: diez años de gobierno en Baja California*, ed. Tania Hernández Vicencio and José Negrete Mata. Mexico: El Colegio de la Frontera Norte and Plaza y Valdés.

Valenzuela Arce, José Manuel. 1997. *A la brava, ese*. Mexico: El Colegio de la Frontera Norte and Escuela de Trabajo Social, Universidad Nacional Autónoma de México.

———. 1998. *El color de las sombras: chicanos, identidad y racismo*. Mexico: El Colegio de la Frontera Norte, Universidad Iberoamericana, and Plaza y Valdés.

———. 2000. "Formas de resistencia, corredores de poder: arte público en la frontera México–Estados Unidos." In *Intromisiones compartidas: arte y sociedad en la frontera México–Estados Unidos*, ed. Néstor García Canclini and José Manuel Valenzuela Arce. San Diego and Tijuana: Fondo Nacional para la Cultura y las Artes and inSITE97.

Wallace, Claire. 2001. "Youth, Citizenship and Empowerment." In *Youth, Citizenship and Empowerment*, ed. Helena Helve and Claire Wallace. London: Ashgate.

Wyn, Johanna, and Rob White. 1993. *Rethinking Youth*. London: Sage.

# 13

## NGOs, Environment, and Gender in Tijuana

SILVIA LÓPEZ ESTRADA

Urban residents in the Mexico-U.S. border region are strongly affected by the impacts of globalization and industrial restructuring, processes that have accelerated under the North American Free Trade Agreement (NAFTA). The environmentally harmful impacts of these processes include auto emissions, industrial pollution from emissions and industrial waste, health and safety risks in the workplace attributable to contaminants used in the *maquiladora* industry, and pollution produced by an ever-increasing number of households in the region's rapidly expanding urban areas.

To address contamination issues and to reduce environmental risks in their living and working spaces, social actors have developed a variety of strategies tailored to a range of action arenas. Women's participation has been a key element in these strategies at the household level, at the community level, and also within nongovernmental organizations (NGOs).

Within this context, this essay analyzes the actions of three women's NGOs in Tijuana on gender and environmental issues. I suggest that women's NGOs in Tijuana that work on environmental issues have paid little heed to a gender perspective, while women's NGOs that address issues of reproductive health have given little attention to issues of the environment. Nevertheless, there is now an emerging interest within both types of organization to link their efforts for sustainable development based on women's participation. This essay is based on a review of the literature on gender and environment, and on interviews with representatives of women's NGOs working on environmental and reproductive health issues in Tijuana.

---

Translation by Sandra del Castillo.

## THE GENDER/ENVIRONMENT/SUSTAINABLE DEVELOPMENT DEBATE

Since the 1970s, the global environmental crisis has been at the center of discussions of development. The aim has been to work toward sustainability, defined as "a pattern of development that reduces to a minimum the degradation of the ecological basis for production and habitability" (Gallopin, Gutman, and Malleta 1989, cited in Velázquez 1996).

Margarita Velázquez, writing from a social perspective, assessed the focus of Gallopin and colleagues and defined sustainable development as:

> a set of processes that necessarily imply finding different modes of development that avoid the progressive exhaustion of the earth's resources on which human life depends, at the same time that they allow sufficient production of goods and services to satisfy the basic needs of the global population and improve the quality of life for present and future generations (Velázquez 1997).

We must add to this definition the perspective of historically and culturally determined gender relations.

Despite the widespread recognition among development planners of the role of women in this process—in particular, women's interaction with their physical surroundings, their role in environmental degradation, and the impacts of environmental issues on their lives[1]—there has been little study of the environment-gender interaction as a means of implementing practices for sustainable development. Women's contributions in the use and management of natural resources have remained on the margins. At best, gender considerations are merely appended to environmental projects.

The study of the links among gender, environment, and development is still at an early stage. To advance this focus, we must recognize that the division of labor by sex and age is a central determinant in resource use and management in contemporary societies (Velázquez 1997). We can distinguish at least two theoretical approaches within the related academic

---

[1] These include, for example, the increase in women's workload as they gather firewood, haul water, and so on, as well as the impacts of pollution and exposure to chemicals, both in the workplace and in their communities (Sen and Grown 1988).

debate. One, promoted by development agencies, emphasizes resource management while minimizing the deleterious effects of economic development; it accomplishes this by viewing women as the recipients of economic assistance and development's environmental impacts. In contrast, organizations like Development Alternatives for Women in a New Era (DAWN)[2] assert that environmental degradation is linked to the Western development model. Such groups emphasize development's deleterious impacts on women in southern countries, and they propose changes for an alternative development that channels more economic resources to the world's poorest groups, women among them (Sen and Grown 1988).

Looking at women's work from an economic perspective, the division of labor has clearly given women a special role in managing natural resources. This role is a by-product of the historical evolution of a patriarchal social structure that assigned the economic production role to men and gave to women the less valued roles related to economic reproduction.

Adopting a cultural perspective, the sex-based division of labor gave women a proximity to nature, which underlies their portrayal as privileged and natural caretakers of their natural surroundings. Women have amassed knowledge about the natural environment that is unique to them and more relevant than the knowledge men and women share. Women's relationship with nature is reciprocal, harmonious, and mutual (Braidotti et al. 1994: 93).

Within this line of thought, the work of Mies is particularly notable (see, for example, Mies 1996). Mies envisioned a dual relationship between women and nature, operating first through biological reproduction, and second through women's efforts to provide for their families' basic needs. Shiva proposes the existence of a practical relationship between women and the natural environment embedded within the feminine principle (respect for life in nature and society), and she proposes this relationship as the basis for sustainable development (Shiva 1991, 1994; Mies and Shiva 1993). For both Mies and Shiva, the dominant development model is patriarchal and based on a reductionist model of science and technology at the service of the global market, a model that threatens to destroy women,

---

[2] DAWN was established during the World Conference on Women in Nairobi in 1984.

nature, and everything non-Western. Both authors propose an alternative development model (Braidotti et al. 1994).

These authors' perspective has been criticized as essentialist, because they largely ignore the role of other factors, such as race, social class or caste, or the gender and kinship systems that prevail in every society (Braidotti et al. 1994; Velázquez 1997). Shiva's focus has also been characterized as biological given her assumption that the supposed relationship between women and nature exists as a function of women's reproductive capacity (Velázquez 1997). And finally, it has been argued that equating women with nature reinforces women's continued subordination to men (Braidotti et al. 1994: 98).

These various authors do not consider the history-specific contexts in which the women/nature linkages occur as part of broader socioeconomic systems that determine men's and women's sociocultural practices in production and reproduction. They do, however, question the dominant model as the only possible model. They note the violence that development wreaks on people and nature and its destructive effects on cultures and lifestyles, and they highlight the validity of popular knowledge in the search for alternative development models that adhere to principles of sustainable development and environmental protection (Braidotti et al. 1994).

Bina Agarwal (1991) develops an environmental feminism, a focus that integrates various elements from the women-and-development debate. Basing her work on India's environmental crisis, Agarwal analyzes material reality and the ideological construction of meanings. She views women as social actors interacting with their environmental surroundings because they suffer the effects of environmental degradation in gender-specific ways at the same time that they act to resolve them. Agarwal notes that environmental movements have been composed primarily of poor women who, because of their socioeconomic marginality, have been forced to maintain a reciprocal relationship with nature. This suggests that this relationship has been constructed socially and culturally, and that it is not biologically determined. As a result, Agarwal proposes that the relationship between women and the environment is structured by a class and gender organization of production, reproduction, and distribution (Agarwal 1991: 8).

## WOMEN'S NGOS, ENVIRONMENT, AND HEALTH

Women's nongovernmental organizations have drawn attention to women as privileged agents in managing health and the environment and have highlighted the need to involve women in strategies for sustainable development. These NGOs constitute alternative spaces for policy discussions in which women can represent their own interests and develop new and unique forms of action. In general, women's NGOs are characterized by tolerance and alternative models, and they place openness to negotiation at the core of efforts to achieve their objectives.

These feminine spaces based on alternative models of social relations are the sites of much discussion and debate, reflection and training, political maneuvering and participation, and advocacy to influence public policy making. They also fulfill a recognized role as mediators between women's needs and governmental social policies to the degree that they link the interests of popular sectors with groups that have technical-professional capacity (Tarrés 1998).

In the area of reproductive health, various regional-level studies have demonstrated the importance of NGOs in building citizenship based on the defense of sexual and reproductive rights and in constructing reproductive health as a social project. A key task of NGOs is to inform women of their reproductive rights and to create mechanisms to protect those already formally guaranteed (González Montes 1999).

In terms of the environment, in addition to supporting demographic policies that respect reproductive rights and promote access to quality health care, NGOs have opposed the consumption patterns that are contributing to poverty and environmental degradation. They call for a clean urban and rural environment, and they promote development policies that protect the atmosphere and support environmental education. These commitments were ratified at the Johannesburg World Summit on Sustainable Development.

It is through international conferences that women's organizations have introduced their perspective on reproductive health and the environment, underscoring the need to empower women as a prerequisite for the sustained survival of all. Several such conferences were held in the 1990s, including the Global Women's Assembly on Environment and the World Women's Caucus for a Healthy Planet. The latter culminated in the

Women's Action Agenda 21, through which women of different positions and from diverse geographical areas joined in their criticism of the dominant development model and proposed a system of social responsibility focused on human needs (Braidotti et al. 1994: 91).

On Mexico's northern border—where economic and social dynamism has meant the broad participation of women, and where the vanguard of Mexico's political transition is visible in state reform and party alternation—NGOs have seen a blossoming of opportunities to participate in the public sphere. They have conquered their fears of losing autonomy and have come to serve as interlocutors as they have gained a degree of recognition among officialdom.

According to some analysts (see, for example, Verduzco Chávez 2000), environmental NGOs in Mexico's northern border region are composed primarily of women.[3] In Tijuana, this is true of organizations such as the Playas de Tijuana Housewives Association (Amas de Casa de Playas de Tijuana) and the Border Environmental Education Project (Proyecto Fronterizo de Educación Ambiental), both of which are made up entirely of women. The same pattern tends to apply to organizations active in reproductive health.

In general, environmental NGOs and those working on reproductive health try to integrate the agreements reached in international conferences into their local programs and work agendas. Yet, despite the fact that international conferences on the environment widened the horizons of the women's movement in the 1990s as NGOs introduced the gender-environment relationship and women's role in development as key points in the discussion, I suggest that environmental NGOs in Tijuana are not conscious of the need to include a gender perspective in their programs and activities.

Even though women's environmental NGOs clearly see the destruction of natural resources as a result of the development model, the role of women as environmental agents is less clear in terms of the reciprocal relationship women hold with their work and home environments. In other words, the role of women as key actors in the use and management of natural resources seems to go unnoticed in these organizations.

---

[3] The exception is conservationist groups, in which men predominate.

Yet there is a nascent and growing relationship between these two types of women's organizations. For NGOs working in the area of reproductive health, their daily encounters with poor and working women have revealed the risks these women face in the factories and in their communities as a result of industrial pollution. And even though environmental organizations have not prioritized a gender perspective in their programs, they have given financial support for environmental education to some reproductive health groups.

Until now, women's organizations have focused primarily on industrial pollution as it affects urban areas, including industrial waste products from maquiladoras, the installation of hazardous-waste treatment plants, and the impacts of both in their communities.[4] The issue of industrial pollution is particularly relevant in Tijuana, where many industrial parks are located within densely populated residential zones.

The focus within the factories falls on the toxic effects that various industrial materials have on the health of women workers. To address these problems, women's organizations have lobbied on public policy design and strengthened their organizational ties with the authorities and with urban communities.

The impacts of environmental degradation on households have received less organizational attention, on the presumption that, within the home, these costs of the environmental crisis have been privatized through domestic practices of resource use and management.[5] This perspective has been documented in studies conducted in various regions of Mexico, including along the country's northern border (see Gaxiola, this volume). Even so, some environmental organizations have promoted educational projects in the use and management of environmental resources and have implemented projects on waste recycling, composting, backyard gardens, and so on.

---

[4] Environmentalism along Mexico's northern border has tended to shift from species protection to quality-of-life questions in urban settlements (Verduzco Chávez 2002).

[5] Some of these practices involve keeping the dwelling habitable, disposing of trash, using and managing water, and raising fruits, vegetables, and small animals in the yard.

In the following section, I consider the arguments outlined above in terms of the experiences of three women's nongovernmental organizations: two environmental NGOs and one reproductive health NGO. It should be noted that these three organizations have been studied previously regarding their participation in the environmental movement and their effectiveness in influencing public policy (Verduzco Chávez 2000). However, they have not been examined from a gender perspective.

### The Playas de Tijuana Housewives Association

The Playas de Tijuana Housewives Association arose around community demands for public utilities, garbage collection, and so on.[6] This NGO grew in importance when it opposed the building of a waste-oil incinerator in the Playas de Tijuana neighborhood. According to some analysts (see, for example, Verduzco Chávez 2002), the organization's membership in the binational Environmental Health Coalition contributed to its success in this action.

Blocking construction of the waste-oil incinerator gave the organization a notable success, and it is building on this success by continuing its environmental activities (Fontecilla 1998; Verduzco Chávez 2002). For example, in 1998 this group blocked the opening of a public prosecutor's office in Playas because, they argued, the office would spur the arrival of diners, stationery shops, copy centers, and street vendors, all of which threatened community safety. Given that Playas is a middle-class residential community, the position of the Housewives Association resonated widely.

The Playas Housewives Association works primarily to advance environmental demands and raise environmental awareness (Fontecilla 1998). Its mission is to protect the well-being of family and community through social action based on a woman's place at the heart of the family. Because members of this organization are not familiar with the gender perspective, their environmental demands are not gender specific. Yet there is broad consensus that women working together can resolve problems within their communities. They have the capacity to take on a range of actions, espe-

---

[6] This group had previously belonged to the Red de Mujeres de Baja California (Baja California Women's Network), but it left this group, perhaps due to differences in demands, focus, or ideology.

cially if they are organized in nongovernmental organizations. Women are not viewed as having unequal access to environmental resources, and their greater involvement in resource management in their homes and communities is seen as part of their reproductive responsibilities. Members of the Housewives Association take their lead from the organization's director, who believes that women have an advantage over men in the public arena given that the authorities, seeing the group's members as the "weaker sex," generally refrain from physical means of control.[7]

This organization provides environmental education through conferences and lectures at schools and professional institutes, and in other organizations and communities. Though no concrete programs are yet under way, the organization has plans to implement community programs in gardening and composting.

Although the Housewives Association did extensive research to support their opposition to the waste-oil incinerator, such an investigative approach is rare. In political activism around environmental issues, the organization's objectives and timetable respond to the demands of society, which tends to make their activities cyclical. As one member noted, "We come together when there is a problem, and when the problem is resolved we return to our homes." Yet the organization has strong mobilizing capacity when calling upon the community to demonstrate, protest, and support the organization's demands. This capacity is due in part to the NGO leader's prior membership in the Ciudad Satélite Housewives Association in Mexico City[8] and to the experience that members of the Playas Housewives Association have gained over time in their interactions with local government officials and politicians.

---

[7] Like other women's organizations whose demands are not gender specific, the Playas Housewives Association has taken advantage of this perception to press its demands and maintain a public presence without fear of physical reprisals. See, for example, the case of the mothers of the "disappeared," as examined by Maier (1998).

[8] According to a study by Tarrés (1998), this community spurred a permanent mobilization to demand the installation of public utilities. Women were active participants, building their own groups and networks. The director of the Playas Housewives Association was a member of one of these groups.

The Playas de Tijuana Housewives Association has recently been called to action over the planned construction of a storage facility for liquefied natural gas in southern Playas de Tijuana. This NGO, along with other environmental organizations, met with representatives of the three levels of government to oppose the Marathon Oil Company's proposal because, they allege, this land use change would entail dire consequences for the community.[9]

The Playas Housewives Association has built a history of involvement at the forefront of a number of social causes. Yet the group has few links with other local-level social organizations, largely because it has tried to build its strength through alliances with binational organizations.

Within a framework of globalization and economic liberalization—and the impacts of both on the border area—membership in the Environmental Health Coalition and other networks such as the Border Ecology Project has encouraged Housewives of Tijuana to enter areas other than the environmental arena, including issues linked to social justice such as the case of undocumented migration.

**Border Environmental Education Project**

The Border Environmental Education Project (PFEA) was established in 1991 to encourage broader involvement in environmental policy and education on the Mexico-U.S border. Its members are professionals who work as advisers or consultants and do environmental education activities with the public at large. The PFEA gears its activities toward providing the public with information on environmental topics and encouraging citizen participation; supporting the development of environmental education; developing strategies and alliances to influence public policy; and promoting spaces for networking and collaboration.

This NGO focuses on managing resources and waste products in urban areas, covering such topics as efficient water use, reuse, and conservation; appropriate garbage and trash disposal; recycling of organic waste products; and forestation. The group works with schools through teacher training, and in communities through the training of outreach volunteers.

---

[9] The Playas Housewives Association sent a formal petition to the Mexican Congress through then-congressional deputy Alejandro Monraz.

The project's regional focus is based on the idea that the environment does not recognize political borders, though the organization does recognize cultural differences and works to ensure that they are respected. It views people as a part of nature and stresses that development of human communities must be integrated with natural systems (*Boletín CEAC*, Spring–Summer 2002).

Although the Border Environmental Education Project is composed principally of women and women are the primary users of its environmental education services, this organization does not adopt a gender perspective in its programs and activities. Nevertheless, it does acknowledge the importance of the differential environmental impacts on men and women, and it expresses an interest in incorporating a gender perspective in its programs.

The group's efforts have been strengthened through international cooperation. Of particular note, the binational Environmental Education Council for the Californias (EECC) has supported its research efforts, policies, and dissemination and community development activities through a program of small grants for environmental programs in the border region. It is through the EECC that the Border Environmental Education Program has been able to network with women's organizations with a specific gender focus, such as Factor X.

## Factor X

The majority of environmental organizations in Tijuana work from a city or community perspective. Factor X was unique in that it defended environmental rights from the workers' perspective. Although some observers consider this organization's environmental actions to have been marginal, its activities merit note because they helped reverse the impacts of environmental deterioration. Unfortunately, Factor X closed its doors in 2004. Some of its members joined other organizations in order to continue their work with women workers in the maquiladoras.

Factor X was dedicated to raising awareness among female maquiladora workers about their rights as workers, with a special focus on building capacity so that these women would be able to defend their labor rights. It also had an interest in reproductive rights, and in this sense the linkages it made between environment and gender went beyond the issue of population growth.

Unlike the Border Environmental Education Project and Playas de Tijuana Housewives Association, Factor X's goals and actions were infused with a feminist philosophy. Factor X divided its activities into three areas: training, services, and research. This organization was particularly concerned with the pollution generated by the maquiladoras and the effects this produced on the health of women workers.[10] The key environmental goal advocated by Factor X was clean and healthy maquiladoras that posed no health risks to women workers. The organization advanced toward this goal primarily through training efforts.

Factor X developed an extensive and detailed two-year training program. The basic course, which graduated ten women annually, lasted twenty-six weeks and covered human, labor, and gender rights; class and gender identity; cleanliness and safety in the workplace; and Mexican labor law. Environmental deterioration was an important part of the curriculum, the goal being to raise women workers' awareness of the inherent risks in exposure to toxic materials.

In addition to educating women workers about their gender and labor rights, Factor X also trained them to serve an outreach role within their communities. The women received a training manual that helped them train other women in their community or workplace; at the end of the course, each graduate recruited five women and taught them about their rights as workers, how to identify risks in the workplace, and how to advocate for better working conditions. In 2000, Factor X received a small grant from the EECC to develop an extended version of its training manual to cover an array of issues linked to environmental risks in the workplace.

As one of the few organizations involved in the areas of affirmative action and the defense of women workers' rights, Factor X established links with numerous local, national, and international NGOs and with local government, and it was a member of many local and national networks.

---

[10] The deleterious health impacts of some industrial chemicals, especially for pregnant women, have been documented in a number of border cities (Denman 1998).

## DISCUSSION AND CONCLUSIONS

The three women's organizations active in environmental and reproductive health issues discussed above share a concern about the effects of industrial pollution on public health. Nevertheless, Factor X, because of its action arena and gender perspective, viewed the environment-gender relationship as going beyond questions of population growth, and it emphasized the consequences of industrial pollution for women maquila workers.

A second characteristic that these NGOs share involves linkages with binational organizations. These links have been crucial for the development of environmental NGOs, and they have helped further the programs and research of reproductive health NGOs such as Factor X, which, unlike the environmental groups, also developed close ties at the local level through networks like the Red de Mujeres de la Península de Baja California (Baja California Women's Network).

As is to be expected, these cases confirm that environmental and reproductive health NGOs have followed different paths, depending on their specific areas of concern. While environmental organizations such as the Border Environmental Education Project and the Playas de Tijuana Housewives Association have concentrated on combating environmental pollution at the city and community level, groups like Factor X focused on addressing environmental risk factors in the workplace.

Factor X is the only one of the three to have defined its goals in terms of women's interests. The Border Environmental Education Project adopts a binational regional perspective that as yet does not consciously or consistently consider the differential impacts of environmental degradation on men and women. And the Playas de Tijuana Housewives Association maintains a traditional posture that privileges the interests of family and community over those of women specifically.

The lack of articulation between gender and environmental groups does not appear to stem from a lack of financial resources, which affects all women's NGOs evenly, but rather from a lack of familiarity with a gender perspective.

Nevertheless, local reality may be compelling these NGOs to give more attention to linkages between these issue areas. This means that both types of organization will have to adopt a more integral focus that considers the interaction between gender and environment.

In the meantime, women's reproductive health organizations have begun to incorporate environmental problems into their broader agendas on women's rights. This concern has brought them in closer contact with environmental groups as they try to gain expertise on environmental issues. A lesson emanating from these various experiences is the importance of raising awareness among social groups about the link between environment and reproductive health.

In parallel fashion, the environmental groups should make efforts to include a gender perspective in their focus areas. This would highlight the gender differences in access to and use and management of environmental resources, as well as the differential impacts of environmental deterioration on men and women and the differentiated ways in which the sexes contribute to reducing damage to the environment. In other words, training and environmental education programs must raise awareness about people's roles in production and reproduction in order to advance the participation of both men and women in sustainable resource use in their households and communities.

**References**

Agarwal, Bina. 1991. *Engendering the Environment Debate: Lessons from the Indian Subcontinent*. East Lansing, Mich.: Center for Advanced Study of International Development, Michigan State University.

Braidotti, Rosi, et al. 1994. *Women, the Environment and Sustainable Development: Towards a Theoretical Synthesis*. London and New Jersey: Zed Books, with INSTRAW.

Denman, Catalina. 1998. "Salud y maquila: acotaciones del campo de investigación en vista de las contribuciones recientes," *Relaciones: Estudios de Historia y Sociedad* 19, no. 74: 73–100.

Fontecilla, C. A. I. 1998. "Calidad de lo urbano: representaciones sociales," *Ciudades* 38 (April–June).

González Montes, Soledad, ed. 1999. *Las organizaciones no gubernamentales mexicanas y la salud reproductiva*. Mexico: El Colegio de México.

Maier, Elizabeth. 1998. *Género femenino, pobreza rural y cultura ecológica*. Mexico: El Colegio de la Frontera Sur and Potrerillo.

Mies, Maria. 1996. *Women, Food and Global Trade: An Ecofeminist Analysis of the World Food Summit.* Trans. Kristin Browne. Bielefeld, Germany: Institute für Theorie und Praxis der Subsistenz.

Mies, Maria, and Vandana Shiva. 1993. *Ecofeminism.* Halifax: Fernwood.

Sen, Gita, and Caren Grown. 1988. *Development Crisis and Alternative Visions: Third Women's Perspectives.* London: Earthscan.

Shiva, Vandana. 1991. *La biotecnología y sus consecuencias en el Tercer Mundo: documentos informativos.* Montevideo, Uruguay: Instituto del Tercer Mundo.

Shiva, Vandana, ed. 1994. *Close to Home: Women Reconnect Ecology, Health and Development Worldwide.* Philadelphia, Penn.: New Society Publishers.

Tarrés, María Luisa. 1998. "De la identidad al espacio público: las organizaciones no gubernamentales de mujeres en México." In *Organizaciones civiles y públicas en México y Centroamérica*, ed. José Luis Méndez. Mexico City: Porrúa.

Velázquez, Margarita. 1997. "Desarrollo y participación: el uso de los recursos naturales de bosques y selvas. Una aproximación desde la perspectiva de género." In *Género, análisis y multidisciplina*, ed. Margarita Velázquez and Leticia Merino. Cuernavaca: Centro Regional de Investigaciones Multidisciplinarias, Universidad Nacional Autónoma de México.

Velázquez, Margarita, ed. 1996. *Género y ambiente en Latinoamérica.* Mexico: Centro Regional de Investigaciones Multidisciplinarias, Universidad Nacional Autónoma de México.

Verduzco Chávez, Basilio. 2000. "Contribuciones del ambientalismo a la movilización de la sociedad civil: un modelo interpretativo de la experiencia en la frontera México-Estados Unidos," *Región y Sociedad* 13, no. 22: 3–47.

———. 2002. "Conflictos ambientales: la internacionalización de la defensa de las comunidades contra instalaciones contaminantes." Guadalajara: Universidad de Guadalajara.

# 14

## Accessible Information Technology for Equitable Community Planning

ALVEN H. LAM, LAURA M. NORMAN, AND ANGELA J. DONELSON

### THE GEOPOLITICAL COMPLEXITY OF CROSS-BORDER PLANNING

The U.S.-Mexico border stretches for 1,951 miles from the Pacific Ocean to the Gulf of Mexico. More than 11 million people live within the border region, which includes 25 U.S. counties (in four states) and 39 Mexican *municipios* (in six states). Each year, approximately 300 million people, 90 million cars, and 4.3 million trucks cross the border between the two countries, making this the busiest border in the world. Since the implementation of the North American Free Trade Agreement (NAFTA) in 1994, the number of commercial vehicles crossing the border has increased by 41 percent. Two-way trade has almost tripled the size of cross-border cities, also known as sister cities, both economically and in their rapid population growth (Lam and Sorzano 2002). Table 14.1 lists some sister-city pairs on the Texas-Mexico border, along with their populations; the cities on the Mexican side tend to be much larger in population than their U.S. "sisters."

Table 14.1. Sister-City Pairs on the Texas-Mexico Border

| Texas City | 1990 Population | Mexican City | 1990 Population |
|---|---|---|---|
| Laredo | 125,000 | Nuevo Laredo | 250,000 |
| El Paso | 600,000 | Ciudad Juárez | 900,000 |
| Brownsville | 100,000 | Matamoros | 300,000 |
| McAllen | 85,000 | Reynosa | 300,000 |

*Source*: U.S. Department of Housing and Urban Development, 2002.

The U.S.-Mexico border region has seen the rapid expansion of *colonias*, which are predominantly Hispanic, economically disadvantaged, unplanned settlements. Many colonias emerged in the 1950s as Mexicans came to the United States through the Bracero Program to work in U.S. agriculture. However, when mechanization eliminated the need for many of these low-cost workers, the Bracero Program was terminated (in 1964), leaving a large unemployed population in the border area. In an effort to offset some of this unemployment, the Mexican government launched the National Border Program (PRONAF) in 1961 to promote border tourism, and the Border Industrialization Program (BIP) in 1965 to spur large-scale development on the Mexican side of the border through incentives for establishing twin-plant manufacturing operations, or *maquiladoras*. The BIP prompted many industrialists to set up small U.S. operations on the Arizona side of the border and large assembly operations on the Sonora side.

The workers absorbed by these programs remained in the border colonias, which commonly lack sewers, clean water, safe and sanitary housing, and other essential services, such as electricity and paved roads. Today, more than 1,000 colonias are recognized in Texas, approximately 140 in New Mexico, and 80 in Arizona (Texas Department of Housing and Community Affairs 2001; Donelson and Holguin 2001). The U.S. Department of Housing and Urban Development (HUD) estimates that at least 1.5 million people live in colonias along the border.

As the economies of border communities have grown since the 1960s, so has the complexity of their geopolitical and social environments. Because border communities are interdependent, they pose a challenge to developing and implementing impartial political and decision-making processes. Since the early 1990s, federal and quasi-federal agencies have granted hundreds of millions of dollars in loans and grants for projects in these substandard areas in the four U.S. states bordering Mexico. But state and local governments also need integrated tools with which to assess the cost of providing adequate housing and meeting basic infrastructure needs in these growing communities. The use of geographic information systems (GIS) to monitor growth and change in border communities is one approach to addressing this problem.

This chapter describes how a project on the Arizona-Sonora border is providing accessible and affordable technological tools to access public records with the goal of enhancing community planning. The Department of Housing and Urban Development and the U.S. Geological Survey's (USGS) Geography Discipline have developed the Colonias Monitoring Program, a joint project to create Internet-enabled GIS to help border cities address shared issues. The use of GIS technology may help democratize decision making by making information about economic, social, environmental, and urban-growth trends more accessible to decision makers, residents, and nongovernmental organizations working on both sides of the border.

The Colonias Monitoring Program has helped border communities to inventory and analyze their growth, housing, and infrastructure through a GIS platform. This program aims to empower local citizens with tools previously available only to those who could afford expensive mapping software. It should also make demographic and planning information accessible to local nongovernmental organizations that are preparing grant and loan applications to improve their communities. With accurate information, communities can access funding through federal programs for colonias, such as HUD's Community Development Block Grant and Rural Housing and Economic Development Program, the U.S. Environmental Protection Agency's Border XXI Program, and the U.S. Department of Agriculture's Rural Utilities Program and Rural Housing Service.

The findings and simulations generated by the Colonias Monitoring Program will provide the rationale for—and validate the need to understand, improve, and guide future development from—a sustainable and comprehensive approach. At the international level, this program provides the opportunity to lead people into a more inclusive participation in their communities' development, eventually affecting policy making in both Washington, D.C., and Mexico City.

The tools created through an online GIS service can be utilized in the field of urban planning to evaluate potential growth scenarios in border communities. The program can also be used to achieve long-term benefits for people living in the colonias through partnerships with organizations created to sustain border communities' growth, housing, and infrastructure. Another purpose of the Colonias Monitoring Program is to provide recommendations for further collaboration in the sister-city areas and to support parallel growth in a productive, mutually complementary capacity.

## THE CASE STUDY: DOUGLAS AND AGUA PRIETA

The sister cities of Douglas, Arizona, and Agua Prieta, Sonora, were chosen as the site of the HUD-USGS joint project, partly because of long-standing agency efforts to coordinate their economic development projects. These sister cities were also chosen because of their remote location (figure 14.1) and comparatively small size—especially in contrast to larger binational centers like San Diego/Tijuana and El Paso/Ciudad Juárez. Their remote location and small size have historically made access to technology and urban services a challenge for these border communities.

Figure 14.1. The Arizona-Sonora region, showing Douglas, Arizona, and Agua Prieta, Sonora.

Douglas was founded in 1900 as a copper-smelting center (Martynec, Peter, and Hardaker 1994). By the 1920s, farming and cattle-raising were also well established in the region (Kearney 1995; Kent 1983), with agriculture both serving and expanding upon the economic base developed by the mining industry and the railroads that were brought in to support the mining interests (Myrick 1967). The region's agriculture depended heavily on low-cost Mexican labor (Weaver 2001). Agua Prieta was founded as a transit stop for mining products in 1899, two years before the construction of a major highway to connect copper mines in Mexico with U.S. markets. Agua Prieta served as both border crossing and railroad terminal.

The late 1950s and early 1960s marked a profound change in the base of the entire regional economy. In southern Arizona, mining and agriculture gave way to a service economy. Meanwhile, the BIP's incentives for establishing maquiladoras were driving large-scale development on the Mexican side of the border. Indeed, the entire region is still undergoing the transition from copper and cattle to today's in-bond-manufacturing and tourism industries, a shift that has significantly increased the region's population by attracting migratory flows from throughout Mexico.

Douglas and Agua Prieta are well suited by location to international manufacture and commerce. Businesses based in Douglas benefit from the maquiladora concept by utilizing the labor force of Agua Prieta. The region's maquiladora employment boomed in the 1980s and 1990s, but it declined precipitously in 2001, largely because of delays in cross-border trade following the terrorist events of September 11, 2001, recession in the United States, and increased manufacturing activity in countries such as China. Despite the tough global manufacturing market, however, Mexico remains an attractive site for direct foreign investment (Cañas and Coronado 2002), suggesting that the border region may need to redefine itself once again to accommodate to a changing economy.

**Methodology**

Partners in the Colonias Monitoring Program have contributed geospatial data to develop base maps of colonia boundaries in Douglas and Agua Prieta. The partners include Mexico's National Institute of Statistics, Geography and Informatics (INEGI) and Ministry of Social Development (SEDESOL), the U.S. Census Bureau, the Border Environment Cooperation

Commission (BECC/COCEF), Cochise County, Arizona, the city of Douglas, and the *municipio* of Agua Prieta, Sonora, as well as HUD and the USGS. Areas previously identified by federal agencies (USDA, Infonavit, Foviste) were also included in the study.

With the help of community members in the two cities, the project identified water and sewer lines, substandard housing, and colonias. The project office in Douglas suggested that the boundaries for the Colonias Monitoring Program be defined by the requests for infrastructure coming from the neighborhoods. In Agua Prieta, community members identified the poorest neighborhoods for inclusion in the project.

Community members in Douglas and Agua Prieta met regularly to identify and collect information for the data layers incorporated into the program, which included transportation, digital orthophoto quarter quadrangles (DOQQs), digital raster graphics (DRGs), Landsat imagery, colonia boundaries, hydrography, Census 2000, public facilities (sewer and water lines), geographic names, and local attractions. New Turf Youth Advocates, a local youth group, helped identify community resources and created a geospatial coverage using GPS readings, maps, and a digital camera. The Douglas Public Works Department & Housing Authority, the head of a local nonprofit organization (Turning Point), the director of Agua Prieta's National System for Integral Family Development (DIF), the coordinator of the Take to the Hills nonprofit, and a minister at Lily of the Valley Presbyterian Church in Agua Prieta assisted in creating new maps of their respective communities.

### Demographics

Douglas, Arizona, consists predominantly of Hispanic families, many of whom have resided in the United States for generations. Mean family size is 20 percent larger than the U.S. average, and the median age is 28 years. Douglas's population totaled 21,336 in 2001, and median household income was $26,490 (versus the U.S. average of $41,369; http://www.infods.com/freedata/). The city's poverty rate is 55 percent (http://www.ezec.gov/ezec/az/border.html).

We can derive the population of the colonias in Douglas by comparing our newly derived colonia boundaries with U.S. Census Block Group Information from 2000 (figures 14.2, 14.3).

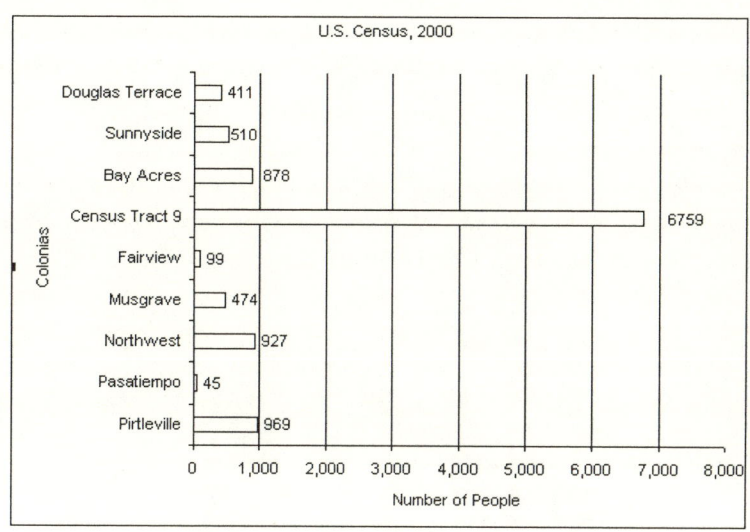

Figure 14.2. Population data for newly designated colonias in Douglas, Arizona (U.S. Census, 2000).

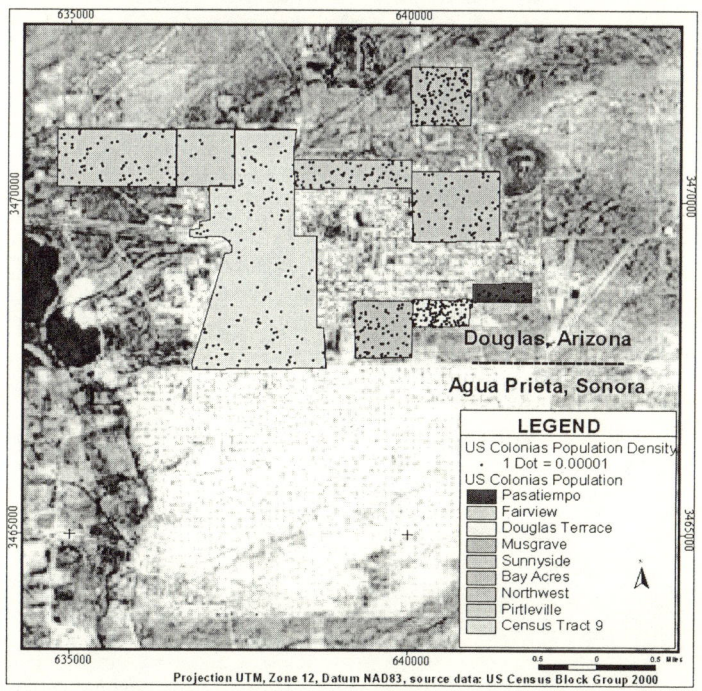

Figure 14.3. Colonias in the U.S.-Mexico border area, ordered from lowest to highest population and density (U.S. Census, 2000).

The population of Agua Prieta and its suburbs has been estimated by INEGI and Mexico's National Population Council (CONAPO). Estimates range from 112,000 to 132,000 within the city limits, and from 173,000 to 185,000 including the suburbs (COCEF/BECC 1998).

It is clear from GIS analysis of satellite imagery that the colonias surrounding Douglas have expanded in several waves of urban sprawl, reflecting the inflow of new immigrants to the area (figure 14.4) (Norman et al. n.d.).

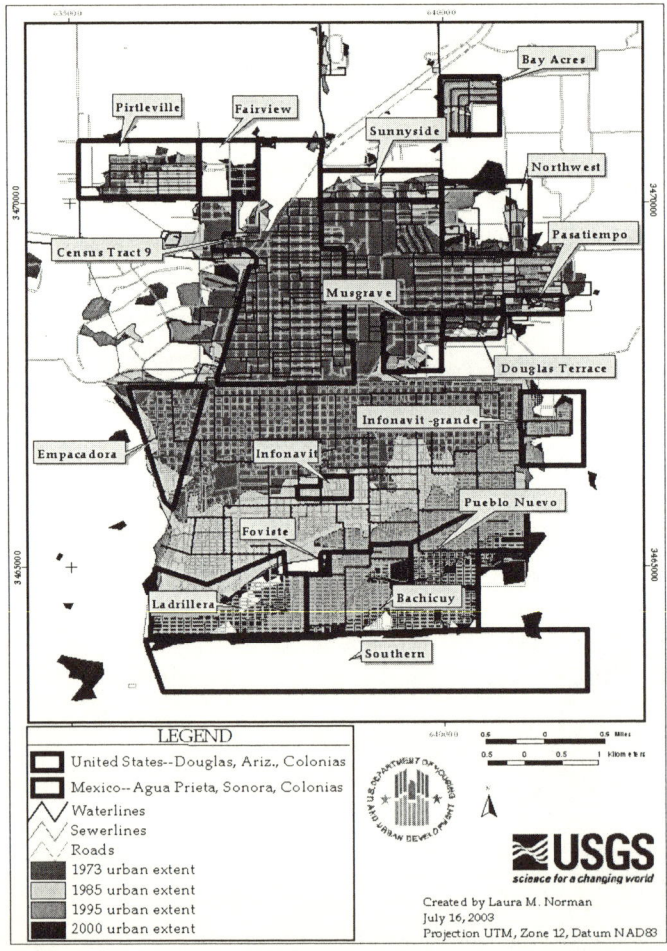

Figure 14.4. GIS analysis of satellite imagery showing the colonias surrounding Douglas and Agua Prieta.

Satellite imagery was used to create a timeline of urban growth that can be forecast on the basis of historical trends. Following this timeline, the region's urban area in 2010 would cover some 7,800 acres, a significant increase from 2000. Dividing datasets at the border to compare the growth on either side reveals that Douglas is growing very slowly relative to Agua Prieta. According to the linear regressions in figure 14.5, the urban area on the U.S. side would grow by about 400 acres (to a total of 3,150 acres), while the urban area on the Mexican side would increase by about 1,000 acres (to 4,600 acres) by 2010.

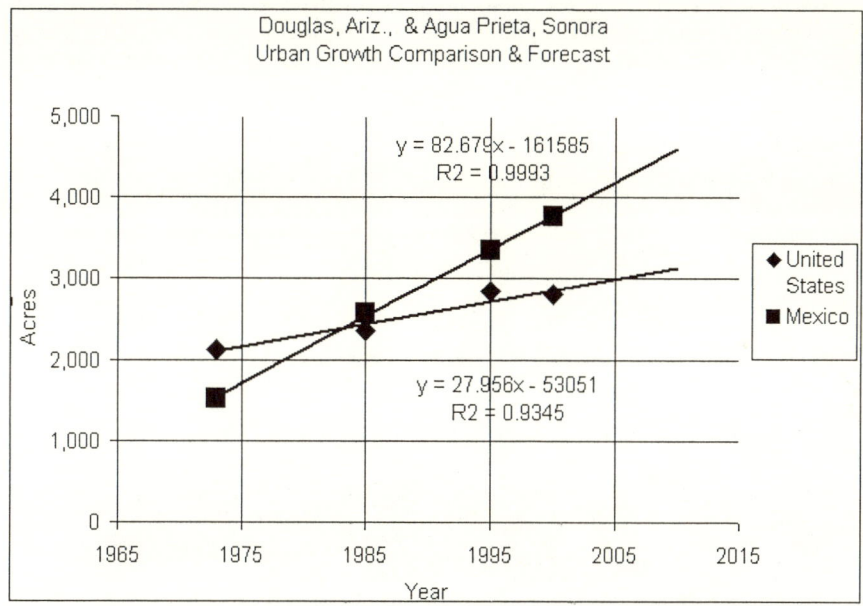

Figure 14.5. Scatter plot and linear regressions showing urban growth in the Douglas and Agua Prieta areas, with a 10-year forecast.

**Colonia Descriptions**

Through a combination of geospatial, tabular, and remote-sensing analysis, we have been able to make some assumptions about the growth rate for each of the newly defined colonias and to generate maps and reports portraying conditions in the colonias (Norman et al. 2004).

Colonias on the northern side of the border tend to be older settlements that have increased steadily in size. For example, Pirtleville colonia was established prior to 1973, grew extensively until 1985, and has been sprawling slowly ever since. Pirtleville has both sewer and water lines (figure 14.6). By contrast, Fairview seems to be the most recently developed colonia; although there were houses in the area before 2000, Fairview was not recognized as urban until then, which may explain why it lacks all infrastructure. The colonias of Bay Acres and Northwest appear to have been established in 1995 and have grown little; the former has water lines but no sewerage. Sunnyside, Musgrave, Douglas Terrace, and Pasatiempo colonias were recognized as urban in 1973 and have been growing slowly but steadily since then; Sunnyside has both water and sewer lines, but Pasatiempo and Douglas Terrace have only water. It is clear that newer colonias (Fairview, Bay Acres, Northwest, and Musgrave) are the ones lacking water and sewer lines; delineating these urban areas will assist in obtaining funding to implement these systems.

Figure 14.6. Housing in Pirtleville colonia, Douglas (photograph by Angela Donelson).

Colonias in Agua Prieta appear predominantly in areas where settlement is recent. The oldest is Empacadora, west of the railroad tracks. It is poor, lacks sewer lines, and is known as a "dangerous" area (author interview with Reverend Jesús Gallegos). Other colonias—including Infonavit, Infonavit Grande, and Fovista—were established as federally subsidized housing areas in the 1980s and 1990s; they are home to many migrants from southern Mexico who come (often with large families) to work in the maquiladoras. These colonias provide well-constructed but very small apartment-style housing, with only one bathroom for all of the tenants. Each "dwelling" measures about 20 by 20 feet and houses six or more people. Pueblo Nuevo and Bachicuy colonias, both established about 1995, are in a flood zone. The lack of sewer lines in these areas has led to the use of outhouses, whose overflow during flooding infects the water supply with fecal coliform bacteria and causes intestinal infections in children (author interview with Reverend Gallegos). Ladrillera was inhabited in 2000 (figure 14.7) and Southern colonia sometime after that. Agua Prieta continues to grow at a rapid rate, and new colonias are appearing continually.

Figure 14.7. Housing and makeshift sewer drainage into a wash in Ladrillera colonia, Agua Prieta (photograph by Silvia Villalobos de Zúñiga).

## IMPLEMENTATION OF THE COLONIAS MONITORING PROGRAM

The geospatial database created for the Colonias Monitoring Program has been uploaded to a map service for Web-based distribution, and there have been open meetings with the publics of both sister cities. A user assessment in December 2002 to identify stakeholders and potential applications of a binational GIS attracted participants from the Southeast Arizona Governments Organization (SEAGO), Southeast Arizona Behavioral Health Services (SEABHS), Turning Point, the University of Arizona, New Turf Youth Advocates, the governments of Douglas and Agua Prieta, HUD, and the USGS. Participants discussed updating and creating digital versions of old maps and using the information to monitor urban growth, track disease, encourage community development, and identify resources. Data sets were then created, incorporating ideas gathered through the various meetings and from solicited members, including the U.S. Border Patrol, the Arizona Department of Environmental Quality (ADEQ), and the Institute for the Environment and Sustainable Development of Sonora (IMADES).

The geospatial database was presented in a two-part workshop in September 2003, the dual aim being to demonstrate the binational Web-based mapping service for Douglas and Agua Prieta and to describe its purpose (to support urban planning and community development in the border communities). The first workshop meeting included a slideshow presentation of the database, a live demonstration, and a presentation by New Turf Youth Advocates. The second meeting was a hands-on workshop to introduce the dataset to the community; no previous GIS experience was necessary. Attendees included a volunteer from a Tucson-based planning company, who acted as facilitator and GIS expert, members of the Douglas Department of Public Works, the Douglas Housing Authority, the U.S.-Mexico Border Philanthropy Partnership, Acosta y Asociados, the *Douglas Daily Dispatch*, the Agua Prieta Emergency Response Commission, SEABHS, SEAGO, the University of Arizona, the Cochise County Housing Authority, New Turf Youth Advocates, Focus Future (a nonprofit binational organization), the Cochise County Health Department, the Agua Prieta municipal government, and Cochise Community College. Participants expressed interest in helping update and utilize the Web-based mapping service for various tasks in the future—such as planning housing developments based on flood-zone information; outlining access to wells and sewer and water lines; and mapping local resources. Evaluation forms distributed at the end of the meeting elicited strong support for the program.

The initial plan was to turn the maintenance of the datasets over to the cities themselves. However, owing to the high costs of the required hardware and software, as well as the need for trained personnel to host the database, neither city can currently play this role. Instead, a Web portal was opened to support the HUD-USGS joint project at http://codd.art.srnr.arizona.edu/colonias. This was accomplished through a collaborative effort with the University of Arizona's School of Renewable Natural Resources and the newly established Center on Impacts of Urban Development in Southern Arizona's Desert Environment (CIUDAD). The Web site provides instruction on how to use the information and how to use the Internet to access assistance, write grants, and acquire funding for colonia-like neighborhoods. Steps are being taken to secure GIS training for city planners so that the cities and their residents can update these data in the future. Nonprofit organizations and volunteers have also been instrumental in disseminating information about the project.

The creation of a Web-based interface for interactive online mapping will greatly assist in the monitoring of colonias along the U.S.-Mexico border. The lack of basic water and waste systems has been identified as a primary contributing factor to the health problems experienced by colonia residents (Ratcliffe 2003). By identifying the areas in need of improvement, these may become designated as colonias and thus be able to secure access to specially targeted programs and funding.

Our goal now is to demonstrate applications of this GIS technology. The mapping Web site can improve public access to public records. Furthermore, the future of urban planning, construction, and renovation requires the accurate representation of local surface features, making a successful GIS a useful recruiting tool for potential investors. Public works and emergency-response services can also benefit from a public-use information-delivery system. Finally, and most relevant to the Colonias Monitoring Program, the identification of those land areas that lack adequate infrastructure or housing will greatly assist in assigning funding for development.

A binational comprehensive master plan, or model, is in development to support the Colonias Monitoring Program. In developing this model, we will begin by refining the existing pilot projects and looking for ways to sustain and maintain the data integrity and currency, and to justify additional projects for more border communities in the future. We plan to incorporate resources from universities and other organizations working with HUD and the USGS to develop applications that benefit people living in colonias. This model is intended to become both a consumer and a generator of data, creating a demand for continuation and enhancement of this research.

## SUMMARY

The Colonias Monitoring Program exemplifies a paradigm shift regarding the dissemination of public records at the international level. The access provided by this new technology allows information on urban neighborhoods and the implications of urban growth to be more accessible and affordable, which, in turn, can promote sustainable development along the U.S.-Mexico border by providing local citizens with knowledge of their surroundings. Partnerships with other federal, state, and local organizations and with community members should improve both the quantity and accuracy of the acquired data. The Web-based mapping service consolidates and makes available demographic and urban-planning information to local nongovernmental organizations that are preparing grant and loan applications to improve their communities. Community planners only need access to the Internet, which empowers everyone with tools previously available only through expensive mapping software.

### References

Cañas, Jesús, and Roberto Coronado. 2002. "Maquiladora Industry: Past, Present, and Future," *El Paso Business Frontier* 2.

COCEF/BECC (Comisión de Cooperación Ecológica Fronteriza/Border Environment Cooperation Commission). 1998. "Agua Prieta, Sonora, Plan Maestro; Para el Mejoramiento de los Servicios de Agua Potable, Alcantarillado y Saneamiento de la Ciudad de Agua Prieta, Sonora, y Levantamiento de Redes Hidráulicas." CONTA 98-02.

Donelson, Angela, and Esperanza Holguin. 2001. "Homestead Subdivision/Colonias and Land Market Dynamics in Arizona and New Mexico." Paper presented at the research workshop "Irregular Settlement and Self-

Help Housing in the United States," Lincoln Institute of Land Use Policy, Cambridge, Mass., September 21–22.

Kearney, Milo. 1995. *Border Cuates: A History of the U.S.-Mexican Twin Cities*. Austin, Tex.: Eakin Press.

Kent, Robert. 1983. "Agriculture and Ranching." In *Borderlands Sourcebook: A Guide to the Literature on Northern Mexico and the American Southwest*. Norman: University of Oklahoma Press.

Lam, Alven H., and Shannon H. Sorzano. 2002. "Housing Challenges in the Colonias along the U.S.-Mexico Border." Paper presented at the Association of European Schools of Planning XVI AESOP Congress, Volos, Greece.

Martynec, Sandra, Duane E. Peter, and Chris Hardaker. 1994. *Cultural Resources Survey and Monitoring of the Douglas-Naco Arizona Sector of the US-Mexico Border*. Plano, Tex: Geo-Marine, Inc.

Myrick, David F. 1967. "The Railroads of Arizona: An Approach to Tombstone," *Journal of Arizona History* 8, no. 3: 155–70.

Norman, Laura M., Angela J. Donelson, Edwin Pfeifer, Alven H. Lam, and Kenneth J. Osborn. 2004. "Analyses of Urban Sprawl and Colonias Development in Douglas, Arizona, and Agua Prieta, Sonora, on the US-Mexico Border: A Process Application Using GIS and Remote Sensing." USGS Open File Report.

Ratcliffe, Michael R. 2003. *Spatial and Demographic Data for Colonias*. Proceedings of the 42nd annual meeting of the Western Regional Science Association, February 26–March 1, 2002.

Texas Department of Housing and Community Affairs. 2001. "Colonias Program Overview," http://www.tdhca.state.tx.us/overview.htm.

Weaver, Thomas. 2001. "Time, Space and Articulation in the Economic Development of the U.S.-Mexico Border Region from 1940 to 2000," *Human Organization* 60, no. 2: 105–20.

# Part V
# Conclusions and Policy Implications

# 15

## Cross-Border Regional Policy Collaboration: Lessons from San Diego–Tijuana

JANE CLOUGH-RIQUELME

The North American Free Trade Agreement (NAFTA), signed in 1993, sparked a surge in cross-border collaboration in the transfrontier metropolitan areas[1] along the U.S.-Mexico border. The NAFTA framework provided new opportunities to strengthen existing economic, social, cultural, and political networks and linkages (Herzog 1990). Cross-border collaboration has flourished between local governments, civil society, and the private sector in the San Diego–Tijuana region as the cities that constitute this binational border region have tackled a variety of shared issues.

This essay examines one example of a growing trend in transfrontier metropolitan areas of local governments facilitating cross-border planning at a regional level, often catalyzing federal government programs. First, it briefly reviews the history of cross-border collaboration within the context of U.S.-Mexican relations. It then describes the development of the San Diego Association of Governments' (SANDAG) Committee on Binational Regional Opportunities (COBRO) as an institutional mechanism for binational collaboration within a regional context. Third, it reviews the policy areas examined by SANDAG through COBRO to assess what advances have been made. Fourth, it summarizes the impacts that the efforts of this stakeholders' working group have had in the binational region, with a focus on environmental issues. Finally, it highlights key issues that continue to be raised in cross-border policy collaboration.

---

[1] Herzog coined this term in his seminal work, *Where North Meets South: Cities, Space, and Politics on the U.S.-Mexico Border* (1990).

## CROSS-BORDER COLLABORATION IN THE CALIFORNIAS IN THE CONTEXT OF U.S.-MEXICO RELATIONS

In 1989 the Bilateral Commission on the Future of United States-Mexican Relations identified some key long-range shifts that would rejuvenate—and complicate—relations between the two countries. Commission members argued that the shifting global context and the internal politics of the two nations would make them ever more interdependent. At the same time, they pointed to the fact that the bilateral agenda was becoming more complex and that border issues would become increasingly important (Bilateral Commission 1989; see also Guillén López and Ordóñez Barba 1995; Shirk 1999; Domínguez and Fernández de Castro 2001).

Despite cyclical shifts in U.S.-Mexican relations at the federal level, communities in the U.S.-Mexico borderlands, from the Californias to Texas and Tamaulipas, have for years been dealing with everyday practical issues affecting their quality of life. Outside the realm of federal-level protocol, this regional phenomenon was coined "citizenship diplomacy" to imply that local governments and civic organizations had taken it upon themselves to initiate dialogue with their counterparts in the other country in order to build relationships and resolve common issues (Thorup 1993).

As transfrontier metropolises such as San Diego–Tijuana grew in size and complexity, the need arose to address issues of transborder planning (Herzog 1990). Lynch and Appleyard, in their now famous report to the City of San Diego, *Temporary Paradise?* (1974), examined the region from a bioregional perspective, without thought to the international border, and drew the attention of city and regional officials to the critical connections between the urbanized areas on either side of the border.

Cross-border dialogue in the Californias has become even more complex and sophisticated since Lynch and Appleyard authored their report. Elected officials, planners, researchers, chambers of commerce, and civic organizations from Tijuana, Mexicali, Tecate, Rosarito, Imperial County, and the San Diego region have dealt with myriad issues as their economies have expanded, populations have swelled, and pressures on the region's natural assets and built infrastructure have intensified (Ganster 2000).

A binational community forum organized by the University of California, San Diego and El Colegio de la Frontera Norte (COLEF) in 1985 considered the desirability and feasibility of a transborder planning agency for the San Diego–Tijuana region. Conference participants included public officials representing the local, state, and federal governments in Mexico and the United States, researchers, journalists, community and regional planners, and interested citizens. The public officials argued that the political obstacles to creating such an entity were "insurmountable," but the planners, researchers, and citizens disagreed. Some contended that the hindrance was a lack of will to face issues of urban growth in a binational region. The overall conclusion was that, for the time being, informal arrangements seemed to be the most effective and efficient (Herzog 1986).

Transborder land-use planning, though not widely accepted at the time, was defined by the then director of urban and environmental studies at COLEF, Carlos Graizbord, as follows:

> In its proper conceptualization, transborder land-use planning clarifies our understanding of international problems and conflicts such as pollution, suboptimal use of natural resources, inefficient land-use allocation, and duplication of services (Graizbord 1986).

One conclusion from the 1985 conference was that cross-border dialogue between business sectors might be less conflictual and more productive than discussions focused on land use or water. The San Diego Chamber of Commerce and the Chamber of Commerce in Tijuana (CANACO Tijuana) initiated discussions at that time, but exchanges were intermittent and unfocused. In 1997, San Diego Dialogue (SDD), a policy institute based at the University of California, San Diego Extension, initiated its "Forum Fronterizo" luncheon series, in which regional civic and business leaders could discuss issues of concern for the mutual prosperity of both nations in the binational region.[2] Indeed, the 1990s saw a proliferation of cross-border conferences and community forums in a variety of sectors and on a variety of issues, including health, economy, infrastructure, environment, water, and energy—all attempting to develop mutually beneficial strategies (Ganster and Sánchez Rodríguez 1999; Spalding 1999).

---

[2] For a full listing of issue papers prepared for the Forum Fronterizo, see http://www.sandiegodialogue.org.

## COBRO: EXAMINING CROSS-BORDER POLICY ISSUES IN THE LOCAL SPHERE

The San Diego Association of Governments, which is the regional planning agency that unites the eighteen cities and unincorporated areas of San Diego County, has been a leader in facilitating cross-border dialogue since the early 1990s. SANDAG serves as a forum for decision making on issues of regional concern and encourages regional leaders to make interregional and binational concerns an integral component of regional planning.

SANDAG began as a voluntary organization. This Council of Governments is now the Metropolitan Planning Organization and Regional Transportation Planning Agency directed by the State of California to facilitate regional comprehensive and transportation plans that coordinate the land use and transportation priorities of the local jurisdictions. SANDAG's Board of Directors includes mayors, council members, and county supervisors from the region's nineteen local governments (eighteen cities and the county). Among SANDAG's innovative principles for policy formation has been the agency's understanding that San Diego forms a transfrontier metropolis in conjunction with Tijuana.

Recognizing that a better understanding of binational, border-related planning issues is key to improving quality of life in the region, in 1996 SANDAG sponsored the creation of the Committee on Binational Regional Opportunities, which included stakeholders from both sides of the border, including elected officials, businesspeople, academics, representatives from nongovernmental organizations (NGOs), and community groups.[3] Its mission was to inform the SANDAG Board of Directors on both short- and long-term binational-related activities, issues, and actions; make recommendations on binational, border-related planning and development; and identify ways to assist and coordinate with existing efforts in the binational area.

These efforts complement those of the Border Liaison Mechanism (BLM), a joint government instrument in which representatives from sister cities and states on the border come together to discuss issues of mutual interest.[4]

---

[3] For more on SANDAG and the Borders Program, see www.sandag.org.

[4] For more on the BLM, see http://www.state.gov/r/pa/ei/bgn/35749.htm.

Over the years, COBRO has addressed border-related issues such as transportation infrastructure, cross-border communication, homeland security, and water and energy supply. During its annual binational conferences, border stakeholders have discussed issues, devised strategies for addressing them, and made recommendations to be pursued by COBRO's members through their respective agencies.

COBRO was so successful in demonstrating the importance of looking at binational, interregional planning issues that SANDAG, in its recent reorganization and consolidation, decided to dedicate one of its five policy advisory subcommittees to transboundary planning.. The Borders Committee advises the SANDAG Board of Directors on issues that mutually impact San Diego and surrounding counties, Native Nations, and Mexico. Through interregional partnerships, such as that created with the Western Riverside Council of Governments, elected officials are addressing planning issues through dialogue and coordinated strategies. Today, COBRO constitutes SANDAG's binational stakeholder working group, advising the Borders Committee on border-related issues with the support of technical staff from the region's municipal planning institutes, as well as from business chambers, universities, and NGOs in San Diego and Baja California. The group meets monthly, alternating (when possible) between San Diego and Tijuana, allowing maximum public participation from both countries.

## POLICY ISSUE AREAS EXAMINED THROUGH COBRO

Since its founding, COBRO has convened annual binational conferences to address border-related planning issues of concern to its membership. The conference findings and policy recommendations serve as a regional binational agenda for area stakeholders. The following sections review select environment-related policy issue areas that COBRO has addressed, along with its recommendations and the current status of those policy areas.

### Water Supply

Water supply poses a serious challenge in the San Diego–Tijuana region, and any solutions will require significant binational collaboration. COBRO has highlighted water as a resource that has far-reaching impacts both north and south of the border, particularly for the region's future economic vitality. San Diego and Imperial counties and the municipalities of northern Baja California all rely heavily on water delivered from the Colorado River.

Population projections suggest that approximately 3.3 million people will live in the San Diego County Water Authority service area by 2010, in addition to 2.15 million in and around Tijuana. This total population of some 5.45 million people is expected to generate demand for approximately 848,000 acre-feet (1.05 billion m$^3$) of water annually. This means a 47 percent increase in population and a 24 percent increase in water demand from current levels (SANDAG 1998).

Multiple factors affect water demand, including population size, migratory patterns, economic conditions, rainfall, water leakage, household size, agricultural demand, and conservation efforts, such as behavioral changes and permanent conservation measures (low-flow shower heads and ultra-low-flush toilets, for example). Likely options for assuring long-term water reliability in this arid region include a mix of increased conservation, maximization of local supplies, water recycling, and desalination.

A key recommendation of COBRO's 1997 conference was the importance of adopting a watershed approach as an overriding principle for any inter-regional planning strategy. San Diego and Tijuana share the Tijuana Watershed, a fact that affects water and wastewater management issues for both.[5] Conference participants recommended establishing a binational convening forum to facilitate regular transborder communication and cooperation regarding political, technical, and water management–related issues. It was suggested that the forum should comprise federal, state, and local water agencies from both nations. The binational forum would facilitate information and technology exchanges in various subareas, promote and assure an open public-participation process on both sides of the border regarding the development of water infrastructure projects in the binational region, explore the potential for joint participation in a binational aqueduct to carry water from the Colorado River to Tijuana and San Diego, and examine opportunities for regional-level binational storage projects such as joint reservoirs.

---

[5] Two-thirds of the watershed is in Tijuana, but it drains northwest through San Diego to the Pacific Ocean via the Tijuana River Estuary.

COBRO's recommendations gave rise to the Border Water Council for San Diego County and Tijuana, whose innovative structure included active participation from federal, state, and local water entities from both sides of the border (Domínguez and Fernández de Castro 2001: 143). Through the Border Liaison Mechanism, the two consuls general provided a structure in which the interests of water agencies from Mexico and the United States could be communicated from the local level to state and federal levels through the U.S. Department of State and the Mexican Ministry of Foreign Affairs (SRE). The Border Water Council was ultimately absorbed into the BLM as one of its working groups.

In 1999 the San Diego County Water Authority and Mexico agreed to study the feasibility of a binational pipeline, and the International Boundary and Water Commission (IBWC) signed Minute 301, a binational agreement outlining the terms and conditions under which the study would be undertaken. In 2002, San Diego and Tijuana collaborated on a feasibility study for a binational aqueduct that would bring Colorado River water from the Imperial and Mexicali valleys to urbanized San Diego and Tijuana (San Diego Water Authority 2003). Negotiations continue with regard to the various options available for a conveyance system. It is hoped that a mutually beneficial and environmentally sound option will prevail. As seawater desalinization is becoming more cost effective, the San Diego County Water Authority and the State Commission for Water Services in Tijuana (CESPT) are pursuing possible joint projects on this front as well.

Over the years, a project that originated with researchers at San Diego State University has grown into a binational watershed advisory council, with support from both the federal and state levels. A very diverse set of stakeholders from both sides of the border meets quarterly to discuss their shared concerns. They have developed a vision statement and are crafting strategies for protecting the watershed.[6]

**Population Growth**

Another issue that COBRO has highlighted is population growth and its impacts on education and the economy in the binational region. If the strength of a national economy is increasingly defined by population

---

[6] For more information about this group, see http://trw.sdsu.edu.

growth rates, educational levels, and the country's ability to create new high-technology products, then a society's ability to compete in the new knowledge-based industries and markets will increasingly depend on developing a workforce that, in addition to traditional skills like reading, writing, and mathematics, also has skills that foster the discovery and application of knowledge.

COBRO's conference on this issue underscored the San Diego–Tijuana region's growing interdependence. For example, since the implementation of NAFTA in 1994, California's trade with Mexico has exceeded $20 billion annually, overcoming such obstacles as fluctuations in the peso-dollar exchange rate and differences in economic indicators which, in the past, had hindered a stable economic relationship.

This binational region has great potential to succeed in highly competitive global markets if it takes advantage of its geographic location and shared resources. In this context, the *maquiladora* industry has been an important factor in the development of the binational market. *Maquiladoras* have helped fuel steady growth in private-sector employment, accounting for up to 70 percent of Baja California's new jobs, though this in-bond-assembly sector also carries significant environmental and social costs (see Kopinak, this volume).

As the binational economy evolves from basic manufacturing toward high-tech industries, the importance of educational institutions capable of forming a competent, technical labor force becomes evident. The San Diego–Tijuana region must collaborate on strategies to maintain a competitive workforce through appropriate training and educational opportunities for the region's residents. Because San Diego has a relatively aging population and Tijuana has a relatively young population, there are synergies with reference to the availability of a local labor force. Indeed, Tijuana has relatively high educational levels, both in real terms and relative to the rest of Mexico.

Acknowledging the interdependence of issues of growth, educational attainment, and economic prosperity, recommendations emanating from the COBRO conference focused on improved communication between educational systems in San Diego and Baja California through the establishment of a Border Education and Culture Council within the Border Liaison Mechanism. Conference participants emphasized the importance of reducing red tape and creating a more direct dialogue between educational agencies. They also encouraged more interaction with and within the business sector. Finally, they recommended assessing infrastructural needs in the region in order to increase the area's competitiveness.

San Diego–Tijuana is rapidly gaining a reputation for having a highly educated and innovative workforce. In recent years Tijuana has attracted highly skilled workers from other parts of Mexico, and it has worked hard to train existing human resources. U.S. and Mexican educational institutions are collaborating in a variety of fields. The Universidad Iberoamericana in Tijuana has for the last several years been partnering with the School of Education at California State University San Marcos in a teacher exchange program called Border Pedagogy.[7] The San Diego County Department of Education has been a partner for several years in a migrant education program and has collaborated with the Mexican federal government to offer distance learning through community technology centers.[8] Many of the leaders of such initiatives have worked on both sides of the border, adding an additional level of understanding to the process. For example, the new director of the University of California Institute for Mexico and the United States (UC MEXUS), which coordinates the University of California system's engagement with Mexican universities, was formerly director of urban and environmental studies at El Colegio de la Frontera Norte in Tijuana.

### Energy, Transportation, and Trade

The San Diego–Tijuana region can potentially become one of the foremost trade centers in the Western Hemisphere, but not without the appropriate supporting infrastructure. Energy experts have noted that this binational region is an "energy island"; due to the lack of energy-generating resources in the region, San Diego and Baja California import almost all of their energy (SANDAG 1999; Sweedler 1999).

Since its 1999 annual conference, COBRO has been examining the relationship between energy, transportation infrastructure, and improved economic prosperity through trade. Recent changes in the energy sectors of

---

[7] For more information, see http://geocities.com/probemsanmarcos.

[8] For more on these centers, called *plazas comunitarias*, see http://www.sdcoe.k12.ca.us/new/pca070605.asp.

both the United States and Mexico have created new opportunities to create binational partnerships. Changes in the energy sector are altering how energy is produced, transmitted, and distributed, with significant impacts along the U.S.-Mexico border. In particular, because of its geography, Baja California is part of the North American grid, not the Mexican national grid. This has profound implications in terms of possible cross-border cooperation to ensure energy security in the region. As the largest energy user, transportation will be directly affected by the direction taken to increase the supply of energy in the region.

Developing cross-border energy-related infrastructure is essential for the economic prosperity and quality of life of the region's inhabitants. Baja California's demand for power is expected to grow by 6 to 7 percent per annum for the next ten years, and Mexico's demand for natural gas is expected to increase almost 9 percent over the same period. San Diego's energy demand is expected to grow 3 percent annually (SANDAG 1999).

A binational regional strategy would focus on taking advantage of the new regulatory changes in the United States and Mexico to develop an environmentally sound cross-border energy infrastructure, create administrative mechanisms to facilitate cross-border collaboration, and diversify the energy portfolio of San Diego and Tijuana, with an emphasis on increasing the use of renewable resources. With these ideas in mind, COBRO has recommended prioritizing border infrastructure, forming a border energy issues group, including border infrastructure needs and financing issues in SANDAG's Regional Comprehensive Plan (RCP) and the Regional Transportation Plan (RTP), and pursuing state and federal financing options.

One outcome of the COBRO conference on binational energy, transportation, and trade was the establishment of the Border Energy Issues Group (BEIG), overseen by the chair of the Borders Committee and the consul general of Mexico in San Diego. A core mission of the BEIG is to promote binational cooperation and planning to ensure that regional energy needs are met in an environmentally sound manner and to achieve consensus on key binational energy issues and opportunities. The BEIG is currently developing standardized criteria for the siting of energy facilities, promoting strategies that include renewables, and supporting programs and policies that encourage energy conservation—all the while drawing attention to the fact that any regional energy strategy will necessarily have to incorporate binational energy issues.

**Effective Cross-Border Communication**

Cross-border communication and collaboration was the subject of the 2000 COBRO conference, which focused specifically on two aspects of communication—information technology and human relations. A study on the emergence of cross-border networks in the environmental sector demonstrated that the proliferation of organizations on the border has made relationships much more complex and diverse. It is possible to analyze these interactions on three levels, from the most informal to the most integrated: convergence, collaboration, and joint planning. According to a study by Francisco Lara (2000), organizations in San Diego generally operate at the level of joint planning, while organizations in Tijuana's environmental sector operate at the collaborative level. However, the majority of the transborder relationships occur at the level of either collaboration or convergence. COBRO conference participants argued that cross-border cooperation in the construction of cross-border networks can be conceptualized as a collective search for a common territory and opportunities for mutual benefit (SANDAG 2000).

Various mechanisms have evolved for using information technology to bring about more fluid transborder communication. One is the successful implementation of BECCnet, an e-mail discussion group hosted by the University of Arizona's Udall Center and funded by various sources, including the Mott and Ford foundations. Set up as a listserv prior to the establishment of the Border Environment Cooperation Commission (BECC), BECCnet's members (numbering at least 470) had substantive input on the development of BECC processes and procedures. BECCnet's director, Robert Merideth, noted, "It has provided a framework for these discussions by reducing space and time barriers." BECCnet is a clear example of border citizenship within the context of NAFTA and highlights the importance of combining social organization and technology (SANDAG 2000).

The Internet has been a crucial facilitator for keeping binational stakeholders up to date on developments in their field. Three examples relevant to the San Diego–Tijuana region, and to the U.S.-Mexico border more generally, are Border EcoWeb, Border 2012 Community Net, and Ventana Ambiental México. Border EcoWeb, a bilingual clearinghouse begun in 1997 through a cooperative agreement between San Diego State University and the U.S. Environmental Protection Agency, facilitates public access to environmental information about the U.S.-Mexico border that is available on the Internet. The site was designed based on a user survey to ensure that it would meet the needs of border environmental stakeholders.[9]

As part of its efforts to engage more citizens in the next phase of U.S.-Mexico border environmental policy making, Border 2012 initiated a citizen participation Web site called Community Net that both informs the public and serves as an interactive dialogue among communities facing similar issues. The site was designed and is maintained by young environmental professionals who began their careers working on the conservation of Baja California.[10]

Ventana Ambiental México is a borderwide initiative of the U.S.-Mexico Chamber of Commerce.[11] This Web site's main purpose is to provide U.S. companies with a database of information on Mexican federal, state, and municipal environmental laws.

One concern regarding all of these Web sites is their sustainability over the long term. Such sites are often initiated through grants, and it is up to the collaborating agencies to find funds for long-term funding and site maintenance.

No matter how effective technology is in facilitating communication, collaboration can only occur if real-life social networks and organizations are already in place. There are many cases of regional transborder collaboration that began at the grassroots but was sustained and ultimately evolved into federal-level programs for the border region. Three examples come, respectively, from the border environmental education movement, environmental justice community, and health care sector. Each became a broad-based border-wide example of what Lara (2000) calls "joint planning," and all three arose through the efforts of local binational communities.

---

[9] Border EcoWeb is at http://www.borderecoweb.sdsu.edu.

[10] See http://www.border2012.org.

[11] Ventana Ambiental México is at http://www.ventanaambientalmexico.com.

The first is the Border Health Initiative, which began as local health centers doing outreach on transboundary health issues in their communities. Community clinics were seeing patients who were migrating back and forth between Mexico and the United States and, in the process, falling through the cracks of the health care system in both countries. The clinics made a very strong case for the need for a "border-blind" health policy framework, catalyzing the establishment in 2000 of the U.S.-Mexico Health Commission, which addresses cross-border health issues such as tuberculosis, HIV/AIDS, and substance abuse, with U.S. and Mexican health officials doing joint planning.[12]

The second example is the Environmental Education Council for the Californias (EECC),[13] which began as a group of concerned environmental educators from San Diego and Baja California. Over time they demonstrated the importance of bringing local networks into broader borderwide initiatives. The EECC now provides technical support to the federal Border 2012 Program, advising various working groups on how to incorporate environmental education into their efforts.[14]

The third case of regional transborder collaboration beginning at the grassroots is Encuentro Fronterizo.[15] Begun with a small grant to two environmental educators, one in Mexico and the other in Arizona, this initiative has blossomed into a broad binational grassroots phenomenon. Encuentro Fronterizo consists of conferences held every eighteen months at some point on the U.S.-Mexico border. These conferences bring together more than four hundred representatives from NGOs and academic institutions in states on the border. Encuentro's binational secretariat operates "virtually" from both the United States and Mexico through a network of dedicated environmentalists via Internet and communications technology.

These three initiatives demonstrate the need to mobilize human resources and technology within social networks if cross-border efforts are to be sustained. Creating a Web site in the absence of a social base is fruitless. A group with good intentions but little use of technology will have only a

---

[12] See http://www.borderhealth.org.

[13] See http//www.eecc.net.

[14] For more on Border 2012, see http://www.epa.gov/border2012.

[15] For further information, see http//www.encuentrofronterizo.org.

limited impact. Federal programs that lack community support are destined to fail. But grassroots initiatives that evolve into broad-based programs and gain recognition from local, state, and federal government have succeeded in a binational context.

## COBRO'S IMPACTS

### Binational Councils

Recommendations emanating from COBRO conferences have led to the establishment of a number of targeted binational councils.[16] One is the San Diego Alliance for Border Efficiency, which coordinates local stakeholder efforts to voice regional concerns about federal programs that may affect the movement of goods and people across the border. Committee members have organized letter campaigns, visited Washington, and represented stakeholders in outreach events held by the U.S. Department of Homeland Security.

The Border Energy Issues Group (BEIG) is examining the binational region's energy situation and exploring ways to develop a set of regulations pertinent to binational energy planning. It is encouraging energy efficiency programs and the development of renewable energy technology. Most importantly, BEIG is exploring the best mechanism for coordinating the three levels of government in a binational context in order to encourage a regional energy strategy that serves both the United States and Mexico.

### Reports and Studies

Since its first conference, in 1997, COBRO has identified key information gaps, and several major studies have been conducted in response to recommendations made by COBRO participants. In 2002, for example, the San Diego Water Authority completed a binational feasibility study of the various alignment possibilities for a binational aqueduct to carry Colorado River water from the Imperial and Mexicali valleys to San Diego–Tijuana.

---

[16] Some of the councils have received support from SANDAG and others from other members of COBRO, such as the San Diego Water Authority. Some were created within the Border Liaison Mechanism, others were not.

This study reflected recommendations from the Border Water Council which was established following the first COBRO conference.

The San Diego Region–Baja California Cross-Border Transportation Study, published in 2000, resulted in the Cross Border Travel Forecasting Model, which assists local, state, and federal agencies on both sides of the border to plan roads, highways, and other transportation infrastructure.

Another study, the Survey and Analysis of Trade and Goods Movement between California and Baja California, Mexico, assessed cross-border shipping patterns among the key private-sector stakeholders in binational commerce. These included maquiladoras (both assemblers and manufacturers), customs brokers, shippers (of both agricultural and non-agricultural products), and transportation companies. The study was completed in 2003.

Finally, SANDAG recently wrapped up a study on the economic impacts of border wait times on the economies of San Diego and Baja California. The study was conducted by a consulting firm, but SANDAG organized a stakeholder advisory group to monitor and advise on the design and implementation of the study. Study findings confirm that the economies and populations of San Diego and Baja California are intimately connected. Although they differ in relative magnitude, the economic impacts in San Diego and Baja California are significant. At today's typical border-crossing time (an average of 45 minutes, according to survey respondents), San Diego County loses over 8 million trips a year, which could mean losses of $1.28 billion in revenue after adjusting for revenue gains due to local forgone trips to Mexico. The retail sector is the most strongly affected (SANDAG 2005).

**Tools and Resources**

COBRO has spurred the development of a variety of tools and resources. Some have been produced by SANDAG as a result of conference recommendations, while others have come out of collaborations among various member agencies of COBRO.

BorderBase (www.borderbase.org), developed by SANDAG, serves the border planning network in the Californias. Plans are in place to expand its use and to revitalize the advisory council to make it more responsive to community needs.

SANDAG recently updated the San Diego–Tijuana Interactive Atlas, a Web site in the GIS section of SANDAG's Web site that contains comparable census data from 1990 and 2000 for the United States and Mexico.[17] A user can identify a variable of interest and get a map showing the pertinent data for the entire San Diego–Tijuana metropolitan region.

Working in collaboration, Tijuana's Municipal Planning Institute (IMPlan), San Diego State University, and SANDAG created a land use map showing comparable land uses on both sides of the border. On the reverse of the map is a spatial image revealing the urban "footprints" of the region's cities all the way to the Salton Sea.

Finally, SANDAG and COBRO members are working with the Regional Workbench Consortium (RWBC), a collaborative network of university and community partners dedicated to enabling sustainable city-region development. The RWBC promotes multidisciplinary research and service learning aimed at understanding how problems of environment and development interrelate across local, regional, and global scales. Taking a forward-looking perspective, RWBC focuses on the Southern California–northern Baja California transborder region, especially the San Diego–Tijuana city-region and the coastal zone. RWBC's 3-D imaging tools and slider technology for looking at shifting land use provided crucial input to the Regional Comprehensive Plan as citizens examined land use changes in the region over time.

**Policy Impacts**

Local stakeholders have played a crucial role in the development and implementation of federal programs such as the SENTRI pass (Secure Electronic Network for Travelers Rapid Inspection), which enables prescreened passenger vehicles to cross the border in dedicated "fast-pass" lanes. COBRO member agencies advocated for this federal program and for its adoption in the San Diego–Tijuana region. A survey conducted by San Diego Dialogue in 1994 revealed that 90 percent of daily cross-border traffic at the San Ysidro Port of Entry could be attributed to commuters, a fact that accounts for much of the extraordinary success of the SENTRI program. The program significantly improved conditions for business and trade in the

---

[17] The census variables have been made comparable through a rigorous process.

region, and it has since been extended to cargo lanes and, more recently, to pedestrian traffic.

Member agencies of COBRO have been working diligently in support of various border infrastructure projects, including the Otay Mesa southbound truck lane, a cross-border terminal, the Interstate 905 freeway, and construction of a rail link to the east. Member agencies have been united when advocating with state and federal legislatures, and they have come a long way in coordinating their message and strategies.

COBRO member organizations are pursuing a variety of environmental initiatives for establishing binational conservation corridors. This border region is one of the world's most important areas in terms of biodiversity, but it is also a focal point of rapid urbanization. Through the efforts of organizations such as ProNatura, Conservation Biology Institute, and the International Community Foundation, local stakeholders are raising awareness among federal agencies about the need to protect these sensitive areas through binational, regional collaboration and federal support.[18]

## CONCLUSION: CHALLENGES AND OPPORTUNITIES FOR IMPROVED BORDER COLLABORATION

Despite significant advances in many policy areas, much remains to be done in the San Diego–Tijuana binational region. Several common themes emerge around the challenges and opportunities that exist for improved border collaboration. First is the issue of governance. Conferences, commissions, and policy institutes have examined border affairs within the context of U.S.-Mexican relations and have concurred on the crucial need to create "binational authorities on border affairs" (Bilateral Commission 1989: 166). A first step in this direction was the recent reactivation of the Border Liaison Mechanism. Questions to be answered now are: Is it enough to move forward on key policy and planning issues with regional impact, or is there a need for some type of transborder planning agency or commission? Could existing structures serve to facilitate this process?

The State of Baja California recently formed an inter-municipal planning commission to examine land use and transportation priorities and to

---

[18] See www.consbio.org/cbi/applied_research/lcbi.

identify ways to coordinate urban development in a regional context.[19] This commission is working closely with COBRO to examine the Otay Mesa–Mesa de Otay binational corridor in an effort to coordinate planning strategies for any new ports of entry while mitigating potential environmental impacts.

A second area to consider is data sharing. Sound, accurate data is the basis for effective planning. Strides have been made, but a need remains for a concerted effort, such as a project using the San Diego–Tijuana region as a test case for a methodology born of true collaboration from the beginning. What can we do to enhance data sharing? As part of its decentralization policy, the Mexican government mandated the creation of quasi-independent municipal planning agencies. A Municipal Planning Institute (IMPlan) was established in Tijuana in 2000, and this was followed by the establishment of a Municipal Research and Planning Institute (IMIP) in Mexicali. These agencies are key links to long-term planning and data sharing. IMPlan, SANDAG, and area universities have already collaborated successfully on a variety of projects, but much more could be done.

Both U.S. and Mexican stakeholders need to understand more about each other's systems of governance and their impacts on transborder planning. The region needs to work harder to present a united front vis-à-vis the centers of power and decision making in their respective countries. Communication is often more frequent between sister cities on opposite sides of the border than between regions on the same side of the border. The Border Health Initiative discovered, for example, that there was less communication between Mexicali and Tijuana or between San Diego and El Centro than between San Diego and Tijuana.

Finally, another mechanism that could enhance binational regional efforts is financing. Funding agencies need to adopt policies that allow truly binational organizations to utilize their funds in this context rather than splitting funding between the United States and Mexico. Even private foundations have guidelines counterproductive to the growing trend for binational organizations, such as requiring that specific funds be spent on one side or the other of the border, thereby interfering with the organiza-

---

[19] For more on regional planning efforts in Baja California, see http://www.bajacalifornia.gob.mx/sidue.

tion's integrated plans. Funding should reflect the reality of the border region; if authentic border projects are to be undertaken in a binational manner, the funding should follow suit in order to ensure the projects' success.

There are over sixty million trips annually across the San Diego County–Baja California border. Over 90 percent of these trips begin or end in San Diego County or in the Tijuana/Tecate region (SANDAG 2005), confirming the reality that the San Diego–Tijuana transfrontier metropolis is a single urban landscape divided by a political boundary. It is up to stakeholders in this binational region to embrace that reality and let it serve as a framework for the future. As former COLEF president Jorge Bustamante wrote in 1992,

> There is one aspect of the relationship between the two countries that nobody in either can change. That is geography.... As we demystify the Mexico–United States border, we prepare to live in a world enriched by the pragmatism and inventiveness of people in borderlands (p. 490).

## References

Bilateral Commission on the Future of United States–Mexican Relations. 1989. *The Challenge of Interdependence: Mexico and the United States*. Lanham, Md.: University Press of America, in collaboration with the Bilateral Commission.

Bustamante, Jorge A. 1992. "Demystifying the United States–Mexico Border," *Journal of American History*, September, pp. 485–90.

Domínguez, Jorge I., and Rafael Fernández de Castro. 2001. *The United States and Mexico: Between Partnership and Conflict*. New York: Routledge.

Ganster, Paul, ed. 2000. *The U.S.-Mexican Border Environment: A Road Map to a Sustainable 2020*. SCERP Monograph Series, No. 1. San Diego: San Diego State University Press.

Ganster, Paul, and Roberto Sánchez Rodriguez. 1998. *Sustainable Development in the San Diego–Tijuana Region*. La Jolla: Center for U.S.-Mexican Studies, University of California, San Diego.

Graizbord, Carlos. 1986. "Trans-Boundary Land-Use Planning: A Mexican Perspective." In *Planning the International Border Metropolis*, ed. Lawrence A. Herzog. La Jolla: Center for U.S.-Mexican Studies, University of California, San Diego.

Guillén López, Tonatiuh, and Gerardo Manuel Ordóñez Barba, eds. 1995. *El municipio y el desarrollo social de la frontera norte*. Mexico: Fundación Friedrich Ebert/El Colegio de la Frontera Norte.

Herzog, Lawrence A., ed. 1986, *Planning the International Border Metropolis: Transboundary Policy Options for the San Diego–Tijuana Region*. La Jolla: Center for U.S.-Mexican Studies, University of California, San Diego.

Herzog, Lawrence A. 1990. *Where North Meets South: Cities, Space, and Politics on the U.S.-Mexico Border*. Austin: Center for Mexican American Studies, University of Texas at Austin.

Lara, Francisco. 2000. "Transboundary Networks for Environmental Management in the San Diego–Tijuana Border Region." In *Shared Space: Rethinking the U.S.-Mexico Border Environment*, ed. Lawrence A. Herzog. La Jolla: Center for U.S.-Mexican Studies, University of California, San Diego

Lynch, Kevin, and Donald Appleyard. 1974. *Temporary Paradise? A Look at the Special Landscape of the San Diego Region*. Report to the City of San Diego.

SANDAG (San Diego Association of Governments). 1998. Report prepared for the first Binational Summer Conference on Binational Water Challenges and Opportunities.

———. 1999. Report prepared for 3rd Annual Binational Summer Conference on "Energy, Transportation, and Trade."

———. 2000. "Building a Strong Region through Effective Communication." Proceedings from 4th Annual Binational Summer Conference.

———. 2005. "Economic Impacts of Border Wait Times at the San Diego–Baja California Border Region." Executive Summary of Study Findings.

San Diego Water Authority. 2003. *Transformation. 2003 Annual Report*.

Shirk, David. 1999. "New Federalism in Mexico: Implications for Baja California and the Cross-Border Region." Briefing paper prepared for the San Diego Dialogue's Forum Fronterizo.

Spalding, Mark J., ed. 1999. *Sustainable Development in San Diego–Tijuana: Environmental, Social, and Economic Implications of Interdependence*. La Jolla: Center for U.S.-Mexican Studies, University of California, San Diego.

Sweedler, Alan. 1999. "Energy Issues in the San Diego–Tijuana Region." Briefing paper prepared for San Diego Dialogue's Forum Fronterizo.

Thorup, Cathryn L. 1993. "Redefining Governance in North America: The Impact of Cross-Border Networks and Coalitions on Mexican Immigration into the United States," DRU-219-FF. Santa Monica, Calif.: Rand Corporation.

# 16

# Equity and Justice in Binational Environmental Policy

Stephen P. Mumme

This essay offers a few reflections on the efforts to advance equity and justice in binational environmental policy. Before proceeding, some clarification is in order. The concepts of environmental equity and environmental justice are certainly complex. However, both are essentially socio-centric and ethical, referring to a socially desirable relationship between human beings and their physical environment. Environmental equity, following various usages in the literature (Bryner 2002; Getches and Pellow 2002; Wescoat et al. 2002), refers to a state of environmental affairs or socio-ecological relations characterized by the norm of fairness in determinations of ecological conditions and fairness in the distribution of benefits and burdens across society issuing from those conditions. The concept of environmental equity thus refers to both the substantive and the procedural norms and practices associated with sustaining or modifying an ecological or environmental state of affairs, and it is implicated in virtually all constructions of the notion of sustainable development. Environmental justice, a narrower construct, may be taken to mean both the state of attainment and the process of attaining a fair distribution of burdens and benefits arising from an environmental or ecological state of affairs (Getches and Pellow 2002). Though some may wish to dispute this construction, I have generally found it useful to view environmental justice as instrumental to the state and practice of environmental equity.

Equity, conceived as both substantive and procedural fairness, is certainly implicated in any meaningful discussion of policy aimed at environmental protection and sustainable development in the border area. At the border, our environmental problems and binational cooperation to solve these problems are inherently embedded in the socioeconomic reality of a profound asymmetry in matters of resource entitlements, the human capacity to produce and consume, and the mix of social and political opportunities that are grounded in access to information, mechanisms of communication, and systems of governance. This asymmetry confronts and often confounds policy at every turn as we attempt to deal with specific environmental problems, be it water availability and quality, air quality, toxic substances, the handling of waste streams, or safeguarding biodiversity.

Thus there is a sense in which equity is a part of every discussion or debate on environmental policy in the border community, and particularly where binational cooperation is involved. Equity considerations certainly inform the difference in national perspectives when representatives of the two countries sit at the table to define and discuss environmental problems. It is equity—in this case, a concern with substantive equity—that focuses Mexican attention on the provision of basic needs as a structural element in binational problem solving, and equity that informs thinking on the need for subsidies, supports, and adjustments in bankrolling binational solutions to shared environmental problems in the border region. Concerns with substantive and procedural equity are expressed directly or indirectly in the La Paz Agreement, the Border 2012 Program, and the goals and procedures of the Border Environment Cooperation Commission (BECC). Equity concerns guide thinking at the Good Neighbor Environmental Board and the Northern Border Sustainable Development Council. And equity concerns are indirectly a part of the formal construal of sustainable development in binational and trinational environmental agreements.

Yet despite this general awareness of the importance of equity in binational environmental decision making and the importance of achieving environmental equity in principle, there are differences in how each nation approaches the problem at the domestic level (particularly in the aspect of environmental justice) and certain shortcomings in how the pursuit of equity is currently framed and implemented at the binational level. To better appreciate this, it is useful to reflect on national differences toward both the substantive and procedural aspects of achieving equitable solutions to environmental problems on the border today.

## BINATIONAL POLICY AND SUBSTANTIVE ENVIRONMENTAL EQUITY

Achieving substantive environmental equity has been an important goal of binational environmental programs since the mid-1990s. Substantive environmental equity, conceived as either the attainment or the guarantee of sufficient capacities to ensure adequate life quality and human development according to defined international standards (see the United Nations Human Development Report, 2002), is considered a critical part of the foundation of any long-term program of sustainable development. In this sense, substantive environmental equity is both an end and a means of binational cooperation for the improvement of the border environment and a point of concurrence as the two governments treat with each other. As seen above, environmental justice—conceived as the substantiation of particular rights, entitlements, and obligations—may be instrumental to attaining and sustaining substantive environmental equity. A policy focus on environmental justice, however, has until recently been more of an expressed emphasis within U.S. domestic environmental programs, notwithstanding the fact that the right to a healthy environment is constitutionally guaranteed in Mexico but not in the United States.

Differences in national approaches to the problem of realizing substantive environmental equity affect binational environmental policy. For Mexico, the pursuit of substantive equity is processed through a policy prism focusing on the human development of border communities; an emphasis on economic development, on public health, on housing and other basic needs; plus an emphasis on compliance and enforcement of Mexico's environmental laws and regulations. Although infrastructure development figures prominently in U.S. policy for border communities, equity considerations at the policy level tend to stress the provision of environmental justice, framed in the context of U.S. civil rights law at the constitutional and statutory level and normally defined as the prevention or remediation of discriminatory risks or threats to the public health of identified minorities.

Evidence of this may be found in contemporary binational programs for environmental protection. The recently expired Border XXI Program, for instance, gave greater emphasis to building up needed border infrastructure for environmental improvement, both physical and social, than it did to the achievement of environmental justice (EPA 2001). Its spending priorities centered on the development of sanitation and water infrastructure, objectives the two countries could agree on, rather than prosecuting environmental injustice, an institutional aim more fully developed and embedded in U.S. domestic environmental policy. Its policy successor, the Border 2012 Program, makes no specific mention of environmental justice as a goal (EPA 2003). In the matter of infrastructure development, neither the BECC nor its institutional partner, the North American Development Bank (NADB), had the authority to function very well in supporting an agenda of environmental justice even though siting and remediation issues were periodically raised by border activists over the past decade. Their capacity to address these issues recently improved with an expansion of their mandates to accommodate a wider range of environmental functions (BECC 2001). Mexico's recent development of a national environmental justice program with a border component allows the possibility of a greater approximation of national programs as these are deployed in border environmental policy, but it does not fundamentally alter its policy priorities.

A brief comparison of national programs supports this view. In the United States, the national environmental justice program of the Environmental Protection Agency (EPA) focuses on alleviating the adverse impacts of environmental hazards and siting issues on protected class and minority communities as well as those communities officially defined as poverty zones. As operationalized at the border (see table 16.1), this means community empowerment; government responsiveness to expressed environmental justice concerns; integrating this policy priority in federal, state, and tribal programs; and risk reduction through an emphasis on compliance with national environmental law and cleaning up environmental media (such as water, air, and soil).

The new environmental justice program of Mexico's Environment Ministry (SEMARNAT) is certainly sensitive to many of the issues associated with the U.S. approach and has the constitutional advantage of proceeding from a federal obligation to protect public health and preserve and protect the environment (*Constitución* 1998: Arts. 4 and 27; SEMARNAT 2002a; Environmental Law Institute 1996: 6–8). With such a constitutional guarantee, Mexico's citizens do not carry the burden of establishing discrimination in order to legitimately claim a right to a safe environment, only the burden of establishing that environmental conditions are hazardous and ecologically unsound or a threat to public health. Mexico's notion of environmental justice thus remains centered on government obligations and the enforcement of environmental regulations (table 16.1). In a broader sense, Mexico's national environmental justice program is focused less on marginal national minorities and more on improvements in Mexican environmental administration as a whole. Promoting public participation, enhancing public awareness of environmental law, and strengthening administrative performance of environmental agencies are expressed as major priorities and are certainly important for empowering economically marginalized communities and society as a whole.

Table 16.1. U.S. and Mexican Border-Area Environmental Justice Programs Compared

| Basic U.S. Approaches | Basic Mexican Approaches |
| --- | --- |
| • Empower communities and build local capacity to participate in environmental decision making and binational activities. | • Give force to environmental commitments in the border area and involve the Attorney General's Office in binational environmental affairs. |
| • Ensure EPA's responsiveness to environmental justice concerns, including development of a strategy to integrate environmental justice into all aspects of the Border XXI Program and other binational activities. | • Guarantee full compliance with Mexican law in the actions and procedures of the Attorney General's Office. |
| • Assume a leadership role in working with federal, state, and tribal agencies to encourage integration of environmental justice into their border programs. | • Assume a leadership role in international environmental affairs for compliance and application of law with the assistance of local authorities at the state and municipal levels. |
| • Reduce risk, exposure, and other adverse environmental impacts in the border region by ensuring compliance with environmental laws and the cleanup of natural resources. | |

*Sources*: For the United States: EPA 2001: 16. For Mexico: SEMARNAT 2002b: 13–14.

The pursuit of substantive equity in binational environmental policy is thus manifest in important differences in domestic realities and priorities. At the most general level, there is binational consensus on the need to meet basic needs and provide essential infrastructure that will contribute to the health and protection of the human and natural environment on both sides of the border. There is also a shared commitment to the importance of reducing low-income communities' "disproportionate adverse exposure" to environmental risks. Yet substantial differences remain. Mexico is still building up the administrative infrastructure for environmental enforcement, while the United States is able to target a wide range of specialized needs. This suggests that while both countries have made significant progress in identifying and prioritizing the economic dimension of substantive environmental equity, they are not as close in dealing with social aspects of substantive equity. In part, this is a function of different official notions or definitions of "at-risk" communities. It also follows from different systems of governance and substantial asymmetry in the fiscal and technical capabilities of public administration at the different levels of government. Whatever the contributing causes, important differences remain with respect to available resources and the identification of target groups in pursuing environmental equity on the two sides of the border.

## BINATIONAL POLICY AND PROCEDURAL ENVIRONMENTAL EQUITY

Binational environmental policy also aims at building up procedural equity, both as an end in itself and as a means of attaining substantive environmental justice in the service of sustainable development and the betterment of human communities in the border zone. Procedural equity may be defined as the establishment and strengthening of procedural mechanisms that ensure public awareness and scrutiny of environmental conditions, provide a democratic process of crafting needed environmental laws and standards, support and reinforce the application and administration of environmental law (and the extension of its benefits to all members of society), and provide adequate mechanisms for public input in the administration of the law and fair access to judicial remedies for environmental disputes (for discussion, see Bryner 2002: 44–47). As a component of environmental equity, procedural equity is particularly important to the empowerment and improvement of marginalized and less privileged groups on the border and their opportunity to remedy adverse environmental conditions (Neighbor 1999: 2).

The provision of procedural equity as an element of environmental equity and sustainable development has been a core objective of nongovernmental and civic groups on both sides of the border. In a region characterized by high levels of social marginality on both sides, it is rightly viewed as the more important transformative norm in sustainable development and vital to building local and regional capacity for environmental governance.

There can be little doubt that this is a critical area of innovation in binational environmental policy. As a basic value and policy objective, the opening and strengthening of new venues for public participation in environmental decision making is a component of every binational environmental program in play in the border today. The amplification of arenas for public input and participation is seen in the citizens' participation and transparency provisions of the BECC (BECC 2002), Border 2012's public forums and advisory groups and emphasis on local and decentralized environmental policy development, the development of new citizens' forums at the U.S. Section of the International Boundary and Water Commission (IBWC 2001), the establishment and implementation of watershed councils in the United States and *consejos de cuencas* in Mexico (GNEB 2003), the creation of citizens' advisory bodies by federal and state environmental authorities, and the articulation of standards for public participation in environmental decision making by domestic and binational government agencies. Minority and at-risk communities have greater access to information sources, public hearings, *foros de consulta*, and decision-making venues than ever before.

Yet obstacles to citizen empowerment and environmental justice remain on both sides of the border and are evident in binational environmental practices rooted in economic and political asymmetry, the embeddedness of centralizing and corporatist procedures, the novelty of new participatory mechanisms, and structural disparities and differences between the two national legal systems (see, for example, de Mello Lemos 1999: 58; Alfie Cohen 2003: 55–56). A proliferation of environmental data generated by the new border environmental programs is still underutilized due to problems of availability and access, especially on the Mexican side of the border. BECC's public meetings are still asymmetric when the participation of U.S. and Mexican civic and environmental groups is compared. Tribal and indigenous groups have been neglected in binational environmental forums—though this is changing and is an emphasis within the new Border 2012

Program (EPA 2003: 6). Legal restrictions limit the participation of nongovernmental advocacy groups in Mexico's recently established *consejos de cuencas*, and the new citizens' advisory forums in the United States remain at risk of domination by government agencies, irrigation districts, and municipal utilities.

Both U.S. and Mexican environmental justice programs profess to support public participation and citizen access to environmental justice, but the Mexican program is more an administrative mechanism for fielding complaints and achieving compliance with environmental law, while the U.S. system supplements administrative mechanisms with civil and criminal legal procedures that are meant to be accessible to protected groups for redress of grievances. The very fact that U.S. citizens and nongovernmental groups are able to use litigation to challenge administrative decisions, improve environmental practices, and redress discriminatory practices marks a significant differential between the two countries in advancing an agenda of environmental justice. While in principle marginalized communities in Mexico have access to judicial remedies and action forcing administrative mechanisms, in practice few of them are able to make use of legal remedies technically available under Mexican law, a fact tacitly acknowledged by Mexico's environmental inspectorate, where improved citizen access to remedies is an official priority (PROFEPA 2001: 10–11). And despite the salience and high politics surrounding Mexico's historic neglect of indigenous communities, Mexican government programs are not yet oriented toward mitigating adverse environmental conditions based directly or indirectly on status discrimination.

In sum, while the governments have made significant progress in recognizing the need to pursue an agenda of environmental equity and justice and committing agencies and programs to this purpose, real differences remain in socioeconomic and political circumstances as well as programs and approach. Achieving greater substantive parity in environmental protection in the border region depends not only on government commitment to environmental improvement in specific areas and practices but on a fundamental strengthening of procedural opportunities and citizen engagement for environmental protection within and beyond government agencies and programs. This is the larger challenge that lies ahead.

## ADVANCING ENVIRONMENTAL EQUITY AT THE BINATIONAL LEVEL

Strengthening binational cooperation for environmental equity and justice in the border community in the face of persistent national asymmetries and procedural obstacles remains a formidable task. The binational programs, commendable as they are, are in a sense only as good as the governments that support them and the social capacities they are able to mobilize. In this sense, achieving environmental equity in the border region is heavily contingent on the larger social and political processes of democratization and economic development.

With this in mind, the contributors to this volume offer a number of valuable insights on the problem of environmental equity in the border region that are relevant to the strengthening of binational efforts in this issue area. On the substantive side, Nora Bringas, Roberto Sánchez, Tito Alegría, Kathryn Kopinak, and Ruth Gaxiola draw attention to the need to understand the intended and unintended social costs of particular forms and strategies of border development, strategies that may be unsustainable over the long term and that contribute directly to environmental degradation and the greater risks shouldered by marginalized communities. There is little doubt that the bilateral government agencies and programs dealing with environmental equity have been reluctant to challenge basic development strategies, viewing their role as reactive and mitigative rather than proactive and preventive of environmental harms. Binational programs that advance procedural environmental equity will inevitably be venues for competing visions of sustainable development and more locally situated agendas of environmental improvement.

John Friedmann, Basilio Verduzco, and others point to the importance of local empowerment as a multidimensional process of opportunity and involvement across a spectrum of human dimensions. Substantive environmental equity from this perspective cannot be separated from the fulfillment of basic needs, locally situated economic improvement, and the opportunity to build local social capital through education and skills-building investments. Procedural environmental equity is contingent not just on the design of binational institutions but also on an enabling political environment based on mutually reinforcing systems of participation in national political processes and national and binational administrative agencies and programs. It depends as well on the capacity of local and regional groups for an autonomous production of knowledge, which points to the importance of building and supporting strong nongovernmental advocacy and resource organizations.

Building social awareness of environmental risks and enhancing social capacity to monitor, assess, and mobilize social efforts to alter unsustainable environmental practices are certainly critical preconditions for the effective functioning of new opportunities for public participation in border programs and the strengthening of procedural environmental equity. Laura Silván, Silvia López, and Alejandro Monsiváis, each in their respective ways, draw the point that national and binational commitments to environmental education and capacity building not only need to be intensified in the border zone but also need to be undertaken in the full awareness of the diversity and complexity of the border's social fabric. Engaging youth in environmental activities contributes to civic consciousness and higher levels of political participation by young adults. Building environmental awareness is not just an end in itself. It supports cultural integrity and other sustaining values and practices that create economic opportunity, enrich social life, and support ecosystems.

In sum, a focus on environmental equity and justice in the context of binational efforts to protect the environment and promote sustainable development directs our attention to some of the most vital challenges for border development today. The United States and Mexico have certainly made progress in recognizing the importance of this aspect of environmental protection and incorporating its principles in their national environmental programs aimed at the border area. Moving beyond the policy rhetoric and developing more cooperative efforts will tax the political commitment and resources of both countries as advances in environmental equity and justice are predicated on the most central questions in sustainable development as it plays out on the U.S.-Mexico border.

## References

Alfie Cohen, Miriam. 2003. "Rise and Fall of Environmental NGO's along the U.S.-Mexican Border." In *Cross-Border Activism and Its Limits*, ed. Barbara Hoogenboom, Miriam Alfie Cohen, and Edit Antal. Amsterdam: Centre for Latin American Research and Documentation.

BECC (Border Environment Cooperation Commission). 2001. *Border Environment Cooperation Commission, 2001 Annual Report*. Ciudad Juárez: BECC, www.cocef.org.

———. 2002. *BECC-NEWS*, Autumn, www.cocef.org.
Bryner, Gary. 2002. "Assessing Claims of Environmental Justice: Conceptual Frameworks." In *Justice and Natural Resources*, ed. Kathryn M. Mutz, Gary C. Bryner, and Douglas S. Kenney. Washington, D.C.: Island Press.
*Constitución Política de los Estados Unidos Mexicanos*. 1998. México, D.F.: Anaya Editores.
de Mello Lemos, Maria Carmen. 1999. "Public Participation in the BECC: Lessons from the Acuaférico Project, Nogales, Sonora," *Journal of Borderlands Studies* 14, no. 1 (Spring): 43–64.
Environmental Law Institute. 1996. *Decentralization of Environmental Protection in Mexico: An Overview of State and Local Laws and Institutions*. ELI Project # 931500. Washington, D.C.
EPA (U.S. Environmental Protection Agency). 2003. *Border 2012: U.S.-Mexico Environmental Program*. EPA-160-R-03-001. Washington, D.C.: EPA, May 5.
———. 2001. *U.S.-Mexico Border XXI Program: Progress Report, 1996–2000*. EPA160/R/00/001. Washington, D.C.: EPA.
Getches, David H., and David Pellow. 2002. "Beyond 'Traditional' Environmental Justice." In *Justice and Natural Resources*, ed. Kathryn M. Mutz, Gary C. Bryner, and Douglas S. Kenney. Washington, D.C.: Island Press.
GNEB (Good Neighbor Environmental Board). 2003. *Sixth Report of the Good Neighbor Environmental Board*. EPA 130-R-03-001.Washington, D.C.: U.S. Environmental Protection Agency.
IBWC (International Boundary and Water Commission). 2001. *U.S. Section Strategic Plan*. El Paso: U.S. Section, IBWC, www.ibwc.state.gov.
Neighbor, Howard. 1999. "Mobilizing Low Income Minorities to Fight Environmental Injustice." Paper presented at the meeting of the Association for Borderlands Studies, Fort Worth, April 21–24.
PROFEPA (Procuraduría Federal de Protección al Ambiente). 2001. *Programa de Procuración de Justicia Ambiental, 2001–2006, versión resumida*. México, D.F.: PROFEPA, www.semarnat.gob.mx/programas/documentos/presentacion/programa_ja/index.shtml.
SEMARNAT (Secretaría de Medio Ambiente y Recursos Naturales). 2002a. *Programa de Procuración de Justicia Ambiental, 2001–2006*. México, D.F.: SEMARNAT, www.semarnat.gob.mx.
———. 2003b. *Programa de la Frontera Norte (resumen avanzada)*. México, D.F.: SEMARNAT.
United Nations. 2002. *Human Development Report, 2002*. New York: Oxford University Press.

Wescoat, James L., Sarah Halvorson, Lisa Headington, and Jill Replogle. 2002. "Water, Poverty, Equity, and Justice in Colorado: A Pragmatic Approach." In *Justice and Natural Resources*, ed. Kathryn M. Mutz, Gary C. Bryner, and Douglas S. Kenney. Washington, D.C.: Island Press.

# 17

## Looking Ahead: Equity in the U.S.-Mexico Border

ROBERT L. BACH

These are difficult times along the U.S.-Mexico border, and from where we are now, looking ahead to a renewal of the region may appear to be an idyllic quest. The binational region is, of course, not a newcomer to poverty, disease, environmental degradation, violence, and social strife. Yet, in the last five years or so, the border region appears to have lost one of its core assets—a self-conscious appreciation of its value as a cross-border community.

Many observers blame current conditions on a dramatic shift in U.S. attention following the terrorist attacks of September 11, 2001. Equally to blame, perhaps, are the grandiose trade and immigration schemes advanced prematurely by Presidents Fox and Bush. With expectations and political ambitions inflated by the economic bubble that each rode to election in 2000, the presidents' "visions" of hemispheric free trade and open migration have proven both illusory and perhaps even counterproductive.

From the outset, the Fox-Bush strategy for a second decade of NAFTA-led growth was simple. If the economy could expand fast enough, the few who benefit from aggregate growth could be swept along politically in sufficient numbers to sustain popular support—even in the face of growing inequality and persistent poverty. Growth had to be substantial enough, though, to prevent the overwhelming majority of people who were poor and disadvantaged from demanding priority attention. Former Mexican Foreign Minister Jorge Castañeda warned of the consequences of this strategy. He noted that rapid trade and mobility–based integration with the United States would create key constituencies and power centers that would be indifferent to the course of events in Mexico. It would weaken the chances of meaningful reform in Mexico (Castañeda 1996).

Nowhere has the fate of this growth-first strategy been more pronounced than at the U.S.-Mexico border. In 2002, speaking in McAllen, Texas, in defense of free trade, outgoing Assistant Trade Representative Richard Fisher asserted that the test of NAFTA and free trade was how well they did in improving the well-being of communities along the border. After a decade of effort, the conclusion has to be that they have not achieved this promise. What has happened along the U.S.-Mexico border is an accelerating drift toward regional conflict and chaos amidst persistent economic hardships and sustained inequality.

The failure, however, did not result from efforts to promote trade, as some critics have argued. Rather, the flaw was that, to focus on trade, strategists gave up on the difficult work needed to improve and sustain the institutions and social investments that border residents had committed to their local, binational communities. These equities were not side issues, as the growth-first perspective cast them. Rather, they were key ingredients to a strategy that could generate and sustain growth (Bach 2003).

## BORDER STAGNATION

The stagnation that currently characterizes the U.S.-Mexico border region reflects a larger political-economic strategy gone astray. Forgotten, even dismissed from policy priorities, is the task of addressing the capacity and willingness of communities to respond to their regional and local challenges. Gone is an aggressive focus on the rule of law, replaced in only a few years by the incentives and enticements of inflated market expectations. Inequality and the corruption that too often underlies it have grown and become more deeply seated in institutions and routine practices. National governments and international agencies, meanwhile, wait for expanded trade and mobility to deliver their promised benefits.

Overall, political institutions and civil society have lost ground to unfettered market initiatives. Across the expanse of the border region—on both sides of the border—local governments struggle with electoral stalemates, corruption, and scandals. In some areas, gangland violence is a persistent reality. And recently two U.S. governors declared states of emergency along their borders in order to release funds to local border communities burdened by the chaos and criminality of cross-border activities.

Civil society organizations continue to wrestle, almost heroically, with these tough everyday realities. Yet, while the number of organizations has increased and their resources have improved in the aggregate, the overwhelming majority, especially in Mexico, remain small, fragile agencies with a single program task (ICF 2004). Philanthropic support, which spearheaded numerous border initiatives in the past decades on issues ranging from conditions in colonias to environmental cleanups, has withdrawn into more narrow efforts to build capacity among local community foundations working separately on opposite sides of the border.

These disturbing conditions and trends along the U.S.-Mexico border are only partly the result of the region's own making. Many of these problems reflect—and in some cases were the direct result of—global trade and development strategies fostered by international financial institutions and the U.S. and Mexican governments. These dominant perspectives, however, have begun to acknowledge, even if reluctantly, that past strategies have failed. Facing sustained criticism of the World Trade Organization, NAFTA, and other trade frameworks, even the World Bank and International Monetary Fund have begun to acknowledge the limitations of their past efforts. At the center of this awakening is recognition of the value of equity in promoting sustained development. However, for equity to be at the core of development strategies, these leading institutions have to take additional steps to revise their programs and objectives. An equity-led agenda requires that priority be given to peoples' core basic needs and disadvantages. Equity also requires local communities to have a willingness and a capacity to participate in the development effort.

## FIRST STEPS: ACKNOWLEDGING THE NEED FOR RENEWAL

The Johannesburg World Summit on Sustainable Development (WSSD) occurred at a critical moment in the transition of worldviews and strategies on economic development. The collapsing worldview that gave priority to growth was well recognized by the Johannesburg conferees and gave hope for the renewal of a more comprehensive and sustainable strategy. Participants realized the possibility, even urgency, of building a new agenda that put the needs and capabilities of local communities first. Yet the Summit itself produced few initiatives to move that new agenda along.

The plan for the Johannesburg Summit was to celebrate the victories of an engaged civil society ten years after launching the global initiative in Rio de Janeiro in 1992. That initiative was designed to mobilize civic organizations around the world to help steer economic growth strategies for the benefit of a wider population and beyond a narrow set of issues concerned primarily with aggregate expansion. Civil society engagement would help turn economic development into sustainable development by inserting the values and priorities of the poor, the vulnerable, and the least advantaged into international and national development strategies.

Even before it started, however, the Johannesburg Summit disappointed. United Nations leaders acknowledged officially that they had only minimal expectations in the run-up to the Johannesburg meeting. Looking back over ten years, the UN, member governments, and even civil society supporters could find little evidence to justify a celebration. Concrete results of a decade of engagement were minimal. As one civil organization noted, about the only sector that benefited after Rio was civil society organizations. They held many more meetings, were given more opportunities to address governments, and collected far more money. At the same time, environmental conditions, inequality, and vulnerability continued to worsen throughout most regions of the world.

In a way, the WSSD marked the end of an era in which strategies of global development that focused first on market-led expansion, combined with consultations from civil society organizations on negative side effects, dominated. But it did not generate a new strategy. Faced with a rather dismal record and collapsing expectations, conferees in Johannesburg took a clearly practical and subtle turn. One of the only areas on which governments and civil society participants could reach agreement was the value of using the Millennium Development Goals as performance measures within international agreements and program assessments.

As minimal as these steps appeared, however, they may have helped to outline initial steps that regions and communities, including the U.S.-Mexico border, could take toward developing a new agenda. Though certainly not aimed at the border region, the refocusing on performance measures offers a valuable tool with which binational organizations could reevaluate their activities. For too long, governments and civil society organizations have not held themselves accountable for progress made or not made toward the lofty goals routinely celebrated in international and binational forums. Lack of accountability is particularly prevalent along the U.S.-Mexico border, where broad statements of mutual, binational intent have failed to produce measurable progress toward goals of poverty reduction, environmental improvement, and so on. In the health arena, for instance, for over half a century Mexico and the United States have met regularly in a Binational Health Commission to discuss ways to improve cross-border public health. Without clear performance goals, however, each successive year's meeting has ended with yet another call for more action and additional resources, even though, in most areas, officials could show no measurable progress toward reducing disease and health risks on both sides of the border.

A focus on performance measures and accountability would provide a disciplined mechanism to reinforce and follow through on changing policy and institutional priorities that address core basic needs, poverty, and inequality. As several international economists have argued, improvement in just a few of these basic needs could have an enormous impact on both the well-being of the world's population and the productivity of the global economy (Sachs 2005). The border region could prosper as well. Impoverished and ill-nourished populations cannot contribute adequately to a nation's economic wealth, and the resources redirected to their care, even minimally, are a drain on, rather than a source of, productive investments.

Shifting priorities also require new institutional champions that have a focus on performance and accountability. In Johannesburg, conferees recognized that leadership had to move away from international financial institutions like the World Bank and International Monetary Fund, among others, that had sponsored the charge toward a singular focus on growth. New agencies and groups were needed that put equity and accountability first.

## TOWARD A NEW CROSS-BORDER AGENDA

If there had been a World Summit–like conference that focused solely on the U.S.-Mexico border, perhaps the participants would have identified the elements of a new agenda. At the very least, either explicitly or implicitly, there may have been a collective recognition of the stagnation that has befallen the region, especially in the last five or six years. By itself, that recognition would be a step forward. For example, in contrast to the efforts of both the U.S. and Mexican governments to find reasons to celebrate ten years of NAFTA, a border equity conference might have focused more on the region's simple but contradictory realities. Performance under NAFTA has been mixed, growth has produced both positive and negative outcomes, and, at the very least, the political discourse and support behind the regional plan have obscured the underlying difficulties created or ignored by a trade-and-mobility-first development agenda.

Such a conference would have certainly mirrored the discovery in Johannesburg of the value of equity as a core concept for understanding both the growth and distributional consequences of different development strategies. In Johannesburg, peoples' basic needs moved to the foreground of discussion, along with the contribution that human resources development could make to broad growth strategies.

A conference on the U.S.-Mexico border would have also focused more intensely on inequality. Recent studies have shown that most developing countries, including Mexico, face an "inequality trap" (Ferreira and Walton 2005). Inequality, rather than an unfortunate and temporary consequence of growth policies, undermines and reduces prospects for economic expansion. Profound, systemic inequality reduces the capacities and incentives for large-scale participation in productive activities. At the same time, aggregate economic growth does little to reduce this systemic inequality and, in many cases, actually deepens it. Even when opportunities do emerge, those who are already disadvantaged have fewer capabilities to respond effectively (Mazumder 2005).

Conferees in a U.S.-Mexico border summit would also have likely added to an understanding of equity as a core ingredient to growth and development. Equity involves a focus both on the fairness of outcomes, such as income and health, and on equality of opportunity and expectation. It also involves investment in human needs and aspirations. A key ingredient is the social character of this investment, the ways in which a community of local residents makes both a collective and personal commitment to the region.

Binational border residents have sunk their social capital deeply into this area over decades of struggle and commitment. They have found in the border region a community in which they belong. Unfortunately, programs of trade and market–forced mobility miss the value of this place-specific and community-organized social capital. The U.S.-Mexico border is more than a place of transit, as implied in most growth strategies. It is a place in which people have established a stake. They invest, produce, and belong. A renewed focus on equity would include ways to promote the use of this social capital to support and sustain economic growth.

Perhaps in this way, a U.S.-Mexico border summit might have joined the larger debate unfolding worldwide over the rules and consequences of growth strategies. Whether the target of opposition is the World Trade Organization or NAFTA, the critical, strategic insight is that the same processes that produce and sustain inequalities undermine the efficiencies and positive benefits of economic growth. World Bank researchers recently acknowledged that the potential benefits for the world's poor of extensive WTO trade deals "are significantly lower" than previously thought (Blustein 2005). By building an equity agenda, U.S.-Mexico border communities might have helped to demonstrate how to give priority to peoples' needs by creating a range of options and alternatives and by creating incentives for all sectors to engage in and pursue new opportunities (Goldstein and Udry 2002).

## PRIORITY TO TRANSPARENCY IN GOVERNANCE

A U.S.-Mexico border summit, like that in Johannesburg, might also have identified mechanisms that would be needed to overcome the orthodox, excessive reliance on market activities. In Johannesburg and elsewhere, the international community embraced a perspective that recognized the value of political institutions to economic growth and sustainability. Quite simply, growth requires effective political and social institutions. It does not occur without them. For a U.S.-Mexico border conference, of course, such a rediscovery would have been a bit ironic. A Western Hemisphere audience would have remembered well how the interlacing of economics and politics has shaped development and freedom. Not too far in the past, the United States and Mexico were deeply involved in a hemisphere in which strong antidemocratic political institutions achieved dictatorial control by ruling an economy that provided monopoly privileges and benefits. Globalization and trade openings emerged, then, not as a simple growth strategy but as a component of progressive political change. Trade openness helped to win political freedom. In Mexico, of course, these political changes remain only one free election away from faltering and returning the country to political-economic stalemate.

Effective governance and its linkages to the economy are as critical to progressive change today as they were in the transition from authoritarian rule. Yet today, effective governance has to focus on the privileges of power rooted systemically in growth-first economic strategies. The United Nations Development Programme (UNDP), which has led the international community's debate with neoliberal growth strategies, has argued for several years that democratic political institutions are the forerunners of effective and sustainable economic development. Democratic governments are much more likely, the UNDP argues, to intervene in market systems to provide a safety net for the neediest members of society and to promote policies that engage popular participation, improve public health, and greatly expand the involvement of neglected and disadvantaged sectors into economic activities. In particular, democratic governance is the most effective framework for organizing the competing and often contentious interests contained within diverse modern societies. Democracy provides the foundation to address the inequalities that weaken and undermine current growth-oriented development efforts.

Effective governance is much more, therefore, than the "market imperfections" that orthodox growth strategies label political and institutional activities. In purely market terms, governance puts limitations on international trade and movement. When those limitations occur at borders and reduce the volume or increase the price of goods and workers transiting the area, government represents large distortions in the potential value of cross-border market exchange.

Those limitations, however, are the rules and outcomes of political institutions that support and sustain the economic activities. Far from "distortions," they reflect and represent the full interests within a community, rather than the privileged position of a few. Government makes market exchange possible by supporting an array of rules, laws, and social supports. It fails if market activities continually reproduce economic hardships and inequality and if they lead to neglect of the basic needs of those whom, in a democracy, governments are created to serve and represent. The so-called limitations on market activities are actually positive steps that communities and political systems take to ensure equity and to sustain economic growth.

In this sense, border communities are rare political and economic zones because, within their neighborhoods, towns, and binational cities, these multiple pressures and objectives mix in the most practical ways. Though the grand strategic debates may occur in the halls of Geneva-based agencies, or in Washington, D.C., think tanks, or in Mexico City offices, equity-based priorities and decisions are rooted in the everyday realities of people living along the borders. NAFTA lost this connection to people on the border. As a result, it does not fundamentally address the core equity interests and needs of border communities. As international agencies and others are finally realizing, the result will be that the economy will sputter, social conflict will increase, and popular support will falter.

Less orthodox perspectives that focus on equity-based development have identified several of the ways in which effective political institutions support economic growth. One of the most important ways involves transparency in decision making and program implementation. Transparency encourages popular participation in priority-setting processes. It helps to ensure a fair playing field with institutional rather than personal or arbitrary rules. And it broadens the range and diversity of interests and viewpoints engaged in implementation. This diversity of interests and skills, according to the UNDP, has a positive impact on both democratic decision making and the productivity of the local economy.

Transparency also offers one of the most effective mechanisms to confront and combat corruption—which is a leading cause of poor economic performance, inequality, and neglect of basic needs. Governments and even international financial institutions have recently taken up a campaign against corruption because of the scale of its negative impact on economic performance. The character of corruption has also changed in the last decade or so, becoming more deeply ingrained in market-led policies. No longer is corruption simply the wayward behavior of individuals engaged in open payoffs and graft that has haunted both the reality and mythology of the binational region for decades. Rather, this new, systemic corruption is embedded in the strategies of market growth.

Corruption now has a more systemic character. By converting public authority into private gain, it creates an uneven economic, social, and political playing field. It misdirects and wastes resources. And it reinforces privileges that unfairly block broader sectors of society from participating in opportunities. A sure sign of this systemic corruption is the narrowing of public policy debates and options. Authorities narrow public debate by asserting that problems are "inevitable" and that the course of action they propose is the only way to address inexorable trends.

All along the U.S.-Mexico border, binational towns, communities, and cities struggle with ways to find transparent forms of political leadership to make the most effective strategic decisions. Battling systemic corruption is a recurring challenge. Just west of Ciudad Juárez and El Paso, for example, local community organizations have mobilized to draw attention to what they believe is yet another incidence of carefully crafted, behind-the-scenes deals that could dramatically reshape their binational community. The object of their opposition is a plan to develop a new binational city, for which private investors and local governments, in an effort to stimulate growth, have agreed to support the building of new industrial parks, housing complexes, and commercial outlets. Of course, all development decisions generate controversies, and the larger they are, the greater the conflict. Yet in this case, these local civil organizations are especially upset by traditional maneuvers that appear to be private profiteering and backroom deals. They are calling for a deliberate, transparent decision-making process in which independent studies of the impact of the proposed development on local residents, water supplies, and the environment can be publicly discussed.

Whether this particular development project is a good idea or not for the border region, the lack of effective governance threatens to undermine initial support for the investment. As global research now shows, lack of support jeopardizes the ability of a project to sustain itself past its initial construction. In this case, the complaints of local civic organizations clearly mirror arguments that emerge routinely from governance processes that lack transparency and exhibit systemic corruption. Local residents want to know, for instance, if public resources will be misdirected and wasted on this new project rather than used for other priority programs. They also raise the issue of narrow decision-making processes and ask whether public resources and decision making will result in unfair personal gain. Reportedly, the 8,000 acres on which this new project will take shape are owned by a single wealthy landowner. Local activists for transparency also raise the larger question about what this governance process means for Mexico's transition to democracy. They contend, for instance, that the lack of a public decision-making process undermines Mexico's political reforms, reinforcing a "partyocracy" in which the privileges of a one-party state are intertwined with benefits to a small sector of the population (*Ciudad Juárez News* 2006).

The persistent dilemma over cross-border migration also reflects this systemic corruption of political institutions and its negative impact along the border. The obscured "dirty little truth" in migration policy debates involves the well-documented privilege that employers and wealthier segments of local communities enjoy because of the workplace and living conditions of illegal migrant workers. Employers benefit from uneven and unfair competition when hiring these workers, compared to those employers who do not violate the law. Even the local household that hires an illegal worker for informal jobs prospers from lower wages, no benefits, and the workers' vulnerabilities. Authorities acknowledge this privilege but accept its "inevitability." Some academic researchers also argue that these circumstances represent a "structural necessity." Rarely, though, do they proceed to point out that the "necessity" appears to be a systemic privilege embedded in illegality, violation of community norms and rules, and dependent upon authorities not enforcing duly enacted laws.

Recent policy debates also show how systemic corruption breeds efforts to make new rules that incorporate this privilege and vulnerability into seemingly normal practices (Bach 2005). Recent proposals for a new contract labor program, for instance, reflect how otherwise strong political opponents have made common cause through deals and carefully crafted publicity to protect and expand the well-documented and illegal privileges now enjoyed by specific groups of private-sector employers. Yet this privilege occurs at the expense of the basic needs of workers and the vulnerabilities of their families and communities. The deals are cast, however, as "essential" mechanisms to promote regional economic growth.

Even the value of migrants' remittances may exacerbate inequalities and vulnerabilities because there are few options available to these workers. The connections that markets produce—for example, between employer and worker and between banker and borrower—when they are built on inequalities of influence and wealth may increase vulnerability and reproduce disadvantage and lack of opportunity (De Ferranti et al. 2004). Several of the current migration proposals reinforce the dependence of workers in Mexico on long-distance migratory journeys to gain work and earn wages to remit home. In doing so, they reproduce and expose migrants to the vulnerabilities and exclusions of either an illegal market or an indentured contract scheme.

**EMPHASIS ON PERFORMANCE**

Clearly, a core thrust of the Johannesburg meeting, and perhaps its primary contribution to a discussion of the future of border communities, was its commitment to accountability and performance in development programs. As noted previously, development programs, especially those along the U.S.-Mexico border, have for far too long been free to fail without consequence. A focus on performance and accountability as incorporated into the Millennium Development Goals could be a source of renewal for border program investments.

The primary challenge to adopting a performance-based accountability agenda is to properly align new outcomes and priorities with the way that institutions and local communities can engage in a transparent process of decision making. If it is true that today's institutions are aligned to reproduce inequality and lack of participation, border communities need a sustained strategy to reset priorities and generate political support for them. Civil society organizations along the border, which normally would be expected to lead such a movement, are woefully inadequate for the task. Part of the problem is that border organizations are simultaneously aligned as critics of prevailing trends and deeply divided by the border itself—defining their interests as Mexican or U.S. rather than in terms of cross-border program performance.

Holding border organizations accountable for their performance is not an easy task. The persistent increase in cross-border routine activities underlies a deep structural change in how organizations must work in the

U.S.-Mexico region to be effective. Currently, there is an institutional mismatch between the way in which families and communities organize their social relationships and the ways that programs, agencies, and juridical entities are able to represent and serve them.

This institutional mismatch arises from the structure of transnational communities and the routine cross-border social relationships that form them. The problem is that, in governance terms, this "institutional mismatch" is a form of structural disenfranchisement and disempowerment. Which government, for instance, represents a community that has part of its members inside one nation and part in another? To which institution does a community as a whole petition for help if the institution itself does not cross the border and lacks authority to work on both sides? To which government jurisdiction and to which service institutions can a person expect to have access for submitting a grievance or satisfying a basic need?

Institutional mismatches are fairly familiar to the community development field in the United States. Urban sprawl during the last decade, for instance, has clearly expanded the realities of community life beyond traditional city boundaries. So-called metropolitan economies now encompass both city and suburb, and people routinely travel back and forth to work and visit. Yet institutional and government boundaries cut across these economic and social relationships and create havoc in terms of governance and service. Institutions of authority, including traditional community and neighborhood-based associations, no longer have power over all parts of the activities important to their citizens, residents, and members. Mayors can only partially influence the local economy, for instance, if many of those who work in the city live in the suburbs, are taxed under a county's jurisdiction, and vote in totally separate elections. No one government entity, no single organization, represents the interests, assets, and desires of the people who organize their lives on this regional as opposed to city scale.

When communities and economies "sprawl" across boundaries that represent national governments, the severity of the institutional mismatch often becomes itself a defining feature of community organization. Members of the same community are separated from each other, disenfranchised from participating in activities that could otherwise serve the entire group, and unable to seek service from a single entity. No government, service institution, or organization is accountable to these cross-border community members.

Not surprisingly, transnational border organizations and even the philanthropic institutions that fund them face huge challenges in forging new cross-border governance frameworks. Currently, institutions at the border are still rooted in separate nation-states. Philanthropic programs are divided between domestic and international initiatives, and community organizations fight over identities as either Mexican or American groups. On many issues, however, organizing locally often requires working transnationally. Rare examples of such cross-border organization only help to underscore the point. In a few instances, an independent union movement in Mexico has been able to use the transnational structures of the textile industry to design its own cross-border organization and to coordinate consumer groups in Canada, the United States, Mexico, and Central America to help pressure specific companies. This transnational reach gave local activists the power to organize on the same scale and level as the industry. Some *maquiladora* workers have also been able to use a combination of U.S. and Mexican legal systems to improve working conditions and get redress for wrongful dismissals.

The value of transnational approaches to organizing equity-based border development strategies is considerable. A good example may be the way that public health organizations need to restructure their activities to combat health risks that routinely stretch and circulate across the border. According to the U.S. Department of Health and Human Services (DHHS), health professionals have reached a consensus that accepts a close link between an individual's health and "the health of the community and environment in which individuals live, work, and play." DHHS reports that health is profoundly affected by the "collective beliefs, attitudes, and behaviors of everyone who lives in the community." In a transnational community, these collective beliefs and attitudes, the environment of work and play, occur across borders. The "community" has simply expanded geographically and socially, stretching across borders to link family and community members living in different locations. The result is that the health of any and all individuals, whether migrant or nonmigrant, who are part of cross-border community relationships is dependent on the health and the environment of work and play in all parts of that region. From the realities of migrants crossing back and forth across the borders, to disease risks shared and transmitted across borders, to general economic and political interdependence, the "community" to which program strategies refer has truly "sprawled" across the international boundary.

Simply put, for public health programs to contribute to a healthy transnational community, their activities much be organized in the same way and on the same scale as the community that they serve. Programs need to reach individuals and families regardless of which side of the border they are on, and attack risk exposures on one side before they become incidents on the other. Arguably, few matters of equity and development matter more than a capability of preventing and responding to disease. Learning to work across borders, building organizations that adequately reflect and interact with communities, may be the only way that health risks can be significantly reduced. How to build those organizations, however, remains a critical challenge for communities and institutions all along the U.S.-Mexico border.

## END REMARKS

Looking ahead, the revitalization of the binational region begins with a renewed appreciation of its communities, not simply as trading partners but as members of a common endeavor. A focus on equity—equality, investment, and social belonging—gives renewed priority to the people of the region and their social institutions. However, the way forward will not be easy, for creating new priorities flies in the face of conventional and dominant political-economic views. A new strategy departs from six years in which the Fox administration ignored the majority of the Mexican population in hopes that the minority that benefits from integration, trade, and migration to the United States will be sufficient to maintain political power. It will also challenge, in the United States, the Bush administration's strategy of ignoring persistent problems and inequalities in employment, education, poverty, and health in the name of faster and ever-less-fettered growth. The border region's binational character, most importantly, will have to challenge the joint U.S.-Mexico strategy of pursuing trade and migration at the cost of the human needs and problems, deep inequality, and pervasive, systemic corruption that such a strategy persistently reproduces.

The most immediate challenges will undoubtedly involve the consequences of the failure of market-led strategies. Efforts to build walls and fences at the border to simply stop markets from working will be mirrored on the social and human side with equally restrictive efforts to enclose migrants' social lives through contract labor programs. With the social and political costs of current strategies accumulating all along the border, reactive efforts to exclude problems and people become rampant and take many forms. Strategies that are rooted in equity will stand as clear contrasts to growth schemes that result in border walls, indentured labor schemes, and a pervasive sense of exclusion.

What has happened to the U.S.-Mexico border in the last five years, then, is not the result of a change in the U.S. government's attention following the 9/11 attacks, as many observers argue. The experiences of the U.S.-Mexico border may be far more profound and damaging than what happened to New York City. The New York region responded to the terrorist attacks with a renewed sense of community, of common commitment to return the area to its former dynamism. New York City became a self-conscious community of hope, in which residents and visitors had a commitment to investment and belonging.

The U.S.-Mexico border was not attacked, but it was excluded. The region will recover only when it begins to renew itself, and that will require a self-conscious assertion by its members to create effective strategies aimed at satisfying core basic needs, reducing inequality, and fostering democratic participation.

**References**

Bach, Robert L. 2003. "Global Mobility, Inequality and Security," *Journal of Human Development* 4, no. 2 (July).

———. 2005. "Western Hemispheric Integration and Migration in an Age of Terror." In *Globalizing Migration Regimes: New Challenges to Transnational Cooperation*, ed. Kristof Tamas and Joakim Palme. Aldershot, U.K.: Ashgate.

Blustein, Paul. 2005. "World Bank Reconsiders Trade's Benefits to Poor," *Washington Post*, December 17.

Castañeda, Jorge G. 1996. "Mexico's Circle of Misery," *Foreign Affairs*, July 1.

*Ciudad Juárez News*. 2006. "Fight over Planned Border City Growing," January 13.

De Ferranti, David, Guillermo E. Perry, Francisco H. G. Ferreira, and Michael Walton. 2004. *Inequality in Latin America: Breaking with History?* Washington, D.C.: World Bank.

Ferreira, Francisco H. G., and Michael Walton. 2005. "The Inequality Trap," *Finance and Development* 42, no. 4 (December). At www.imf.org/external/pubs/ft/fandd/2005/12/ferreira.htm.

Goldstein, Markus, and Christopher Udry. 2002. *Gender, Land Rights and Agriculture in Ghana*. New Haven, Conn.: Yale University.

ICF (International Community Foundation). 2004. "Blurred Borders: Transboundary Issues and Solutions in the San Diego/Tijuana Border Region." San Diego: ICF. At www.icfdn.org/publications/blurredborders/index.htm.

Mazumder, Bhashkar. 2005. "The Apple Falls Even Closer to the Tree Than We Thought." In *Unequal Chances: Family Background and Economic Success*, ed. S. Bowles, H. Gintis, and M. Groves. Princeton, N.J.: Princeton University Press.

Sachs, Jeffrey. 2005. *The End of Poverty: Economic Possibilities for Our Time*. New York: Penguin.

# Acronyms

| | |
|---|---|
| ADEQ | Arizona Department of Environmental Quality |
| BECC | Border Environment Cooperation Commission / Comisión de Cooperación Ecológica Fronteriza (COCEF) |
| BEIG | Border Energy Issues Group |
| BIP | Border Industrialization Program / Programa de Industrialización Fronteriza (PIF) |
| Calit2 | California Institute for Telecommunications and Information Technology |
| CANACO | Cámara Nacional de Comercio / National Chamber of Commerce |
| CEAC | Consejo de Educación Ambiental de las Californias / Environmental Education Council for the Californias (EECC) |
| CECADESU | Centro de Capacitación para el Desarrollo Sustentable / Training Center for Sustainable Development |
| CELADE | Centro Latinoamericano de Demografía / Latin American Demography Center |
| CENIC | Corporation for Education Network Initiatives in California |
| CESPT | Comisión Estatal de Servicios Públicos de Tijuana / State Commission for Water Services in Tijuana |
| CICESE | Centro de Investigación Científica y de Educación Superior de Ensenada / Center for Scientific Research and Higher Education of Ensenada |
| CIEJ | Centro de Investigación y Estudios sobre Juventud / Center for Research and Studies on Youth |
| COBRO | Committee on Binational Regional Opportunities |
| COCEF | Comisión de Cooperación Ecológica Fronteriza / Border Environment Cooperation Commission (BECC) |
| COLEF | El Colegio de la Frontera Norte |
| CONAPO | Consejo Nacional de Población / National Population Council |
| CSCC | California State Coastal Conservancy |

| | |
|---|---|
| CTP | Coastal Training Program |
| CUDI | Corporación Universitaria para el Desarrollo de Internet |
| CUNA | Instituto de Culturas Nativas de Baja California |
| DAWN | Development Alternatives for Women in a New Era / Mujeres para un Desarrollo Alternativa |
| DHHS | U.S. Department of Health and Human Services |
| DIF | Desarrollo Integral de la Familia / National System for Integral Family Development |
| EAP | economically active population |
| ECLAC | Economic Commission for Latin America and the Caribbean / Comisión Económica para América Latina y el Caribe (CEPAL) |
| EECC | Environmental Education Council for the Californias / Consejo de Educación Ambiental de las Californias (CEAC) |
| EPA | U.S. Environmental Protection Agency |
| Foviste | Fondo de la Vivienda para los Trabajadores del Estado / Housing Fund for State Employees |
| FTAA | Free Trade Area of the Americas |
| GIS | geographic information systems |
| GNP | gross national product |
| HUD | U.S. Department of Housing and Urban Development |
| IBWC | International Boundary and Water Commission / Comisión Internacional de Límites y Aguas (CILA) |
| ICF | International Community Foundation |
| IDB | Inter-American Development Bank |
| ILAC | Iniciativa Latinoamericana y Caribeña para el Desarrollo Sostenible / Latin American and Caribbean Initiative for Sustainable Development |
| IMADES | Instituto del Medio Ambiente y el Desarrollo Sustentable / Institute for the Environment and Sustainable Development |
| IMIP | Instituto Municipal de Investigación y Planeación / Municipal Research and Planning Institute |
| IMJ | Instituto Mexicano de la Juventud / Mexican Youth Institute |

| | |
|---|---|
| IMPlan | Instituto Municipal de Planeación / Municipal Planning Institute |
| INEGI | Instituto Nacional de Estadística, Geografía e Informática / National Institute of Statistics, Geography, and Informatics |
| Infonavit | Instituto del Fondo Nacional de la Vivienda para los Trabajadores / National Workers' Housing Fund |
| IRCA | Immigration Reform and Control Act of 1986 |
| MDGs | Millennium Development Goals |
| NADB | North American Development Bank |
| NAFTA | North American Free Trade Agreement |
| NIEHS | National Institute of Environmental Health Sciences |
| NOAA | National Oceanic and Atmospheric Administration |
| NRC | National Research Council |
| NSF | National Science Foundation |
| PAN | Partido Acción Nacional / National Action Party |
| PFEA | Proyecto Fronterizo de Educación Ambiental / Border Environmental Education Project |
| PIF | Programa de Industrialización Fronteriza / Border Industrialization Program (BIP) |
| PRD | Partido de la Revolución Democrática / Party of the Democratic Revolution |
| PRI | Partido Revolucionario Institucional / Institutional Revolutionary Party |
| PROBEA A.C. | Proyecto Biregional de Educación Ambiental / Biregional Environmental Education Project |
| PROFEPA | Procuraduría Federal de Protección al Ambiente / Office of the Attorney General for Environmental Protection |
| PRONAF | Programa Nacional Fronterizo / National Border Program |
| PRONEA | Programa Nacional de Educación Ambiental / National Environmental Education Program |
| RCP | Regional Comprehensive Plan |
| REACCIUN2 | Red Académica de Centros de Investigación y Universidades Nacionales de Alta Velocidad |

Acronyms    357

| | |
|---|---|
| REUNA | Red Universitaria Nacional |
| RNP | Rede Nacional de Ensino e Pesquisa |
| RTP | Regional Transportation Plan |
| RWBC | Regional Workbench Consortium |
| SANDAG | San Diego Association of Governments |
| SCERP | Southwest Consortium for Environmental Research and Policy |
| SDD | San Diego Dialogue |
| SDSU | San Diego State University |
| SEABHS | Southeast Arizona Behavioral Health Services |
| SEAGO | Southeast Arizona Governments Organization |
| SECOFI | Secretaría de Comercio y Fomento Industrial / Ministry of Commerce and Industrial Development |
| SEDESOL | Secretaría de Desarrollo Social / Ministry of Social Development |
| SEMARNAT | Secretaría del Medio Ambiente y Recursos Naturales / Ministry of the Environment and Natural Resources |
| SENTRI | Secure Electronic Network for Travelers Rapid Inspection |
| SRE | Secretaría de Relaciones Exteriores / Ministry of Foreign Affairs |
| STPS | Secretaría de Trabajo y Previsión Social / Ministry of Labor and Social Security |
| TRNERR | Tijuana River National Estuarine Research Reserve |
| UABC | Universidad Autónoma de Baja California / State University of Baja California |
| UC MEXUS | University of California Institute for Mexico and the United States |
| UNDP | United Nations Development Programme |
| UNEP | United Nations Environment Programme |
| USDA | U.S. Department of Agriculture |
| USGS | U.S. Geological Survey |
| WSSD | World Summit on Sustainable Development |
| WTO | World Trade Organization |

# Contributors

**Tito Alegría** is a doctoral candidate in urban planning and development at the University of Southern California and a researcher in the Department of Urban and Environmental Studies at El Colegio de la Frontera Norte in Tijuana, Mexico. His key areas of research are urban development, urban structure, and intra-urban analysis.

**Robert L. Bach** is a and senior fellow at the Inter-American Dialogue at American University. His work focuses on the social issues involved in economic integration, including regional poverty, inequality, and institutional development. He designed the Global Inclusion Initiative at the Rockefeller Foundation and served as executive policy adviser in the U.S. Immigration and Naturalization Service during the Clinton administration.

**Nora L. Bringas Rábago** is a research professor in the Department of Urban and Environmental Studies at El Colegio de la Frontera Norte in Tijuana. Among her publications is *La ciudad compartida: desarrollo urbano, comercio y turismo en la región Tijuana–San Diego* (1995, coauthor).

**Jane Clough-Riquelme** is a regional planner with the San Diego Association of Governments (SANDAG). Her work focuses on borders planning, including tribal liaison and binational and interregional planning with neighboring jurisdictions. She also coordinates planning activities related to environmental justice and social equity for SANDAG. She served as guest editor for two special editions of the *Journal of Environment and Development*: one on sustainable development in the border region and one on water issues on the U.S.-Mexico border.

**Michael Connolly Miskwish**, a member of the Miskwish Clan of the Campo Band of Kumeyaay Indians, has served as a board member for the National Tribal Environmental Council, the Rural Community Assistance Corporation, and the National Tribal Air Monitoring Support Center. He is currently the California representative to the EPA Tribal Operations Committee and co-chairs the Natural Resources Committee for the National Congress of American Indians. He has authored several papers on American Indian environmental management, history, and economics, and has taught at San Diego State University and D-Q University.

**Angela J. Donelson** is a lecturer in the University of Arizona's Department of Geography. She has worked for the U.S. Department of Housing and Urban Development as the Arizona specialist on colonias issues and as a city planner on the U.S.-Mexico border. Her research interests are in community development, housing, and ethnic poverty. Dr. Donelson is the author of "The Role of NGOs and NGO Networks in Meeting the Needs of U.S. Colonias" (*Journal of Community Development*, 2004) and coauthor of "Analyses of Urban Sprawl and Colonias Development in Douglas, Arizona and Agua Prieta, Sonora on the U.S.-Mexico Border: A Process Application Using GIS and Remote Sensing: U.S. Geological Survey" (2004).

**John Friedmann** is Professor Emeritus of UCLA's Department of Planning and is currently an honorary professor in the School of Community and Regional Planning at the University of British Columbia and a member of the Centre of Chinese Studies in the Institute of Asian Research. He has worked extensively in and on Latin American urban and regional development, and is now expanding his focus to include the study of China.

**Ruth Gaxiola Aldama** is a research assistant in the Department of Urban and Environmental Studies at El Colegio de la Frontera Norte in Tijuana. Her areas of interest include urban sustainability and social vulnerability.

**Lawrence A. Herzog** is professor of city planning in the School of Public Administration and Urban Studies, San Diego State University. He specializes in urban/environmental design and planning, and comparative urbanization in the Mexico-U.S. borderlands and Latin America. His work has appeared in both academic and popular media publications. His books include *Return to the Center* (2006), *Shared Space* (editor, 2000), *From Aztec to High Tech* (1999), and *Where North Meets South* (1990).

**Kathryn Kopinak** is professor of sociology at King's University College at the University of Western Ontario in London, Ontario, Canada. Her current research interests include the impact of *maquiladora* employment on international labor migration. She is the author of *Desert Capitalism* (1996) and several articles on Mexican maquiladoras, including "Maquiladora Industrialization of the Baja California Peninsula: The Coexistence of Thick and Thin Globalization with Economic Regionalism" (*Journal of Urban and Regional Research*, June 2003), and editor of *The Social Costs of Industrial Growth in Northern Mexico* (2005).

**Alven H. Lam** is director of international research at the Office of International Affairs, Office of Policy Development and Research, U.S. Department of Housing and Urban Development. Dr. Lam specializes in urban development and housing policy, geographic information systems, local finance and governance, and property taxation. He has managed HUD's research projects and international programs with China, Spain, Mexico, Russia, and UN-Habitat. Prior to joining HUD, he was a research fellow at the Lincoln Institute of Land Policy in Cambridge, Massachusetts.

**Enrique Leff**, a leading Latin American scholar on ecological issues, is coordinator of the Environmental Training Network for Latin America and the Caribbean of the United Nations Environment Programme in Mexico. Dr. Leff is the author of a number of books, including *La complejidad ambiental* (2000), *Justicia ambiental: construcción y defensa de los nuevos derechos ambientales culturales y colectivos en América Latina* (2001), *Saber ambiental: sustentabilidad, racionalidad, complejidad, poder* (2002), and *La transición hacia el desarrollo sustentable: perspectivas de América Latina y el Caribe* (2002).

**Silvia López Estrada**, a sociologist, is a researcher in the Department of Population Studies at El Colegio de la Frontera Norte. Her research interests include family, work, and gender; gender and poverty; women's political participation; and public policy. She has published several articles and chapters on these topics, including "Border Women NGOs and Political Participation in Baja California" (in *Women and Change at the U.S.-Mexico Border*, ed. D. Mattingly and E. Hansen, forthcoming). Dr. López is currently coauthoring a book to be titled *Poverty, Family and Gender in Tijuana*.

**Alejandro Monsiváis** is a research professor in political and economic sociology at the Instituto Mora in Mexico City. His areas of interest include the construction of citizenship, the rule of law, and processes of democratization. He recently published *Vislumbrar ciudadanía: jóvenes y cultura política en la frontera noroeste de México.*

**Stephen P. Mumme** is professor of political science at Colorado State University. His research interests center on comparative environmental politics, with an emphasis on U.S.-Mexico border environmental management. Dr. Mumme's recent studies focus on environmental decentralization in Mexico, its impact on the northern border region, and the politics of reforming transboundary water management.

**Laura M. Norman** is a research cartographer with the U.S. Geological Survey's Southwest Geographic Science Team in Tucson, Arizona. Her research involves applications utilizing satellite data in combination with GIS to address environmental and societal issues and to characterize and quantify temporal change of natural systems within watersheds in arid and semiarid portions of Arizona and Sonora, Mexico. She is coauthor of "Analyses of Urban Sprawl and Colonias Development in Douglas, Arizona, and Agua Prieta, Sonora on the United States-Mexico Border: A Process Application Using GIS and Remote Sensing" (2004).

**Keith Pezzoli** is the supervisor of field research and a lecturer in the Urban Studies and Planning Program at the University of California, San Diego. Dr. Pezzoli is currently co-chair of the Global Planning Educators Interest Group (GPEIG) within the Association of Collegiate Schools of Planning (ACSP). He is also principal investigator of the Research Translation Core of UCSD's Superfund Basic Research Program (2005–2010) and leads the Regional Workbench Consortium, a collaborative, Web-based network of researchers and community partners dedicated to linking science and technology to policy and planning.

**Roberto Sánchez R.** is director of UC MEXUS and professor of environmental studies at the University of California, Riverside. His research looks at the human impact of global environmental change, environmental issues in urban areas, sustainable development, U.S.-Mexico border environmental policies and practices, and ties between trade and environment.

Prior to joining UC MEXUS, Sánchez had been associate professor of environmental studies at the University of California, Santa Cruz, had worked on transboundary issues at the North American Commission for Environmental Cooperation, and had directed the Department of Urban and Environmental Studies at El Colegio de la Frontera Norte.

**Laura Silván** is a social anthropologist at the Escuela Nacional de Antropología e Historia in Mexico City. Since 1990, she has directed the Border Environmental Education Program in Tijuana. She is also a member of the Joint Public Advisory Committee of the North American Commission for Environmental Cooperation, codirector of the Environmental Education Council of the Californias, and a member of the planning committee for the Annual Meeting on the Border Environment.

**Basilio Verduzco Chávez** is a professor in the Department of Regional Studies at the University of Guadalajara. Among his publications is *La ciudad compartida: desarrollo urbano, comercio y turismo en la región Tijuana-San Diego* (coauthored).